Contents

Social and Health Services

Communication Across Cultural Boundaries

Improving Intercultural Interactions

Modules for Cross-Cultural Training Programs

editors

Richard W. Brislin
Tomoko Yoshida

Multicultural Aspects of Counseling Series 3

SAGE Publications
International Educational and Professional Publisher
Thousand Oaks   London   New Delhi

For information address:

 SAGE Publications, Inc.
2455 Teller Road
Thousand Oaks, California 91320

SAGE Publications Ltd.
6 Bonhill Street
London EC2A 4PU
United Kingdom

SAGE Publications India Pvt. Ltd.
M-32 Market
Greater Kailash I
New Delhi 110 048 India

Printed in the United States of America

Library of Congress Cataloging-in-Publication Data

Main entry under title:

Improving intercultural interactions : modules for cross-cultural
    training programs / edited by Richard W. Brislin, Tomoko Yoshida.
        p. cm. — (Multicultural aspects of counseling series ; 3)
    Includes bibliographical references and index.
    ISBN 0-8039-5409-3. —ISBN 0-8039-5410-7 (pbk.)
        1. Intercultural communication. 2. Cross-cultural orientation.
    3. Multicultural education. I. Brislin, Richard W., 1945-
II. Yoshida, Tomoko. III. Series: Muticultural aspects of
counseling; v. 3.
GN345.6.I46   1994
303.48′2—dc20   93-35561

            95 96 97 98 10 9 8 7 6 5 4 3 2

Sage Production Editor: Astrid Virding

Series Editor's Introduction

This volume continues the **Multicultural Aspects of Counseling** series' emphasis on practical and applied issues that define culture inclusively and defines counseling broadly. While each book in the series emphasizes a specific multicultural perspective, this volume focuses on practical aspects of training as one means of helping. Many publications emphasize cross-cultural training methods and teach the reader "how to" do training, while other books emphasize the content of training. This volume emphasizes a balance of method and content.

The book is divided into modules. A module is significantly different from a book chapter. The modules are collections of materials which guide the reader both on the content of a defined unit of training and the method of delivery for that content. This volume recognizes that much multicultural training is cross-disciplinary and cross-field. Each module will share similarities and differences with each other module, approaching cross-cultural training from different disciplines and fields.

Like the other book in the series, this volume goes beyond the rhetoric about multiculturalism to direct action and applied analysis, focused on decision making and change agents. The reader is directly involved in each module with opportunities to interact as a participant and not just as audience. This cross-disciplinary focus is one of the unique features of this volume.

The **Multicultural Aspects of Counseling** series defines culture broadly rather than narrowly. That means in addition to ethnographic variables (nationality, ethnicity, language, religion, and so on) the series volumes also focus on demographic variable (such as age, gender, place of residence), status variable (such as social, economic, educational), and affiliation variables (formal as well as informal). This inclusive definition of culture allows each of these social system variables to become salient, according to the demands of the social context, as the primary cultural feature.

The series takes a psychological perspective but, as in the Brislin and Yoshida volume, that perspective is applied to disciplines outside of psychology. Multicultural training needs requires an interdisciplinary focus because the problems themselves are dynamic, as different aspects of the problems become salient. For this reason the helping dimension of the series is defined broadly enough to include multicultural training as one helping intervention.

This volume emphasizes the educational model rather than the medical model in its approach to counseling. The client is viewed as a student or trainee rather than as a patient. The participants in training may themselves be healthy and normal but still have serious problems where some form of helping is appropriate. The modules in this book present a variety of methods for providing multicultural training.

The volume will increase the reader's awareness through challenging culturally-biased assumptions; knowledge, through presenting factual knowledge and information about a particular method, population, or problem; and skill, through identifying right actions based on appropriate awareness and accurate knowledge. This volume will stimulate the reader to consider a variety of different approaches to training according to the different disciplines, fields, and perspectives where multiculturalism is an important factor. The volume is intended to stimulate readers to develop their own unique approaches for training their own clients, students, and target populations.

Paul Pedersen
Syracuse University
Series Editor

1 The Content of Cross-Cultural Training: An Introduction

RICHARD W. BRISLIN

TOMOKO YOSHIDA

Benjamin Franklin once said that there are two certainties in life that all people will face: They must deal with the inevitability of death, and they must pay taxes. To these, another can be added: People must interact with others from very different cultural backgrounds, whether they are well-prepared to do so or not. There are various reasons for this additional certainty, and all of them are addressed in this collection of materials designed to assist people who want to improve the effectiveness of their intercultural interactions.

Movement Across National Borders

Many reasons for increased intercultural contact relate to the growing internationalization of business (Adler, 1991; and Chapter 3 in this book by Neal Goodman). Materials for various products move across national borders so frequently that it is now difficult to discover exactly where a certain car, video recorder, camera, or business suit was actually made. Conscious attempts by consumers to support their economy by "buying national" are frequently waylaid given that materials can be produced in one country and assembled in another. The demands of today's business world bring executives, and workers desirous of better jobs, to countries other than their own. At times, they will take on the role of sojourners and will return to their own countries after a few years. At other times, they will become immigrants and will seek permanent residence and/or citizenship in the new country.

If new immigrants or sojourners find themselves in need of help, they may seek out the assistance of the new country's social service agencies and counseling centers (Chapter 11 by Colleen Mullavey-O'Byrne). They will also want to place their children in schools and will be concerned with programs to ease their children's transition from past to present school systems (Chapter 7 by Kenneth Cushner). If sojourners and new immigrants have stress-causing problems that lead to the search for professional intervention, they will be concerned with finding counselors and health care workers who are sensitive to their cultural background (Chapter 12 by Paul Pedersen and Chapter 10 by Colleen Mullavey-O'Byrne).

Culturally Diverse Groups Within a Country

Other reasons for increased intercultural contact involve the refusal of minority groups within any large country to become part of a homogenous melting pot. These minority groups can consist of recent immigrants, groups that have been in a country for many generations, and indigenous groups who were in a country when immigrants first arrived. Many people (e.g., Hispanics and African-Americans in the United States, Native Americans in both the United States and Canada, Eastern European immigrants in Australia) who are referred to as "minority group members" in their countries do not want to lose valued parts of their cultures. They do not want to become "carbon copies" of the dominant groups within their country. Further, rather than disappearing on the fringes of society, they want to take respected places within the mainstream of their cultures. As a result, members of various minority groups are placing demands on social service agencies, schools, hospitals, and businesses to recognize and to value cultural diversity (Chapters 6 and 7 by Cushner, Chapters 10 and 11 by Mullavey-O'Byrne, and Chapters 2 and 5 by Richard Brislin).

They are also placing demands on various institutions to value and to respect their native languages. If countries respect language differences, there will be easier access to social services and to health care for people not yet fluent in a country's dominant language (Chapter 16 by Carolina Freimanis on the importance of language interpreters). At the same time, many members of minority groups recognize that people who are fluent in the country's dominant language will have more access to society's benefits. Knowing this, they look to educational institutions for effective language teaching that can assist in their adjustment to the dominant culture (Chapter 15 by Mark Sawyer and Larry Smith).

The Place of Cross-Cultural Training Programs

One response to the fact of increased intercultural contact is to establish formal workshops and seminars that introduce people to the importance of culture, to cultural differences, and to the inevitable stresses that occur as people attempt to adjust to a different culture. The most frequently used term for these workshops and seminars is *cross-cultural training programs* (Bhawuk, 1990; Brislin & Yoshida, in press; Landis & Brislin, 1983). The goal of these programs is to assist people in making adjustments to other cultures so that they work effectively and participate as respected contributors to their communities. Various programs have been established for diverse groups whose members are faced with adjustment challenges, such as international students (Chapter 9 by Paul Pedersen), overseas businesspeople (Chapter 3 by Neal Goodman), and participants in international youth exchange programs (Chapter 6 by Cushner).

Programs also exist for various professionals who are often asked to assist the people who are experiencing the challenges of cross-cultural adjustment. These professionals include social service and health delivery specialists (Chapters 10 and 11 by Mullavey-O'Byrne), teachers in schools with large numbers of culturally diverse students (Chapter 7 by Cushner), counselors with clients from different cultural backgrounds (Chapter 12 by Pedersen), people who can offer their bilingual skills and try to help as language interpreters (Chapter 16 by Freimanis), and language teachers who want to include the importance of culture and cultural differences in their courses (Chapter 15 by Sawyer and Smith).

The Goals of Training

Cross-cultural training programs should be viewed as one of several contributions designed to assist people who cross cultural boundaries. Other factors that will influence people's adjustment include visa regulations; procedures (if any) for the acquisition of citizenship; inclusion of sojourners and new immigrants in a country's national health care plan; societal norms that allow people to seek good jobs without regard to ethnicity, skin color, or gender; and so forth. Cross-cultural training programs can never be a "cure-all" that can alleviate problems better addressed through a country's legal system, a country's social service agencies, or a country's educational institutions. When this important fact is kept in mind, cross-cultural training can make positive and important contributions to people's adjustment (Black & Mendenhall, 1990; Deshpande & Visweswaran, 1992).

Planning for training programs can be improved greatly if program administrators give attention to the goals and recommended content of training that experienced practitioners have identified (Bhawuk, 1990; Brislin & Yoshida, in press). Four goals, all of which can guide the selection of program content, are the following.

1. Training can assist people in overcoming obstacles that could interfere with their enjoyment of their cross-cultural experiences. We know of very few people who have accepted a cross-cultural assignment with the expectation that it would be a thoroughly miserable experience. Rather, people want to find satisfaction in their work and in their everyday lives. For example, Tomoko Yoshida argues in her module that understanding people's differing emphases on external reality (what the "facts" are!) and interpersonal reality (what people's feeling are) can assist individuals in the quest for positive intercultural experiences.

2. People who are experiencing cultural adjustment should develop positive and respectful relationships with others in the culture. These "others" can be long-term citizens in the case of immigrants going through the normal processes of adjustment. The "others" can be members of a powerful and well-established group (e.g., male Caucasians in the United States or Australia) in the case of people from minority groups within a large country. Further, the positive and respectful relationships should be reciprocated: Long-term citizens and members of powerful groups should have favorable feelings toward the people crossing cultural boundaries. The goal of reciprocity often means that both types of people should receive training: those experiencing major cross-cultural adjustment challenges and those in the host country who interact with them frequently. The modules in this book reflect the importance of training for long-term residents of the host country. One example is Paul Pedersen's module on overseas students, which includes large amounts of material for the international student advisers who work with them. Other examples are Colleen Mullavey-O'Byrne's modules aimed at social service workers and health delivery personnel who interact frequently with sojourners, immigrants, and refugees.

3. Cross-cultural training should help people accomplish the tasks associated with their work. People have different tasks to accomplish, and one goal of training is to help them overcome obstacles to productivity. An informal image to keep in mind is that training should assist people in accomplishing tasks with the same efficiency as they would in their own familiar culture. Examples include encouraging overseas students to obtain their degrees in a reasonable amount of time (Paul Pedersen's module); developing effective teams in the workplace that are productive and that can react to change (modules by Richard Brislin, Elaine Bailey, and Tomoko Yoshida); and assisting businesspeople who find themselves on overseas assignments (module by Neal Goodman).

4. Cross-cultural training should assist people with the inevitable stress that they will experience, but it should also encourage people to prevent stress

from becoming debilitating. *Culture shock* (Barna, 1983) is one of the concepts covered most frequently in training programs. It refers to the sense of helplessness, powerlessness, and "fish out of water" feelings that most sojourners and immigrants experience. Culture shock is considered a normal, even desirable, part of the cross-cultural experience and training programs cannot prevent its occurrence. We say "desirable" because if people do not experience culture shock, it often means that they are not moving widely within the host country and instead are staying in enclaves with familiar people from their own culture. Even though some culture shock is not preventable, training can encourage people to understand the stresses they face and to deal with them effectively. An informal image helpful in program planning is to view people, after a normal culture-shock experience, as facing no more stress than they would in their own culture. The job of an air-traffic controller is stressful. However, we can imagine controllers being no more stressed at Narita airport in Japan compared to their work at O'Hare airport in Chicago. Understanding stress and stress reduction is central to the work of language interpreters (module by Carolina Freimanis), cross-cultural counselors (module by Paul Pedersen), and women trying to break through the "glass ceiling" in the workplace (module by Elaine Bailey).

The Content of Training

In making recommendations for decisions concerning the content of cross-cultural training, Brislin and Yoshida (in press) recommended that program planners give attention to four aspects faced by people who move across cultural boundaries: (1) awareness of culture and cultural differences; (2) the knowledge (or "facts" as accepted within a culture) necessary for adjustment; (3) challenges to people's emotional balance that intercultural experiences inevitably bring; and (4) opportunities to identify and to practice various skills, involving visible behaviors, that can assist in people's adjustment.

Awareness of Culture and of Cultural Differences

Many people about to interact extensively with others from different cultural backgrounds are unaware that there is a major influence on behavior summarized by the word *culture*. People are socialized in a culture without much conscious awareness of the fact. They think about culture much like they think about the air they breathe: They take it for granted. People think about culture only when it is taken away from them, and this occurs when they have to interact extensively in another culture. Training, then, should introduce an awareness that there is a major influence called *culture*, that it has major effects on people's lives, and that different behaviors are considered culturally appropriate in different parts of the world. Nonverbal behavior (module by Ted Singelis) is a good example. Most people have learned appropriate nonverbal behaviors in their own culture and are frequently surprised when these same behaviors are *totally inappropriate* elsewhere. For example, many Americans put a great deal of effort into developing a dynamic *individual* public speaking style. In fact, one of us has written (Brislin, 1991) that it is necessary for success in the American world of work. These same Americans are surprised when, on international assignments in most Asian countries, they discover that this same dynamic style may cause problems. A softer style that emphasizes the importance of the total *group* (rather than any one individual) can be much more effective. Becoming aware of these differences is a first step in intercultural success.

Knowledge

Training should cover the knowledge necessary for survival in other cultures, a point made clear by Kenneth Cushner in his module concerned with youth exchange programs. Beyond this necessity, training should also cover knowledge, broadly defined, that is considered important in other cultures. Often, there are not widely accepted facts that people can call on to decide whether an intercultural behavior is appropriate or not. Rather, people in a culture have informal guidelines that make certain behaviors appropriate, and that these informal guidelines are the "knowledge" that they call on. This is a major theme in the module by Tomoko Yoshida on varying views of reality. For example, many businesspeople who find themselves on international assignments are from cultures where punctuality is valued. Appointments scheduled for 11:00 a.m. are expected to begin on the hour! These same businesspeople are bothered when, in other countries, they find their 11:00 a.m. appointments totally unapologetic when they show up at 12:15 p.m. Many intercultural anecdotes such as this one can be analyzed by asking the question, "What's the appropriate knowledge?" In the United States and other nations that emphasize individualism (see modules by Brislin and by Goodman), many argue that appropriate knowledge is that "We should respect the person with whom an appointment has been made." In many other cultures, the appropriate knowledge is that "The person with immediate needs has as much claim to my time as the person waiting for the appointment." The person who did not show up until 12:15 p.m., then, might have helped someone with a flat tire, might have listened sympathetically to a coworker's last minute problem, or may have gone to a school to bring a sick child home. Understanding these differences in appropriate knowledge can be of great assistance in reducing people's culture shock reactions when faced with behaviors that bother their sense of "rightness."

Emotional challenges

When people's sense of rightness is challenged, the reaction is not merely intellectual. People do not respond by saying, "Isn't it interesting that what I thought was correct is considered incorrect in this other culture." Rather, they respond with complex emotions such as frustration, confusion, disgust, and sometimes anger. The importance of understanding emotions is central to helping people achieve the fourth part of the criteria for intercultural success, as discussed above. When people are unable to deal with the emotional challenges of intercultural interactions, severe stress can result that can affect both their mental and physical health.

Many of the modules deal with the emotional hazards of extensive inter-cultural contact. Tomoko Yoshida, Richard Brislin, and Neal Goodman present concepts that allow people to think about their intercultural encounters in new ways so that the line between "challenging" and "distressing" is crossed less frequently. The concepts include the varying emphases people place on hard facts compared to interpersonal relations, the view of people as individual entities versus the view of people as part of a larger group (Triandis, 1989), and the number of rules and norms the people in a culture accept as desirable. Several modules contain guidance for conducting complex role-playing exercises that are meant to introduce people to emotional challenges. These include the modules by Colleen Mullavey-O'Byrne for social service and health care professionals and by Paul Pedersen for counselors. Role-playing is one of the best and most effective methods for introducing emotional confrontations, but it has to be carefully used by cross-cultural trainers (Gudykunst & Hammer, 1983). If used thoughtlessly by inexperienced program administrators, the *training sessions themselves* can become so emotionally charged that trainees will become upset. We have observed training sessions that came to a halt because program administrators were unprepared for the intense reactions that role-playing can cause. We recommend that the role-playing exercises presented by Mullavey-O'Byrne and Pedersen be used (a) only after all materials concerning their use are studied carefully and (b) only by trainers who have had experience direct-ing role-play exercises.

Skills: Actual Behavior

An interesting exercise is to ask people to suggest behaviors that they *know they should carry out* but for one reason or another do not. These behaviors can include stopping the smoking habit, getting more exercise, apologizing to secretaries when one is clearly wrong, writing to one's parents more frequently, not shouting at umpires at Little League baseball games, cutting down on fat in one's diet, and so forth. Most people are able to list these kinds of behaviors that they should carry out but do not. What does this short exercise tell us? It reminds us that the previous steps of awareness, knowledge, and emotional reactions are important but do not provide a complete analysis. For example, many people are aware that they are overweight, know that their health may be threatened, and have become accustomed to emotional confrontations with others because of their weight but still do not go through the steps necessary to shed unwanted pounds. This same process of awareness, knowledge, and emotional challenge but no actual behavior change occurs very frequently in intercultural encounters.

We recommend strongly that culturally appropriate behaviors be identified and (where possible) actually practiced during cross-cultural training. All the module developers give attention to this recommendation. For example, Paul Pedersen encourages the development of listening skills in his module for counselors. Carolina Freimanis suggest ways that language interpreters can increase their effectiveness by improving the recall of material that they have heard presented. Kenneth Cushner suggests that elementary and secondary school teachers develop lists of "proposed actions" when faced with cultural differences in their classrooms. Neal Goodman identifies various behaviors (e.g., business card and gift exchanges) with which American businesspeople will be relatively unfamiliar. All these module developers recognize that intercultural success will frequently be dependent on changing behaviors so that they are more appropriate in other cultures.

People Who Offer Training Programs

The people who can combine a knowledge of goals, program content, and instructional methods in an effective manner are a widely scattered collection of professionals. Some are employed in international program offices in universities. Others are human service professionals, who have themselves participated in many intercultural encounters, in social work agencies, hospitals, and nursing homes. Some are employed by businesses whose executives clearly recognize the benefits that good training programs can offer to their organizations (Tomoko Yoshida is one such person). Given that they are employed full time by one organization, however, they have limited time to offer programs elsewhere in their communities. Some are university professors and/or researchers who are asked to give various kinds of off-campus workshops in their communities (Richard Brislin is an example). Still others are curriculum specialists assigned to their city or state's Department of Education. A few are employed in small consulting firms whose members compete for contracts to offer training programs in various organizations. Although exact statistics on trainers are not available, it is our impression that most people offer training programs as extensions of their full-time jobs (in the field's jargon, they "keep their day jobs" and "moonlight"). Far fewer people make their living solely by developing, marketing, and administering programs.

One feature of the delivery of cross-cultural training, then, is that most programs are organized by people who are not members of the organizations whose members will receive the training. In fact, one of us has argued that this can be a benefit since an odd fact about human nature is that outsiders are often seen as more knowledgeable and insightful than the boring "old shoe" colleagues that are seen every day (Brislin, 1991). Our impression is that the following sequence of steps is likely to occur. A person, whether she or he is an international student adviser, professor, or human service professional, is asked to give a program. The individual from the sponsoring organization has seen or heard about the person through a talk given at a conference, or community service organization such as the Lion's Club, or in general through the process known as "networking" (Brislin, 1991). Assume that the training program is for health service administrators and that the person does a good job. This fact contributes to his or her positive reputation, and more requests for programs are then received.

Once multiple requests are received, people with good reputations as trainers have important decisions to make. They are often asked to give programs that stretch their previous experience and education. For instance, if they gave good workshops for health service administrators, they might be asked to offer a training program in a small business whose executives are contemplating overseas expansion. Or, they might be asked to give a workshop at a small college whose administrators are trying to recruit more international students. The question becomes, Do they accept the invitation? In the past, many good trainers have had to say no, explaining that they do not have access to training materials that are suitable for the proposed workshop group. One of the main goals of this book is to encourage the development of more training programs given the availability of a wider range of materials. We envision, for example, that trainers skilled in programs for international businesspeople will be able to give workshops on college campuses. Or, trainers with experience in programs for health care professionals will be able to offer good workshops through a city's Department of Education. With the availability of modules for various programs, trainers with good reputations will be able to say yes when invited to give different types of workshops. They will be able to increase the range of their offerings given the availability of diverse training modules.

Modules for Training Programs

Although we occasionally refer to the contributions in this book as *chapters*, a better term is *modules*. A module is a collection of materials for a cross-cultural training program that is 6 to 12 hours in length (i.e., 1 or 2 days). Before beginning the development of their training materials, the contributors to this book agreed to a general format that they felt would (a) provide a good structure but that would (b) not stifle their creativity. All agreed that good training must cover awareness, knowledge, emotions, and behaviors in different ways so that trainees are actively engaged and are *not* merely passive recipients of many long lectures. They agreed that trainees can become actively involved in workshops (discussed by Bhawuk, 1990) through the use of various training methods. Consequently, all module developers contributed various types of materials:

- Self-assessment exercises that allow trainees to discover what they know, or what their attitudes are, so that they identify aspects of their intercultural relationships that need attention.
- Case studies or critical incidents that allow trainees to empathize with people who are having difficulties in various intercultural settings, such as in social service agencies, schools, hospitals, and businesses.
- Presentations of key concepts that should provide trainees with concepts and frameworks that will assist in their developing knowledge. This is the most "traditional" of the training methods because the presentations can help trainers prepare short lectures, or the presentations can serve as assigned readings.
- Various exercises that can be used, with minimal costs and demands on equipment, in actual training programs. These exercises include role-plays, group discussions, work on tasks that are dependent on diverse contributions, simulations, and so forth. As discussed above, we strongly recommend that the modules by Colleen Mullavey-O'Byrne and Paul Pedersen be studied carefully before engaging in exercises that could stimulate emotional reactions by trainees.
- Different out-of-workshop exercises, sometimes called "homework assignments." These exercises allow trainees to practice various behaviors in settings similar (and sometimes identical) to those in which actual intercultural interactions will take place. If the training program takes place over a period of time, trainees' reports of their homework assignments can lead to excellent discussions back in the workshop.

We feel that the materials in these modules provide sufficient structure for experienced trainers to expand the range of their offerings. At the same time, the materials allow them to make additions or modifications to meet the needs of the specific organizations that request training and of the specific trainees whose needs will be addressed.

The Organization of the Modules

We have grouped the modules into four major sections that correspond to four types of programs that cross-cultural trainers organize on a regular basis.

Three of the sections are based on the types of organizations in which trainers work most frequently: the business world; schools (elementary, secondary, and tertiary levels), and social service and health delivery agencies. The fourth section is based on the need for a type of program content that trainers universally include: communication across cultural boundaries.

The World of Business

In the section on programs for businesspeople, Neal Goodman covers material necessary for people who are contemplating international expansion and/or who are contemplating overseas assignments. Richard Brislin deals with the necessity of good interpersonal relations in international business. He also deals with a concept that many trainers have found especially helpful in organizing specific pieces of information: cultural differences brought on by socialization in an individualistic culture compared to socialization in a collectivist culture. Understanding this concept is very helpful in preparing people from individualistic countries such as the United States and Canada to work successfully in a collectivist country such as Japan or Korea. The concept is also helpful for people moving in the opposite direction: collectivist to individualistic culture, as with Mexicans engaging in joint trade agreements with representatives of Western European nations.

There is also a module on gender relations in the workplace prepared by Elaine Bailey. The reason for its inclusion is very pragmatic: The same people who develop good reputations as cross-cultural trainers are frequently asked to give gender-relations workshops. Many people argue that the same sorts of concepts and methods needed for good cross-cultural workshops should also be found in good gender-relations workshops. Another pragmatic reason is that, in our experience, *participants* in programs for international business (Goodman) or working well with culturally diverse others (Brislin) frequently bring up issues involving gender in their discussions and questions. A necessity for virtually any trainer, then, is an ability to handle diverse inquiries related to gender.

Education

Cross-cultural training programs can be found at all levels of a country's educational system. Among laypeople, the type of student program that comes to mind most quickly when "cross-cultural training" is mentioned is probably "study abroad" experiences in other countries. Kenneth Cushner presents a set of ideas and methods, based on his extensive work with adolescents, that maintain student attention and prepare them for successful experiences (see Cushner, 1989, for information on program evaluation). Paul Pedersen, again based on extensive personal experience, presents materials useful in working with international students pursuing college degrees at both the undergraduate and graduate levels. In efforts to integrate the concerns of cross-cultural training into other parts of an educational system, Cushner has prepared another module for elementary and secondary school teachers who find themselves working with culturally diverse populations. Neal Goodman makes suggestions for introducing ideas concerning cultural diversity into the university curriculum. He suggests that thinking start with an experience with which all people in higher education will be familiar: interactions between professors and students, and how these are culturally influenced.

Social and Health Services

The movement of people across national boundaries often brings challenges to a country's social and health services for which professionals are not well prepared. Colleen Mullavey-O'Byrne has prepared two modules, based on her extensive experience in Australia, that should prove useful to trainers in different parts of the world. Like many module developers, she focuses on *concepts* that should be useful to many people rather than on materials so specific to cases in one country that they have limited usefulness elsewhere. Another general concept that must be dealt with everywhere forms the basis of a module by Paul Pedersen: People from one culture will often seek help from counselors whose socialization and education took place in a very different culture. How can counselors learn to identify the reasons for people's problems, and how can they demonstrate empathy, when they do not have detailed and firsthand knowledge of every culture whose members they will meet? Although there is no "cure-all" set of answers to these questions, Pedersen presents a number of concepts and methods that should be helpful to counselors.

Communication Across Cultural Boundaries

Within any cross-cultural training program, issues concerning communication between people from different cultural backgrounds are guaranteed to arise. These issues are brought up so frequently that four modules were needed to introduce them. Tomoko Yoshida has analyzed a number of puzzling communication difficulties about which people frequently complain. She argues that many can be understood if a culture's relative emphasis on "reality and the facts" is contrasted with a culture's emphasis on harmonious interpersonal relations. "So why wasn't I told right after the job interview that they didn't think my qualifications are relevant? They were so nice, and so I waited by my phone for a month expecting a follow-up." In calling for an immediate "no, we don't find that your qualifications fit our needs," the person is asking for a view of reality that emphasizes a set of facts. In being nice and not saying no immediately, representatives of the company are trying to maintain smooth relations and to keep (their view of) the person's feelings in mind.

This anecdote also helps introduce the other three modules in the section on communication. Many of the behaviors that the interviewee observed were undoubtedly nonverbal: gestures, body movements, facial expressiveness, and so forth. Ted Singelis provides a framework for analyzing a wide-ranging set of nonverbal behaviors and provides exercises that allow people to "talk about" these often misunderstood aspects of communication. The anecdote also reminds us that language and culture are intimately intertwined. The interviewee heard a set of verbal statements that could have met all the grammatical rules of a language and could have been presented by a person who used perfect diction. Yet there were misunderstandings. When language teachers want to include treatments of a culture's use of language in addition to the more traditional coverage of grammar, vocabulary, and pronunciation, the module by Mark Sawyer and Larry Smith should prove very helpful. At times, people will feel that they have neither the formal language skills nor the cultural knowledge to interact effectively in other cultures. Carolina Freimanis discusses the role of professional and community interpreters in her module. She explains carefully why simply asking bilinguals to help out with potential communication difficulties is no guarantee of success.

A Final Thought

The modules in this book encourage productive and effective intercultural interactions in a wide variety of settings and for a wide variety of reasons. As mentioned earlier, one criterion for intercultural success is that people enjoy their assignments and develop good relationships with others. This criterion clearly moves people beyond a mere acceptance of, and tolerance for, the cultural differences they encounter in their work. We hope, in addition, that many people exposed to these modules will move beyond enjoyment and good relationships. We hope that they will actively seek out the challenges that intercultural interactions can bring. Further, we hope that they can develop a better understanding of themselves given the self-insights that encounters with other cultures can stimulate.

References

Adler, N. (1991). *International dimensions of organizational behavior* (2nd ed.). Boston: PWS-Kent.

Barna, L. (1983). The stress factor in intercultural relations. In D. Landis & R. Brislin (Eds.), *Handbook of intercultural training, vol. 2: Issues in training methodology* (pp. 19-49). Elmsford, NY: Pergamon.

Bhawuk, D. (1990). Cross-cultural orientation programs. In R. Brislin (Ed.), *Applied cross-cultural psychology* (pp. 325-346). Newbury Park, CA: Sage.

Black, J., & Mendenhall, M. (1990). Cross-cultural training effectiveness: A review and a theoretical framework for future research. *Academy of Management Review, 15,* 113-136.

Brislin, R. (1991). *The art of getting things done: A practical guide to the use of power.* New York: Praeger.

Brislin, R., & Yoshida, T. (1994). *An introduction to intercultural communication training.* Thousand Oaks, CA: Sage.

Cushner, K. (1989). Assessing the impact of a culture-general assimilator. *International Journal of Intercultural Relations, 13,* 125-146.

Deshpande, S., & Viswesvaran, C. (1992). Is cross-cultural training of expatriate managers effective: A meta-analysis. *International Journal of Intercultural Relations, 16,* 295-310.

Gudykunst, W., & Hammer, M. (1983). Basic training design: Approaches to intercultural training. In D. Landis & R. Brislin (Eds.), *Handbook of intercultural training, vol. 1: Issues in theory and design* (pp. 118-154). Elmsford, NY: Pergamon.

Landis, D., & Brislin, R. (1983). *Handbook of intercultural training* (3 vols.). Elmsford, NY: Pergamon.

Triandis, H. (1989). The self and social behavior in differing cultural contexts. *Psychological Review, 96,* 506-520.

The World of Business

2 Working Cooperatively With People From Different Cultures

RICHARD W. BRISLIN

The main reason for poor job success seemed to be the inability of [sojourners] to interact effectively with their national counterparts . . . [Sojourners] openly acknowledged that they spent very little of their time socializing with nationals and having host nationals as friends.

Kealey (1988, p. 14)

This module deals with an often neglected dimension of business: human interaction. Even highly qualified people can be unsuccessful if they are unable to get along with others. If one has many allies, small mistakes are often overlooked while accomplishments are highly acclaimed. If one has many enemies, however, the opposite is likely to occur. Through this module people will be exposed to skills necessary for working effectively and cooperatively with people from different cultures. They will also be given an opportunity to analyze their performance and to further develop interpersonal skills.

Contents

Self-Assessment Exercise:
Interpersonal Communication in the Workplace

Please respond to the following eight statements. You can write a short response, or you can use the 5-point scale that follows each statement.

1. When information is conveyed through person-to-person conversations in my organization (sometimes called "the grapevine"), I am one of the first people to learn the information.

5	4	3	2	1
strongly agree	agree	not sure	disagree	strongly disagree

2. When working with others in group activities, I am skillful at encouraging others in the group to make contributions.

1	2	3	4	5
strongly disagree	disagree	not sure	agree	strongly agree

3. When working with others in group activities, I listen carefully and respectfully when others speak.

5	4	3	2	1
strongly agree	agree	not sure	disagree	strongly disagree

4. When high-level executives in my organization share information with me, and when this information is not privileged and sensitive, I share it with my colleagues.

1	2	3	4	5
strongly disagree	disagree	not sure	agree	strongly agree

5. When I learn a skill that is important to job success in my organization, I try to pass on that skill to others.

5	4	3	2	1
strongly agree	agree	not sure	disagree	strongly disagree

6. When people with whom I work are from different backgrounds than myself (e.g., other ethnic groups, other countries), I try to respect differences in the way they behave.

1	2	3	4	5
strongly disagree	disagree	not sure	agree	strongly agree

7. Other people in my organization find me a cooperative and pleasant colleague.

5	4	3	2	1
strongly agree	agree	not sure	disagree	strongly disagree

8. I am good at "reading" the nonverbal signals that others send out when communicating with me.

1	2	3	4	5
strongly disagree	disagree	not sure	agree	strongly agree

In scoring this self-assessment, add up the number of points you gave yourself for each question. The lowest possible score is 8, and the highest possible score is 40. As you read the essay in this chapter (as well as the essays in other chapters on such topics as power, leadership, and individualism-collectivism), try to identify ways that you might change your attitudes and behaviors so that you will eventually be able to increase your score.

Case Studies

Judith's Mistake

Judith found herself in the company of high-level executives much more frequently than she expected.

Hired a year ago, Judith was a division manager in a large multinational organization. Committed to both affirmative action and to the presence of a workforce that mirrored its international outreach, the company had recently hired members of minority groups within the United States as well as nationals from other countries. Judith got on well with members of this diverse workforce and spent a great deal of time with colleagues at about her own level within the organization. This group of colleagues lunched together frequently, kept each other informed of developments within their departments, and occasionally found themselves at the same social gatherings on Friday and Saturday evenings.

After about 6 months in her job, Judith found herself given more and more important assignments by two of the company vice-presidents. Because she was a good public speaker, she was invited to meetings of company executives where she presented the results of the tasks she was given. Given the time that she was spending with the executives, she found herself giving excuses to members of the old lunch group when told of the restaurant that they had selected. When asked about what she had learned about company plans that might be of use to her colleagues, she told them that she was too busy to give them information now, but that she would fill them in on developments as soon as she could.

One of the assignments Judith was given led to the recommendation of a new product line. When the results of tests to determine customer acceptance of the proposed product came back to the executives, however, it was decided that Judith's original recommendation was a big mistake. The executives felt that Judith should have foreseen some of the difficulties and that a lot of money had been wasted on the tests. Judith discovered that there was a price to pay for a mistake as large as the one she made. She was no longer given prize assignments by the vice-presidents. She also found that she was having more difficulties in her day-to-day work within the division that she was originally hired to supervise. Her old lunchtime colleagues, although not obviously rude in their exclusivity, found themselves going out together at noon without Judith.

Questions

In addition to the mistake Judith made with the recommendation for the new product, had she made other errors in her relations with others at the company? What were these errors and how could they have been prevented?

Different Approaches to Their Jobs

Stan and Peter received their assignments to India at about the same time. Interested in international affairs because of some courses they took at an American university, Stan and Peter found themselves seeking employment overseas. Even though they were engineering majors, they had enjoyed the courses they had taken to fulfill their university's general education requirement, and these courses had a strong international component. Another quality they had in common was that they were unmarried. They felt that without the "stay at home" pressures that a family can bring, they should take advantage of any opportunity they could to live overseas, realizing that such experience would undoubtedly be useful in their later career development.

Working in nearby villages in India, Stan and Peter recommended to local farmers that agricultural yields could be increased with a simple yet effective irrigation system. After extensive discussions with the farmers who would be involved, the systems were built and began to function. At this point, Stan and Peter began to diverge in their approaches to their jobs. After a day's work, Stan found himself spending more time with other Americans who happened to be living nearby. He did not ignore his work and in fact was well-liked by his Indian colleagues, but he did not spend much free time with host nationals. Peter, however, spent a lot of his voluntary free time with Indian farmers. He would walk with them to various points along the irrigation canals, explaining the details of construction and giving advice about maintenance. Peter found that one young farmer was especially clever when asking questions about the irrigation system. Consequently, Peter spent a great deal of time with this farmer, answering questions and even posing hypothetical problems that might interfere with the irrigation system. The young farmer enjoyed solving these problems, sometimes going to elders in the village to discover key points of information needed to convince Peter that he had a good solution. Peter noted that the elders seemed to like this young farmer and respected him both for spending time with Peter and for his willingness to seek out additional information.

Eventually, Stan and Peter left India to take assignments in the United States, where both had good careers. However, there was quite a difference in the long-range success of the two irrigation projects. The project in which Stan was involved fell into disrepair and was abandoned. Villagers did not have much good to say about their memories of Stan's sojourn with them. The project in which Peter was involved, in contrast, was both operative and well-maintained. In fact, farmers from a third village used it as a model for developing their own irrigation system.

Questions

What is the difference between Stan's approach to his job and Peter's approach that led to the failure versus success of the two projects? What are the values of various people and how did these values contribute to the two very different outcomes?

Skill Concepts: The Importance of Others in One's Work

Is there a difference in the *image* people have concerning what good managers do and what managers actually do in their day-to-day work? Answering yes, Mintzberg (1975; reprinted 1990) contributed important insights and shattered some popular stereotypes concerning the work of managers and executives. The popular view of the successful manager includes mental pictures of people sitting quietly in their offices contemplating the future of their organizations. They have large amounts of time to read the *Wall Street Journal*, *Business Week*, and the *Harvard Business Review*. Occasionally, they will call in other executives and share ideas about change and expansion. These well-read and thoughtful people then supervise the preparation of plans to put their carefully thought-out ideas into practice. They calmly wait for their subordinates to put the plans into action, only occasionally finding it necessary to intervene in developments and to make minor modifications.

As might be inferred by now, this stereotype or myth has little basis in reality. Following and shadowing managers for days at a time, Mintzberg (1975) found that managers are constantly talking to others at all levels within the organization: with their superiors, with others at their own level, and with their subordinates. Further, there is a great deal of interaction with people outside the organization in activities summarized by the commonly used term *networking*. Managers are constantly interrupted by others: Secretaries try to put through phone calls, subordinates want to have a quick chat about a problem, and visitors to the organization want a chunk of time. They have to run off to meetings, regretting that they haven't had enough time to prepare as well as they would have wished. With all these demands on their time, managers might have as little as 15 minutes a day for careful, uninterrupted thought about their future efforts on behalf of their organization. "Read books?" they complain. "When is there any time? I can glance at some of the trade magazines now and then, but I could always use more time to spend on them!"

If good managers are not solitary and careful thinkers reminiscent of biblical scholars who spend 8 hours a day in their libraries, they must be good at something to get their work done, to earn their promotions, and to contribute to the overall success of their organizations. This conclusion is indeed true, and what good managers do is to work well with others. In everyday terms, they get along with lots of different people, make their subordinates feel appreciated, learn about what's happening in their organization through effective communications with many different colleagues, and in general are liked and respected by others. Through their good interpersonal skills, they get their jobs done. They may not have enough time for as much reading as they would like to do, but they obtain necessary information about important developments through conversations with others. They may not have the time they desire to develop and to put forward their vision for the organization's future, but they are able to collect the contributions of their colleagues if these other people feel comfortable and appreciated when suggesting future directions. When the managers are overwhelmed by the demands on their time, they are able to delegate some of these demands to others. Given the managers' "people skills," these colleagues are willing to share the burden, knowing that the managers will be willing to reciprocate in the future.

What does all of this mean? The extremely important implication is that individuals seeking managerial careers must get along well with many different kinds of people. There are many terms for the necessary behaviors managers must possess: people skills, interpersonal skills, tendency to be liked and respected, the ability to give and to receive information during face-to-face conversations, and so forth. Does all this seem to be common sense? In an *ideal* world, it would be. The ability to work well with others in this *actual* world is not as widespread as *employers* would desire. In surveys of what businesspeople look for when hiring college graduates, a frequent complaint is that job seekers lack good communication skills and good interpersonal skills. They may be very well trained in technical skills (e.g., forecasting using econometric models, computer expertise, and excellent knowledge of business law), but they cannot use these skills in the business world because they can't get along with anyone. If new hires are unfriendly and abrasive in their demeanor, and cannot communicate their knowledge to others during face-to-face meetings and as part of informal conversations, they will be unable to contribute effectively to their organization.

In their book *Management Education and Development: Drift or Thrust into the 21st Century?* Porter and McKibbin (1988) reviewed the criticisms of business school graduates from the point of view of people who might hire them. One of the four categories of common criticisms was "poor communication and interpersonal skills." Porter and McKibbin (1988, p. 99) summarize the problem in words that are hard to misunderstand: "Various surveys carried out in the early 1980's indicated that there was a widespread perception in the practicing world of business that business school graduates were deficient in communication skills—both oral and, especially, written. Often such criticisms also included the area of interpersonal skills, [a capability that] is at least as much related to leadership as to communication." Interpersonal skills are central to success in intercultural interactions, and this important relationship will be discussed throughout this chapter.

Perhaps I can add a personal note to this discussion. I have worked with students for over 25 years. I have had the opportunity to see students in the classroom and to later see a number of them after they had invested a number of years in their careers. Who was highly successful and who was less successful? Who was successful in classroom activities and in test performance, but less so on securing employment after graduation? Who might have gotten "Cs" on their report cards, but later were highly respected and successful within their organizations? The answer centers on interpersonal skills. People who are easy to get along with, who can communicate effectively with lots of different people, and whom *others* seek out for mutual sharing of information, are the students who achieved success. Abrasive, unlikable people, even though they may have received the best grades as students, were far less successful in their careers.

Importance for International Assignments

The importance of interpersonal skills is perhaps even more evident when people find themselves on international assignments and/or traveling extensively in other countries. Researchers interested in the unique challenges that stem from extensive intercultural interactions have asked the question, "What are the qualities of people who are successful on international assignments?" Answers to the question have been summarized in a number of places (e.g., Brislin, 1981; Hannigan, 1990; Hawes & Kealey, 1981; Kealey & Ruben, 1983). Many types of important intercultural assignments could be discussed, and the experiences of international businesspeople provide clear examples. For businesspeople, *success* is defined in terms of goal accomplishments that have a universal aspect: setting up joint ventures, introducing products in another country for the first time, demonstrating improved production capacity, and so forth. One of the *roads* to these goals is good intercultural interaction, a concept that refers to a genuine interest in working with people from other countries as well as the ability to do so. Hawes and Kealey (1981, p. 161) list seven more specific indicators of good intercultural interaction:

1. *Interaction with host nationals socially and on the job.* The opposite side of this indicator refers to people who interact only with people from their own national background who happen to be living in the same overseas site.

2. *Interest in and some knowledge of local language, such as modes of greeting or salutations.* Almost all people appreciate the efforts of visitors to learn some of the local language. If time demands prevent extensive study of another language, the effort spent on learning a hundred commonly used phrases (greetings, polite remarks, commonly used questions to elicit more information) will pay handsome dividends.

3. *Knowledge of local nonverbal modes of communication.* Many psychologists argue that *more* information is conveyed through nonverbal signals than through words and phrases that emanate from peoples' mouths (Damen, 1987). Surely we have all been in social settings where another person said something such as, "We'll have to meet for lunch soon!" The words said one thing, but nonverbal signals (such as the person's body posture, amount of eye contact, or facial expression) conveyed that the luncheon meeting would probably never take place. Knowledge of another country's nonverbal signals that indicate such important messages as interest versus disinterest in a proposal will be very helpful. Businesspeople who complain about "inscrutable" individuals from other countries (Asians are frequently the target of this complaint) are usually saying that they are unable to interpret nonverbal messages. (This topic is treated in more detail in Chapter 14 by Ted Singelis.)

4. *Factual knowledge about the local culture.* This indicator includes knowledge about the "hard" aspects of business such as accounting practices and tax structure, as well as the "soft" aspects such as preferred leadership styles and negotiating tactics.

5. *Expressing concern with and training nationals.* In an important series of studies, Kealey (1988; see also Hawes & Kealey, 1981) asked host nationals about technical assistance advisers who had the best reputations over a long period of time. In other words, Kealey was interested in the sort of adviser who would be remembered fondly by host-country nationals *after* the adviser returned to his or her own country. The advisers who had good long-term reputations were those who provided training to hosts—the advisers had skills to offer and they made sure that *hosts* developed those same skills. Even if their formal job descriptions did not include the expectations that training programs be established and that skills be transferred, the successful advisers took it on themselves to add these tasks to their workdays.

6. *Tolerance and openness toward local culture and conditions, local mentality and customs.* People are very sensitive about criticisms of their culture. If visitors make no attempts to understand cultural differences and to respect local customs, they will have many doors slammed in their faces when they try to accomplish their goals. It is wise to learn local customs and to participate in respected rituals whenever possible. In Japan, for instance, there are frequent social gatherings of company managers during evening hours, and the chief executive officer is often present. During some of these gatherings, many participants provide entertainment—they tell a story, sing a song, play a musical instrument, and so forth. A businessperson from another country is not expected to participate, but if he or she can, this fact will be remembered the next day when the businessperson presents proposals for various cooperative efforts. No joint ventures will be determined by whether or not the visitor can contribute to the merriment of the evening, of course. But such participation (that adds the quality of "human sincerity" highly valued by the Japanese) can

provide the slight "edge" that makes one businessperson stand out from the competition.

7. *Attitudes of collaboration and cooperation.* Forty years ago, it may have been possible for businesspeople from the United States to dictate their wishes to colleagues in other countries. The United States was victorious in World War II, the economies of Japan and Germany were in shambles, and American managers were universally respected as having incredible "know-how." The facts have changed since then. There is no one dominant nation that can dictate the direction of the world's economy. There are many "players" on the economic world stage, and businesspeople must convey attitudes of collaboration and cooperation. They must communicate the feeling that "we all have a great deal to bring to this business venture. Let's work together and cooperate so that we will all benefit." If businesspeople from one country are unable to convey this set of attitudes, they will lose international opportunities to businesspeople from other countries.

The Importance of Good Interpersonal Relationships

A central aspect of all seven indicators of good intercultural interaction is the ability to work well with others. The major difference between interactions with others on international assignments and on assignments within one's own country, of course, is that the others possess many qualities summarized by the word *different*. The others speak various languages, have different skin colors, possess an array of attitudes toward important aspects of life such as work and recreation, eat different foods, and so forth. The ability to get along well with others despite these differences is central to success on overseas assignments. It is useful to review the seven indicators of intercultural interaction again with the importance of good interpersonal relationships in mind.

The first indicator involves interaction on the job and in social activities outside the workplace. If people get along well with others, they are sought out for interactions and are invited to various social gatherings. Others look forward to more interactions. In contrast, abrasive and unpleasant people are avoided and find themselves frozen out of both informal conversations at work and from social gatherings. I argued in an extensive discussion of power (Brislin, 1991) that successful people know that one skill associated with power is the ability to combine the talents of many individuals. If a person gets along well with others, she or he is more likely to know about their various talents and will be in a better position to elicit their cooperation. Cordial people also know about *current* developments in their organization since they are well situated in informal communication networks. In contrast, since few coworkers speak with unpleasant people, these individuals never know what is currently going on in their organizations. They may read about developments later in the company newsletter, but by the time information appears in an open publication, it is not of much use. People who knew about the information (e.g., stock options, promotion opportunities, potential new clients) have already milked it for its benefits.

Good interpersonal relations are even more important on international assignments. Since business people do not always know the language of the country in which they are carrying out negotiations, they are more dependent on the kindness of strangers than they would be in their own country. These others can be language interpreters, go-betweens, officials at the embassy that represents the businessperson's country, and so forth. Even if they can read the local language, they are dependent on the advice of others for information on the exact printed sources than can provide useful advice. When discussions focus on the case of American business people in other countries, there are often discussions of *style*. Counterparts in other countries often make a distinction between the expertise of American businesspeople and their interpersonal style (Adler, 1986). They appreciate the Americans' knowledge but react negatively if this knowledge is not conveyed in an interpersonally acceptable style (Brislin, Cushner, Cherrie, & Yong, 1986). Businesspeople who possess both knowledge and an acceptable style are sought out for further money-making ventures.

One way to either take advantage of one's attractive style developed in one's own country or nurture it if there are some difficulties that need attention is to work on the second indicator of good intercultural interaction. This is the indicator that deals with knowledge of the local language. Host nationals appreciate the efforts of visitors to speak their language and to use common phrases in socially acceptable settings. Most people appreciate efforts even if they are clumsy and halting—the exception may be the French. The stereotype of French speakers is that they are happy to hear their language spoken by visitors—if it is done perfectly. The use of the host national language can be both a road to, and a development from, good interpersonal relations. If businesspeople use the local language, hosts appreciate this and seek them out for further interaction. If businesspeople become serious about their language study and want to become proficient, they have to learn how native speakers use their language in informal settings, or how people *actually* talk. Sometimes this distinction refers to language as learned from books in formal college classes and language as people really speak in informal conversations. The only way to learn the latter, which includes slang terms and trendy expressions, is to interact frequently with hosts. People who interact well with others will have more opportunities to learn informal language.

As businesspeople learn how language is actually used in informal social situations, they will also have the opportunity to learn about nonverbal communication, the third entry on the list of indicators (see also Chapter 14 by Singelis). The classic treatments of this topic written by Edward Hall (1959, 1966, 1976) have long been consulted by overseas businesspeople. One of the major topics he discusses is the uses of and differing attitudes toward time. How people use time can be considered part of nonverbal behavior. For instance, assume that a meeting has been called that would bring together a host country CEO and a visiting businessperson. The meeting was scheduled at 10:00 a.m., but the visitor continues to wait for the CEO to arrive at 10:45 a.m. Should this delay be interpreted as a nonverbal sign that the CEO considers the visitor's business to be low priority? Or should the visitor accept the delay as a *compliment*, realizing that the CEO is giving the message, "I accept you as a close colleague and realize that you understand and are sympathetic with our culture. As you well know, there can be last-minute demands on my time that I was unable to foresee, and my culture's norms say that I must attend to these demands."

Another important nonverbal set of signals to consider centers on ways in which respect is shown for the contributions of others. Verbal signals are obvious: Statements such as "You did well in your presentation" are highly valued by the recipient of praise. Just as important are nonverbal signals. While making the presentation, did others pay attention? Did they show interest in their faces? Did their body posture show involvement in the presentation, or were the people slouched in such a way that they indicated disrespect? Worse, did people engage in other activities such as reading the newspaper during the presentation? If individuals want to convey respect for the contributions of others, they will do well to practice both verbal utterances and nonverbal signals. In intercultural interactions that involve members of a culture's minority and majority groups (e.g., blacks and whites in the United States) or that involve people from more and less economically developed countries (e.g., Japanese businesspeople negotiating in Pakistan), the sensitivity to nonverbal signals is heightened. The representative of the majority group, or the representative of the economically developed nation, may say something positive, but this utterance *must* agree with nonverbal signals. If the nonverbal signals are problematic, such as indications of boredom, aloofness, or condescension, the others in the interaction will pick up these messages. The time spent in *practicing* ways of showing interest and respect through nonverbal means will be rewarded on international assignments.

The fourth indicator of good intercultural interactions involves factual knowledge about the local culture. Facts can certainly be obtained through reading good books, and nothing we say here is meant to downplay this important source of knowledge. As discussed in the first part of this chapter, however, managers and executives have far less time to read books and trade magazines than might be expected. More often, people obtain up-to-date information through short chats with colleagues during the work day and during after-hours social gatherings. The water cooler, coffee pot, and dinner table are often the sources of new information, with the library playing a secondary role. Readers might try thinking through this question. In recent years, think of three interactions you have had with supervisors (e.g., bosses, professors, presidents of voluntary organizations) that were successful because you had important and up-to-date information. Where did you obtain information? Was it from books, magazines, or television? Or was if from conversations you had with other people? If all or part of the information was obtained from conversations with others, how many conversations would not have taken place if you and the others had poor interpersonal relationships?

The importance of good interpersonal relations on international assignments is even more important than in one's own country. There are a number of reasons for this assertion. As will be discussed more fully in the chapter on individualism and collectivism, the preference in many countries is that businesspeople should get to know each other and be comfortable with each other before engaging in serious negotiations. Although Americans believe that it is quite acceptable to "get down to business" because "time is money," people in Asian and Latin American countries want to establish a relationship based on trust before doing business. The American businesspeople who can interact with others in a respectful, pleasant manner will have an advantage over more brusque and impatient colleagues. Another reason is that sojourners in other countries do not know the sources of good printed information, or could not read it if it was handed to them. Sojourners are dependent on host-country colleagues either to guide them to key sources of information or to share it during conversations.

Sojourners should give attention to *their* contributions during these conversations, and these efforts will be a mark of sensitivity toward the fifth indicator of good intercultural interaction: a concern with host nationals that includes the transfer of knowledge and the training of host nationals in new skills. This indicator is especially critical when Americans and others from highly industrialized nations work in less technologically developed countries. As Cialdini (1988) argues convincingly, reciprocity is a universal expectation in human interaction. If one person does something for another individual, the second person should eventually return the favor. There are cultural differences in such details as *when* the favor should be returned (right away or at a later date), but the expectation of reciprocity in some form is universal. In discussing indicator number four concerned with factual knowledge, I pointed out that much information will be obtained through conversations with host-country colleagues. It is easy to be only on the receiving end of important information because host-country colleagues obviously have a great deal to offer sojourners who have only recently arrived on their international assignments. The sojourners should be careful to reciprocate when they can. For example, many sojourners, simply because they will stand out from host-country colleagues by virtue of their skin color, accent, or demeanor, may find themselves in the company of high-ranking executives. If interesting information is conveyed during these sessions, the sojourners should make efforts to share it with colleagues. If the sojourners do not, there can be a great deal of resentment. Recall the first case study in this chapter. Judith found herself in meetings with high-level executives and felt that she was on the "fast track" to promotions. She pulled away from the colleagues with whom she used to spend a great deal of time. When difficulties started to occur within the organization, Judith did not have the support of her former colleagues. She was not able to call on them for help. As my father told me, "Be nice to people as you move up in the world, because you might meet them again on the way down!"

The concern with reciprocity is also part of the second case study, which is drawn from the research of Hawes and Kealey (1981). Even though it was not part of his formal job description, Peter made efforts to establish training programs so that the irrigation system he introduced would be maintained after he returned to his own country. If he had not, the system might have fallen into disrepair and might have been abandoned. Hawes and Kealey argue that technical-assistance advisers who are rated most highly *by host nationals* take the time and effort to prepare for the day when they return home. Such efforts include asking themselves, "What skills are necessary to maintain this construction project and to start others?" The advisers then establish formal and informal programs to transfer these skills to host nationals.

Efforts such as skill transfer and reciprocity will proceed smoothly if sojourners engage in behaviors stimulated by attention to the sixth factor: tolerance and openness toward the local culture and its customs. Host nationals are quick to pick up nonverbal communications that indicate disapproval or condescension. Wise sojourners will ask themselves, "What customs will I surely encounter, and how can I show respect for them?" For instance, in Japan, sojourners will undoubtedly be asked to participate in quality control circles where people give suggestions for improving the company's products. Such activities may be less familiar to American managers if they have worked in companies where workers are rarely asked to make suggestions, especially in the presence of company executives. In the United States, sojourners from Asia might be invited to speak at one of the service organizations such as the Rotary Club or Lions Club. The sojourners may be less familiar with the concept of "service clubs," as they are not as common in Asia. Yet if they turn down the opportunity to speak, they are losing an opportunity to show respect for an aspect of American culture. A list of "the invitations I should not turn down" can be part of the effort to anticipate customs that must be respected. In Hawaii, businesspeople *must* accept invitations to a family's party to celebrate the first birthday of a son or daughter; and they must attend high school graduation ceremonies for a family's 18-year-old. These gatherings are much more important than in other parts of the United States. In Asia generally, invitations to a dinner in someone's home are issued only to people with whom the hosts feel very close. Homes are usually smaller than in the United States, so a host is saying, "I realize that you as an American are accustomed to more elaborate surroundings, but I feel that you value our relationship and will not look down on the size of our home." An American who turns down such an invitation is issuing a grave insult.

If the first six indicators of intercultural interaction are given attention, there should be little difficulty meeting the seventh: displaying attitudes of collaboration and cooperation. If all parties respect each other's culture, and

if everyone involved *knows* that people are trying to collaborate and to cooperate rather than to dictate their own viewpoint, then creative solutions to
difficult problems can be suggested. Adler (1986) presents an interesting case
involving delivery dates for freight shipments from Japan to the United States.
The Americans, who were importing products from Japan, wanted to promise
delivery to *their* customers by a specific date and time. The Japanese, not wanting
to lose face if events beyond their control interfered with the delivery of shipments, were reticent to promise exact times. Because all the people involved
knew about the American concern for time and the Japanese concern with loss
of face, people knew that the problem did not center on lack of respect or an
unwillingness to cooperate. Instead of putting energy into mutual accusations
that charged each other with ethnocentrism and disrespect, the people involved could put their resources into finding a mutually acceptable solution.
The suggested solution involved promising delivery within a range of times
rather than at a specific time. This allowed the Americans to use language
similar to that with which they were accustomed (e.g., "delivery by the end of
the workday on Friday"). It also allowed the Japanese to make promises that
they were confident they could keep (e.g., "the plane is scheduled to arrive
Friday morning, so even with a 6-hour delay beyond our control we can still
keep our promise"). The key to such compromises is a cooperative attitude
based on good working relationships among the people involved.

An Exercise in Cooperation

This exercise is based on ideas found in research dealing with cooperative
group learning (e.g., Aronson, Blaney, Stephan, Sikes, & Snapp, 1978; Johnson
& Johnson, 1987; Kagan, 1989/1990).

The general goal of this exercise is to participate in a workgroup that will
complete a task that no one person can accomplish by himself or herself. Further,
each member of the workgroup must contribute to accomplish the task.

The facilitator will divide the class into groups of about four people each.
Ideally, the groups will be diverse in terms of people's ages, ethnic and cultural
background, previous college major (business vs. engineering vs. liberal arts),
and so forth. The trainer will give each group an article of about four pages
in length on some topic within the general area of intercultural relations.
For businesspeople, for example, the article might be from periodicals such as
Forbes, Fortune, Business Week, Wall Street Journal, Harvard Business Review, and the
like. The aspect of the article that will be different is that it will be divided
into four parts. Each person in the four-person workgroup will receive one of
the four parts. The task is to write a summary of the key points in the article
using no more than 200 words.

Each person in the group must share his or her section with the others. The rule is that no person can *show* his or her section to others: Communication of key points must be done through oral presentations. Others in the workgroup can ask questions of a presenter to draw out the important points. After all members of the workgroup make their contributions, the members must decide on the important points from the four sections, and they must write a summary that incorporates all the key points. This summary will then be shared with the facilitator and with the other workgroups.

Each person should have a number of specific goals in mind:

1. Making a clear presentation of the ideas in his or her section.
2. Listening carefully and respectfully to the contributions of the others.
3. Drawing out the contributions of others when others are unclear or are shy about contributing.
4. Behaving in such a way that the *others* in the group will feel that he or she is a congenial and cooperative coworker.
5. Working cooperatively with others when decisions are made about what the most important points are to include in the 200-word summary.
6. Participating in the decision concerning the final preparation of the 200-word summary that will be handed to the professor.
7. Becoming more aware of one's ability to work cooperatively with others, as stimulated by the self-assessment exercise and as discussed in this chapter.

After the summary is handed in to the facilitator, each person should return to the initial self-assessment exercise and should review the seven specific goals of the exercise presented in the last paragraph. Each person should ask himself or herself, "What specific behaviors might I change so that I will be able to work *better* with others in the future?" Then, each person can ask, "What behaviors and skills have been identified in this chapter that might be transferable to other aspects of my life (e.g., family, volunteer activities in my community, interactions with friends, etc.)?" Hand the written answers to your facilitator.

Out-of-Workshop Projects

Based on what you have learned in this chapter, complete the following out-of-class activities that can help you consolidate this new information.

1. Think of five people you know who have been successful in their chosen fields. *Success* may be marked by criteria such as promotions, presence on the "fast track," respect of many others, and so forth. Then, think of five people you know who have clearly been less successful. Review the material presented in this chapter. Do the attitudes and behaviors summarized by the

phrase "working well with others" differentiate between the successful and the less successful? Are the less successful being held back because of their inability to work well with others? What, specifically, are they not doing well (consult the concepts in the self-assessment scales and the goals presented at the end of the exercise)? Would the successful people be even more so if they worked better with others?

2. Think of a person with whom you work but with whom you don't get along particularly because of an unfortunate incident or a "spat" sometime in the past. Make efforts to make up with this person. Especially if the incident occurred a while back, an opening remark to the other person might be something such as, "I don't remember all the details of the reason we had that unpleasant encounter, but let's put it aside. We can help each other and work with each other more effectively if we can put the incident behind us. I'm willing to forget it and start fresh. How about you?" Then, keep track of the benefits that come your way because you now have an adequate working relationship with the other person. These are benefits that accrue (e.g., key information, introductions to prominent people, opportunities for career development) that would not have come your way without the patched-up working relationship. Note that we are not recommending that people become best friends, only that you and the other person maintain an adequate working relationship.

3. We do *not* recommend the following possibility unless people are good at accepting firm suggestions from others. You might ask yourself the question, "Who has frequently observed my behavior in the workplace, especially my interactions with colleagues, superiors, and subordinates?" Then, give the self-assessment scales from the first part of this chapter to the person whose name you write down in answer to the question. Ask the person to fill out the scale with you in mind. Instead of "I" in the eight questions, the person would have your name in mind (e.g., if your name is Harry, Question 2 would read, "When working with others in group activities, Harry is skillful at encouraging others in the group to make contributions.") Then, discuss the results with the person who filled out the scales. Be sure to make the other person feel comfortable when giving you this feedback on your behavior.

References

Adler, N. (1986). *International dimensions of organizational behavior*. Boston: Kent Publishing.
Aronson, E., Blaney, N., Stephan, C., Sikes, J., & Snapp, M. (1978). *The jigsaw classroom*. Beverly Hills, CA: Sage.
Brislin, R. (1981). *Cross-cultural encounters: Face-to-face interaction*. Elmsford, NY: Pergamon.
Brislin, R. (1991). *The art of getting things done: A practical guide to the use of power*. New York: Praeger.

Brislin, R., Cushner, K., Cherrie, C., & Yong, M. (1986). *Intercultural interactions: A practical guide*. Newbury Park, CA: Sage.

Cialdini, R. (1988). *Influence: Science and practice* (2nd ed.). Glenview, IL: Scott, Foresman.

Damen, L. (1987). *Culture learning: The fifth dimension in the language classroom*. Reading, MA: Addison-Wesley.

Hall, E. (1959). *The silent language*. Garden City, NY: Doubleday.

Hall, E. (1966). *The hidden dimension*. Garden City, NY: Doubleday.

Hall, E. (1976). *Beyond culture*. Garden City, NY: Anchor.

Hannigan, T. (1990). Traits, attitudes and skills that are related to intercultural effectiveness and their implications for cross-cultural training: A review of the literature. *International Journal of Intercultural Relations, 14*, 89-111.

Hawes, F., & Kealey, D. (1981). An empirical study of Canadian technical assistance: Adaptation and effectiveness on overseas assignment. *International Journal of Intercultural Relations, 4*, 239-258.

Johnson, D., & Johnson, R. (1987). *Learning together and alone: Cooperative, competitive, and individualistic learning* (2nd ed.). Englewood Cliffs, NJ: Prentice Hall.

Kagan, S. (1989-1990). The structural approach to cooperative learning. *Educational Leadership,47*(4), 12-15.

Kealey, D. (1988). *Explaining and predicting cross-cultural adjustment and effectiveness: A study of Canadian technical advisors overseas*. Hull, Quebec, Canada: Canadian International Development Agency.

Kealey, D., & Ruben, B. (1983). Cross-cultural personnel selection criteria, issues, and methods. In D. Landis & R. Brislin (Eds.), *Handbook of intercultural training, vol. 1: Issues in theory and design* (pp. 155-175). Elmsford, NY: Pergamon.

Mintzberg, H. (1975, July/August). The manager's job: Folklore and fact. *Harvard Business Review*, pp. 49-61. Reprinted in the same journal, January/February 1990.

Porter, L., & McKibbin, L. (1988). *Management education and development: Drift or thrust into the 21st century?* New York: McGraw-Hill.

3 Cross-Cultural Training for the Global Executive

NEAL R. GOODMAN

For all practical purposes, all business today is global. Those individual businesses, firms, industries, and whole societies that clearly understand the new rules of doing business in a world economy will prosper; those that do not will perish. . . . It is no longer business as usual. Global competition has forced . . . [executives] to recognize that if they and their organizations are to survive, let alone prosper, they will have to learn to manage and to think very differently.
I. Mitroff quoted in Adler (1991, pp. 4-6)

Businesspeople are perhaps the largest group of people who have lived overseas for extended periods of time. Since many of those who traveled in the past had little or no concept of culture and cultural differences, countless stories of their mistakes and blunders prevail. Although many of the stories are quite humorous in retrospect, most were very painful experiences at the time. This module aims at increasing the readers' awareness as to the importance of being knowledgeable as well as skillful in communicating with culturally different others. Various exercises and simulations are used for this purpose. A list of knowledge areas is also provided as a guideline so that readers become aware of the sources of many different problems.

Contents

IV. Applications

V. Additional Activities

Self-Assessment Exercise: Cross-Cultural Awareness

Please indicate the degree to which you would answer the questions listed below. There is no passing or failing answer. Please use the following scale, recording your score in the space before each question.

1 = definitely no   2 = not likely   3 = not sure   4 = likely   5 = definitely yes

___ 1. I can effectively conduct business in a language other than my native language.

___ 2. I can read and write a language other than my native language with great ease.

___ 3. I understand the proper protocol for conducting a business card exchange in at least two countries other than my own.

___ 4. I understand the role of the Keiretsu in Japan or the Chaebol in Korea.

___ 5. I understand the differences in manager-subordinate relationships in two countries other than my own.

___ 6. I understand the differences in negotiation styles in at least two countries other than my own.

___ 7. I understand the proper protocols for gift giving in at least three countries.

___ 8. I understand how a country's characteristic preference for individualism versus collectivism can impact on business practices.

___ 9. I understand the nature and importance of demographic diversity in at least three countries.

___10. I understand my own country's laws regarding giving gifts or favors while on international assignments.

___11. I understand how cultural factors impact on the sales, marketing, and distribution systems of different countries.

___12. I understand how differences in male-female relationships impact on the business practices in at least three countries.

___13. I have studied and understand the history of a country other than my native country.

___14. I can identify the countries of the European Community without looking them up.

___15. I know which gestures to avoid using overseas because of their obscene meanings.

___16. I understand how the communication style practiced in specific countries can impact on business practices.

___17. I know in which countries I can use my first name with recent business acquaintances.

___ 18. I understand the culture and business trends in major countries in which my organization conducts business.

___ 19. I regularly receive and review news and information from and about overseas locations.

___ 20. I have access to and utilize a cultural informant before conducting business at an overseas location.

Suggestions for Facilitators

Have the trainees list the areas in which they feel the strongest or the weakest.

1. Ask individuals to: (a) place a tag on the items they have listed where they feel they have a strong knowledge base; (b) use the numbers allocated to questions in the assessment to link the tagged items to the relevant question in the self-assessment; (c) identify the items where they feel "weakest" and would like to have more knowledge; (d) link these to items in the questionnaire in the same way as they linked the strong items. Then instruct the participants to circulate around the room and try to find someone who has knowledge about a topic that they would like to know about. Have the participants report what they have learned.

2. (a) Ask the individuals to meet in small groups to identify areas of strengths and weaknesses and discuss strategies for overcoming areas of weaknesses. (b) Ask each group to nominate a representative to report the outcome of their discussion to the large group.

Case Studies

Thailand

John has recently been sent by his company to Bangkok to head up a staff of Thai account executives. After 3 months on site, he is beginning to settle in and become familiar with his Thai associates. One day after dictating a letter to his secretary, John is interrupted by a phone call from the United States. He excuses himself but not before asking his secretary to bring him the letter as soon as it is ready. During his phone conversation, the secretary knocks on the door and John motions for her to come in and give him the letter. He quickly scans it, puts it in the envelope, licks the envelope and stamp and returns the letter to the secretary. The secretary appears to be upset but John cannot interrupt the conversation. Later in the day John asks his secretary if everything is all right. She says yes, but John senses that there is something wrong.

Discussion Question

What could John have possibly done to upset his secretary?

Discussion Notes

In many countries, the royal family is held in high esteem. Jokes about the royal family and provocative questions about royalty should be avoided. In Thailand, the king is regarded with great love and admiration. If properly coached before going to Thailand, John was probably well aware of the importance of the king in Thai society. What he failed to consider in this scenario was that given the high regard for the king, the king's picture appears in many places, including postage stamps. By licking the stamp that had a picture of the king on the reverse side, John was showing great disrespect for the king. This was very upsetting to the secretary. The secretary would not wish to cause her boss to lose face by telling him of his disrespectful behavior, so he will probably continue to act in a disrespectful manner.

This example illustrates the importance of the differences in Power Distance between societies (Hofstede, 1980; see also Chapter 8 in this book by Goodman for further discussion of Hofstede). Power Distance refers to the degree to which a society accepts the idea that power is to be distributed unequally. In his research, Hofstede found Thai society to be far higher in Power Distance than the United States. In High Power Distance societies, there is generally greater social distance between people of different statuses, greater use of titles, more respect for age, and a reduced likelihood that a subordinate would correct the behavior of a person who has superior status.

The Netherlands

A U.S.-based corporation operates a subsidiary in The Netherlands from its corporate headquarters in New York. Marge has been given the responsibility to coordinate the joint operations between the United States and The Netherlands at a major international trade fair in Germany.

After meeting with her Dutch counterparts in The Netherlands, all parties agreed to stay in regular communications via phone and fax. Marge came away from her visit feeling very optimistic about working with her Dutch colleagues. Originally, she was concerned because one of her American colleagues told her that the Dutch can be very difficult. Shortly after returning to New York, Marge started working rigorously on the project, often putting in 12-hour days at the office. She would frequently call her Dutch counterparts early in the day (by 10:30 or 11:00 a.m. New York time) but found her Dutch associates unavailable or unwilling to spend a great amount of time on the phone with her. She was beginning to feel upset by the apparent lack of involvement in the project being exhibited by her Dutch colleagues. She also began to sense resentment by her Dutch associates regarding her calls. Even her faxes marked urgent were often not responded to until the next day and in one case not for several days. The original optimism that Marge felt regarding the cooperation she would get was quickly fading. She sought out the advice of the American colleague who had previously warned her about working with the Dutch. He told her that the Dutch are just difficult to work with and that she should try to do all the work herself.

Marge then proceeded to take the initiative in all decisions with little consultation with the Dutch. This only made the situation worse.

Discussion Questions

How do you explain Marge's difficulties with her Dutch colleagues? What advice would you give Marge?

Discussion Notes

An important element of all human communication is the ability to make correct interpretations of other people's messages. Jones and Nisbett (1972) claim that people interpret their own behavior differently than do people observing it. They argue that people usually attribute their own behavior to situational factors (e.g., deadlines and workload), whereas observers attribute the behavior of others to the traits or qualities of "those people." This is particularly true when a *misunderstanding* occurs between the actor and the observer. The process whereby we observe, interpret, and judge the actions of others is known as the *attribution process* (Triandis, 1975). The tendency that observers overestimate the significance of an actor's *traits* in determining their behavior and underestimate the force of situational factors is known as the *fundamental attribution error* (Gudykunst & Kim, 1984; Ross, 1977).

In examining the situation regarding Marge and her Dutch associates, one of the first considerations must be to avoid a jump to trait attributions—"Those Dutch are arrogant and uncooperative"—at the expense of gaining a fuller understanding of situational factors. Had Marge been more understanding of Dutch culture and society, she may have managed the situation better.

Research by Geert Hofstede (1980), a Dutch social psychologist who examined the business styles in 50 countries, identified four dimensions of national culture. One of these dimensions is Masculinity/Femininity. An important aspect of this dimension has to do with the degree to which people live to work (Masculine) or work to live (Feminine). In Masculine societies, work plays a far more central role in people's lives than in feminine societies. Quality of life, close family relations, and more separation between work and one's private personal life is more characteristic of Feminine societies than of Masculine societies. In the context of this case, Marge is coming from a Masculine society in which working well beyond the regular 5:00 p.m. end of the day is quite common and expected. Dutch society by comparison is a highly Feminine society in which the time after 5 p.m. is one's own and will not be sacrificed nearly as readily as in the United States. This is not to say that the Dutch do not work as hard as the Americans. They may very well be able to use their time more efficiently. Furthermore, when nearing an important deadline, the Dutch will make whatever sacrifice is needed to get the job done. However, it may very well have been Marge's expectation that her Dutch colleagues regularly work until 6:30 or 7:00 p.m., just as she does.

Another aspect of Dutch society that is important here is that most Dutch food markets close by 6:00 p.m., so unless the employees get to the store shortly after work, they will not have the opportunity to shop for fresh products for their evening meal.

Had Marge considered some of these cultural and situational factors, she might not have so readily jumped to make negative trait attributions about the Dutch. These will only become a self-fulfilling prophecy if she communicates her feelings to the Dutch. What could Marge have done differently? Knowing something about Dutch culture and lifestyles, Marge simply could have made her calls to the Netherlands at 8:30 a.m. New York time, which would have corresponded to 2:30 p.m. Dutch time, thus giving her Dutch colleagues ample time for discussions and responding to faxes. Her routine calling at 10:30 or 11:00 a.m. always caught her Dutch colleagues just as they were preparing to end the work day. The success of any cross-cultural cooperative effort depends on a level of trust and understanding that goes far deeper than a similar monocultural endeavor.

United States/France

A French tourist fell on a patch of ice in front of an exclusive store in New York City. After returning to France, he developed complications resulting from the fall. After a few months his condition worsened so he wrote a letter to the American store asking for the name of the company's insurance carrier. After waiting 3 months for a reply, he sent a second letter via a private mail service. Two weeks later he received a reply that said, in part, "We see no justice in your alleged claim since on the day you claimed to fall, 9/2/92, it was 90 degrees F in New York and there was no possibility of there being ice on the sidewalk."

Discussion Question

How do you explain this situation?

Discussion Notes

In France, as in most of Europe, dates are written in the following sequence: Date/Month/Year. The tourist wrote that he fell on 9/2/92, which was of course February 9, 1992, not September 2, 1992.

Skill Concepts

The term *globalization*, which was a mere "buzz word" a few years ago, has now become one of the most salient realities for any organization. Most organizations today must look beyond their borders for new ideas, marketing, manufacturing, sourcing, strategic alliances, and potential competitors in their traditional "home" markets. The ways in which organizations have developed strategies to deal with the reality of globalization vary significantly (Adler, 1991).

Although the organizational dynamics will vary based on the degree of globalization, one constant is that the person, the international executive, will be the contact, the person on the firing line in all cross-cultural interactions. Every person who works or anticipates working in the international arena must contend with the serious and very costly mistakes and misunderstandings caused by differences in business practices and social customs. These negative outcomes are less likely to eventuate when those who work internationally or with personnel from other countries develop an ongoing commitment to acquiring the skill for effective international communication.

The purposes of cross-cultural training for international executives are these:

- To increase awareness of how to overcome the hidden cultural assumptions that interfere with effective intercultural interaction.
- To expand their repertoire of culturally appropriate behaviors.
- To understand how cultural factors impact on job performance.

Even the most competent and effective executive at home can be seriously undermined by the ubiquitous and unseen forces of cultural differences. This is not to say that these forces are deliberate, intentional, overt, or conscious efforts to undermine the well-intentioned executive. Rather, they are subtle, evasive, unconscious, and hidden factors. The lack of cross-cultural understanding by executives in today's global economy results in increased time to get the job done right, increased travel time and costs, increased frustration, poor job performance, decreased revenues, poor working relationships, and lost opportunities. By paying attention to some of the critical factors that can directly impact on the success of an international executive, those executives and their companies could dramatically improve their performance and profits. What are these key factors? Below I will examine a few of the critical factors for international business effectiveness.

Understanding the Importance of Culture

It is critical to begin with an understanding of just how profound a role culture plays in our lives. Humans have evolved to a point where culture has replaced instinct in determining our every thought and action. What we think and how we choose to act is a result of what we have been taught in our culture.

Survival is based on how well we learn to adapt to the specific culture in which we find ourselves. An American placed in a North African desert whose culture didn't teach him or her where and how to dig for moisture-laden roots would die of dehydration rather quickly. Similarly, an executive who has learned how to survive in the business world in one culture may find it impossible to survive in another culture. The one key advantage that we have is that once we are aware that there are cultural differences, we can learn from them. Any executive who engages in business relationships with people from another culture must learn their culturally prescribed ways of doing business.

There are many cultures to which a person belongs. There are the cultures of the individual's neighborhood, region, generation, ethnic group, religion, social class, workplace (often referred to as *corporate culture*), and others. For our purposes here, I will be referring to national culture, with the clear under-standing that there are great variations within national cultures. In many respects, one can think of culture as being analogous to an iceberg. As with an iceberg, there is the part of culture that is clearly in sight and there is a larger part of culture (the most dangerous part) that is submerged, out of sight, below the water-line, waiting to destroy any business venture if people are unaware of its hidden danger.

The cultural items above the waterline are the cultural artifacts that usually show up in travelogues. These include: food, festivals, fashions, music, art, and architecture. The hidden dimensions of culture include issues such as ethics, values, conceptions of justice, eye behavior, male-female relationships, notions of cleanliness and sanitary practices, learning styles, and motivation to work, among others. It is these items that can undermine the best inten-tioned executive, unless of course the executive charts a course of action that considers the cultural variations in social and business protocol.

History and Geography

It is not enough for executives to know a little history and geography of the country with which they are dealing. Rather, it is vital to know how these factors impact on business practices. One thing to consider is the historical relationships between countries. An American company held a St. Patrick's Day party in London and invited British associates, while a Japanese firm held its Christmas party on December 7. Neither party did much for the public image of either company. An executive who is hosting several European counterparts must consider historical and linguistic factors in designing the most appropri-ate seating assignments. Savvy corporations have international protocol offi-cers who spend considerable time on such important details.

Most Americans (in this context I am referring to U.S. citizens) are surprised at the degree to which non-Americans view the world, their place in the world, and their business relationships in a historical context. American businesspeo-ple would be well advised to carefully examine past historical relationships and to emphasize their corporate history and achievements of their organization. A simple example of the relationship between history and business practices is the historical necessity of close group cooperation for the cultivation of rice in Japan. As recently as 100 years ago, more than 80% of the Japanese population was employed in rice cultivation. Cultivating rice required a considerable amount of community effort and cooperation. Individual needs were secondary to those of the group. In Japan today, loyalty to the group, group decision making, and consensus building are essential parts of Japanese business customs. The parallel to the historical practices of rice cultivation is hardly coincidental.

Social, Demographic, and Business Trends

All business relationships must be viewed in the context of the trends that are occurring in the society. For example, a company marketing electronic items to teenagers in a society where the teens have no disposable income is wasting its time and money. Businesses must look at trends such as the privatization of industries as important potential opportunities. However, without a deeper understanding of the culture a company may not consider factors such as the importance of patronage in the workplace (even with privatization) when considering some of the hidden costs of entering a new country.

The unification of Europe into a single economic community with unified standards and legally enforceable directives is a trend that every businessperson must be aware of. Likewise, an understanding of trends such as the importance of the "green" issue on the manufacturing, marketing, and packaging of products is absolutely essential in today's environmentally sensitive climate. One trend that began in the United States and is very slow to catch on elsewhere is the smoke-free workplace. Some European executives have insisted on the right to smoke while working in the United States on a 2- to 3-year assignment. When told that this was not permissible, some executives have returned to Europe.

Another major social trend demanding sensitivity is the movement in U.S. businesses to value diversity. The initiatives taken in the United States in this regard are not understood in many countries around the world. An example of this is the role of women in the workplace. The number of women in the workplace and the types of work women do vary significantly from culture to culture (Adler & Izraeli, 1988).

Politics and Economics

The linkage between government and business is generally strong in all countries. Astute international executives need to understand how the linkage operates for each country in which they do business. In the case of Japan, the Ministry of International Trade and Investment (MITI) has played a major role in funding research projects to certain groups. In Japan, a number of conglomerates called *Keiretsu* exist. Keiretsu means "affiliated" or "series." The term refers to the grouping of companies in Japan, which includes the parent company, subsidiaries, and subcontract firms. Many Keiretsus are grouped around a major bank or trading company. Members of the Keiretsu, which can be as varied as beer breweries and cement manufacturers, often cooperate with one another in what amounts to an exclusive network of relationships. Anyone looking for a joint venture partner needs to understand how their partner fits within the Keiretsu system. A similar grouping of companies known as *Chaebol* exists in Korea.

An example of how a lack of political savvy can impact on a business cost occurred recently during a major trade show. A large electronics firm had prepared 40 thousand 25-page full-color brochures in four languages to distribute at a major international trade show. The company was hoping to use the trade show to attract representatives of the Chinese government who would help them with the necessary permits to build a manufacturing plant in China. In the brochures there was a page that prominently listed all of the company's international manufacturing sites. Among those listed was the Republic of China, which is the name the Taiwanese government uses. However, the name is considered unacceptable by the government of the People's Republic of China. Had the brochure listed the site as Taiwan, there would be no potential embarrassment. A day before the trade fair opened, a top-level executive of the company noticed the inappropriate listing. After a few hectic phone calls it was decided to discard all the brochures, which cost over a half million dollars to produce.

Communication Styles

The differing communication styles of a culture can cause serious misunderstandings. One of the most respected analyses of differences in communication style is provided by Edward T. Hall (1966, 1976). According to Hall, cultures can be characterized as having a *high-context* communication style or a *low-context* communication style. A high-context communication or message is one in which most of the information is either in the physical context or internalized in the person, while very little is in the coded, explicit, transmitted part of the message. A low-context communication is just the opposite; that is, the mass of the message is vested in the explicit code (Hall, 1976).

In high-context societies, the meaning of a message can only be understood within the context of the message. Most homogeneous societies are high-context. In these societies, knowing a word or a character has little meaning without knowing the context in which it is used. Because of the need to fully understand the contextual meaning of symbols, Hall argues that high-context communication is a widely shared cohesive force that has a long history. It is also slow to change and works to unify the group using it.

Examples of low-context societies include Germany, the United States, most of Scandinavia, France, and the United Kingdom. When executives from low-context (Western) cultures work with people from high-context (Asian) cultures, a commonly heard complaint expressed by the Westerners is that the Westerners cannot "read" or understand their Asian associates, even when they know some of the language. This is because they are missing the context in which the message is being sent. So although there may be many different meanings to the word *maybe* in Japan, ranging from "maybe" to "no," the Westerner will miss the context and therefore not receive the proper message.

Verbal and Written Communications

If an American were to come home from work and say that during the day she gave a speech and it "bombed" and afterward the proposal she had been working on for 6 months was "tabled" at the executive board meeting, it would be clear to most Americans that this executive had a pretty miserable day. To the British, however, she had a marvelous day. In the United States, to have your speech bomb is synonymous with disaster, it was a horrible failure, whereas in Britain it was a splendid success. In the United States, to have your motion tabled implies that the motion has been put *off* the table with no further discussion at that time, whereas in Britain having your motion tabled means it is being put *on* the table for discussion. In international business situations, there will be many occasions where there will be differences in the meanings of words. For example, in the past in some East European countries the "cost" of an employee's salary was not counted as a cost to the company because the society "profited" by employing someone.

In addition to the fact that words may have many different meanings, the same can be said for many other aspects of written communication. An important example of these differences is the way dates are written. In the United States, the order is Month/Day/Year. In most of the rest of the world, the order is Day/Month/Year. It is always safest to write out the month. Another point of contention is the decimal point and comma in writing numbers. Americans place a comma to distinguish between thousands, while using a period to separate units. In Europe the reverse is true, so 1,333.20 (U.S.) equals 1.333,20 (Europe). More than one business relationship has been destroyed when decimals and commas were misinterpreted by people or computer programs.

The use of translators is one way to overcome communication problems. However, be careful to properly brief translators before and after the translation session in order to be certain that the intended messages were conveyed (insights on these and other issues can be found in this book, in the module by Freimanis). In the case of written translations, it is often advisable to have important documents translated twice, once from the first language into the second language and then a second time (by a different translator) back from the translation into the first language. Two examples from European hotels illustrate potential translation mistakes. In an Austrian hotel catering to skiers: "Do not perambulate the corridors in the hours of repose in the boots of ascension." In a Zurich hotel: "Because of the impropriety of entertaining guests of the opposite sex in the bedroom, it is suggested that the lobby be used for this purpose."

Nonverbal Communication

There are wide cultural variations in kinesics (body movements) as well as in the sense of time and space. When it comes to gestures and facial expressions, it is best to remember that there are no universals. A laugh in one context can mean happiness or embarrassment. Americans have a hard time reading the facial expressions of Asians because the lexicon of facial expressions is unfamiliar to the Americans. Gestures such as the OK sign in the United States (making a circle with the thumb and forefinger) have different meanings around the world (obscene in Brazil, zero in France, and money in Japan). The very degree of body movements is culturally defined. Italians and Latin Americans tend to use motion with their hands a lot when they speak; most Asians find this distracting. The degree to which eye contact is made and sustained also can cause some cross-cultural discomfort. Spaniards tend to stare right into your eyes to the point of distraction even for some Americans who have been raised to believe that looking someone in the eye is a sign of trust (for further treatments of nonverbal behaviors, see the module by Singelis in this book).

The sense and use of space will also vary between cultures. Germans, for example, tend to keep their office doors closed and one does not enter someone's office until being invited in. However, once in a team meeting, Germans will stand closer and touch more than Americans. Japanese offices are wide open so all members of the group can see and hear what is going on. A pivotal place for the key person in a Japanese office is near the center of the office. Those at the periphery (near the window) are less essential. In the United States, a private office with a window is a prized possession.

In the United States, it is common to stand at an arm's length when engaging in a social or business conversation. In the Arab world and some Latin American countries, the comfort level is much closer. This results in a little dance between an American stepping back away from an Arab who then feels detached and moves closer to the American, and so on. Although time is a universal, how it is dealt with is not. The notion that time is money is countered by the need to develop relationships (which takes time) in many societies. Americans, for example, will prefer to get down to business shortly after meeting a counterpart. For many, this abruptness is rude and impersonal. In most countries around the world, people prefer to do business with those with whom they have a relationship. These relationships take time, effort, and expense. They must be nurtured. By American standards of time (quarterly reports, etc.) the long-term benefits of the relationship are not valued because of the need to show short-term benefits from one's work. Such shortsightedness will severely impact on an international executive's effectiveness.

In business discussions, executives who are used to getting things done in a hurry are often exasperated when meeting with those who like to silently contemplate for a while before responding to a question. To break the deadening silence, the former executive is likely to speak up before the latter has even had a chance to respond.

Slang, jokes, and acronyms are generally to be avoided on international assignments. Any form of slang such as sports terminology will only confuse matters. A U.S. executive scolded his Polish account executive by declaring that he "fumbled the ball" and "punted" when he had the "whole nine yards" right in his hands. He then told him that he better "hit a home run" with the next account or else he will find himself "out in left field." Jokes simply do not translate well nor are they used in the same context. One astute Japanese executive who had to give a dinner speech to a group of Americans, and who understood that Americans enjoy a joke at the beginning of a speech, began his speech with an apology (the common way to begin a speech in Japan) that he did not have a joke. This was enough of a joke to get the speech off to a good start. Acronyms likewise should be avoided because they may have different meanings in other cultures and people are often embarrassed to ask for the meaning of the acronym. In the event that acronyms are necessary, a glossary should be provided.

Introductions, Greetings, and Titles

A handshake will be an acceptable greeting around the world. However, the strength, length, and duration of the handshake will vary by culture. Of course, Japanese will still bow to each other and it is advisable for foreign visitors to bow slightly when shaking hands. Mexicans who know each other will hug and East Europeans may kiss. In many European countries it is common to shake hands with everyone in the room before and after each business meeting.

Business card exchanges are an important part of any international business meeting. Variations include where to keep your cards, when to exchange cards, what information should be on the business card, which languages the card should be in, and what to do with the business card once you have received it. One rule to follow: Always bring five times more cards than you think you will need. To explore the nuances of a business card exchange, we will examine the exchange as carried out by an American in Japan.

First, the cards should be in English on one side and Japanese on the other. The Japanese side should have a logo or other marker that will allow the American to know which direction their name is facing. It is important that the company and title be prominently positioned. The cards should be kept in a card holder in the vest or jacket pocket. Never keep the cards in a wallet or a pocketbook. The presentation of the card is done at the beginning of the meeting. Cards are presented with the giver's name (Japanese side) facing the recipient. The card can be delivered by one or preferably two hands accompanied by a slight bow. On receipt of a card, it should be studied carefully to determine the status of the person the executive is meeting. Since meetings usually involve more than one person, each card received should be placed on the table, like an open deck of cards, in front of the recipient so that the executive can tell who he or she is speaking with. The recipient should avoid shuffling the cards, placing them in one's wallet, or writing on them in the presence of the giver. The business card is the symbolic embodiment of the organization; therefore it should be treated with the utmost respect.

As a general rule, use people's titles when on international business assignments. Learn the appropriate titles for each country. People with Ph.D.s should always be referred to as "Doctor." In many countries, people will be referred to by their title only. For example, "Chief Engineer, can you tell us how this operation works?" In Germany, a male who has a Ph.D. is referred to as "Herr Doctor (last name)"; the wife of the Ph.D. is referred to as "Frau Doctor (last name)." The use of first names in business will also vary by country and age. Be alert to these differences. German executives who have worked together for 25 years will still refer to each other as "Herr (last name)."

Entertainment and Gift Giving

Cultural differences in business entertaining include issues such as who one entertains and where, and how one entertains. In countries in which status is important, it is not advisable to invite people of different statuses to the same dinner party. Americans will often invite people to their homes, whereas in some societies the home is considered too private, unworthy, or embarrassingly small to serve as an appropriate forum for business entertaining. In some countries there is a "help yourself" approach to entertaining done in the home. This approach does not work well when entertaining people whose culture teaches them to wait to be asked three times before accepting an offer of food. In one instance, a Chinese guest went an entire evening without eating though he was quite hungry because he was too embarrassed to take food after only being asked to do so once. In another case, an American woman executive was being entertained at tea in London. After having the tea served, the American woman helped herself to cream and sugar rather than waiting to be served. The English woman was embarrassed by the implication that she was not serving quickly enough. In many countries in Asia, it is common to go out after work and have a meal and a few drinks in order to establish and maintain harmonious relationships. Likewise, it is appropriate to invite a client or associate to play a game of golf.

Gift giving has its own set of protocols. As a general rule, a small gift from your home country is appreciated. A gift that is tied to the particular interest of the individual (such as a jazz CD for a jazz enthusiast) is especially appreciated. Gifts for children are also well received. Be careful that the "hometown" gift you are bringing to Singapore was not made in Hong Kong. Because many gifts carry symbolic meanings (such as, clocks imply death in China), it is always best to seek the advice of a cultural informant before selecting gifts. The giving of large gifts, or payments for special services promised or rendered, should only be undertaken after consulting the legal department in the home and host culture. The provisions of the U.S. Foreign Corrupt Practices Act, which are quite complex, hold an employee liable for acts committed on behalf of his or her employer. Companies can be fined up to $2,000,000 and individuals can be fined up to $100,000 and imprisoned up to 5 years. Individual fines cannot be paid by the company.

Marketing, Sales, Quality, and Packaging

Because markets are now international, each organization has to struggle with the demands of the cultural differences in local markets (Buzzel, Quelch, & Bartlett, 1992; Sheth & Eshghi, 1989; Terpstra, 1988). Those companies whose executives had hoped that a unified Europe would allow for a uniform marketing approach have been surprised at the need to remain sensitive to the cultural preferences of each country (Quelch, Buzzel, & Salama, 1991).

Major cultural differences in selling techniques include the relationship between the salesperson and the customer. "Cold calling," which is the relatively unannounced call or visit to a prospective customer, is virtually nonexistent in many countries in which there is a close and long-term relationship between a salesperson and a client based on mutual trust. As one insider advises his colleagues: "In many foreign countries, personal relationships are more important than company regulations and products. Developing relationships takes time, but it is crucial to the selling process" (Flynn, 1987).

International trade fairs have become extremely important venues for conducting business, yet very few domestically based sales organizations have an understanding of how to take advantage of the opportunities that these shows present. Unlike U.S. trade shows, at which there is an open display of one's goods and services and a lot of looking but no buying, a European trade show is relatively closed and only open to those who are there to conduct business. The U.S. company often will spend a lot of money to set up an open display with personable sales people with little seniority or authority. The exhibit is saying, in effect, everyone and anyone is welcome but do not ask too many questions or expect to conduct any serious business. A comparable German exhibit will be more like a fortress where savvy gatekeepers will quickly weed out all but the most important clients who, once allowed into the inner sanctum, will meet directly with senior managers. The message that this exhibit is sending out is that only very special people are welcome and that it is a privilege to be allowed to stay.

Distribution systems likewise vary from culture to culture. The success or failure in penetrating a market will be directly related to having the right contacts. In countries with large conglomerates, such as Japan with the Keiretsus and Korea with the Chaebols, many companies have found it to be advantageous to join forces with these organizations in order to benefit from their well-established and substantial distribution systems. Grey market products (products that may or may not be legitimate but are sold at steep discounts by unofficial distributors) are a hidden factor that must be considered in many countries.

In some societies, the first thing people care about is quality ("Is it the best?"); in other societies, the first thing on a customer's mind is the cost ("How cheap is it?"); and in other countries, the concern is style ("How does it look?"). The color, size, and quantity of items need to be considered in the packaging of any product. The color blue is for funerals in some countries, smaller items are preferred over large items, and the number of items in a package can be critical. For example, a golf ball manufacturer unknowingly packaged their golf balls in groups of four and then sent 50,000 units to their Asian distributor who promptly sent them all back, advising the manufacturer to repackage the golf balls in packages of three. In many of the countries where the golf balls were to be distributed, the number 4 was equated with death whereas the number 3 is symbolic of long life. For golfers who are known to be superstitious, the number of golf balls in each package was more important to the distributor than the quality of the product.

Decision Making and Negotiations

Any executive who enters into a cross-cultural negotiation process without adequate preparation is in for a number of surprises. The variables that need to be addressed include: cross-cultural differences in the concept of negotiations, selection of negotiators, role of individual aspirations, protocols, types of issues, nature of persuasion, value of time, basis of trust, risk taking, internal decision-making processes, and forms of agreement (Moran & Stripp, 1991; Weiss & Stripp, 1985). There have been several analyses of failed negotiations and suggested strategies for improved effectiveness (Casse & Deol, 1985; Cohen, 1991; Fisher, 1980, 1988).

The nature and timing of decision making is likewise culturally determined. In Japan, there is a great deal of attention paid to getting everyone's approval for a project before a decision is made to take on the project. The process known as *ringi sho* allows each person responsible for the implementation of the project to consider his or her responsibility to the project *before* it is approved. In an American company, decisions are made by an individual who will consult with a few senior advisers. Once a decision has been made, then those lower down in the process will be notified and expected to make the necessary changes to implement the plan. When Japanese and American firms agree to work on a common project, differences in decision-making style frequently impede success. The Americans may make a proposal that the Japanese study very thoroughly. Not only do the Japanese examine the proposal, they will prepare plans for the implementation of the project, such as allocation of personnel and resources. During this long process, the Americans have given up hope since it is apparent to the Americans that the Japanese are "dragging their feet." Once the Americans are informed that the Japanese wish to go ahead with the project, then the Americans first begin to consider how to implement the project. This of course is very disconcerting to the Japanese, who are ready to act immediately. To the Japanese, the Americans cannot be very sincere or serious if they have not already thought out the implementation process.

An executive who now works with the Commonwealth of Independent States reports that when Russia was run by the Communist Party, an official who ran a business could demonstrate his power by his ability to make decisions arbitrarily. The problem of implementation was someone else's problem.

Managing

The management of a global organization requires special skills and attitudes (Bartlett, 1989; Davidson & de la Torre, 1989; Harris & Moran, 1991; Mendenhall & Oddou, 1991; Phatak, 1989). There are some key cultural differences that are most significant when managing people who are from other countries. These differences have been described by Geert Hofstede as Four Dimensions of National Culture (Hofstede, 1980). The Dimensions are the following:

- *Power Distance:* The degree to which a society accepts the idea that power is to be distributed unequally.
- *Uncertainty Avoidance:* The degree to which a society feels threatened by ambiguous situations and tries to avoid them by providing rules and refusing to tolerate deviance.
- *Individualism:* The degree to which a society believes that individuals' beliefs and actions should be independent of collective thought and action.
- *Masculinity:* The degree to which a society focuses on assertiveness, task achievement, and the acquisition of things as opposed to the quality of life.

In any intercultural management situation, it would be advisable to examine how Hofstede's model helps to explain any differences in expectations or behaviors (for further elaboration of the Dimensions see Goodman's module, Chapter 8 in this book).

Applications

Sharing Information

Provide your group of participants with the topical headings from the previous section, Skill Concepts (e.g., politics/economics; communication styles). Create groups of 3 to 5 and have your students come up with as many examples as they can describing cross-cultural differences for each category.

Encountering a New Culture

(This application is based on an exercise developed by Paul Pedersen, 1988). Ask two members of the group to assist you by playing the role of consultants in this activity. Choose one male and one female, but do not make a point of the gender-selection process. Ask the consultants to read the following instructions outside the room and prepare appropriate questions for the group.

Simulation Instructions

To the consultants: Congratulations on being selected as a consultant. A prestigious multinational corporation is thinking of building a production plant in Zawambia. Your job is to learn as much as possible about the culture of these people and prepare a report on their culture. Your only limitation is that you must ask only "Yes" or "No" questions of the people of Zawambia. You can end your visit when you think you have obtained sufficient information for your report.

If you have any questions about the game, please ask them before the game begins. Prepare your questions now. Do not go back into the room to start the interview until you are instructed to do so.

To other participants:

1. While the consultants are reviewing their instructions, state the following to the remainder of the group: "You are members of the old and proud culture of Zawambia. The consultants are coming here to study your culture. There are three important rules that you must learn and practice: (1) You may talk only to people of the same gender (including consultants); (2) you have a two-word vocabulary, yes and no; and (3) your response to any question is based on whether the person asking the question is smiling or not. If the person is smiling, answer yes; if not, answer no." (If there are not at least two males and two females in the group, choose alternative criteria, such as those wearing glasses and those not wearing glasses.)
2. Begin the activity when the consultants are ready.
3. After the consultants have completed their questioning of the Zawambians, lead a group discussion by choosing some of the following questions and writing them on a flip chart:

- How would the consultants describe the Zawambian culture?
- Were the Zawambians cooperative?
- How did the consultants feel during the activity?
- How did the Zawambians perceive the consultants?
- Did the consultants notice any special communication patterns by the Zawambians?
- What were the Zawambians' rules?
- How do you explain any misunderstandings that occurred?
- Are there any similarities between the activity and any other prior experiences?
- What helpful hints have you learned from the activity?
- What does it tell you about cross-cultural misunderstandings?

4. During the discussion, include the following key points:
   - Different cultures (just as different companies or departments) often interpret the same event differently.
   - One is likely to seriously misinterpret other cultures if one evaluates them solely in terms of one's own values, expectations, and behavior.
   - It is often dangerous to try to play by the other culture's rules if you do not have a basic understanding of the culture.
   - Differences between cultures are generally seen as threatening and described in negatives terms.
   - People are rarely aware of the impact their language has on an outsider.
   - People often feel that their own language is superior and that people who speak their language are smarter.
   - Along with excitement and curiosity, apprehension, loneliness, and lack of confidence are common when visiting another culture.
   - Developing a close friendship with a sensitive person from the other culture who can serve as one's cultural informant and advocate is one of the best strategies for understanding and working in the other culture.

Cross-Cultural Encounters

1. Divide the total number of participants into groups of three or four. Ask the groups to discuss the following topics and to record salient points on newsprint:
   - Any cross-cultural experiences that the participants have engaged in and the nature of the experience (e.g., tourism, living overseas, having a neighbor from abroad, or having a coworker from a different cultural background).
   - The positive and negative outcomes of these experiences.
2. After 15 minutes of recording responses, a representative of each trio should present the trio's collective experiences to the full group. Lead a discussion on the varied types of intercultural experiences that are part of living in today's world.

American Cultural Values and Stereotypes

1. Divide participants into two groups. Ask one group to consider these questions: "What are some basic values of your country? How are these values manifested in the workplace?" List responses on a flip chart. Responses might include freedom, individualism, materialism, and practicality. Ask the other

group to consider this question: "What are some of the stereotypes of your country that foreigners have of you?" Write responses on a flip chart and discuss how these stereotypes might have originated. Responses could include: friendly, informal, rude, ignorant of others, disrespectful, wasteful, promiscuous, concerned with a quick profit.

2. Arrange participants into a "fishbowl" (two concentric circles). Participants from the first group should be placed in the inner circle. Ask them to discuss for 5 to 10 minutes the possible implications that may result in a cross-cultural situation, given the list of values they generated. Then have participants from the second group occupy the inner circle. Ask them to discuss the possible consequences of the stereotypes they listed and what, if anything, a person can or should be doing to counteract these stereotypes.

References

Adler, N. (1991). *The international dimensions of organizational behavior* (2nd ed.). Boston, MA: PWS-Kent Publishing.

Adler, N., & Izraeli, D. (1988). *Women in management worldwide.* Armonk, NY: M.E. Sharp.

Bartlett, C. (1989). *Managing across borders.* Boston, MA: Harvard Business School Press.

Buzzell, J., Quelch, J., & Bartlett, C. (1992). *Global marketing management.* Reading, MA: Addison-Wesley.

Casse, P., & Deol, S. (1985). *Managing intercultural negotiations.* Washington, DC: SIETAR International.

Cohen, R. (1991). *Negotiating across cultures.* Washington, DC: U.S. Institute of Peace Press.

Davidson, W., & de la Torre, J. (1989). *Managing the global corporation.* New York: McGraw-Hill.

Fisher, G. (1980). *International negotiation: A cross-cultural perspective.* Yarmouth, ME: Intercultural Press.

Fisher, G. (1988). *Mindsets: The role of culture and perception in international relations.* Yarmouth, ME: Intercultural Press.

Flynn, B. (1987, June). Homing in on foreign sales customs. *Business Marketing,* pp. 91-92.

Gudykunst, W., & Kim, Y. (1984). *Communicating with strangers: An approach to intercultural communication.* Reading, MA: Addison-Wesley.

Hall, E. T. (1966). *The hidden dimension.* New York: Doubleday.

Hall, E. T. (1976). *Beyond culture.* New York: Doubleday.

Harris, P., & Moran, R. (1991). *Managing cultural differences.* Houston, TX: Gulf Publishing.

Hofstede, G. (1980). *Culture consequences: International differences in work related values.* Beverly Hills, CA: Sage.

Jones, E., & Nisbett, R. (1972). *The actor and the observer.* Morristown, NJ: General Learning Press.

Kohls, R. (1984). *Survival kit for overseas living.* Yarmouth, ME: Intercultural Press.

Mendenhall, M., & Oddou, G. (1991). *International human resource management.* Boston, MA: PWS-Kent Publishing.

Mitroff, I. (1987). *Business not as usual.* San Francisco: Jossey-Bass.

Moran, R., & Stripp, W. (1991). *Dynamics of successful international business negotiations.* Houston, TX: Gulf Publishing.

Pedersen, P. (1988). *A handbook for developing multicultural awareness.* New York: Praeger.

Phatak, A. (1989). *International dimensions of management.* Boston, MA: PWS-Kent Publishing.

Quelch, J., Buzzel, R., & Salama, E. (1991). *The marketing challenge of Europe 1992.* Reading, MA: Addison-Wesley.

Ross, L. (1977). The intuitive psychologist and his shortcomings: Distortions in the attribution process. In L. Berkowitz (Ed.), *Advances in experimental social psychology* (vol. 10). New York: Academic Press.

Sheth, J., & Eshghi, A. (1989). *Global marketing perspectives.* Cincinnati, OH: South-Western Publishing.

Terpstra, V. (1988). *International dimensions of marketing.* Boston, MA: PWS-Kent Publishing.

Triandis, H. (1975). Culture training, cognitive complexity, and interpersonal attitudes. In R. Brislin, S. Bochner, & W. Lonner (Eds.), *Cross-cultural perspectives on learning.* Beverly Hills, CA: Sage.

Weiss, S., & Stripp, W. (1985). *Negotiating with foreign businesspersons.* New York University Graduate School of Business Administration Monograph No. 85-9. New York: New York University Graduate School of Business Administration.

4 Gender Relations in the Workplace: Using Approaches From the Field of Cross-Cultural Training

ELAINE K. BAILEY

TAKE TIME TO LISTEN to the voice of our strength, to the quiet brag of our hearts. We can, we can, we can. Then let our strength fuse with that of millions and surge to the moment of change moving always towards another time another place of our own making. Let our newly blossoming anger assault unrelenting the injustice that women and every oppressed class live daily.

Esther Ramani
"Sangharsh," India

Although many of us like to believe that sexual discrimination no longer exists, statistics show that women still earn significantly less than men and hold less important positions and that even when they do hold similar positions they earn less than men. This module raises our awareness of the many "invisible" barriers and forms of discrimination that women face in the workplace. Readers are given an opportunity to examine their biases, to reframe them in a positive fashion, and to explore ways to achieve more equity in the workplace for women.

Contents

Self-Assessment Exercise: Socialized Roles in the Workplace

Research has identified the following reasons men and women give for not wanting a female as a member of the work group or as a manager. Respond to the following statements as they relate to most women in your organization. Indicate the degree to which you agree or disagree with these statements by placing the appropriate number in the blank in front of the statement. The response may be placed in different contexts, which can range from your personal beliefs to observations of the behavior of others. It is critical that you reply from your belief and experience base and NOT in a "politically correct" manner. Statements may be reworded if it makes you more comfortable expressing your agreement or disagreement.

strongly agree	agree	not sure	disagree	strongly disagree
5	4	3	2	1

_____ 1. Women are unable to project the confidence necessary to succeed in the workplace.

_____ 2. A woman does not have the power to influence males in the organization.

_____ 3. Females do not know the "rules of the game."

_____ 4. In attempting to succeed many women "come on too strong."

_____ 5. It is difficult to effectively interact with women in the workplace.

_____ 6. Working for a woman reflects negatively on a male's abilities.

_____ 7. Women take jobs from qualified men.

_____ 8. Women in positions desired by males are seen only as "tokens."

_____ 9. Women are too emotional to make rational, logical decisions.

_____ 10. Women have difficulty managing stress, pressure, overtime, and travel away from home.

_____ 11. Women have a higher turnover rate and a higher absenteeism rate than men.

_____ 12. Women ignore or are unaware of the political side of the organization.

_____ 13. Women do not want responsibility, promotions, or job changes that increase authority and responsibility.

_____ 14. Family-related social problems are created by women working.

_____ 15. Women have problems managing other women.

_____ 16. Women in the workplace create sexual tension that distracts from work performance.

_____ 17. Group work is difficult for women because they are not "team players."

_____ 18. Women are not as committed to the organization as men because of family and other outside interests.

_____ 19. Women do not understand modern workplace technology.

_____ 20. Women work to supplement the family income.

You may wish to write and rank your own statement.

_____   _____

_____

This exercise is designed to explore some commonly held beliefs about females in the world of work. To provide a "safe" environment for "honest" exchange, divide into groups of four. Within these groups randomly assign half to argue the "strongly agree" perspective while the other half supports the "strongly disagree" perspective on items selected by the facilitator. The two sides are to defend their "assigned" points of view. The advantages to this approach are that (1) some of the participants will be provided the opportunity to examine an unfamiliar viewpoint and (2) other participants will be provided an opportunity to discuss otherwise "unacceptable" points of view. One of the downfalls of gender workshops is that some individuals feel as though they cannot honestly verbalize their feelings and beliefs. As a result, individuals will say what is expected or "politically correct" during the workshop while maintaining previously held beliefs and behaviors. This process provides an opportunity to honestly convey beliefs and feelings regarding the issues.

Skill Application Through Involving Self and Others

Select one or two of the statements you scored as a 4 or 5. If you had no 4s or 5s, choose a 3. On an individual basis determine the following: (1) the origin of the belief about the statement; (2) the implications for men and women in the workplace; and (3) how you might reframe this perception. To clarify your perceptions and attitudes, form groups of three or four participants. Each participant is to select one of the assessment statements for group discussion and reflection. Each small group will be expected to report to the larger group on the following: (1) the main themes that evolved; (2) differing points of view; (3) the possible basis for these perspectives; and (4) how change can be initiated.

Assessment Worksheet

Statement Example: "Women would prefer not to work outside the home."
a. Origin: Television was a major influence factor by casting women in stereotypical roles of only being a housewife and mother. Literature from nursery rhymes to textbooks placed women within the ranks of jobs traditionally termed *women's work*. The expectations and behaviors communicated by educators perpetuate sex-role stereotyping.
b. Implications within organizations: Biased human resource decisions are made regarding all dimensions of women's careers when they are not viewed as serious career candidates for recruitment, selection, promotion, and training.

c. Reframe: Some individuals, both men and women, would not work if it was not an economic requirement. However, most people derive a sense of personal purpose, satisfaction, and value from their work. Equity should be a primary consideration in making all workplace decisions.

Statement (from the original best of 20, or your own additions) _____

_____

a. Origin _____

_____

b. Implications _____

_____

c. Reframe _____

_____

Statement _____

_____

a. Origin _____

_____

b. Implications _____

_____

c. Reframe _____

_____

Statement _____

_____

a. Origin _____

_____

b. Implications

_____

c. Reframe _____

Skill Concepts: Workplace Reality

John Naisbitt, author of *Megatrends 2000* and coauthor of *Reinventing the Corporation*, has said that the changing role of women in our society is the most significant change in this century. More than 1,000 million females, nearly a third of the world's female population, are projected to be earning incomes by the year 2000. Although some may not agree on the degree of significance, most would agree that the increase in the number of women in the paid workforce has wide-ranging effects. More women are entering the workforce than ever before. Women between the ages of 15 and 64 will approach 50% of the female workforce in developing countries by the year 2000, and women in industrialized countries will comprise nearly 60% of the female workforce (Ness, 1989).

Less conservative estimates project 6 out of 7 working-age women will be involved in the world of work by the year 2000. Almost two thirds of the new entrants into the American labor force between 1985 and 2000 will be female, increasing dual-career families from 55% in the late 1980s to 75% (Faludi, 1991). In a cross-section survey of companies in the United States, 73% of the companies already report that 30% or more of their workforce is female. Forty-seven percent of the companies in the survey have a greater than 50% female population (Towers Perrin and Hudson Institute, 1990).

A decrease in the number of younger workers and appropriately skilled workers will prompt organizations to explore new ways of recruiting women, especially those who are educated but not currently working. In addition to the possibility of bringing new skills and styles to the workplace, the fact that there are increased numbers of working women has generated a great deal of speculation about whether or not women and men work in the same ways, and if they differ, how they differ. What strengths each sex brings to the workplace and how management styles might change as a result of the influx of women are examples of important discussion topics. However, little is discussed concerning the stereotypes and biases of both men and women that interfere with the more basic issues of types and levels of positions women hold in organizations, their level of compensation, and the quality of their work life. Organizational practices consistent with the needs and expectations of women require organizational change that is dependent on stereotypes and myths being explored and then altered.

Stereotypes and Socialization

Socialization of individuals into sex roles is a process by which sexes assume different personality characteristics, preferences, and skills. This process implies that cultural views of the "proper" attitudes and behaviors for each sex are communicated through the messages of parents, significant others, media, teachers, and friends. The messages become internalized as appropriate sex-role behavior and continue to be reinforced. These patterns of behavior provide the foundation for stereotyped sex-role behavior (Epstein, 1988). Stereotypes are passed from generation to generation buried under numerous layers of justifications and reinforcement. A vast variety of laboratory experiments conducted by psychologists have compiled considerable evidence about processes that reinforce stereotypes. The influence of stereotypes to compel individuals to conform to stereotyped expectations results in behavioral confirmation, better known in organizational behavior literature as *the self-fulfilling prophesy*. Individuals tend to observe and recall aspects of an individual's behavior that are consistent with the stereotype and reject evidence that contradicts the stereotype. The issue is further complicated by the fact that stereotyped individuals often subscribe to the stereotypes about themselves. Only a restructuring of the socialization through the education of all parties to the stereotype will lead to erosion and eventually successful release from the constraints imposed by this insidious cycle.

For generations, people survived by remaining within prescribed roles, adapting to the pattern of thought, belief, and behaviors of their cultural group and subgroups. However, survival today is dependent on people rapidly adapting to our cosmic global village through transformations that offer seemingly unlimited choices and opportunities. We change our environment and are changed by it, and in the process traditional customs, values, attitudes, and beliefs are disrupted. As our culture and social institutions change, we must learn to change sex-role expectations based on outdated stereotypes. Our capacity for such learning is a requirement of survival in today's rapidly changing world environments. Yet, inequities remain as life choices and decisions are made by both men and women based on patterns of gender socialization from previous eras.

Role Ambiguity and Role Stress

Historically, the household served as the force that perpetuated gender differentiation from generation to generation. The skills, characteristics, and roles they supported centered on authority and compensated employment for men with domestic work and child rearing the role of women. However, compensated employment and employment outside the traditional role has been an add-on for generations of women in poor and working-class families, minority women, immigrant women, and women rearing children alone. These "hidden working mothers" comprise a significant portion of employees in all national economies and only recently have their numbers been revealed. In the United States three-quarters of all working women are in their childbearing years. More than half of all mothers work, even those with young children, and many are returning to the workplace shortly after childbirth. In 1988, 60% of all school-age children had mothers in the workforce, up from 30% in 1970. Women with children under 6 years of age are the fastest-growing segment of the workforce ("Human Capital," 1988).

Significant role conflicts between workplace requirements and caretaker responsibilities are experienced by most employed women. The stress from the multiple expectations of each role result in role overload, which creates additional job and family problems. Often multiple role expectations create role conflict, which results in additional stress. The fact that a "second shift" of from 15 to 18 hours a week is required of most women has been well documented. This leaves little time for after-work socializing, overtime, weekend work, or networking on the golf course. However, when women hit the glass ceiling, an often-documented statement is that women are just not ready to make the same sacrifices for their careers as men (Kelly, 1991). Comments of this nature reshuffle the blame for career obstacles back to women rather than examine individual and organizational stereotypes. A reevaluation of organizational policies and practices following an examination of gender stereotyping could lead to constructive changes in formal and informal organizational policies and practices.

Self-Image

It is apparent that our various self-images are threatened by accelerating changes within our environment as traditional roles are altering under the impact of contemporary events. Old absolutes give way and uncertainty is left for men as well as women. Not only is the self-concept for many in doubt, but traditional role images in society are being altered as well. What is a woman, a black, a teacher, a manager, a parent? Rapid change requires continuous redefinition of our self-image relative to our roles as well as the role expectations we have of others. Our self-image is a consequence of a continuous feedback loop based on personal trait projection, ethics, style, and the image we project to others. How others perceive us can never be divorced from our self-perception as this feedback reinforces or alters self-perception (Sitterly & Duke, 1988).

Cynthia Fuchs Epstein has been involved for two decades in research addressing the changing roles and self-concepts of men and women. She discovered that gender differences are mostly mindsets reflected through behavior. Her book *Deceptive Distinctions: Sex, Gender and the Social Order* (1989), contains insights into how men and women live, work, and relate to each other. Epstein found that the differences are largely created and kept in place by social, not necessarily biological, forces, and therefore are susceptible to change. The arena of sex characteristics versus gender identity remains yet to be resolved. Current research is under way addressing the significance of biological characteristic differences.

One significant area Epstein addresses is sex typing and job placement. Women and men are still often typecast and stereotyped in their counseling and placement into careers as well as in their development of career aspirations. Women are still placed in low-prestige and low-pay positions. There appears to be little fit or logic between women's careers and their attributes. "At every level of experience and education women are concentrated in lower-level occupations and at lower ranks within occupations" (Epstein, 1988, p. 152). This holds true worldwide in socialist, communist, and Western capitalist societies. Culture over time establishes guidelines and individuals act according to those norms. Behaviors based on these norms form patterns of what is normal, natural, and therefore acceptable sex-typed work.

Compensation Gap

As much as 45% of the pay gap is caused by sex segregation in the workforce. Some estimates, on the correlation between females employed and pay, state the relationship that for every 10% rise in the number of women in an occupation, the annual wage for women drops by roughly $700. In the United States, a resegregated workforce was one reason why women's wages fell in the 1980s; in 1986, more working women were taking home poverty-level wages than in 1973 (England, 1992). The clerical female workforce climbed to nearly 40% by the 1980s; female bookkeepers increased from 88% to 93% between 1979 and 1986; black women were resegregated into traditional female jobs; the lowest civil service jobs increased in the percentage of female employment from 67% to 71%; at the top level the proportion of women in senior executive services had not improved since 1979, remaining at 8% (Faludi, 1991).

"In 1986 working women made only 64 cents to a man's dollar which was actually slightly worse than the year before—and exactly the same gap that working women faced in 1955. The 70 cents figure (often used in the media)— came from a onetime Census Bureau report that was actually based on data from another year and departed from the standard method for computing the gap. It inflated women's earnings by using weekly instead of the standard yearly wages—thus exaggerating the salary of part-time workers, a predominantly female group" (Faludi, 1991, p. 364). Even the 64 cents to the dollar figure is inaccurate because as much as half of that improvement was due to men's falling wages, not women's improving earnings. Take out men's declining pay as a factor and the gap had closed only 3 cents on the dollar. In 1988, women with a college diploma were still making 59 cents to their male counterparts' dollar. In fact, the pay gap was now a bit worse than 5 years earlier. Black women, who had made almost no progress in the decade, were also at the 59-cent differential. The pay gap for older and Hispanic women was even worse. In 1968, older women made 61 cents to a man's dollar; in 1986, their wages were 54 cents to a white male's dollar (Faludi, 1991). The pay gap widened in almost all female employment fields. This led communications professor Elizabeth Lance Toth, who tracks women's status in her profession, to report, "In a forty-year career, a woman will lose $1 million on gender alone" (Faludi, 1991, p. 336).

Power and Powerlessness

Power is vested in those who control the largest share of resources or perceived rewards and have the ability to exercise significant influence. Reward through selection, compensation, performance evaluation, promotion, assignments, new equipment, or furnishing are only a few examples of the resources typically under male control. Organizational cultures sanction rewards for sexual differences between men and women and penalize individuals when they move toward minimizing the differences.

Women are in a double-bind, as few are in nontraditional positions and even fewer are in high enough positions to influence in the traditional manner. Yet, organizations are pointing to the few women promoted as the beginning of a trend and justify past discrimination on the basis that no qualified women were available in the workforce. However, reports of droves of female careerists in the professions have been inflated. Between 1972 and 1988 women increased their share of professional jobs by only 5%. In fact, only 2% more of all working women were in professional specialties in 1988 than 15 years earlier, and that increase occurred by the early 1980s with no change since (Faludi, 1991). Let us look at top executive suites and women appointed to boards. Women comprise 40% of all executive, management, and administrative positions (up from 24% in 1976), yet they remain confined mostly to the middle and lower ranks, and the senior levels of management are almost exclusively a male domain. A 1990 study of the top Fortune 500 companies by Mary Ann Von Glinow of the University of Southern California showed that women were represented in only 2.6% of corporate officers' ranks (the vice presidential level and higher). Of the Fortune Service 500 companies only 4.3% of corporate officers were women, even though women constitute 61% of all service workers. "This means that at the current rate of increase, it will be 475 years —or until the year 2466 —before women reach equality with men in the executive suite" (England, 1992).

The situation is worse on corporate boards, where only 4.5% of corporate directors are women. Only one woman in 1986 held the rank of CEO and Chair of the Board of a Fortune 500 company. She inherited the company from her father and her husband. Today, there are only four more women at the top, with one woman as founder of the company she oversees, one acting, and one sharing the position with her husband. Even the many reports of the rise of female entrepreneurs founding their own companies masked the reality in that the majority of white female-owned businesses had sales of less than $5,000 a year.

The blue-collar work world offered no better news. For example, the ranks of female carpenters fell 0.5% in 5 years and construction inspectors from 7% to 5.4% between 1983 and 1988. Women made the most progress in the blue-collar professions as motor vehicle operators—more than doubling their numbers between 1972 and 1985—but that was only because women were being hired to drive school buses, typically a part-time job with the worst pay and benefits of any transportation position. Official equality policies seldom if ever tackle these deeper aspects of organizational culture.

Teamwork

Team membership begins with being accepted as someone with something to contribute. Many women are not accepted "on the team" because of being viewed as not knowing what teamwork is all about. Men view other men as having learned through team sports what it means to submit to discipline, pursue excellence, and experience pain, failure, and risk. Team experiences provide a vehicle for learning how to relate to others, to learn one's role in a social organization, to realize and understand one's limitations, and to learn the rules of the game. Learning the "rules of the game," which is learning how the rules are interpreted, is as critical to success in an organization as it is on a team. One only learns and is privileged to know the interpretation if he or she is allowed to play. Being a team player is a basic classification and if you fail to be accepted all other positive traits will be discounted. The older male often sees his role as "the coach" for younger male employees to smooth the path for acceptance. The "old boy network" was established and is perpetuated through this process. This is the first stage in the successful career progression of a male employee.

In contrast, traditional sex-role stereotypes place women in restricted roles of surrogate daughters, wives, lovers, or mothers. Women are often judged by sex-role traits such as attractiveness, social skills, and "knowing their place" rather than ability, talent, and potential. The female protégé may become trapped in the role of the privileged female with real or implied sexual connotations. Women are often accused of capitalizing on their sex rather than abilities. Sex-role stereotyping will diminish in the workplace as women willingly forfeit the need for male approval and men learn to value the abilities and contributions of women.

Some Conclusions

If we are to have synergistic leadership and true equality in the workplace, male and female stereotypes and biases must be addressed. Changes in career counseling, training, and job placement require both men and women to move beyond traditional role concepts and stereotyping to realize true equality in the workplace. Over one half of the human race, women, are too frequently excluded from the decision-making process and the halls of power because of biases, prejudices, and outdated role expectations. Human development will never achieve its potential as long as women are denied their right to share fully in the management of our social institutions and organizations. There are many factors throughout the world that constrain female leadership, but there are three that must be overcome if true synergy is to be achieved: (a) obsolete mindsets that restrict the role of women to wife and mother; (b) women's own inadequate self-images that psychologically handicap them from greater self-fulfillment; and (c) male stereotyping of women's roles in organizations, which underutilizes female talents or misuses women's competencies. Each of these constraints requires massive reeducation and attitude change. As long as beliefs, attitudes, and traditions prevail in which distinctions are made about people's intrinsic worth on the basis of sex stereotypes, true organizational synergy will be thwarted. Equal treatment that frees men and women to grow and develop fosters mutual trust as persons of both genders are unrestricted in their roles.

Skill Application Through Observation and Analysis

Case Study: The Job Interview

Cynthia was a recent university graduate entering the job market. She was well prepared for a professional position and had several interesting interviews. The firm she was interviewing with today seemed to be the ideal organization offering a position with many challenging opportunities. Three managers conducted a team interview with her and then introduced her to other employees in the department. At noon, Leon and Curt invited her to join them for lunch. She was expected to continue with interviews and meet with other firm members following lunch. Leon and Curt told her they were taking her to the most prestigious private club in town.

As they entered the dining room a man in an official-looking blazer approached them. "I must apologize but ladies are not allowed in the Men's Grill; however, I can seat you in another dining area," he said. Leon and Curt appeared to be surprised. The three of them were seated in a small, side dining room which was empty. Leon and Curt apologized profusely and appeared to be extremely uncomfortable. Cynthia couldn't decide what to do, however, she sat through the meal. At first she was embarrassed for Leon, Curt, and the firm, but them she began to get angry. Why hadn't Leon and Curt done something or at least left for another restaurant?

Cynthia concealed her feelings during the afternoon, but found it difficult to concentrate on the remaining interviews. She found herself distracted and wondered how often the club was used for meetings and entertaining clients. Would she be excluded from informal networking opportunities afforded the male employees? She also wondered if this situation was an exception or was it an indication of other discriminatory actions condoned by the firm? Two weeks later, she received an excellent offer from the firm in terms of the position, compensation, and benefits, but she had serious doubts about taking the position.

Questions

1. Should Cynthia have asked to leave the restaurant?
2. What should Leon and Curt have done?
3. Should the firm take any action? If so, what?
4. What would you do?
5. Have you had a similar experience? Describe how you managed it.
6. Should Cynthia accept the job offer? What would you do?

Research-Based Advice and Analysis

The following information can enhance or redirect the discussion if these solutions do not surface from the groups. The possibility exists that Cynthia can talk with other women in the organization during the interviews or informal discussions. The embarrassment of the situation may have been dispelled by directly addressing the issue at lunch with Leon and Curt. Sometimes an immediate, direct approach is the best way in which to address sensitive issues. Research prior to the interview on the human resource management practices of the organization can answer many questions in this area. For example, one could inquire as to how many women have been promoted, how many women have been hired, how many women sent to training and what types of training, and if the organization has an Affirmative Action Plan. Have there been any lawsuits or grievances against the company? The level of social responsibility in which the company engages and the community image provide additional information. The battles one chooses to fight as well as the timing of each battle are critical success factors (Brislin, 1991).

Case Study: Ms. Vice President

Susan was one of the first female vice presidents for a large national technology firm. She had worked very hard to move up the corporate ladder to the vice-presidential level. Susan and her husband, Stephen, mutually agreed to postpone having a child until both were well established in their careers. Following Susan's promotion to the vice presidency, both agreed not to postpone having a child any longer. Their child, although healthy, seemed to have more than the average bouts of illness. The day-care facility had no sick-care program, and home-day nursing care was unavailable. The responsibility for sick child care became the responsibility of Susan and Stephen. Although Stephen agreed to equally share in the parenting responsibilities, he seemed to have more difficulty taking days off from work for child care. His excuses seemed plausible and Susan's employer was more than supportive, so she assumed the responsibility for more of the sick-care days.

Susan seemed to manage the additional responsibility and continued her high level of performance within the organization. Based on her presentation skills and performance, Susan was asked to represent the company's West Coast operation at a national conference in New York City. She was extremely pleased to be the recipient of this honor and at the same time was ambivalent about accepting this assignment. Stephen, although extremely supportive and outwardly proud of her accomplishments, had not been enthusiastic about her few previous trips away from home. Susan was concerned about how Stephen would react to this trip because of the time and distance involved. She was also concerned about the issue of sick-child care if their child became ill during her absence.

Questions

1. Should Susan accept this speaking assignment?
2. What impact will her decision have on her career?
3. What options does she have available to her?
4. Have you been in a similar situation? If so, how did you handle it?

5. What would you do in this situation?

Research-Based Advice and Analysis

The following information can enhance or redirect the discussion if these solutions do not surface from the groups. Susan and Stephen can talk with others in their organizations to see how different parents cope with issues such as this one. Single parenting, although not an explicit issue in this case, is frequently brought up in group discussions. The high divorce rate coupled with out-of-wedlock birth and single parent adoptions create additional strains on women. Many divorced fathers contribute little or nothing to the financial or emotional support of their children when they are not present in the family. Empirical studies show that fathers average only 12 minutes per day in primary child care, women average an additional 18 hours per week doing home labor, and working wives spend 15 fewer hours at leisure each week than their husbands (Kelly, 1991, pp. 80-81). When presented with scheduling conflicts, child care takes precedence. In addition to child care, time and emotional investment in household maintenance are still the primary responsibility of the female. Research still puzzles over the failure of males to increase their housework participation as women spend more hours in work outside the home (England & Farkas, 1986).

Case Study: Upstaged Monique

Monique was called to an impromptu department meeting to assist with design and development of the advertising campaign for a new client. Following an intense morning of discussion, Monique was asked to become the account executive with two support staff. Sheryl requested to be part of the team as they have worked exceptionally well in the past. Derek, recently recruited from a competitor, was assigned to the team. Derek is aggressive and let it be known he has never been assigned a female manager. Monique is confident she can work well with Derek, as she has never had problems with her male colleagues in the past. Following 2 weeks of very productive team effort, Monique is prepared to present the team's campaign at the regularly scheduled monthly meeting. This meeting is attended by all upper-level management personnel.

At the outset, Derek positioned himself to be in control of the projection device for the presentation and spread his notes across the front of the table. Monique was surprised by this action because during their preparation for the presentation Derek showed little interest in participating. However, to present a united front she made no comment. Early in the presentation Derek began interrupting Monique to add information that implied ideas were his or that she was forgetting significant details. As the meeting progressed, Monique began to lose control of the presentation as Derek began to field questions that the other male staff seemed to direct to him rather than her. Monique became more and more frustrated as she tried to regain control, which she seemed to be unable to accomplish. At the close of the meeting the managers clustered around Derek commenting on the quality of the campaign and how pleased they were to have him "on board."

Questions

1. How did Monique lose control?
2. What mistakes did Monique make?
3. What impact will this have on her career?
4. What should Monique do now?
5. Have you been in a similar situation? If so, how did you handle it?
6. What would you do in this situation?

Research-Based Advice and Analysis

Ideas are power because ideas bring recognition through contributions that typically represent money to the organization. Good ideas are rare, valuable, and hard to come by. Often, women are unaware of the worth of their ideas and fail to realize that ideas are the most vulnerable property one owns. The noncreative but smart individuals are constantly looking for others' ideas, and meetings are ideal for idea-pickpockets. Information and ideas are often viewed as public property within organizations unless they are put in writing. The difference between the contributions of men and women at meetings is that men more often edit ideas and in the editing stake a claim. Women see their contribution adding to or building on the ideas of others and give credit to the generator of the initial idea (Trahey, 1977, p. 97).

A second critical issue in this case addresses the differences in communication style between men and women. Research has validated that in cross-sex conversations men and women communicate very differently than in same-sex conversations. There is a significant difference not only in the nonverbal communication but in the verbal aspects of the communication as well. Men tend to verbalize more than women; they try to dominate through interruption and control the topic of discussion (Tannen, 1990).

Field Exercises

1. Below are listed some recommendations for change in organizational and work culture. Write a commitment and action plan for one realistic change (over which you have control) in your workplace environment to be implemented on return to your organization.

Planned Change in the Work Culture

a. Emphasize quality of work life, rather than just quantity of goods and services.
b. Promote concepts of interdependence and cooperation, rather than just competition.
c. Emphasize consciousness of corporate social responsibility and goals rather than just technical efficiency and production.
d. Restate relevant traditional values such as personal integrity, work ethic, respect for others' property, individual responsibility, and social order.
e. Encourage the capacity for intuition, creativity, flexibility, openness, group sensitivity, and goal-oriented planning.

Innovative employees assist people and their social institutions to build on, yet to transcend, their cultural past.

2. Identify through interviews or observation "invisible" gender barriers that prevent career advancement. Write critical incidents based on the identified barriers. This can assist in raising personal awareness as well as establishing the reason for unfair practices.

3. Identify one major stereotype barrier for women in your organization. How can this stereotype be altered to assist women to achieve their personal career goals?

4. Select items from the following list of socialized roles and validate or invalidate them within your organization with specific examples.

Gender Role Socialization

A Woman Is Taught	A Man Is Taught
• To do what she's asked	• To control
• To be pleasing to a man	• To score, to achieve
• To hurt no one's feelings	• To pursue goals, take charge
• To look good	• To discuss women's bodies
• To be taken care of	• To have a dream
• To compete for male attention	• To work as a team
• To care for others before self	• To take risks, challenges
• To follow rules	• To make the rules, decisions
• To let others make choices	• To put women on a pedestal
• To be friendly, helpful	• To expect service from women

5. Request or require participants to keep a journal of their experiences and observations for the duration of the training. It should reflect observations and experiences that occur during each session. Special attention should be given to attitudes and practices that encourage sex equity and those that perpetuate sex bias.

6. Interview a female in a nontraditional job and a male in a nontraditional job to discover the issues surrounding sex job stereotyping. Include their perception of the impact of their job choice on family life, economic situation, and how others view their job choice.

References

Brislin, R. (1991). *The art of getting things done: A practical guide to the use of power.* New York: Praeger.

England, P. (1992). *Comparable worth: Theories and evidence.* New York: Aldine de Gruyter.

England, P., & Farkas, G. (1986). *Households, employment, and gender: A social, economic and demographic view.* New York: Aldine de Gruyter.

Epstein, C. F. (1988). *Deceptive distinctions: Sex, gender, and social order.* New Haven, CT: Yale University Press.

Faludi, S. (1991). *Backlash: The undeclared war against American women.* New York: Crown.

Human capital: The decline of America's workforce. (1988, September 19). *Business Week* (Special Edition), No. 3070, pp. 100-141.

Kelly, R. M. (1991). *The gendered economy: Work, careers, and success.* Newbury Park, CA: Sage.

Naisbitt, J. (1990). *Megatrends 2000.* New York: John Monrow.

Ness, S. (1989). *Women in the world of work: Statistical analysis and projection to the year 2000.* Geneva: International Labor Office.

Sitterly, C., & Duke, B. (1988). *A woman's place: Management.* Englewood Cliffs, NJ: Prentice Hall.

Tannen, D. (1990). *You just don't understand: Women and men in conversation.* New York: Ballantine.

Towers Perrin and Hudson Institute (1990). *Workforce 2000: Competing in a seller's market.* Valhalla, NY: Towers Perrin.

Trahey, J. (1979). *Jane Trahey on women and power: Who's got it? How to get it.* New York: Rawson Associates Publishers.

5 Individualism and Collectivism as the Source of Many Specific Cultural Differences

RICHARD W. BRISLIN

The liberty of the individual must be thus far limited; he must not make himself a nuisance to other people.

John Stuart Mill
On Liberty (1859)

A good deal of confusion could be avoided, if we refrained from setting before the group, what can be the aim only of the individual; and before society as a whole, what can be the aim only of a group.

T. S. Eliot
Mass Civilization and Minority Culture

Should a person be viewed as a single entity or should she or he be viewed as dependent on the existence of other human beings? This fundamental question leads to the discussion of individualism and collectivism. Through this module one will understand why individualists and collectivists disagree on many core beliefs such as: "Which is more important, an individual's rights or the group 'face'? Do you or do you not take a once in a lifetime career opportunity that can adversely affect your company? Is group harmony more important than the pursuit of 'truth'?" Through this module, readers will gain valuable insights regarding their own values and behaviors, while familiarizing themselves with the concepts so they are able to use them in their everyday lives.

Contents

Self-Assessment Exercise:
Your Individualism-Collectivism Orientation

Assume that you are in the United States and want to have a good career in an American corporation. Please answer the following questions about your behavior in the workplace. Please use the following scale, placing the appropriate number in the blank before each question.

5	4	3	2	1
strongly agree	agree	not sure	disagree	strongly disagree

___ 1. I would offer my seat in a bus to my supervisor.

___ 2. I prefer to be direct and forthright when dealing with people.

___ 3. I enjoy developing long-term relationships among the people with whom I work.

___ 4. I am very modest when talking about my own accomplishments.

___ 5. When I give gifts to people whose cooperation I need in my work, I feel I am indulging in questionable behavior.

___ 6. If I want my subordinate to perform a task, I tell the person that my superiors want me to get that task done.

___ 7. I prefer to give opinions that will help people save face rather than give a statement of the truth.

___ 8. I say "No" directly when I have to.

___ 9. To increase sales I would announce that the individual salesperson with the highest sales would be given the "Distinguished Salesperson" award.

___ 10. I enjoy being emotionally close to the people with whom I work.

___ 11. It is important to develop a network of people in my community who can help me when I have tasks to accomplish.

___ 12. I enjoy feeling that I am looked upon as equal in worth to my superiors.

___ 13. I have respect for the authority figures with whom I interact.

___ 14. If I want a person to perform a certain task I try to show how the task will benefit others in the person's group.

Now, imagine yourself working in one of the following countries. Choose the one about which you have the most knowledge because of actual overseas experience, reading, having friends from that country, classes that you have taken, and so forth.

Japan	Mexico	Brazil	Philippines	Hong Kong	Thailand
Taiwan	Peru	Venezuela	India	Argentina	Greece

If you do not have enough knowledge about any of these countries, imagine yourself working on a class project with three foreign students from any of these countries.

The next part of the exercise is to answer the same 14 questions, but to answer them while imagining that you are working in one of the countries listed above or working on a class project with three students from that country. Imagine that you will be living in that country for a long period of time and want to have a good career in a corporation there. Use the same scale and place the appropriate number (5 for strongly agree, 4 for agree, 3 for not sure, 2 for disagree, and 1 for strongly disagree) in the space corresponding to each of the 14 questions.

____1.   ____8.
____2.   ____9.
____3.   ____10.
____4.   ____11.
____5.   ____12.
____6.   ____13.
____7.   ____14.

The scoring of this exercise is different from most in that it involves comparison of the two sets of numbers, the one for imagining a career in the United States and the one for imagining a career in one of the other listed countries. Let's call the first time the questions were answered "the first pass" and the other time "the second pass." In scoring, give yourself 1 point according to the following guidelines.

Question 1: Give yourself a point if your number in the second pass is higher than in the first pass.

Question 2: Give yourself a point if your number in the first pass is higher than in the second pass.

Question 3: A point if number is higher in the second pass.

Question 4: A point if number is higher in the second pass.

Question 5: A point if number is higher in the first pass.

Question 6: A point if number is higher in the second pass.

Question 7: A point if number is higher in the second pass.

Question 8: A point if number is higher in the first pass.

Question 9: A point if number is higher in the first pass.
Question 10: A point if number is higher in the second pass.
Question 11: A point if number is higher in the first pass.
Question 12: A point if number is higher in the first pass.
Question 13: A point if number is higher in the second pass.
Question 14: A point if number is higher in the second pass.

If you scored 6 or more points, this means that you are sensitive to the cultural differences summarized by the concepts of *individualism* and *collectivism*. You are sensitive to the fact that different behaviors are likely to lead to the accomplishment of goals and to success in one's career depending on the emphasis on individualism or collectivism in the culture (Bhawuk & Brislin, 1992). Before reading this chapter on this important distinction, see if you can find reasons for the difficulties people had in the following two case studies. Some of the difficulties are due to mistakes in behavior that were the bases of the 14 items in the exercise.

Skill Application Through Observation and Analysis: Two Cases

On International Assignment in Greece

Mike had been assigned to Greece to work in one of the fast-developing overseas branches of the American-based company at which he was considered "an up and comer." Mike's grandparents were originally from Greece, and he spoke a few phrases that he used to use when visiting his grandparents. Mike was never sure whether or not his ethnic background had much to do with the reasons for his selection, but he was eager to face the challenges on an overseas assignment.

Mike had a very pleasant personality, found it easy to meet new people, and so found himself in many conversations with Greek nationals within a few weeks of his arrival. Given that he was able to use some Greek phrases in these conversations, host nationals asked where he learned them. On informing his new colleagues that his grandparents were from Greece, the host nationals were anxious to learn the name of the exact village to which Mike had ancestral ties.

After about a month, Mike began to be disturbed by the topics covered during his informal conversations with host nationals during lunch breaks and during after-hours social activities. Hosts asked Mike about his salary, his religious preferences, whether or not he had attended a prestigious university in the United States, whether or not he had a lady friend, and whether he'd like to meet some nice Greek women. Realizing somehow that the general term *intercultural sensitivity* he had heard about might include answering such questions, Mike tried to be as honest as possible in his responses. On learning that Mike made a good salary, it was not long before colleagues asked him for loans.

Mike found his sensitivity challenged even more when one host national asked him to help arrange a face-to-face interview with the Business School dean at Mike's alma mater. The host national wanted his son to study for an MBA at Mike's old school. Finally, becoming visibly upset at the totality of all these personal inquiries into his private life, the requests for loans, and requests for other favors, Mike informed his Greek colleague that he didn't know the dean very well. Seeing his irritation, Mike's colleagues kept their distance for a few weeks and didn't know if they would ever be as close to Mike again.

Questions

Are there reasons summarized by the terms *culture* and *cultural differences* for the difficulties experienced by Mike and his colleagues? Working alone or in small groups, write short answers to these questions: What does Mike feel about the inquiries and requests? What do the Greeks feel when they make these inquiries and requests?

On International Assignment in India

Florence had long wanted to travel to exotic places. She had to work her way through college and so never had the financial resources to spend a junior year abroad, as did many of her classmates. So when she completed her degree program and landed a good job with a major multinational, she looked forward to the day she would be able to apply for an overseas assignment.

The opportunity for such an assignment came after about 3 years. There were two openings in India, and there were five good applicants already "on board" in the organization. One was Nemi, an Indian national who had lived in the United States for the last 10 years, having left India at age 22 to pursue graduate education abroad. Florence interviewed for the job with Charles, the organization's vice president in charge of overseas operations. Charles took a liking to Florence and had the intuitive feeling that, despite the fact that she was younger than the other applicants, she would be resourceful enough to do well on an overseas assignment. He liked the fact that Florence had worked her own way through college, as he long ago had to do the same thing. He had waited on tables in a fraternity house, and he noted that Florence had worked in the student union cafeteria.

Charles announced that Florence and Nemi were the two selections. Florence had always gotten on well with Nemi during the few times their paths had crossed in the American headquarters, and she was pleased that Nemi would be her colleague given his command of Hindi and his knowledge of Indian culture. Shortly after her arrival in India, Nemi and Florence received a telegram from Charles asking them to examine the possibility of obtaining some raw materials from a rural area about 300 miles from a big city in India. From the tone of the telegram, it was clear that Charles was positively inclined toward the possibility. Nemi and Florence worked hard on their task but found themselves on opposite sides of the fence when it came to forwarding their recommendation to Charles. Florence felt that the removal of raw materials would have negative environmental consequences for two nearby villages, especially the quality of the villages' air and water. Nemi agreed that Florence's concerns might have some validity, but that these were outweighed by benefits that villagers would receive, such as employment in good-paying jobs. Florence and Nemi negotiated back and forth, trying to come up with a common set of recommendations with which they could both be comfortable. Florence was willing to consider Nemi's position on employment in her own thinking but was very uncomfortable when he added the argument, "Remember, Charles is basically in favor of this project." This argument did not seem relevant to Florence. After all, Charles was thousands of miles away and knew practically nothing about the impact that the project would have on villagers.

Questions

Write short answers to these questions. Is there an element in the disagreement between Florence and Nemi that has a basis in culture and cultural differences? What value is Nemi emphasizing that does not appear to be as strongly held by Florence?

Skill Concepts: The Importance of Individualism and Collectivism for the International Manager

"The United States is the major exporter of modern organization theories, but its position of extreme individualism in comparison to most other countries makes the relevance of some of its theories in other cultural environments doubtful" (Hofstede, 1980, p. 219).

The Importance of Individualism and Collectivism

In understanding the nature of culture and cultural differences, a number of analysts have proposed that the distinction between individualism and collectivism is among the most important, if not the single most important, concepts for the understanding of interpersonal interactions during intercultural encounters (Bhawuk & Brislin, 1992; Hofstede, 1980; Hui, 1990). The distinction refers to priorities in people's goals. In individualistic societies, such as the United States, people are socialized to pursue their own goals. When there is a conflict between a person's own goals and those of the person's group, the individual goals are emphasized and the group goals downplayed. People in individualistic societies are rewarded for "doing their own thing," that is, making their own plans and working toward their accomplishment. In collective societies (mainly in Latin America and Asia), people are willing to downplay their own personal goals for the good of a group. People value their group allegiances and are willing to place the goodwill of their group above the pursuit of their own plans. "Loyalty to the group and to one's organization" are valued more than doing one's own thing.

Does all this seem rather abstract and unimportant? The general explanation of individualism and collectivism is admittedly at a rather high level of generalization, but it can be applied immediately to clarify important facts about intercultural interactions. Let's look at an example from international business dealings. Assume that executives in both individualistic and collective societies feel that their managers are behind the times in terms of modern computer technology and applications. "It feels like the 1960s around here," one executive complains when looking at both the available hardware and software. One option under consideration is that long-term training programs should be established. Large numbers of managers could be sent to school for 4 full months, and their normal duties would be carried out by others on an overload basis. Where is it more likely that the decision will be made to actually institute such programs? Is it more likely to be in a collective or an individualistic society? Hofstede (1980) suggests that long-term training programs are more common in collective societies. A major reason is that executives can expect that the people trained will still be with the company 10 and 15 years from now. Recall the explanation of the collective society: People feel loyal to a group and are willing to downplay their own plans. Some people undoubtedly are tempted by attractive job offers elsewhere, but their collective upbringing in their cultures has prepared them for a greater sense of loyalty to their organization.

However, consider the plight of executives in individualistic countries. If they pay large amounts of money for long-term training, there is no guarantee that the managers will be with the company 2 or 3 years from now. If the training is for managers within the automobile industry, a manager who works for Ford today may be working for General Motors next year. To rub salt into the wound, from the point of view of the executives, people in individualistic countries will probably list the long-term training experience on their resumes when they seek new jobs. In individualistic societies, people pursue their own goals. When they discover that another organization has an attractive package of salaries, benefits, and working conditions to offer, they are more likely to move to the other organization than people in collective countries. Incidentally, executives are quite vocal about the problem raised here. When asked to comment on what they find lacking in the American business school graduates whom they hire, one of their complaints was a lack of loyalty to the organization (Porter & McKibbin, 1988; another complaint was a lack of interpersonal skills, covered in the module by Brislin, Chapter 2 of this book).

In his multinational survey, Hofstede (1980) found that the United States was the world's most individualistic nation. Other countries high in this quality were Australia, Great Britain, Canada, The Netherlands, and New Zealand. Countries highest in collectivism are in either South America or Asia. They include Venezuela, Colombia, Pakistan, Peru, Taiwan, and Thailand. Although not among the most collective countries, Japan is far more collectivist than the United States.

Aspects of Individualism and Collectivism

Research on individualism and collectivism (Bellah, Madsen, Sullivan, Swindler, & Tipton, 1985; Triandis, 1990; Triandis, Brislin, & Hui, 1988) has indicated that there are a number of aspects that follow from the generalization of "pursuit of one's own goals" (individualism) compared to "loyalty to one's group" (collectivism). It is always dangerous to make sweeping statements concerning how people behave, and generalizations about individualists and collectivists are no exception. Keeping in mind that there will always be people whose behavior varies from the generalizations, I feel that the following statements about individualism and collectivism are helpful guides.

Individualists are socialized to be self-reliant and to have more of a sense of separation from their extended family and from their community. People do not expect members of their extended families to be major supporters when they seek out employment and develop their careers. Uncles, aunts, and cousins may have a piece of advice or two, but individualists are less likely to expect major forms of help such as "the inside track" on the best jobs. Individualists are expected to "stand on their own two feet" and to develop a set of personal skills that they can call upon throughout their career development. Individualists are more likely to be utilitarian in their thinking about how they use their time and what projects they should undertake. They will work very hard if they decide that the outcomes of their investments of time and energy will bring benefits to them. They are less likely to invest time and energy if the benefits are to accrue to their group, in contrast to them, personally. They believe that competition has an important part to play in the business world and are willing to compete with colleagues for scarce resources, such as promotions to executive positions. Given that they are expected to develop their own skills, they expect to see competence rewarded. Individualists become very uncomfortable when another reason besides competence and ability is used to hire or to promote people in organizations. "Nepotism" has negative connotations because it places a kinship relation above competence in hiring and promotion decisions. There is a discomfort with authority and more distrust of people in power. If individualists are expected to be self-reliant and to develop an effective set of career skills, they then find it difficult to defer to authority figures unless those people clearly have more expertise in a certain topic area. When a vice president says, "I think that we should accept the first of these three options," an individualist lower in the organizational hierarchy is less likely than a collectivist to accept this view in an unquestioning manner. An individualist is likely to say, "What the hell does the vice president know? I have spent a lot more time researching the options, and I think that the second of the three is far superior." Individualists are also interested in pursuing a varied life (Schwartz, 1990) and constantly seek new challenges, begin new hobbies, and move from job to job in the quest for new stimulation. "I just wanted a change" is a common answer given to the question, "Why did you leave your old job? You seemed pretty happy there and you were well-paid." This question will be especially common when collectivists interact with individualists, and this will happen more and more frequently as the business world becomes even more international than it is at present. Collectivists are likely to feel closer to their organization. Especially given the facts that people are well-paid and happy in their work, collectivists see little reason to change organizations.

The most important distinction between collectivists and individualists is the emphasis placed on the feelings and opinions of group members and the psychological closeness between a person and others (Kagitcibasi, 1990). Collectivists are more willing to downplay their own goals in favor of group preferences. They are more likely to be concerned about how their decisions will affect others in their valued groups. For instance, if a person receives a scholarship to pursue a graduate-level degree in another country, a collectivist is likely to consult with others in the extended family. The opinions of grandparents, uncles, aunts, and cousins will be seriously sought. One topic of concern will be the impact on the extended family. Will the person be able to fulfill his or her obligations to the group, such as care of elderly parents? Will others in the collective be able to take over these duties? Will the honor of a person receiving an advanced degree extend to the entire family so that all people can take pride in accomplishment? These concerns are much more likely to be raised in collective societies (Hsu, 1981).

A key point in understanding international management is that one's organization can be looked upon as a collective. This is especially true in collective countries that have achieved stunning economic success since World War II, such as Japan. The same time, energy, and loyalty that once were put into one's extended family have been extended, in a few countries, to one's organization (Triandis, Brislin, & Hui, 1988). Since people's sense of their own personal identity is wrapped up in their organization, they work hard for the good of their company because they experience a sense of self-worth if their company does well. This is in sharp contrast to an individualist, who can experience a sense of self-worth by working hard on his or her own goals, independent of the overall objectives of an organization.

There is more sharing of material and nonmaterial resources in collective countries. People talk more with each other! If one person learns a key piece of information or develops a new skills, there is more likelihood of sharing it with others. People spend more time with each other in social activities and are more willing to sacrifice their own preferences (e.g., going to a baseball game) for the preferences of the group (e.g., others want to take a hike into the mountains). An individualist might say, "O.K., see you next week. I'll go to the game while you people take your hike." A collectivist would be more likely to join the hike. There is a greater willingness to conform to the views of others in the group. Collectivists may have a private opinion, but they are more likely to keep it to themselves if they see that their opinion might cause a disruption in the group. There is more concern with maintaining the approval of one's group and more emphasis on helping others (and oneself) to save face. Here, *face* means the respect and affection of others, and people avoid embarrassing encounters that might cause others in their collective to feel that they have lost status, affection, or respect. There is a greater feeling of involvement in the lives of others. Intercultural misunderstandings have been caused by people's unwillingness to burden members of the collective with various problems and troubles. If members of a collective thought that they had offered membership to a person, they expect that person to share the benefits and responsibilities of the collective. "We thought that you were one of us. We learned that you could have used $5,000 for a business expansion. You went to a bank. Why didn't you come to us?" Membership in a collective involves behaviors that can be thought of in terms of both sides of a coin. It is very comforting to have a collective when help is needed: investments in business, care for elderly parents when there is an opportunity for an extended business trip, and introductions to influential and prestigious people who are somehow connected to the collective. The opposite side of the coin, of course, is the set of responsibilities that goes with collective membership. Others in the collective will feel free to ask for favors, borrow money, take advantage of the introductions to high-status people one might know, and generally become involved in one's personal life. If one wants privacy and does not want to share personal details such as one's current income and the names of romantic companions, he or she should not become involved with a collective!

The Distribution of Rewards

Another distinction between individualist and collectivist cultures occurs when there are rewards to be distributed. If different people in a group contribute in varying degrees to the accomplishment of a task, how are the rewards for task accomplishment to be distributed? Readers might find the following short exercise useful in clarifying the distribution-of-rewards issue.

Assume that you are employed in a company (for profit) that contracts to do construction work (e.g., roads, sewage treatment facilities) in rural areas of the community where you live. The company recently received a contract for $800,000 dollars (U.S.) to build a road. Given a number of fortunate circumstances, such as good weather, the project was completed for $700,000. It is now the end of the fiscal year and the board of directors has decided that the extra $100,000 can be distributed the way people (who were involved in the road construction project) decide. The following people are somehow involved. All have been in the company for at least 5 years and get along well with each other.

Person A was the hardest worker and was clearly responsible for supervising a great deal of the actual day-to-day work on the project. At least 40% of the day-to-day work on the project was done by him. Persons B, C, and D were solid but not spectacular contributors. They were competent workers but not outstanding. Each contributed about 15% of the actual day-to-day work on the project. Person E is a very high status and wealthy person in the organization and in the community. Although he did not engage in any of day-to-day work on the road construction project and did not write the proposal for funding, it is known within the organization that he called upon his connections and used his influence so that the original $800,000 contract would go to the company.

Person F is a contributor much like B, C, and D. His contribution was about 15% of the work needed for the project's completion. His father died recently, however, and person F has considerable expenses associated with the funeral, nursing care for his mother, and the education of his much younger brothers (his father left no estate).

Note that the contributions of A, B, C, D, and F total 100% of the project's workload.

You are unassociated with the project but are asked to help in the decision making concerning the distribution of the $100,000. How would you distribute the money?

If you need to make other assumptions or to presuppose other facts so that the negotiations can proceed, please write these down here.

Assume that you are working in an individualist society. What is the final distribution of money?

	Amount	*A Few Words of Explanation (Why)*
Person A		
Person B		
Person C		
Person D		
Person E		
Person F		
Another person		
Total = $100,000		

Now assume that you are working in a collectivist society. What is the final distribution of money?

	Amount	*A Few Words of Explanation (Why)*
Person A		
Person B		
Person C		
Person D		
Person E		
Person F		
Another person		
Total = $100,000		

The major difference in the distribution of the $100,000 within individualist and collectivist societies centers on the concepts *equity* and *equality*. Individualists prefer an equitable distribution of rewards. Equity refers to the distribution of rewards based on people's contributions. Person A in the story contributed 40% of the work. Consequently, he should receive approximately 40% of the rewards, or approximately $40,000. The other people should receive rewards based on their contributions. For the people whose contributions were 15% each, then the rewards would correspond to this figure.

Equality refers to a distribution pattern where all people receive the same level of rewards. If there were five people who contributed to the project, each would receive approximately 20% of the rewards. Even though all the people involved realize that person A contributed more than the others, the collective norm is that rewards should be equally distributed. Recall the discussion of collectivism. People feel close to their group and are willing to downplay their own preferences in favor of group goals. After recommending a roughly equal distribution of rewards, collectivists justify their decision with arguments such as the following: "It is more important to keep the group functioning smoothly than to single out any one person for attention. If one person gets more, there is the danger that this will disrupt the group because of jealousy. Even though a few people don't contribute as much on this project, if we keep the group together they may be able to contribute more to the next project." Individualists, in contrast, justify an equitable distribution with a quite different set of arguments: "We've got to reward individual accomplishment. Person A will see less reason to work hard on the next project if we don't reward him today for his efforts on this recently completed project."

There are a number of other differences in the distribution of rewards. Collectivists are more likely to give attention to person F who has a special set of needs. They are likely to give him more than that given to others in the group. Or, in the space within the exercise that calls for additional assumptions necessary to complete the task, collectivists are likely to write something such as, "I assume that the company has already taken care of Person F's special needs, independent of the distribution of money brought in by profits on this road construction project." Collectivists are also likely to give more attention to person E whose status and influence were instrumental in obtaining the project funds in the first place. In general, collectivists are more respectful of status and are more deferent to authority figures (Hofstede, 1980; Triandis, 1990). They are more sensitive to the fact that status figures want respect and that there can be dangers if "we don't take care of people in power." They are likely to vote a solid $10,000 to person E in recognition of his efforts, even though this person clearly does not need the money. If individualists give any special attention at all to person E, they decide on some sort of nonmonetary recognition. For instance, individualists might vote to name the road after the high status person.

Why is there more deference to authority and more sensitivity to status in collectivist societies? One reason is that such deference helps to keep the group together. We are not arguing that collectivists always have the same opinion as their group. Rather, we are arguing that when they have their own opinion or set of preferences, they are more willing to put them aside and to adopt the group goals. When members of a collective have varying opinions, it is functional to have respect for an authority figure who can say, "I've listened to everyone's opinion and I have decided that we will take this specific course of action." Given respect for the decision, the collective remains intact and people pursue the recommended course of action. If people are not willing to defer, they will pursue their own preferences and the collective is likely to be weakened. In other words, without respect for authority, the people will become much like individualists and will "do their own thing."

Another interesting result of this exercise is that individualists will sometimes vote themselves some money for making the recommendations. This reflects an aspect of individualism discussed earlier: People are good at calculating the rewards and costs of various courses of action as these actions apply to themselves. When rewards exceed costs, they remain in the work settings that bring this favorable ratio. When costs exceed rewards, they are likely to leave such settings, or at least wish that they could leave. In voting themselves money for completing the exercise individualists say, "You've asked me to act much like a person in a consulting firm who comes in and helps a company make tough decisions. Do you expect consultants to work for free?"

Advice for Individualists and Collectivists Who Move Across Cultures

Arguing that changes around the world (e.g., internationalization of business, migration, desire for democracy) will bring individualists and collectivists into more and more contact, Triandis, Brislin, and Hui (1988) provided sets of advice for people moving across cultural boundaries. They provided 23 pieces of advice for individualists moving to collective cultures, and another 23 for collectivists working in individualist cultures. For example, collectivists have to learn to develop a network of influential people within their communities. A network refers to a set of people who interact so that they can be mutually useful. One person knows a good tax accountant and shares this information because someone else knows a good newspaper reporter who enjoys working with carefully placed "leaks." Members of a network are not necessarily one's friends. Collectivists, accustomed to the emotional support of a group, find the "mutual usefulness" aspect of developing a network to be difficult if not actually distasteful. In contrast, individualists have to be willing to become more emotionally close to their coworkers. Whereas individualists sometimes hear the piece of advice (in their own countries) to keep one's social life and business life separate, there is not this sharp distinction in collectivist societies. Collectivists want to feel emotionally tied to the people with whom they work. This fact is key to understanding the first case study. Mike felt that his sense of privacy and his personal life were being invaded. His Greek coworkers, however, were complimenting Mike by offering him membership in their collective. It must be kept in mind that it is great to have a supportive collective who can come to one's aid and who can grease the wheels for interactions with influential people in society at large. But it must also be kept in mind that there are obligations to the collective, and these include sharing personal information and resources such as money and one's "contacts."

Another piece of advice for collectivists in an individualistic society is that any arrogance or aloofness associated with being a boss must be downplayed. Individualists enjoy feeling that they are equal or nearly equal to their superiors. They do not enjoy hearing superiors making such statements as, "I'm the boss and because of that we will do it my way." The privileges of status should not be overplayed in individualistic societies. Bosses may have access to company cars, elite dining facilities, and beautiful offices, but these should not be bragged about and should not be used as bludgeons with subordinates. The advice for individualists in a collective society is nearly the reverse. Individualists may have to learn to be more "bossy" with their subordinates and to accept the trappings of status such as fine cars (when some of their subordinates have to take the bus) and servants. Being bossy, and accepting the behaviors of a high status person in a collective society, can be quite difficult for individualists intimately familiar with Thomas Jefferson's arguments that "All men are created equal and are endowed by their creator with certain unalienable rights . . . " This concern with status is central in understanding the second case study. Nemi was socialized as a collectivist and is much more willing to defer to the wishes of his vice president. Florence, socialized to feel that her views are equal or are even superior in merit to the vice president's (since she has studied the issues and the vice president has not), is far less willing to go along with a recommendation simply because it is the preference of a high-status figure.

Skill Application Involving Self and Others

The Pursuit of Happiness

People using the module should divide into groups of three or four. The members of each group will consider various features and skills of people and will discuss whether these hypothetical individuals will be happier in an individualistic society or in a collective society. At times, group members will not be able to suggest a general answer and instead must respond, "It depends on . . . ," and then write in additional information. Group members should develop reasons explaining why they are choosing the individualistic society option, the collectivist option, or the "it depends" option. Reasons can be written in the spaces corresponding to the intersection of rows and columns in the following table.

In Which Type of Culture Will These People Find More Happiness?
(Be sure to give a few words "why.")

	Individualistic	*Collectivist*	*It depends on . . .*
1. Unattractive people			
2. Inventors (in search of patents)			
3. Women			
4. People who organize long-term training programs			
5. Good public speakers			
6. A person with a famous uncle			
7. Graduate students			
8. Shy people			
9. Plastic surgeons			
10. Manufacturers who take patents and make commercial products			
11. Lawyers			
12. High-status people			
13. People with mental health difficulties			
14. Hardworking but unimaginative people			
15. Gracious and charming people			
16. People seeking their first jobs after their formal studies			

Complete these sentences with a few phrases that summarize some of the ideas that you identified when discussing the two types of societies:

Individualism works well when . . .
Collectivism works well when . . .

Here are a few thoughts for your consideration. When people have certain problems that might interfere with their quest for happiness, it is very useful to have a supportive collective that can marshall its forces behind such people. So when a person is unattractive, shy, unimaginative, or mentally ill, it is possible that a collective will try to help that person out. A shy person, for instance, might say, "I'm shy, but so what? When it comes time for me to meet potential marriage partners, my collective will arrange introductions." I have taught people from both individualistic and collectivistic cultures. It is a month before graduation. People about to receive their degrees run into each other on campus. What's a common question in an individualistic culture? "How are your job interviews going?" Collectivists (e.g., from Mexico or Thailand) have told us, "I have a tough time understanding why Americans ask this question all of the time. The fact is that my uncles are arranging for me to have a choice of jobs waiting for me when I arrive home."

In comparison, individualists have to go out and reap the benefits of society by themselves—they will not necessarily have a supportive collective to give them extensive help. So if they are gracious and charming and if they are also good public speakers, they will be able to meet and to be remembered by others who might have benefits to offer. Some people make a living helping individualists. If a person is unattractive, this can interfere with making a good impression on others. So plastic surgeons can help. If a person has a problem reaping the benefits of society, there (to repeat) will not necessarily be a supportive collective to help. The person may have to hire to a lawyer to protect his or her rights.

Authority and status are important in collective societies. Having a famous uncle can be helpful. Just being a graduate student conveys high status in many collective societies. In fact, graduate students from Asia often face a loss in status when coming to the United States for advanced degree work. In individualist countries, graduate study is not seen as high status in and of itself—it is seen as the road to greater achievement at a later date. Ambitious people will probably find more happiness in an individualistic society because they can "do their own thing" and do not have to constantly consult their collective. This leads to a few "it depends" answers. Ambitious women will probably find more happiness in an individualistic society because they will be judged on their own merits rather than on the merits of their husband or family (a more collective phenomenon). Women who want to raise children and nurture family members (as their major roles in life) will be happier in a collective society. When people have achieved high status through their own hard work, achievements, and accomplishments, they will probably find more happiness in an individualistic society. When they have high status because of the prominence of someone else to whom they are related, they will be happier in a collective society.

Another contrast involves the invention of new products and the production, marketing, and improvement of the same products. There are more patents in individualistic societies (Hofstede, 1980), demonstrating the support such societies give for people pursuing their own unique ideas. But to produce, market, and improve such products over a period of years, the efforts of many people are needed, not all of whom can be motivated by the search for individual glory. Because collectivists work well in groups and are able to downplay their own preferences in favor of group goals, they may be better able to bring new products to the marketplace. The classic example is videocassette recorder (VCR) technology. The inventions and the patents are American; the production and marketing are Japanese.

Skill Practice

Out-of-Workshop Exercises

1. Review the self-assessment exercise at the beginning of this chapter. When I used the phrase "first pass," this refers to behaviors more appropriate in individualistic societies. The phrase "second pass" refers to behaviors more

appropriate in collective societies. Review the 14 behaviors, and explain why each is more appropriate in one or the other type of society.

2. Consider friends that you have had with whom you were once very close but are now not so close. Was there anything about the individualistic or collective nature of their backgrounds (compared to yours) that led to difficulties? These difficulties, in turn, might have led to the people involved becoming less close. Remember, there can be people whose background is very collective even if they live in an individualistic society. For instance, an American female student once reported, "I realize the United States is individualistic, but my background is very collective, especially the extreme closeness of my family. I was dating an attractive man. He had some great features—smart, good job, tall, movie-star good looks. But we broke up. He didn't like my sisters all that much, and I never could live with someone who wasn't close to my family."

3. Draw a square that is 6 inches on each side. Draw a small picture of yourself in the middle. Then, draw a small picture of other people who are important in some way to your life—keep within the 6-inch square. The tendency is that if people are important to the individual doing the drawing, then those people are drawn closer to the individual's picture of himself or herself. Is this true in your case? Consider the three or four people who are closest to you. If there was a major change in your life, would this change affect these other people?

References

Bellah, R., Madsen, R., Sullivan, W., Swindler, A., & Tipton, S. (1985). *Habits of the heart: Individualism and commitment in American life.* Berkeley, CA: University of California Press.

Bhawuk, D., & Brislin, R. (1992). The measurement of intercultural sensitivity using the individualism and collectivism concepts. *International Journal of Intercultural Relations, 16,* 413-436.

Hofstede, G. (1980). *Culture's consequences: international differences in work-related values.* Beverly Hills, CA: Sage.

Hsu, F. (1981). *Americans and Chinese: Passage to differences* (3rd ed.). Honolulu: University Press of Hawaii.

Hui, C. (1990). Work attitudes, leadership styles, and managerial behaviors in different cultures. In R. Brislin (Ed.), *Applied cross-cultural psychology* (pp. 186-208). Newbury Park, CA: Sage.

Kagitcibasi, C. (1990). Family and home-based intervention. In R. Brislin (Ed.), *Applied cross-cultural psychology* (pp. 121-141). Newbury Park, CA: Sage.

Porter, L., & McKibbin, L. (1988). *Management education and development: Drift or thrust into the 21st century?* New York: McGraw-Hill.

Schwartz, S. (1990). Individualism-collectivism: critique and proposed refinements. *Journal of Cross-Cultural Psychology, 21,* 139-157.

Triandis, H. (1990). Theoretical concepts that are applicable to the analysis of ethnocentrism. In R. Brislin (Ed.), *Applied cross-cultural psychology* (pp. 34-55). Newbury Park, CA: Sage.
Triandis, H., Brislin, R., & Hui, C. (1988). Cross-cultural training across the individualism-collectivism divide. *International Journal of Intercultural Relations, 12,* 269-289.

Education

6 Cross-Cultural Training for Adolescents and Professionals Who Work With Youth Exchange Programs

KENNETH CUSHNER

It is through necessity that the means of perception are developed. Therefore, oh man, increase your necessity.

Jalaludin Rumi
13th-century scholar

In America, one can drive for days and still be in the same country. In other parts of the world, national border lines are crossed much more commonly in a day's travel. Although we talk of a global world, many people still grow up in relatively homogenous environments. This module introduces youth exchange programs as a means to develop an international perspective among our adolescents. It warns, however, that merely dropping off the youths in a different country does not accomplish our intended mission. It can, in fact, backfire. Cushner describes the various components of successful youth exchange programs.

Contents

Self-Assessment Test

Read the following list of questions regarding international youth exchange programs. Grade yourself according to how well you think you could answer the question. A grade of A assumes that you would be able to write a truly excellent, accurate, and comprehensive answer. A grade of F indicates that you would not know where to begin. A grade of B indicates that you would be able to write a good answer. A grade of C means you would be able to respond in an adequate manner. A grade of D means you would write an inadequate answer. Write your grade at the end of each question.

Questions

1. Education for an international perspective is of concern to many in these increasingly global times. Given your knowledge of the culture learning process, how can the educational process best bring about an international perspective?
2. What is the history of international youth exchange? Approximately how many exchange organizations are in existence today?
3. In what critical ways do exchange programs differ from traditional international travel programs?
4. What are the best conditions for orientation for youth exchange? When should orientation begin and end? What should the focus be of effective orientation programs?
5. At what key times during the exchange experience are students likely to experience strong negative emotions? How might this be most effectively handled?
6. What have been some of the documented outcomes of the international exchange experience? How do these differ from outcomes of more traditional school experiences that may address international concerns?

Case Studies: Critical Incidents

The purpose of the following critical incidents is to encourage you to identify and discuss issues related to the experience faced by students who participate in international youth exchange programs. You will be presented with a few situations that have actually occurred in conjunction with adolescent sojourns. You will be asked to offer explanations and suggested resolutions to the proposed incidents, and you should do so both individually as well as in groups. The more diverse your discussion group is in terms of knowledge and experience, the more lively and informative your discussion is certain to be.

Disappointing Questions

Mrs. Steiner, the new school coordinator of international exchange programs, had completed the difficult task of selecting three students who were to have the opportunity to spend a year abroad as foreign exchange students—one in France, one in Japan, and one in Venezuela. Her next major task in this role was to arrange for an orientation program for these students and their families. After weeks of planning, contacting foreign embassies, and meeting with prior exchange students, Mrs. Steiner had quite a comprehensive program planned and ready to deliver. The highlight was to be extensive dialogue with former exchange students and host nationals from France, Japan, and Venezuela. This, Mrs. Steiner was certain, was to be the most beneficial aspect of any orientation, especially after having spoken at great length with the previous students who spoke so often about the cultural differences students would encounter.

The evening for the orientation finally arrived, just days before the new students' departure. To Mrs. Steiner's surprise, although the various presentations were quite informative and interesting, the students seemed quite uninterested in the cross-cultural aspects of the various presentations. At the end of the presentations, most of the students' questions centered on what they should pack, what articles they would not be able to find in the various countries, and how long it would take for letters and packages to reach them in their new homes. Mrs. Steiner was quite confused by this response and somewhat hurt that much of her effort seemed rather useless.

Discussion Questions

1. How might you explain the students' apparent disinterest in matters of culture and cross-cultural interaction during their orientation program?
2. What might be the most appropriate content for this phase of an orientation program? How is the best way and when is the best time to address issues of culture and cross-cultural contact?
3. How would you conceptualize and design an orientation experience for young people who will spend a year on an international exchange program?

Same Native Language

John had left his home in Wisconsin only 36 hours earlier and found it quite amazing that he was now in New Zealand along with 75 other students who came from 14 countries. He, as well as these other students, were about to embark on the experience of a lifetime—that of spending 1 year living with a new family and attending school in New Zealand. As was customary, new arrivals into New Zealand would spend about 2 days at a brief "Gateway Orientation," sleeping off their jet lag and being introduced to essentials of life in their new home. All along, John was certain he would have a relatively easy time adjusting to his new country. This sense was reinforced during the Gateway Orientation when he observed students from such places as Japan, Thailand, and France struggling with their English. Why, John's native language was the same as those in New Zealand, so what could possibly go wrong? He left the Gateway Orientation rested and eager to merge with his family and new school. He confidently said goodbye to the orientation staff, expecting to see them a few weeks later at another gathering.

At the next gathering of students and staff from around the country, John was singled out by local volunteers as having quite severe adjustment problems. His host parents thought him abrasive, and his host brothers and sister complained that he was nosy and too inquisitive. John complained that people were too literal, maintained only "surface-level" relationships, and did not appear to be sincerely interested in developing close interpersonal relationships.

Discussion Questions

1. If you were a counselor for the exchange organization, where might you focus your discussion with John?
2. What element of the exchange experience is often overlooked, as in the case with John here, and is probably at the center of this problem?
3. What is the connection between language learning, trust, and relationship building?

Skill Concepts: The Need
for the Adolescent Exchange Experience

An American Perspective

The vast size and relative geographic isolation of the United States, coupled with the historical tendency to encourage assimilation and a "melting pot" ideology, has resulted in a nation of people who have rather limited experiences with those from other countries. American students, as well as many American adults, are oftentimes rightly accused of being rather parochial, highly ethnocentric, and internationally naive. In addition, the tendency to stress an individualistic orientation in American society may serve to further prevent many young people from developing a sense of connectedness with others as well as their relationship with the world.

The development of an international perspective, although recognized by many as one of the great shortcomings of American education, may not easily come about in the rather traditional classroom and educational environment in which many of our young people find themselves. Challenging the perspectives of students in relation to the development of a worldview has been attempted throughout the social studies curriculum for many years, albeit with limited success. Although a significant amount of useful information can be presented in the classroom, little evidence exists to suggest that sufficient motivation emerges as a result of these predominantly cognitive efforts to enable students to apply this new knowledge in the real world.

Increased interest in the role that experiential learning can play in developing an international perspective has developed over the years. Experiential learning, as opposed to a didactic or cognitive approach, provides opportunities for students to engage in real-life and/or simulated encounters that simultaneously engage cognitive, affective, and behavioral domains. Hansel (1988) cites four factors that set experiential learning for international development apart from traditional classroom learning:

1. In the experiential context, the student's motivation comes from the situation itself. Survival within the family, community, or school becomes the motivating factor for further learning, not external factors such as grades imposed by a teacher.
2. The experience itself is direct and real—not vicarious. Students must use all their senses as well as all of their information and problem-solving skills to accommodate their new surroundings, not just the cognitive domain as is so often the case in the classroom setting.
3. Immediate feedback is provided in the day-to-day living situation. As such, individuals must question, adapt, and respond in a manner they feel appropriate, and in return, promptly learn from their mistakes in understanding and their errors in thinking and behavior. Individuals can then decide to change or not.
4. Learning in this manner is holistic. It is assumed that relationships between parts are better grasped when experienced as an entire system than when each part is studied individually, which is often the case in a traditional approach to teaching.

This chapter is written with the idea that well-developed, sustained, and monitored immersion within another culture can aid one in having a successful experience as well as having a lasting, significant impact on the international development of young people.

Characteristics of an International Exchange Experience

Each year, tens of thousands of young people take the opportunity to spend anywhere from 1 month to 1 year living in another culture. Although such exchanges can occur between the ages of 12 and 25 for school, academic preparation, or simple culture learning, the majority of these immersion experiences occur with students between the ages of 15 and 19 completing an academic year abroad.

Today, there are literally dozens of international student exchange organizations that offer homestay programs. The concept of international student exchange and homestays can be traced back to the 1930s to work done at The Experiment in International Living. The Experiment pioneered the idea of homestays as a means by which individuals from one culture could learn about another. International homestays became more commonplace in the post-World War II years when NATO alliance youth were encouraged to take up residence in the United States and American young people were encouraged to spend time living in Europe. AFS Intercultural Programs, for instance, the nation's largest international student exchange program today, traces its roots to these times when American Field Service volunteer ambulance drivers began an exchange between France and the United States. More recently in the United States, the Council on Standards for International Educational Travel was established as a nonprofit organization committed to establishing standards for international educational travel. Today, each year literally tens of thousands of youths from at least 60 nations around the world participate with one of the well over 50 recognized and monitored programs to live with families in countries other than their own (Herwig & Herwig, 1990).

International educational programs are basically of four types: (1) *academic* in nature, officially recognized and accredited by educational institutions usually responsible to an accrediting agency; (2) *religious, fraternal, or service* in nature, through organizations such as church or temple groups, fraternal orders, or community service organizations that offer selective, restricted programs in the context of the objectives of their own group; (3) *private, nonprofit* in nature, through groups such as foundations, schools, or charitable organizations that operate under official not-for-profit status; and, 4) *commercial* in nature, through groups that are established profit-making businesses that market travel, study, and exchange programs.

Although the various exchange programs may emphasize travel and sight-seeing, language study, cultural contact, or educational study, exposure of participants to some degree of cultural contact and the potential for significant culture learning is of most importance in this discussion. Merely sending youths overseas to live for a considerable period of time does not guarantee that they will learn more than if they remained at home. In fact, poorly conceived and monitored programs may actually do more harm in terms of encouraging the development of previously nonexistent negative stereotypes or by creating such a stressful situation for the participants that they avoid further contact with foreign nationals.

Characteristic of all successful homestays are a number of factors that provide insight into the needs and perspectives of participants as well as guidance for program administrators, the predominant one being *total immersion*. By total immersion, Grove (1989, p. 2) means "no less than the participant is completely, constantly, and more or less exclusively in contact with the people and culture of the host community. No other type of international exchange program routinely comes closer to attaining the complete immersion of its participants than an intercultural homestay program." Unlike an old friend, relative, or houseguest who comes to visit for a short while, the international exchange student lives full-time for an extended period of time in the home of a host family. With short-term visitors, families put on their best behavior. In addition, the short-term visitor is usually from the same culture and rather familiar with routines and the use of various facilities, therefore not requiring instruction or explanation for many of the daily habits encountered in the host's home.

Families hosting international exchange students have a tendency to try to put the exchange student into some familiar category—in this case, that of a short-term, rather familiar visitor. Most people, however, do not have extensive experiences relating to others from foreign cultures. Many are ignorant that knowledge often thought to be common, such as how to use shower curtains or where to place toilet paper, may not be known and therefore must be taught. A comfortable category in which to place the exchange student may not exist for the host family, thus leading to awkward and uncomfortable situations.

Participants from abroad are also expected to fully immerse themselves in the day-to-day activities of the host family. The student usually enters the homestay experience intent on learning about another culture and the insider's perspective. However, even though the student is an inside learner, he or she is essentially an outsider to long-standing family ties, family history, and that special ingroup feeling that develops in many families. This relationship building takes considerable time and energy, thereby introducing some interesting opportunities and obstacles that must be overcome. One particular and often-times overlooked situation concerns the use of language, particularly when student and host family share a common language, as students from one English-speaking country would encounter when they go to another English-speaking nation. Many students moving between countries that seemingly share a common language make the assumption that there will be few, if any, adjustment difficulties. After all, everyone speaks the same language—or so it seems. When student and family from two *different language* backgrounds come together, a considerable amount of time is spent learning to communicate. In addition to the slow process of language learning, trust and understanding develop between student and family. By the time language facility has improved, a certain understanding of one another has developed. Discussion around rather sensitive and personal issues can now emerge knowing that a certain degree of trust has been developed. On the outside, speakers of the *same language* may appear to communicate and understand one another. Critical problems often present themselves as individuals may delve into rather sensitive issues, oftentimes unknowingly, long before any real sense of trust and understanding has been developed. This is especially evident when students from the United States take their rather forthright and apparently open attitude with them to another English-speaking country. Such was the case of John in the critical incident presented earlier. John's reference to "literal" implied that his family avoided discussion of deeper, perhaps more sensitive issues, that he wished to discuss.

The immersion experience also must continue for a significant amount of time, the least of which, according to Grove (1989), is 1 month, with little opportunity for continuous face-to-face contact with others from their home country. This length of time is critical for any real culture learning to occur. The concept of culture shock is instructive here. Individuals engaged in an international immersion experience significant emotional transitions that begin to move away from a sense of euphoria. For many, this transition occurs only after the first few weeks in another culture. It is the growth that occurs as one lives through the emotional changes one is encountering, while having little opportunity to escape from the realities of this new life, that is significant. It may be far too easy and comfortable for some sojourners to remain with those whose way of life is familiar to them than it is to fully participate in the lives of others, as is the case in a homestay program.

Orientation and the International Exchange Experience

Most readers of this book are quite familiar with the concept of culture shock, the U-curve hypothesis, and, in general, the process of cross-cultural adjustment. Basically, when we speak of adjustment in the cross-cultural context we are speaking of the process that individuals adopt in their efforts to adjust to their cross-cultural immersion experience. In general, an individual's adjustment is analyzed in terms of four dimensions (Brislin, 1993): the subjective dimension (how well the individual feels she or he is doing); an objective dimension (how well others think the sojourner is doing); task effectiveness (how well the individual is doing in achieving the objectives of the sojourn); and lack of invisible signs (such as somatic complaints, high blood pressure, headaches, etc.). These four aspects of adjustment are looked at across four domains: the degree to which the sojourner has made a good cultural adjustment; the degree to which the sojourner identifies with the host culture; the degree of cultural competence; and role enculturation.

Typical of all individuals, and certainly characteristic of each exchange student, is the tendency to experience certain ups and downs in life—perhaps somewhat exaggerated in adolescents. Complicating matters is the fact that the exchange student will not have her or his usual and typical means of emotional support, at least not during the early days and months of the experience. Also typical of most adolescents, those ups and downs may be a little higher or lower than in other individuals. Although no two students will experience the same emotional responses at the same time, there are certain experiences and stages during a sojourn that can be anticipated and instructive (Grove, 1989; King & Huff, 1985). Perhaps most critical for program administrators to consider then is that sustained support for all participants—student, host family, and natural family—must be considered. Sustained support considers orientation, supportive counseling, and assistance, as well as crisis counseling if required. Critical aspects of student orientation will be considered here.

Pre-Departure

Orientation for student sojourners really begins the moment an individual applies to the program of her or his choice. Although an international exchange experience can be quite stressful and demanding, the potential for significant intercultural learning and personal growth is great. Very early in the marketing and application process, potential exchangees should be made aware that the experience is far more than an informal tour or vacation package. Students should be encouraged to begin to question their own abilities to adjust and adapt to new and different circumstances, while the organization should strive to screen out applicants who may be at risk to themselves (e.g., severe depression) and others (e.g., interpersonal conflict) in this potentially stressful situation. Careful screening of both student participants and host families must occur at this time.

Surprisingly, significant and detailed orientation experiences for students immediately prior to their departure have not been shown to have great impact on students. Students are typically too involved with emotional good-byes with family and friends and too busy shopping for items for the year to pay much attention to significant issues about their host country or culture. In addition, learning theorists looking at the role of prior knowledge in the attainment of new information have demonstrated that up to 80% of what individuals learn in any educational encounter may be directly dependent on what that individual already knows (Bransford, 1979). Most Americans, and certainly most American youth, have had few, if any, significant encounters across cultures. As a result, information typically provided in cross-cultural orientation programs before the experience begins falls on "deaf ears," as prior categories and frameworks may not be present in the minds of the participants. Adolescents seem to miss much of what is presented in many pre-departure orientation programs that emphasize aspects of culture and cross-cultural interaction. Such was the case in the first critical incident when Mrs. Steiner's planned orientation program was not well received.

With this in mind, pre-departure orientation should be brief. Early communication to students should prepare them to expect those aspects of the experience with which they are most certain to be able to identify—among them, their role as a cultural ambassador. As such, students should be encouraged to become better able to answer questions about their own country and culture; to be able to engage in dialogue around political events; and to be able to defend a position taken by their own nation vis-à-vis world events. This in and of itself may require significant effort on the part of many American youth who are oftentimes rather politically naive and inexperienced. Students should be encouraged to read the *New York Times* or the various weekly newsmagazines for a few months before their departure. At the same time that students are beginning to read about their own nation and culture, they are beginning to develop categories around the concept *culture* that should be useful when they begin to analyze similar dimensions in their host country.

In addition, pre-departure orientation may prepare students for the demands of travel and extended residence in the host country. Orientation should also encourage language study; might introduce students to general geographical, historical, and political aspects of the host country; and should provide the opportunity to discuss anxieties and apprehensions about the forthcoming experience in terms of the adjustment process. Opportunities for natural families to meet with exchange personnel should also be made available.

During the Experience

Most newly arrived exchange students are usually at the peak of an emotional high as soon as they land in their new country. Their arrival signals the culmination of months of anticipation, weeks of preparation, and days of good-byes. For new host families, too, seeing their exchange student finally get off the plane sets into motion a series of fun-packed activities, introductions, visits, and scenic tours. Soon, all may witness *arrival fatigue* on the part of the student. Obviously tired from the extended travel and subsequent changes in body time, arrival fatigue also is complicated by the fact that although the student has arrived in body, he or she may not have arrived in mind. Although welcomed in a new home by an extremely well meaning family, the lack of familiar surroundings and known family and friends, as well as constant bombardment of new language, brings on a sense of overload. Although the length of time any one individual experiences arrival fatigue may vary, eventually the optimism resurfaces and the students are able to carry themselves around with considerable ease.

Very early in the experience, the exchange student typically focuses attention on the similarities between people and cultures rather than on the differences. Hosts, just like back at home, are seen to enjoy family times together, watch television, go to work and school, and so forth. The differences noticed early in a sojourn are typically perceived as "quaint" or "interesting." During this time, sometimes called the *settling in* phase, the differences between cultures slowly become apparent and the potential for significant "culture shock" is present. Students, as well as host families, often confront such concerns as disconfirmed expectations, the need to belong, a high degree of ambiguity and uncertainty, and so forth (see "Emotional Experiences" in the 18-theme culture-general framework, Chapter 7 in this book; and Brislin, Cushner, Cherrie, & Yong, 1986). Overly positive expectations on both sides, in terms of what the "perfect host family" or "perfect exchange student" will be like may cause an otherwise promising experience to become fraught with problems. Or, students may have unrealistic expectations about what the host culture and experience will be like based on what they perceive to be accurate from viewing television and films. Students may come with the unrealistic expectation that their foreignness will be a focus of positive attention, only to find that entry into an ingroup may take considerable time. Or, students such as John in the second critical incident may have unrealistic expectations as to their ability to adjust to the new world around them.

Although students may begin to confront some critical issues and face potentially stressful times, relationships are usually deepening and a high degree of trust may be developing with the host family. It is during this time that the greatest potential for relationship-building exists. *If* the student and host family are aware that culture shock is quite possible and that it is quite normal for sojourners to react negatively to the stresses and changes they encounter, the support and encouragement that can be provided by the family (as well as perhaps the community) can help facilitate a more positive adjustment. Culture shock is often best explained to students and families at this time in one of two ways. In some instances, students begin to realize that what happens in the new environment seems to be rather irregular and unpredictable, ambiguous and uncertain. When one's world is perceived as such, when one's behavior seldom achieves the expected outcome, or when one's normal behavior may be perceived by others as abnormal or strange, it becomes difficult to maintain any sense of order and to ever believe that one will achieve a sense of belonging and "fit in." Another reason students may experience a high degree of culture shock may be the result of the realization that they themselves are in a sense culture-bound and set in patterns of thinking and behaving that may not be universally accepted, and may in fact be in question in the new environment. Internal "soul-searching" may result in depression or exaggerated behaviors, thus creating problems in the host family or school situation. Although students are learning about the new culture from the minute they step foot in the new country, it is not until this phase of culture shock passes that students are truly able to begin significant culture learning.

The well-established exchange organizations have found it useful to consider post-arrival orientation as an ongoing process that should be addressed at various times throughout the exchange experience. Understanding some of the immediate questions and needs of students will help to structure an arrival orientation. Concern over such issues as toileting procedures, sleeping practices, and eating habits are great and should be attended to at the earliest possible time. An immediate post-arrival orientation that lasts more than 24 hours might also address such issues as laundry, currency, postage, individual security and safety, use of telephones, and so forth. Addressing such issues helps make individuals feel safe and comfortable in their immediate surroundings while they sleep off their jet lag and familiarize themselves with their immediate and new surroundings.

It is not until students have been in country for anywhere from 3 to 5 weeks that they themselves may begin to raise questions about the role of culture and behavior. Now, having their own personal experiences that may have generated questions in their minds, students are ready and able to make full use of the range of cross-cultural orientation strategies and concerns. Once students have had ample opportunity to interact and observe hosts, then questions around communication, politeness, community events, social patterns, cultural values, role distinctions, and nonverbal behavior can be adequately addressed. Students now have a foundation from which further learning can develop.

At various times throughout the academic homestay, exchangees should meet to process their experience as well as to raise questions and share concerns. Addressing issues of intercultural effectiveness or cross-cultural competence

can, and should, become a major focus of orientation programming throughout the sojourn itself. One of the major goals of any orientation program is to
increase the likelihood that each individual will become as effective as possible
during the exchange experience.

Effectiveness is the subject of great debate on the part of trainers and exchange
organization volunteers. A four-part criterion for success has been proposed
by Brislin (1993) that, again, includes: (1) a subjective dimension addressing
how well one feels about the cross-cultural encounter; (2) an objective dimension looking at how well hosts think an individual is doing; (3) task effectiveness, or how well one is achieving the goals of one's sojourn; and (4) a lack of
invisible signs, emphasizing good health and well-being. Attention to each of
these is really designed to assist students in achieving as much as possible from
their sojourn experience in terms of increased knowledge about themselves as
well as others while improving their communication skills in a variety of ways.
Successful orientation programs have demonstrated the ability to reduce the
severity of culture shock (Cushner, 1989; Grove, 1989). Participants tend to feel
more in control of their experience and have acquired concepts and vocabulary
that can be brought to bear on daily problems and obstacles that they are certain
to encounter.

Post-Return

There are typically three times during the exchange experience when
unanticipated strong emotions emerge. Holiday periods may be one of those
times when a strong sense of loneliness and homesickness can occur. Then,
toward the end of the exchange experience, a student's emotions may again
be in flux. A sense of excitement about returning home is mixed with feelings
of sadness as one considers leaving those who have come to mean so much.
But perhaps the most unanticipated difficulties may arise once the student
returns home and reverse culture shock or reentry shock sets in. Never expecting there to be difficulties returning to one's natural home, and shortly after
returning and sharing photos and memories with others, returnees (as they are
often called) soon begin to feel as if they don't belong. Something feels amiss
and quite different; and it may take some time until one realizes that it is
usually he or she who has changed the most.

The experience of reentry shock can be as disorienting and alienating as
initial culture shock. In addition, it may take some time before the returnee finds
ways to integrate his or her experiences, finds individuals who can understand
the changes he or she has grown through, and begins to put the real educational outcomes of this overseas experience to work. Reverse culture shock is
more likely to cause problems for individuals under certain conditions: (1)
Those who have spent time in cultures significantly different from their own
may have an especially difficult time on reentry, as when Japanese students

return to a rather traditional lifestyle from a more dynamic one in the United States or Western Europe. (2) Those who have spent a long period of time away from their natural home, and especially those who were better adjusted during their sojourn experience, may have a difficult reentry. (3) A rather thorough and involved post-return orientation may also be especially needed when returnees come home to developing countries from experiences in an industrialized nation.

As a result of successful reentry, individuals truly begin to internalize the international experience. Wilson (1988) suggests that successful returnees find ways to integrate their experience into their lives. Returnees should be encouraged to use their newly attained knowledge and skills as they reenter their home society by doing such things as offering new perspectives on world issues, recognizing cultural relativism in people's comments, becoming bridge-builders between cultures in their home or school community, and exploring expanded career and educational opportunities. But caution must be advised regarding the need to belong. It is not uncommon for adolescents on their return to be perceived as "snobs" as they eagerly share their privileged experiences.

Outcomes of the Exchange Experience

Although many will report that an international exchange experience is the most impactful experience of their lives, the real issue for educators is the kinds of measurable outcomes that emerge. The AFS Impact Study is cited as the most extensive attempt to analyze the outcomes of an extended international homestay (Hansel, 1985, 1988). Over 2,500 students from around the world responded to 17 self-rating scales designed to measure learning and personal growth as a result of a year abroad. Four characteristics demonstrated an especially strong relationship to the exchange experience and the development of an international perspective, especially in terms of values, attitudes, and perspectives concerning factual knowledge. Learning seemed to be most extensive in the following areas:

1. Understanding other cultures (characterized by an interest in learning about other people and cultures as well as an ability to accept and appreciate their difference)
2. Awareness and appreciation of host country and culture (characterized by considerable knowledge of the people and culture of the student's host country as well as an understanding of their place in world affairs)
3. Foreign language appreciation and ability (characterized by an ability to communicate with people in a second language and to take advantage of the opportunities resulting from bilingualism)
4. International awareness (characterized by an understanding that the world is one community, a developing capacity to empathize with people in other countries, and an appreciation of the common needs and concerns of people of different cultures)

In addition, as a result of the experience abroad, students appear to be less materialistic, more adaptable, more independent in their thinking, more aware of their home country and culture, and better able to communicate with others and to think critically (Hansel, 1988). Students in the control group who did not go abroad showed very little learning in these areas and had little opportunity in their normal life in the United States to develop this sort of international perspective.

Skill Applications

The training manual *They Are Talking About Me and Other Stories About Exchange Students* (Cushner & Grove, 1990) is a modified version of the culture general assimilator (see Chapter 7 in this book; and Brislin et al., 1986) designed to be used in the orientation for English-speaking adolescents preparing to live overseas. The adolescent version incorporates 25 critical incidents, categorized into three major components: Transition and Change, Roles and Relationships, and Things and Categories. Each section of the manual contains a series of critical incidents, a short essay introducing major ideas, and a series of interactive exercises designed to illustrate key concepts. This manual was the basis of a rather comprehensive study of the impact of a culture general assimilator as an orientation tool for youth exchange participants (Cushner, 1989). Results of its use indicated that individuals who received culture-general assimilator training were better able to identify dynamics that mediate cross-cultural interaction and adjustment; were better adjusted, as determined by responses on a culture shock adjustment inventory; and were more efficient in their interpersonal problem-solving ability. In addition, those in the treatment group required fewer family transfers throughout their stay.

Another valuable exercise for those responsible for adolescent exchange programs is to reconceptualize the orientation experiences of participants. One might begin by identifying an individual who will be responsible for the expansion of orientation programs as recommended in this module. If none exists, a person should be designated to take responsibility for this process. In some instances, a community volunteer may be responsible for preparation of students going overseas as well as orientation of those who have come to live in their community. In other cases, a teacher or school counselor may be charged with the task of monitoring student adjustment. In any case, a redesign of the orientation provided to youth participants should consider it as an ongoing process that must accommodate different needs at different times. Such an approach may help more effectively facilitate individual as well as institutional goals. With this in mind, the following exercises are presented as samples of what might be utilized at various stages in the exchange experience.

Field Exercises

Pre-Departure

One way to encourage young people to begin thinking about the transition and related experiences they are certain to confront throughout their overseas stay, and to serve as an icebreaker at a pre-departure orientation, is to have them begin thinking about major transitions they have experienced in their lives. Ask students to recall a major transition they have encountered, such as the first time going to summer camp, a move to another part of a state or country, or a transition to a new school. On a piece of paper, have them trace out their emotional responses from the time they began the experience to when they began to feel comfortable and "at home."

Ask small groups of students to come together and introduce themselves according to their graph. Have each student state, as specifically as possible, the causes of the major fluctuations in his or her graph. Can each recall what caused the emotional peaks and valleys? What strategies do each recall employing that helped facilitate the experience?

Trainers can use this exercise as a "jumping off" point to discuss issues related to adjustment, transition, the U-curve hypothesis, and so forth. Students often find it useful to have a model of adjustment in their minds, even if it is the rather simplistic U-curve hypothesis. Students tend to retain this rather simple model in their minds and find it easy to identify their emotional state at various times throughout an experience (see Chapter 9 by Pedersen in this book). It is not uncommon to have young people who are familiar with the adjustment process approach a counselor at times of stress with an opening line such as, "I think I'm at the bottom of my U." A wise youth counselor then knows it's time to talk.

During the Experience

Generally, only after a period of time have sojourners had enough encounters to reinforce the notion that "significant cultural differences" exist between student and host. It is during the experience, then, that the greatest potential for culture learning can take place. Attuning the sojourners to the many subtle differences around them is a useful approach to take in that it accomplishes at least two objectives: (1) participants become aware of the attribution process in themselves and others (one of the major objectives of attribution training using the culture assimilator), and thus become better able to make isomorphic attributions about the motivations of others' actions; and (2) participants begin to build a culture-specific profile of one another, thus deepening their understanding and levels of trust.

The exercise Red Flags: A Technique for Improving Cultural Awareness (developed by Elijah Lovejoy and described in Grove, 1989) is an approach to developing isomorphic attributions and greater understanding of others. This exercise asks individuals to recognize the powerful and oftentimes inaccurate subjective judgments they may make about others. Red flags may be negative, positive, or reciprocal in nature.

Negative red flags may consist of such attributions as: they are dirty; they are rude; they are hypocrites; and they are stupid. Consider cleanliness, for example. People in most cultures place a high value on cleanliness. Differing definitions or customs around cleanliness, however, often become the basis for negative judgments. Americans, who often pride themselves on their degree of cleanliness, are often perceived as dirty by the Japanese. When Americans bathe, they tend to soak, wash, and rinse in the same water, although they would never consider doing this with their clothes or dishes. The Japanese use different water for each step of the bathing process and find the American way difficult to understand—and even dirty. Americans, however, oftentimes judge Australians in the same manner when they are observed to wash and rinse the dinner dishes in the same water and merely allow them to drip dry. What other negative red flags can you identify?

Positive red flags, although relatively rare, do occur. In such cases, things may appear better or more pleasant than they really are. Some examples of positive red flags include: they are so friendly; we are going to be intimate friends; and they are so generous. Many visitors to the United States, for instance, are often taken by the warm reception they experience in the first few days in the country. Visitors are often greeted with big smiles, invitations to meals, and encouragement to stop by any time—only to find that such offers are rarely realized. What at first may be interpreted to mean that visitors will have many new friends may soon be interpreted that these same Americans are two-faced and insincere. What other positive red flags can you generate?

Reciprocal red flags generally refer to those reactions of a host in response to something the visitor does. Examples include: they are angry at me; they are surprised at me; and they are laughing at me. The following incident is a good example of a reciprocal red flag (King & Huff, 1985).

Although she had made an easy initial adjustment during her first few days in the United States, Margarita, from Mexico, quickly became worried when her host father would hug and kiss her at bedtime. She was certain that he was trying to seduce her. She was obviously concerned and quite worried over what she was going to do. And there was nobody with whom she could speak. She had no friends yet, she couldn't bring her concern to the rest of the family, and her own natural family was thousands of miles away. She began to avoid conversation with her host father and on occasion was cold and rude. Out of sheer frustration, the host father sought out a coordinator in the community and suggested that Margarita move out. In this case, Margarita's misinterpretation of the host father's behavior resulted in her avoidance and left him feeling alienated and unwanted.

The general message in pointing out red flags is to alert sojourners to the kinds of powerful subjective responses they are likely to feel in themselves.

Once these have been recognized, the individual can question their origin, attempt to reframe the meaning, and thus gain a greater understanding of the meaning behind another's actions. Sojourners should keep a journal, recording periods of strong emotion and exploring the situations accordingly.

Post-Return

For an international sojourn to have the greatest impact possible on the future direction of the participant, it is critical that individuals reflect and integrate their learnings once they return to their home country. The following activity should be introduced to returnees approximately 3 to 5 weeks after their return. It provides an opportunity to present students with a framework for relating the research literature concerning returnees to their own personal experience (modified from Grove, 1989).

Group leaders should introduce students to some form of the following statement:

> Intercultural learning through a youth exchange homestay program involves growth and change in a number of unanticipated ways. Many people consider the international homestay experience to be a turning point in their lives. Over the years, researchers have been documenting the changes that people experience as a direct result of the international experience. Below are short descriptions of some of the ways in which people have noted change in themselves. (1) Relate each of these in terms of your own overseas experience, and (2) explore how these changes might impact your future educational and career plans.

A. Central to all intercultural homestays is the move from a familiar environment to a new and quite different environment. In such a situation, individuals are constantly confronting crises which they must learn to handle effectively. Personal values and skills may change as a result. Exchangees often report the ability to think more creatively and critically; to become more aware of their own needs; to accept more responsibility for themselves; and to deemphasize material things. How are these reflected in your experience? How might these changes affect your future? What behaviors might exchangees engage in to continue these benefits?

B. Each exchangee becomes fully involved in the daily lives of other people. Developing and maintaining interpersonal relationships with people from diverse backgrounds, thus, is essential. Such skills are often transferable to other settings in your life. Interpersonal relationship building may result in a deeper concern and sensitivity toward others; an increased adaptability to changing social circumstances; a valuing of human diversity; an ability to communicate more effectively and freely with others; and an ability to enjoy oneself in others' company. How are these reflected in your experience? How might these changes affect your future?

C. During a stay in another culture, individuals are exposed to countless dimensions of that culture. Most people on an intercultural homestay become more knowledgeable and sensitive about other cultures. This may be expressed as an increased knowledge about a host country and culture; an increased sensitivity to aspects of one's own culture; and a greater understanding of the nature of cultural differences. How are these reflected in your experience? How might these changes affect your future?

D. Finally, living in another country often helps people to recognize that the world is one large, global community in which problems are oftentimes shared. Such global awareness, which helps individuals to take their place in a global society, may be seen in a deeper interest in world affairs; an awareness of global linkages; and a commitment to work to search for solutions to some of the world's global problems. How are these reflected in your experience? How might these changes affect your future?

References

Bransford, J. (1979). *Human cognition: Learning, understanding and remembering*. Belmont, CA: Wadsworth.

Brislin, R. (1993). *Understanding culture's influence on behavior*. Ft. Worth, TX: Harcourt Brace Jovanovich.

Brislin, R., Cushner, K., Cherrie, C., & Yong, M. (1986). *Intercultural interactions: A practical guide*. Newbury Park, CA: Sage.

Cushner, K. (1989). Assessing the impact of a culture-general assimilator. *International Journal of Intercultural Relations, 13*(2), 125-146.

Cushner, K., & Grove, C. (1990). *They are talking about me and other stories about exchange students*. New York: AFS Intercultural Programs.

Grove, C. (1989). *Orientation handbook for youth exchange programs*. Yarmouth, ME: Intercultural Press.

Hansel, B. (1985). *The impact of a sojourn abroad: A study of secondary school students participating in a foreign exchange program*. Unpublished doctoral dissertation, Syracuse University, Syracuse, NY.

Hansel, B. (1988). Developing an international perspective in youth through exchange programs. *Education and Urban Society, 20*(2), 177-196.

Herwig, K., & Herwig, K. (Eds.) (1990). *1991 advisory list of international educational travel and exchange programs*. Leesburg, VA: CSIET.

King, N., & Huff, K. (1985). *Host family survival kit: A guide for American host families*. Yarmouth, ME: Intercultural Press.

Wilson, A. (1988). Reentry: Toward becoming an international person. *Education and Urban Society, 20*(2), 197-210.

7 Preparing Teachers for an Intercultural Context

KENNETH CUSHNER

It is often hard to learn from people who are just like you. Too much is taken for granted. Homogeneity is fine in a bottle of milk, but in the classroom it diminishes the curiosity that ignites discovery.

Vivian Gyssin Paley (1979)

In an increasingly global world one need not step out of one's community to experience "culture shock." Many teachers who have grown up in a relatively homogeneous society are now faced with the challenge of educating a heterogeneous group of students. This module not only provides the reader with facts and figures pertaining to the multiethnic reality many educators must face but also introduces strategies to help understand and solve problems that arise from cultural differences. Readers are also provided with exercises that assist in analyzing as well as solving cross-cultural classroom problems.

Contents

I. Self-Assessment Test

II. Case Studies: Critical Incidents

III. Skill Concepts: Diversity in Education

IV. Skill Applications

V. Field Exercises

Self-Assessment Test

Read the following list of questions regarding teacher education and the education of children in a diverse society. Grade yourself according to how well you think you could answer the question. A grade of A assumes that you would be able to write a truly excellent, accurate, and comprehensive answer. A grade of F indicates that you would not know where to begin. A grade of B indicates that you would be able to write a good answer. A grade of C means you would be able to respond in an adequate manner. A grade of D means you would write an inadequate answer.

Questions

1. What percentage of children in schools in your country in the 1990s are children of color?
2. What are the projections for the demographics of cultural diversity in your nation's schools for the year 2025?
3. What percentage of your national teaching force are people of color?
4. What is the percentage of women in the teaching force in your country during the 1990s?
5. What are the projections for the percentage of teachers representing diverse groups as well as the gender balance of your nation's teaching force into the next century?
6. How many Limited English Proficient (LEP) students are in your nation's schools?
7. What percentage of your nation's teachers speak a second language?
8. Characterize the experience of first-generation immigrant or refugee children in the classroom. How do the processes of acculturation and adjustment enter the picture?
9. How might the teacher today, faced with students from so many backgrounds, begin to understand the complexities of the multicultural experience?
10. How do such concepts as assimilation, melting pot, and pluralism affect the education of children in your country?
11. Identify 3 to 5 aspects of your own cultural upbringing that may present obstacles as you learn to interact in a culturally diverse classroom setting.
12. What are some key concepts from the fields of cross-cultural psychology and training that can assist teachers as they respond to the needs of a diverse student population? How are these concepts evident in cross-gender interactions? In able-bodied/disabled interactions?

Score your own paper according to the grades you gave yourself for each item. Each grade of A counts as 3 points, a B counts as 2 points, a C as 1 point, a D as 0 points, and a grade of F counts as -1 point. Determine your grade point average.

Case Studies: Critical Incidents

The purpose of the following critical incidents is to encourage you to identify and discuss the experiences faced by numerous children and teachers in culturally diverse school settings. You will be presented with a series of situations that have actually occurred in classroom and school settings. These incidents center around many of the themes in the 18-theme culture-general framework proposed by Brislin, Cushner, Cherrie, and Yong (1986), which have been further developed in Cushner, McClelland, and Safford (1992). You will be asked to offer your own explanations and suggested resolutions to the proposed incidents, and you should do so both individually as well as in groups. The more diverse your discussion groups can be, both in terms of teachers and students, the more lively and informative your discussion is certain to be.

The Rural Elementary School

Renata is a 21-year old Mexican-American student majoring in elementary education at an urban university located a few miles from where she grew up in the Eastern part of the United States. She is about to begin a field experience in a rural elementary school. Having lived in the inner city all of her life and having traveled very little, she is apprehensive and feels unprepared to deal with students from rural backgrounds. After 1 week in the classroom, Renata has encountered many potentially disruptive and unexplained behaviors. For instance, three new students entered her classroom in 1 week. These students are children of migrant farmworkers and they will be living in the community for approximately 1 month. These students have been in 12 schools over the past 3 years. One student missed 3 days of class because one of the work horses was sick. Renata also finds the faculty very low-keyed. She explains it that the faculty display a very "down-home" attitude and are not very wise to the world. And to top things off, one of the parents confronted her after school one day and told Renata that she just doesn't understand the values of the community and that she should "go back to where you belong!" Renata found this especially disturbing because as long as she could remember she had wanted to give all she could to children in school.

Renata met with her university adviser and told her that she wanted to leave the field of education.

Discussion Questions

1. What is behind Renata's problem? If you were the adviser, what would you suggest?
2. How might a teacher best approach people whose value orientations, expectations of educators, and work style are significantly different from one's own?
3. Who should change? Renata? The faculty?
4. What experiences have you had living and/or working with people different from yourself where you had to contend with significant cultural differences? How

did you react to the strong emotions and unexpected stress? How did you cope in such a situation?

Moving From Hawaii

Alice, a 12-year-old sixth-grade student, had recently moved from Hawaii to a small town in Ohio, about 45 minutes outside of Cleveland. Although she was sad to leave her friends in Hawaii, Alice had grown up in a family that traveled quite frequently, moved relatively often, and prided itself on its ability to make easy adjustments. Alice was born in Australia while her parents had been on a 2-year teaching assignment. Alice anticipated few adjustment difficulties. At the start of the year, Alice went to school with little more than the expected "start-of-the-year" jitters.

Alice's language arts teacher was also new to the community and on the first day of school asked the children to stand, introduce themselves, tell where they were born, and of course to comment on "what they did on their summer vacation." In her turn, Alice stood up, introduced herself, said she was born in Cleveland, and spoke about her recent move from Hawaii. Her response was greeted with a few ooh's and aah's as most of the children in the class had spent their whole life in this small community. Alice appeared happy and content with her first day at school.

Discussion Questions

1. How would you explain Alice's reluctance to share her actual birthplace with the teacher and students? Can you articulate what her internal dialogue might be during this experience?

2. What instances can you relate where you were treated as an outsider? How did you finally gain the status of insider?

3. In what situations might you find students, teachers, and/or parents in the role of outsider? What impact might this have on relationships within the school setting?

4. What might a teacher and/or school counselor do to help facilitate the emotional needs of new students?

Eyes on Your Own Paper

Ulrike's parents sent her from Germany to school in the United States with the hope that she would improve her English language skills. Although she had studied English for many years in school and could speak it rather fluently, she did not have a good understanding of the more subtle aspects of the language. This was an area her parents wanted to see more fully developed.

Because of her apparent English language ability, the guidance counselor at her new school placed her with a full academic load. In one case in particular, her biology teacher, Ms. Reynolds, noticed that while taking tests Ulrike seemed to look at her neighbor's paper from time to time. Ms. Reynolds tried to quietly warn Ulrike to keep her eyes on her own paper and that if she needed some help to simply ask and it would be provided. Ulrike, however, never asked for assistance and continued to glance at her neighbor's papers.

Finally, Ms. Reynolds had enough and confronted Ulrike with evidence that she had been cheating. Ulrike responded that she was aware that she looked at a few answers but insisted that she did not cheat on the whole test. She seemed to give the impression that she did not understand why the teacher would be so upset since there are so many tests that she would take. Ms. Reynolds is upset that Ulrike would cheat and feels that she is dishonest and too lazy to study hard.

Discussion Questions

1. What insights could you provide to Ms. Reynolds that would help shed some light on the situation?
2. In what ways does culture influence the manner in which people learn how to learn? How do these differences in learning styles affect educational gain?
3. What might educators do to accommodate differences in learning styles? In what ways do learning styles affect testing and evaluation?
4. What recovery skills might Ulrike employ to alleviate her current problem?

Skill Concepts: Diversity in Education

Perhaps the greatest challenge yet to face the educational system of most nations is how best to address issues of equity and excellence within a context of diversity. Coupled with this task is the growing need that schools and nations face as they prepare their citizenry for the kinds of interactions that are becoming apparent as the world becomes increasingly global in nature. This section discusses the changing demographics of children and teachers in the United States as well as in a global context, introduces a culture-general framework useful for understanding and exploring the kinds of experiences both teachers and students are likely to encounter as they interact across cultural boundaries, and highlights some examples of school-based modifications that effectively address such issues.

In the United States alone at the beginning of the 1990s, roughly one third of the school-age population were children of color. This percentage is expected to increase to somewhere between 44% and 48% by the year 2025. Complicating this issue is the fact that relatively few of those in the teaching force represent minority populations. As of the late 1980s, roughly 88% of teachers in the United States represented the majority culture—that is, white, Anglo, and middle class, with about two-thirds of those being women. This figure, too, is expected to increase resulting in approximately 94% of the American teaching force representing a rather homogeneous, privileged, and cross-culturally inexperienced majority. This pattern of increased diversity in the classroom with an increasingly homogeneous teaching force is being mirrored in many nations of the world, including Canada, Australia, Israel, Great Britain, and New Zealand.

The United States has prior experience integrating significant numbers of immigrants, albeit with mixed reaction and success. During the early part of the 20th century, hundreds of thousands of legal immigrants entered the country through Ellis Island in New York. Although the road for new immigrants into the United States (or any country for that matter) has never been an easy one, the majority of the immigrants in the early part of the century having come from Europe could "fit" the human landscape, so to speak, once they learned the English language. The physical features they exhibited were not all that different from those of the majority of the people already here. Assimilationist ideology was easy to defend—people could conceivably "melt" into the greater pot called "America."

Those entering the United States today come from a much greater diversity of nations and backgrounds. Immigrants from the many diverse countries of Central and Latin America, Asia, and the Middle East are not uncommon. Into the schools they bring not only different ways of thinking and behaving but also diverse ways of communicating. Such diverse languages as Vietnamese, Cambodian, Arabic, Spanish, Russian, and Japanese are found in American schools with increasing regularity. In Florida's schools, for instance, at least 84 different languages are spoken—and the schools are actively working to provide educational services in 50 of these. And they are coming into that state in such great numbers that in 1989, as an example, enough children from Nicaragua alone were entering Dade County to support the building of a new elementary school *each month*. Of course, no such massive building efforts were undertaken, and few of the badly needed teachers were recruited. Increasingly across the country, children are speaking a language other than English at home. Between 30% and 50% of children in such cities as New York, Santa Fe, Hartford, and Providence speak languages other than English (Vobejda, 1992). In Miami, nearly three quarters of the residents speak a language other than English at home, with 67% saying they don't speak English very well. The United States is now the fourth largest Spanish-speaking country in the world! Although bilingualism is increasing among the American population in general (even given the English-as-an-Official-Language movement currently under way!), only 5% of our nations teacher's are themselves truly bilingual.

The plight many immigrants to the United States face today is far more difficult than that of previous times. The desire by many today is to retain their cultural and linguistic identity and to avoid the push to fit in to some pre-existing mold. But even when the English language is effectively learned, the distinct physical features of many of the immigrants today are quite different from those in the mainstream, thus creating a phenotypic barrier. Physical features have a strong impact on people's attributions and until the greater population becomes more accepting and tolerant will be a tremendous obstacle.

But not only teachers must be prepared to accommodate diversity. Today's young people are growing up in a world significantly different from that of their parents. As such, they, too, must be prepared for the kinds of intercultural interactions they are certain to encounter. Consider some of the following.

The world has become much more technologically oriented in the past 50 years. As such, attention must be paid to the ethical and moral use of such technology as well as to the preparation of all its citizenry for the use of such technologies. It has been proposed that the United States is fast becoming two societies—not black and white or rich and poor, but those who are technologically functional and connected worldwide versus those who are technologically illiterate. Niche-marketing by the smaller, well-connected firms who are able to quickly respond to needs will bring success to such firms in the coming years. The large corporate dinosaurs, such as General Motors, will continue to struggle in today's market and economy.

Coupled with this is the fact that the world has become increasingly nuclear—and our own safety and security as a species may depend on our ability to adequately manage these capabilities. Even though the Iron Curtain has crumbled and communism has essentially dissolved, people are still, if not even more so, quite xenophobic. Recent outbreaks in Germany in response to "guest-workers" and in Los Angeles in the wake of the Rodney King incident, as well as the many nationalist movements around the globe point out the necessity, even more essential now, to firmly face issues of racism, prejudice, and intercultural interaction.

Finally, our dependency on international linkages is also greater than ever before. It is estimated that four out of five new jobs presently created in the United States are the direct result of foreign trade. Add to this the fact that over 6,000 American firms have operations overseas and 6,000 international firms have branch offices in this country. It quickly becomes apparent that young people in today's schools stand a great chance of having significant contacts with individuals from backgrounds quite different from their own—not by themselves living in a foreign country during their career but by foreign nationals spending increasing amounts of time in various American communities.

The focus of multicultural education has often been on curricular addition and expansion. This is important in that historically many groups and perspectives have been ignored or otherwise absent from the knowledge base provided in schools. Today, however, efforts must reach beyond a simple infusion of knowledge. Preparation of educators to deliver instruction from an intercultural or international perspective quickly becomes a double-edged sword. Teachers must be prepared to teach young people from a variety of cultural and linguistic backgrounds. At the same time, the knowledge and skills that teachers themselves are learning must become the content that is taught to young people in order for them to gain the skills necessary to live effectively in a global, interdependent world. This double-edged sword will not be easy to satisfy given what we know about our current population of teachers and the process of culture learning. We must begin to seek out concepts that cut across the various diversities that teachers and students will encounter in the schools. Such concepts must assist one in understanding and accommodating interactions across not only cultural barriers but also gender, age, class, and ability lines.

Search for a Common Ground

Each of us is socialized within a given culture to believe that certain things are right and good. That, by its very nature, is the manner in which every individual gains an understanding of his or her world, forms an allegiance to a given group, and seeks to transmit those understandings to others of the group. It should not be surprising, then, to consider the school as an institution that has embedded within it certain values and expectations that have been determined by the majority culture-at-large. If such is the case, schools, which inherently operate from one "majority" culture perspective, reward those whose mode of interaction, communication, and manner of learning are congruent with its method of operation. In contrast, a significant number of students are left out of the process, thus feeling alienated and "unreached." Perhaps the concepts of ethnocentrism and culture shock from the field of cross-cultural psychology capture the essence of the dilemma better than any as we begin to consider the experiences of traditionally marginalized groups as they confront the culture of the school.

The 18-theme culture-general framework proposed by Brislin et al. (1986) forms the essence of many of these problems and provides a context from which to understand relevant issues. This framework suggests that people will encounter similar experiences whenever they interact over a significant period of time with people who have been socialized in a manner different from themselves. Such similar experiences are found to occur regardless of the backgrounds of the actors, regardless of their roles, and regardless of the situation in which they find themselves.

At one level, understanding and accepting the strong emotional responses people will have when involved in intercultural interactions is critical to one's success in this arena. People's emotions will be aroused as they meet with unpredictable behavior on the part of others or when their behavior does not bring about an expected response. This will be true for the student where there is a clash between the culture of the school and that of the child, as well as for the teacher who finds her- or himself in a highly diverse context. But in addition to emotional readiness, gaining the perspective of an insider is critical to establishing any functional relationship among teacher, students, and family. The culture-general framework points out that such differences in work styles, value orientations, and roles are common across cultures, as well as among the various subcultures or subgroups that make up a multicultural nation at large. This framework can also help individuals prepare themselves for the kinds of reactions they will have as they encounter differences in the school and community.

The 18 culture-general themes are categorized into three broad areas of concern and potential misunderstanding. When people from different backgrounds come together, it is common (1) for people's emotions to be highly charged and as a result to experience intense feelings; (2) for people to misunderstand and experience conflicts because of their operating from a different knowledge base; and (3) for people to interpret similar stimuli in different ways because of underlying bases of cultural differences. The 18 themes are found within these three major categories. *People's Experiences That Engage Their Emotions* include anxiety; disconfirmed expectations; the need to belong; ambiguity; and confronting one's own prejudices. The *Knowledge Areas That People Find Difficult to Understand* include work-related behaviors such as decision-making, problem-solving, and the locus of control; orientation in time and space; verbal and nonverbal language use as well as language learning; role-determined behavior; group versus individual orientation; rituals versus superstitions; social hierarchies of class and status; and value orientation. The *Bases of Cultural Differences* include the process of categorization; differentiation; the tendency people have to form ingroups and outgroups; differences in learning styles; and the manner in which people make judgments or attributions about others.

It is important at this juncture to stress that this is not the "melting pot" myth presented under another guise. It is possible to identify common ground without diminishing the importance of cultural/individual differences. Both culture-general and culture-specific approaches need to be presented in balance. You might analyze the case studies presented earlier and demonstrate how they imply *both* general and specific aspects.

Looking at the school context through the lens of the culture-general framework enables us to frame or explain some of the situations encountered almost daily by teachers and students in a variety of contexts while at the same time guiding our goal-setting efforts. Although the entire range of 18 themes cannot be discussed fully here (see Brislin et. al., 1986; and Cushner et al., 1992), a few will be expanded on.

Belonging and Related Concepts

There is probably nothing more critical in the life of an adolescent than "fitting in." The concept of *belonging*—the need people have to fill a niche, to feel that they belong and are at home, and to strive to gain the status of insider with a group with which they wish to identify—is of utmost importance to most young people. New teachers, too, as well as new community members, have a need to feel that their contributions, ideas, and efforts are recognized, heard, and perhaps integrated into the existing fabric. People find meaning, security, and identity by belonging to various groups or networks. When excluded from such groups, people may begin to experience such negative responses as loneliness, alienation, a loss of self-esteem, and a decreased sense of direction and purpose.

Related to the need to belong is the tendency people have to form ingroups—defined as those with whom they feel comfortable and are able to discuss concerns with—and outgroups—those generally kept at a distance, both physical as well as emotional. A difficulty faced by newcomers to most situations is that they are entering a context in which people have already formed their ingroups. The newcomer, as Alice was in the second case study above, has left her ingroups behind. It is important to recognize that those in the new context generally do not need newcomers. A good deal of time is often required before new ingroups are established.

The issue of belonging is of critical importance in the intercultural context. Isolation from a group due to cultural or social incompetence, as well as physical separation, may have a similar impact on the individual. In the cross-cultural context, lack of social skills and language competence required to communicate effectively and to develop and maintain interpersonal relationships can likewise lead to isolation.

Cushner et al. (1992) state:

> Whatever the cause of the isolation, psychologists tell us that people tend to react in the same manner; they become more negative, rejecting, self-deprecating, self-absorbed, less responsive, and perhaps hostile.

It is no wonder that people, especially adolescents in schools, strive so very hard to be a part of the groups that appeal to them. What other "groups" may occur in schools in which individuals, both students, teachers, and families, may desire access but for some reasons may feel left out?

Anxiety

Related to the need to belong is another of the 18 themes—anxiety. Anxiety refers to feelings of discomfort individuals may experience when in an unfamiliar situation. A high degree of anxiety, evident in such school-based settings as test-taking with its accompanying threat of failure as well as with interactions with peers, teachers, and parents, may result in inattention and an inability to operate at higher levels of cognitive processing.

Renata's situation in the first case study demonstrates the link between the knowledge issues of the culture-general framework and people's emotional responses. The migrant students in the school are experiencing significant change—quite regularly, it seems. Their emotional needs must be met if they are to benefit in any educational setting. Billy Davis (1972), who grew up in a family of migrant farmworkers, speaks of the practical experiences teachers assume students bring with them to the classroom from the home experiences, as well as of the resulting anxiety:

No expert in measurement knows better than I the wishful thinking inherent in the concept of culture-free testing. I have sat with cold, damp hands, holding my breath, hoping the teacher would not call on me. . . . We never had a private bathroom, or a kitchen sink, or an oven. I never owned a tricycle, bicycle, or pets (stray dogs are a separate category). We did not "go on vacations," "have company," "take lessons," or "pack luggage." . . . For years I owned no toothbrush, nail file, or pajamas. I could go on. In short, the ordinary middle-class world was strange to me and its terms frightened me.

In addition, in the case study, Renata has come into critically close encounters with people who have vastly different values, expectations, and way of life. Overcoming her own immediate emotional reactions and then striving to learn as much as she can about the people with whom she will interact will prove to be critical to her success in this realm.

Communication Issues

Included in the knowledge areas are issues related to differences in language and communication styles, which seem to cut across the various diversities people will encounter in the schools. Verbal as well as nonverbal messages have significant impact, not only on the interpersonal interactions in the school context but also on the teaching and learning process. Critical to the development of any educational relationship is the degree to which trust and mutual understanding emerge. Because of the extent to which communication differences can result in significant misattributions or misjudgments about the motivations of others, considerable attention should be paid to this area in any teacher training program. Beyond the general cross-cultural communication differences any trainer would be prepared to introduce in a training program, attention to cross-gender communication, as well as communication between able-bodied and disabled individuals, should be stressed.

For instance, communication between able-bodied and disabled individuals often creates a unique set of problems to be addressed. Nonverbal behavior of a disabled person is often misinterpreted and viewed as inappropriate. In a similar manner, the nonverbal behavior of an able-bodied individual may signal discomfort, confusion, or rejection of the disabled individual, thereby further complicating the interaction. As the behavior of one is misjudged, the relationship may be strained, and a cycle of miscommunication may be set up that is difficult to break.

Uncertainty regarding appropriate behavior may result in strained relationships lacking the spontaneity and relaxed tone of more "normal" interactions. Differences in communication patterns between able-bodied and disabled individuals are quite apparent. For instance, able-bodied individuals tend to be more inhibited and nervous when communicating with individuals with disabilities—interpersonal distances are exaggerated, and encounters are characterized by greater anxiety and emotional discomfort. In addition, conflicting messages are often sent, as able-bodied individuals may verbally send positive messages while nonverbally communicating rejection or avoidance. Disabled persons report that their able-bodied communicators tend to glance away from them more frequently, stand farther away, act more nervous, pretend to ignore the disability, and assume that the disabled person is more disabled than he or she actually is. All of these increase the difficulty of communication.

Paul Williams, writing from the perspective of a disabled person, relates a vivid encounter:

> When one of us meets one of you, especially if it is for the first time, we are quite likely to lack many of the skills for successful communication. We may not be able to think of anything appropriate to say, or to put it into the right words, or to control our facial expression. But you also will show a great lack of skill. You will be embarrassed, you won't be able to think of anything appropriate to say, you will tend to talk in an inappropriate tone of voice, you will tend to have a wide grin on your face and ask questions without really being interested in the answer. The handicap is a mutual one. Both of us have difficulty in communicating with and forming relationships with the other. The trouble is that you have lots of opportunities to go off and form relationships more easily. We don't. You can deny your handicap. We can't—we live with it all the time (Shearer, 1984).

The stereotypes of differences between male and female communication patterns are also critical to consider in the educational context (Cushner et al., 1992). Folklore tends to perpetuate the perception of certain stereotypical differences in male and female speech, even though empirical research often indicates this to be inaccurate and biased. For instance, the common belief that women speak more than men does not stand up in the research. In fact, in mixed-sex groups, men tend to speak at least twice as much, interrupt more often, and have a tendency to speak in ways that control both the direction of the talk and the overall situation in which people are speaking (Spender, 1981). Other cross-gender communication findings that are of interest: men are more likely to interrupt women than men; men receive more criticism and reprimands in the workplace than do women; women professionals are touched more often than male professionals; women are more likely to reveal personal information than are men; men use more personal space while they are talking than women; and men tend to initiate more conversation with mixed company at work than do women (see Chapter 4 by Bailey in this book; Cushner et al., 1992; Spender, 1981).

Although there is a lack of empirical research on the subject at the moment, it appears that the real differences in communication patterns between males and females may not be as important as the perceived differences or stereotypes. Although categorization or stereotype formation are inevitable and serve necessary and useful functions, when they are used to enforce inequalities of power and influence, their unquestioned use may cause not only miscommunication but also miscarriages of justice.

Learning Styles

The example of Ulrike above points out numerous issues related to learning styles as well as testing and assessment across cultures. In this particular instance, Ulrike seems to be overwhelmed by the extreme number of tests that American students must complete. In Ulrike's native country, as in many places around the world, most of class time is spent studying, discussing, or otherwise "learning" the specific content of the course with little, if any, time devoted to testing. Testing is simply accomplished at the end of the term with students preparing for one major exam in the field of study to determine if she or he qualifies for the next level. Ulrike may find studying for tests on a weekly (or more) basis too demanding and distracting from the manner in which she is accustomed to learning.

Although slow to change in the minds of some, and slower to change in behavior, it seems that we are beginning to move away from the cultural deficit model that was so often used to explain school failure on the part of some groups. Rather, a cultural difference model is slowly being accepted. This position posits that the cognitive, learning, and motivational styles of many students in our schools are merely different from those most often expected by teachers, administrators, and curriculum developers who, you will recall, in the majority of cases represent the dominant culture. There exists, in a sense, a "culture clash" between the expectations and skills of students and those of teachers. As assimilationist ideology is fading, so too is the expectation that all children should be forced to fit a monocultural school culture that tends to favor white, middle-class values, behavior, and thinking skills.

As learning style preferences are recognized by many to exist within a group, differences are also found across cultures. People learn how to learn in ways that are rather specific to their group. Socialization into one's group not only teaches one what to think and learn but how to think and learn as well. This knowledge, like our knowledge of our own culture, is often tacit. That is, it is not articulated within the culture and is, for the most part, unknown to those outside it. In general then, thinking about differences in learning style suggests that culture significantly influences the manner in which one learns how to learn.

Researchers suggest that individuals *tend* to fall in distinct categories with regard to the manner in which they prefer to learn and, to a large degree, that these preferences are culturally determined. Some propose that there exist field-dependent versus field-independent learners. That is, field-independent learners are parts-specific, can isolate facts as needed, are rather linear in their thinking and approach to problem solving, and tend to test rather well, given the kinds of assessment practices predominantly in use today. Field-dependent learners, on the contrary, must see the big picture, seek to find personal relevance in the task at hand, and require that some sort of personal relationship is established between teacher and student.

Schools tend to stress the cognitive domain, rather low-level thinking, and the memorization of facts. In order to achieve success at the tasks presented in most schools, students are required to adopt a logical and rather linear approach to problem solving, to be highly task- and rule-oriented, and to function within a rather rigid hierarchy. Field-independent or analytical thinkers tend to be rewarded in the school context.

Field-independence tends to be more often associated with the dominant white middle class than with other groups. As a result, one often finds a majority of children from Mexican-American, African-American, Puerto Rican, and Native American backgrounds to be quite unfamiliar with the preferred learning and teaching style of the school when they first come into contact with the school environment. There appears to be a tendency that field-independent students perform better at school tasks than their field-dependent counterparts. It is incumbent on teachers, then, to develop instructional and assessment strategies that complement those that the students naturally bring with them to school.

Cooperative learning is one instructional strategy that seems promising in its ability to accommodate a variety of learning styles while significantly improving the educational achievement of individuals from traditional minority groups (see Johnson & Johnson, 1985; Slavin, 1985, 1989/1990). Characteristic of well-structured cooperative learning groups is positive goal interdependence; that is, common goals for individual as well as group success are expected. Members of the group are accountable to one another. Considerable evidence exists to suggest that cooperative learning encourages students to help one another learn how to learn; increases achievement for the majority of students; results in more positive feeling toward school; improves intergroup relations in the classroom as well as out of school; and improves student self-esteem, time on task, as well as school attendance.

Key Factors in Successful Innovation

The analysis of schools that are successfully addressing issues of diversity suggests that there is no formula that can be widely developed and applied to any particular school setting. Successful innovation seems more likely to occur when school personnel make the effort to adapt what is known about effective schools to their own situation and when some form of partnership develops between the school and local community and businesses. And oftentimes the most successful innovations are rather small. The addition of an Italian language course in a community that has many Italians, although a small step, may serve to let others know that their concerns are recognized.

Successful innovation in schools can be looked at in terms of four dimensions.

1. Sociocultural inclusion refers to building a sense of community from within the school. This helps to remove barriers of access to knowledge, to the mainstream society and culture, as well as to one's own identity. Schools that

accept and integrate various cultures, languages, and experiences throughout the school context help all students learn to negotiate life in a society characterized by diversity. Dialogue among home, school, and community helps greatly to facilitate this dimension. Understanding that people's values may differ is one thing. Providing the opportunity for people to come together to dialogue about such phenomena is another. An effective school becomes a community of dialogue around critical issues related to the education of children.

2. Curriculum inclusion and expansion suggests that people continue to ask if a standard, universal curriculum is best for all students and teachers, just what such a standard curriculum would consist of, or if diversification might be more effective. Inclusive curricula focus on all students and integrate the contributions of many different people and groups to the history and experiences of a nation and the world.

3. Modification of pedagogy should occur so that it reflects the living hand of cultural tradition, including culturally specific learning style differences as well as the social, linguistic, and cognitive requirements of a future characterized by change and diversity. Teaching from such a perspective does not mean throwing out the knowledge and understanding necessary for success in the dominant society. Rather, it suggests that all can, as does the multilingual who can function in two (or more) languages, gain the skills necessary to function in a multicultural society.

4. Finally, methods of assessment that consider the complex interrelationships of race, class, ethnicity, religion, gender, culture, and disability in students are characteristic of effective schools. Assessment strategies that consider cultural and other differences provide students and parents with better indicators of student performance. Portfolio assessment, for instance, is proving to be an effective means of gathering a wide range of evaluative information on students (see Means, Chelemer, & Knapp, 1991; Tharp, 1989).

Skill Applications

The application of many of the concepts from cross-cultural psychology and training to American ethnic groups is proving to be rather fruitful. The following exercise, modified from the *Ethnic Literacy Test—A Cultural Perspective* prepared by Shirla McClain in 1980, is an attempt to bring some of the culture-general themes to light in terms of major American ethnic groups.

Directions: Caution must be taken to avoid the creation of stereotypes when using specific examples to illustrate certain points. Such is the case here. Although fixed statements cannot be sensitive to individual differences to the complexity or the dynamic conditions of any multicultural context, the following statements have been identified, for the most part, as being true. Either individually or in groups: (1) expand on the content of the sentence, perhaps adding limits or examples that do not fit to generalizations where appropriate; (2) explain why the sentence is true; and (3) explore the possible implications of this knowledge for teaching, learning, and assessment. For what other groups do each of these findings hold true?

Communication Differences

1. A Mexican-American child may have difficulty in reading words that begin with two consonants.
2. Non-Standard English is a language system that has rules.
3. Many Appalachians form some possessive pronouns by adding *n*, such as in "his'n" or "her'n".
4. Vietnamese children may experience problems in spelling words that end with a double consonant.
5. Nose wiggling and pointing with the lips are two forms of nonverbal communication used by Puerto Rican Americans.
6. African-Americans may interrupt a speaker with encouraging remarks.
7. Black English is not a synonym for black slang. Rather, it is a form of Standard English that has its own slang.
8. Vietnamese children have great difficulty learning to read polysyllabic words.
9. Touch between teacher and student can have multiple meanings. It can facilitate learning with children of Hispanic backgrounds while alienating children from some Southeast Asian cultures.
10. For some African-Americans, as well as students of Hispanic descent, to avoid eye contact with people of authority is a sign of respect.

Value Orientations

11. The Native-American concept of time is significantly different from that of European-Americans'.
12. Mexican-American religious beliefs include the concept of fatalism.
13. Native-Americans usually prefer private rather than public recognition.
14. Mexican-American students generally prefer to work in groups rather than as individuals.
15. Appalachians have difficulty adapting well to urban life.
16. Among Native-Americans, the concept of private ownership may not exist.
17. Appalachians have strong kinship bonds.
18. African-Americans have a strong work orientation.
19. African-Americans tend to be deeply religious.

Family-Related Roles

20. The concept of an extended family is central for many Native-Americans, Asians, and Hispanics.

21. Mexican-American families are patriarchal.
22. Family roles and responsibilities are rather fluid and flexible in the African-American family.
23. For most Native-Americans and Asians, the elderly are honored and revered.

Field Exercises

Sensitivity to Diversity

Planning for the needs of a diverse student population requires teachers who are sensitive to a variety of interactions as they occur in the school environment, both in terms of interpersonal interaction as well as in terms of teaching and learning. Developing the ability to make accurate judgments or attributions regarding the behavior of others is critical if one is to facilitate mutual understanding. The 18-theme culture-general framework provides the opportunity for teachers to begin to develop a vocabulary as well as concepts to help explain the cross-cultural interactions in which they are engaged.

This exercise requires participants in a training program to make extended observations in a school or classroom, paying special attention to perceived intercultural problems or issues that arise. Record your observations as precisely as possible; identify any and all of the culture-general themes that you believe apply; and finally, propose any action that you feel will help resolve or otherwise shed light on this problem. This exercise can be accomplished under a variety of conditions. For instance, participants might conduct one observation session of an hour during their regular "workday," report back to the group, and follow up with a second observation session. Alternatively, participants can go on a "scavenger hunt," seeking evidence of these issues in schools, newspapers and magazines, television, and so forth. Again, the 18 themes include the following:

- Anxiety
- Disconfirmed expectations
- The need to belong
- Ambiguity
- Prejudice and ethnocentrism
- Work-related behaviors such as decision making, problem solving, and the onus of control orientation in time and space
- Nonverbal behavior, including the use of time and space
- Language use and language learning
- Role-determined behavior
- Group versus individual orientation
- Rituals versus superstitions
- Social hierarchies of class and status
- Value orientation

- Categorization of information
- Differentiation
- Ingroups and outgroups
- Differences in learning styles
- Attributions formation

A simple observation form might be developed, such as the following:

Problem as I Perceive It	Culture-General Themes	Proposed Action
Student does not participate in class discussions.	Role-determined behavior, group vs. individual orientation, and differences in learning styles	Provide all new students an orientation on expected class behavior. Show a film demonstrating "ideal" classroom behavior.

Learning and Teaching Styles

The following, taken from C. Grant and C. Sleeter, *Turning on Learning* (1989), might be used as an introduction to the investigation of learning styles. Below are some items that describe criteria to investigate among individual students. You should decide how best to go about investigating these items. Once sufficient data has been collected, look for patterns based on gender and ethnic backgrounds; but as above, try not to stereotype certain groups as learning in one particular way. Once patterns in student learning styles have been determined, use them as guides for selecting teaching strategies.

Working Alone or Working Together can be investigated by asking a student her or his preference or by observing the student when there is a choice and noting which option is selected most often.

Preferred Learning Modalities refers to the sensory channels or processes the student prefers to use for acquiring new information or ideas, including observation, reading, listening, discussing, experiencing, writing, and so forth. Again, this can be investigated by giving students a choice and recording their preference; recording student success under each condition; or asking individual preference.

Content About People Versus Content About Things can be determined again by asking or by offering a choice (i.e., in story content or math story problems) and noting which is selected most often.

Structured Versus Nonstructured Environment can be observed by noting student preference for a highly structured environment compared to a more open-ended one in which the individual has greater control. Students who seem to get lost or do poorly on open-ended assignments and those who seem bored with structured assignments should be noted.

Details Versus the Whole Picture relates to the distinction between field-dependence and -independence. Student preference for, and success with, detail versus greater comfort with ideas should be noted. For instance, some students may pay great attention to grammar and punctuation when story writing but may have little to say, whereas others may produce good first drafts that are weak in mechanics.

An observation form such as the following may be useful:

Learning Style Record Sheet

Directions: For each student, record data you collect about each item related to her or his preferred style of learning.

Student's Name _____

Method of Data Collection	Findings

1. Style of Working
   Alone
   With others
2. Modality
   Watching
   Reading
   Listening
   Discussing
   Touching
   Moving
   Writing
3. Content
   People
   Things
4. Need for structure
   High
   Low
5. Details vs. generalities

References

Brislin, R., Cushner, K., Cherrie, C., & Yong, M. (1986). *Intercultural interactions: A practical guide.* Newbury Park, CA: Sage.

Cushner, K., McClelland, A., & Safford, P. (1992). *Human diversity in education: An integrative approach.*, New York: McGraw-Hill.

Davis, B. (1972). *The ripe harvest: Educating migrant children.* Coral Gables, FL: University of Miami Press.

Grant, C. A., & Sleeter, C. E. (1989). *Turning on learning.* Columbus, OH: Merrill.

Johnson, D., & Johnson, R. (1985). Student-student interaction: Ignored but powerful. *Journal of Teacher Education, 36*(4), 22-26.

McClain, S. (1980). *Ethnic literacy test: A cultural perspective.* Unpublished document, Kent State University, Kent, Ohio.

Means, B., Chelmer, C., & Knapp, M. (Eds.). (1991). *Teaching advanced skills to at-risk students.* San Francisco: Jossey-Bass.

Shearer, A. (1984). *Disability: Whose handicap?* Oxford, UK: Basil Blackwell.

Slavin, R. (1985). Cooperative learning: Applying contact theory in desegregated schools. *Journal of Social Issues, 41*(3), 45-62.

Slavin, R. (1989/1990). Research on cooperative learning: Consensus and controversy. *Educational Leadership, 47*(4), 52-54.

Spender, D. (1981). *Men's studies modified: The impact of feminism on the academic disciplines.* Oxford, UK: Pergamon Press.

Tharp, R. G. (1989). Psychocultural variables and constants: Effects on teaching and learning in schools. *American Psychologist, 44*(2), 349-359.

Vobejda, B. (1992, April 16). More Americans are speaking little English. *The Beacon Journal,* p. A8.

8 Intercultural Education at the University Level: Teacher-Student Interaction

NEAL R. GOODMAN

As teacher/student interaction is such an archetypal human phenomenon, and so deeply rooted in the culture of a society, cross-cultural learning situations are fundamentally problematic for both parties.

Geert Hofstede (1986)

Too often even those in the field of intercultural communication are oblivious to the differing perceptions of teacher-student interactions. We may lecture about "Low versus High Power Distance" cultures, while insisting on treating our students from High Power Distance cultures as "equals." The assumption that *our* way of teaching is more "advanced" seems to be a hard one to discard. In this module, Goodman applies Hofstede's five concepts to the actual teaching situation. Readers are given an opportunity to assess their own preferences, orientations, and biases while being exposed to potential cross-cultural problems.

Contents

Self-Assessment Exercise: Instruction Styles

Instructions: Below there are 46 statements that are clustered in pairs. Circle the statement in each matched pair that you are most comfortable with. There are no wrong answers. Make your choice as spontaneously as possible. You will have 23 items circled at the end of the exercise. (Adapted from Hofstede, 1986.)

1. A positive association in society is with whatever is rooted in tradition.
2. A positive association in society is with whatever is "new."
3. Impersonal "truth" is stressed and can, in principle, be obtained from any competent person.
4. Personal "wisdom" is stressed and is transferred in the relationship with a particular teacher (guru).
5. A teacher should respect the independence of his or her students.
6. A teacher merits the respect of his or her students.
7. One is never too old to learn; continual education.
8. The young should learn; adults cannot accept a student role.
9. Students expect to learn how to do.
10. Students expect to learn how to learn.
11. Student-centered education (value is placed on student initiative).
12. Teacher-centered education (value is placed on teacher-ordered learning).
13. Students expect teacher to initiate communication.
14. Teacher expects students to initiate communication.
15. Teacher expects students to find their own paths.
16. Students expect teacher to outline paths to follow.
17. Individual students will speak up in class in response to a general invitation by the teacher.
18. Individual students will only speak up in class when called upon personally by the teacher.
19. Individuals will speak up in large groups.
20. Individuals will only speak up in small groups.
21. Large classes are split socially into smaller cohesive subgroups based on particularist criteria (e.g., ethnic affiliation).
22. Subgroupings in class vary from one situation to the next based on universalist criteria (e.g., the task at hand).
23. Students may speak up spontaneously in class.
24. Students speak up in class only when invited by the teacher.
25. The teacher is seldom contradicted and rarely criticized.
26. Students are allowed to contradict or criticize teacher.
27. Confrontation in learning situations can be beneficial; conflicts can be brought into the open.
28. Formal harmony in learning situations should be maintained.
29. Effectiveness of learning is related to the excellence of the teacher.
30. Effectiveness of learning is related to the amount of two-way communication in class.

31. Neither the teacher nor any student should ever be made to lose face.
32. "Face-saving" is of little importance.
33. Education is a way of improving one's economic worth and self-respect based on ability and competence.
34. Education is a way of gaining prestige in one's social environment and of joining a higher status group.
35. Outside class, teachers are treated as equals to students.
36. Respect for teachers is also shown outside of class.
37. Diploma certificates are important and displayed on walls.
38. Diploma certificates have little importance.
39. In teacher-student conflicts, parents are expected to side with the student.
40. In teacher-student conflicts, parents are expected to side with the teacher.
41. Older teachers are more respected than younger teachers.
42. Younger teachers are more liked than older teachers.
43. Acquiring competence is more important than acquiring certificates.
44. Acquiring certificates is more important than acquiring competence.
45. Teachers are expected to give preferential treatment to some students (e.g., based on ethnic affiliation or on recommendation by an influential person).
46. Teachers are expected to be strictly impartial.

Scoring

Step 1: On the chart below, circle the numbers corresponding to the numbers circled on your inventory sheet. (For example, if you circled 1 on the inventory, circle it below in the CS category.) Total the circles in each row and place in the blank.

1	8	9	18	20	21	28	31	34	37	44	45	CS = _____
2	7	10	17	19	22	27	32	33	38	43	46	IS = _____
3	5	11	14	15	23	26	30	35	39	42		SP = _____
4	6	12	13	16	24	25	29	36	40	41		LP = _____

(CS + IS + SP + LP should equal 23)   TOTAL = _____

Step 2: Transfer your scores above to the appropriate blanks below and compute totals for Collectivism/Individualism and Power Distance.

CS (_____) – IS (_____) = _____ Collectivism/Individualism Score

SP (_____) – LP (_____) = _____ Power Distance Score

Step 3: Mark your scores below. Collectivism/Individualism is on vertical line; Power Distance is on horizontal line.

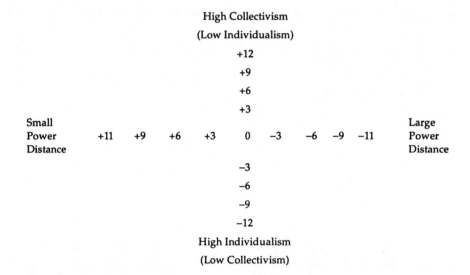

High Collectivism
(Low Individualism)

As faculty search for ways to internationalize their courses, they often fail to note that the very nature of how they teach and how students learn is often culture-bound. The self-assessment that you just completed will be used later to examine cross-cultural differences in student-teacher interaction. However, before we examine the self-assessment, let's turn to some illustrative cases.

Case Studies

Japan

Recently, a major educational joint venture was established between a prestigious U.S. business school and an equally renowned Japanese university. The purpose of the venture was to establish an American-style MBA program in Japan. Although the vast majority of students in the first year's class were Japanese, the professors and some of the students were from the U.S. school.

As the first semester neared the end, the American and Japanese students had gotten over their initial shyness and were getting along very well. The examination period was approaching and one of the first exams for the year was in finance. The professor had distributed a case that would be the basis for the exam. Each student was to prepare a comprehensive spreadsheet and provide exhibits to be attached to the exam. The students were free to use computers and outside reference books. All preparatory work was to be done individually, guided by the U.S. school's honor code that all students signed pledging their commitment to honesty and integrity in their work at school. While the American students were busy at the library and computer center, their Japanese counterparts were nowhere to be seen.

While grading the exams, the American professor noted the near uniformity of the answers of the Japanese students. After some further investigation, he learned that nearly every Japanese student had collaborated during their preparation for the exam in clear violation of the specific instructions of the professor and in violation of the honor code they all pledged to follow.

The American professor was dismayed by the betrayal of the students. He was even more upset by the apparent lack of concern shown by the Japanese administration. The American students who quickly learned of the Japanese "conspiracy" were totally disillusioned. They realized that they could no longer trust their Japanese colleagues whom they otherwise admired for their hard work.

Discussion Questions

How do you explain the behavior of the Japanese students? How do you explain the reaction of the Japanese administration? How should the American professor respond to this situation? How should the American students respond to the situation? A discussion of this case will be presented later in this chapter.

Nigeria

Charles had been an honors student throughout high school and college. On the advice of his professors at a highly regarded liberal arts college in the Midwest, he decided to take his junior year abroad in Nigeria. Charles was excited about studying in an area where there were few Americans. He was hopeful that he could be integrated into the local student culture. By the fourth month at his host university, Charles was beginning to feel comfortable in his new setting. He had made some friends and he was enjoying his classes. Of all his classes Charles particularly liked a class on Nigerian literature. The professor seemed to be particularly attentive to Charles's presence because he had just returned from a visit to the United States.

One day in class the professor was giving a lecture on comedy. During the lecture the professor mentioned that he was very impressed by an American improvisational group he saw at Second City in Cleveland. Charles, noting that Second City is in Chicago not Cleveland, raised his hand and as soon as he was acknowledged he mentioned the correct location. The professor showed no appreciation for Charles's contribution and continued his lecture. At the end of the lecture the professor asked Charles to remain in the classroom. The professor told Charles that he was not to come to any further classes and that he would receive an incomplete for the course. Charles was shaken and felt that this was some sort of a trick, but the professor was very rigid and gave Charles no explanation or alternative. Finally, in desperation, Charles left the classroom feeling that his whole year was going to be ruined.

Discussion Questions

How would you explain the professor's action? What could Charles do to remedy the situation? A discussion of this case will be presented later in this chapter.

Korea

In his early 20s, Harold taught high school history and was an adjunct professor at a nearby community college. When he was 25, he was invited to become an instructor/trainer for a large U.S. corporation based in Chicago. As Harold entered his mid-40s, he was considered to be one of his company's most accomplished instructors.

In fact, he was recently part of a team that developed a new course called "The Qualities of a Master Trainer." Having taught the course several times, Harold had made small changes in the course to get it to the point where he was extremely proud and satisfied with it.

The corporation Harold works for recently opened a subsidiary in Korea and was trying to provide their new Korean employees with the same training opportunities as were provided to its American employees. One of the first courses to be selected for delivery in Korea was "The Qualities of a Master Instructor." This was deemed to be a critically important course because the subsidiary was going to employ a number of new trainers who would be instructing the remaining employees in many courses, including sales, stress management, quality improvement, and career planning.

In light of Harold's seniority, reputation, and experience with the course, Harold was selected to go to Korea to teach the course to the Korean trainers. Harold was indeed a master trainer, although he thought of himself more as a facilitator. His style, which he learned through many years of trial and error, was participatory. He loved to get his trainees involved in his courses. He always projected an informal and easy style in which he was more an equal of his students, not their superior.

Though this was Harold's first business trip abroad, he felt confident in teaching the course he helped to design. Harold's main concern before accepting the assignment was the English language ability of the trainers. He was relieved to learn that they all spoke English fluently.

Harold arrived in Korea on Sunday and tried to stay up to get a regular night's sleep before having to teach the course on Monday morning. When he awoke on Monday he was a bit disoriented but after his third cup of coffee he felt alert and anxious to get to the training center. In the cab on his way to the training center Harold reviewed his notes one final time. He was confident and enthusiastic about meeting his Korean colleagues.

As he entered the training room Harold was pleased to see that the materials were in place, and all the audiovisual equipment was working. He checked out the room carefully and waited the 10 minutes before his students were to arrive. The eight students all arrived together and right on time. He introduced himself and put *Harold* on the board in big letters so they could practice and remember his name. As he engaged in some small talk with the participants before the program, Harold was concerned that some of the students would speak in Korean to each other before responding to him. Also, some of the students spoke in very halting English. He had been told that they were all fluent in English.

Harold began the class with the usual introductions. He introduced himself, told people to address him by his first name, and told the students about his rural upbringing and his prior teaching experience and his experience with the firm. The students introduced themselves but said little about themselves, with the exception of Kim Park who had been to the United States and loved American movies. Harold proceeded with his usual icebreaker, a brief joke about the company. The joke, which generates a lot of laughter at home, did not seem to work. Harold felt that something might have been lost in the translation as he proceeded with the first part of the class.

Harold asked the class what they hoped to get out of this class on the qualities of a master trainer. The students looked back at him with no response. He then asked the participants to contribute an objective they had for the course. Again there were blank stares. Finally, one of the participants responded, saying, "We want to learn the qualities of a master trainer." That was not the type of individual objective he was looking for but at least he had a response. Harold explained that the response was fine and he then asked the participants to provide him with a list of the qualities of a good trainer. After waiting 5 minutes for the participants to generate their lists, Harold asked for volunteers to present their list of qualities. To his dismay no one raised a hand. None wanted to contribute their ideas. Finally, the same student who spoke earlier raised his hand and in a hushed voice said, "A master trainer must possess great wisdom."

Wisdom was not the response Harold was expecting. He already had a list of "good" and "bad" qualities and in all cases in the past the students could generate a list that identified each one. Harold thought the next best thing to do was to present the list to the students, so he quickly went to the board and wrote the following good and bad qualities:

Good Instructor

   A. Relates to his or her students
   B. Shows great enthusiasm
   C. Gets and gives feedback
   D. Puts students at ease
   E. Draws students into discussion
   F. Humanizes him- or herself (tells jokes, etc.)
   G. Shows flexibility
   H. Identifies students' needs and interests
   I. Is prepared and knowledgeable
   J. Uses a variety of training aids
   K. Is him- or herself

Bad Instructor

   A. Monopolizes classroom conversation
   B. Is pompous

C. Is dictatorial
D. Speaks too fast or too slow
E. Reads materials to the students
F. Interrupts answers
G. Fakes it
H. Has distracting mannerisms

The trainees quietly wrote down everything Harold put on the board. Once he was finished writing Harold turned to the group and asked, "What items on the board do you agree or disagree with?" Again, there was no response. Exasperated, Harold announced a short break and asked the participants to come back from the break with at least one question. Harold could not generate much discussion about his course during the break. Mostly people wanted to know what he thought about Korea.

The break was over and Harold, fearing no response again, asked the group for some questions. Again, for a painfully long time, there was silence. Finally the student who had been to the United States raised his hand. Harold excitedly asked, "Yes, what is your question?" The student responded, "Do you know when Sylvester Stallone will make his next movie?"

Harold wanted to get on the next plane to Chicago.

Discussion Questions

What are some of the causes of Harold's frustration? What could Harold have done differently? A discussion of this case will follow later in this chapter.

Skill Concepts

Introduction

In any intercultural encounter, one must distinguish individual differences in personality from group or national characteristics. One of the foremost examinations of national characteristics has been conducted by Geert Hofstede (1980, 1991).

Hofstede is a Dutch social psychologist who designed a massive research study involving the local country employees of subsidiaries of International Business Machines (IBM). The research included a survey of over 116,000 employees at all levels from unskilled workers to top managers. The research was conducted in over 50 countries and in 20 languages. All the employees worked for the same company and they were otherwise matched for characteristics such as job category, age, and gender. Based on this voluminous amount of data, Hofstede identified four *dimensions* of national culture that can serve as a basis for comparing the dominant value systems between national cultures.

It is important to note that Hofstede examined the relationship between nationality and mean values scores. Focusing on the relationship between nationality and mean values scores meant that the country, not the individual respondent, became the unit of analysis. Thus, the dimensions that derived from the research were *ecological* dimensions of collective national cultures and not dimensions of individual personality. However, it is appropriate to think of the dimensions of national culture as examples and measures of the "personality" of each culture.

The Four Dimensions of National Culture

The Four Dimensions of National Culture that Hofstede identified were these:

1. *Power Distance.* The degree to which a society accepts the idea that power is to be distributed unequally. The more this is accepted, the higher the country's ranking in power distance.
2. *Individualism-Collectivism.* The degree to which a society feels that individuals' beliefs and actions should be independent of collective thought and action. The more this idea is accepted, the higher the rank on this measure. Individualism contrasts with collectivism, which is the belief that people should integrate their thoughts and actions with those of a group (e.g., extended family, organizations). In individualistic societies, people are more likely to pursue their own personal goals. In collective societies, people are more likely to integrate their own goals with those of group members.
3. *Uncertainty Avoidance.* The degree to which a society feels threatened by ambiguous situations and tries to avoid them by providing rules and refusing to tolerate deviance. The more a society accepts this idea, the higher its ranking in uncertainty avoidance.
4. *Masculinity.* The degree to which a society focuses on assertiveness, task achievement, and the acquisition of things as opposed to quality of life issues such as caring for others, group solidarity, and helping the less fortunate. The more assertiveness, competitiveness, and ambition are accepted, the higher a country's rank on this measure.

Hofstede found that the more a nation is characterized by masculine values, the greater is the gap between the values espoused by men and women in that nation.

The Four Dimensions and Teacher/Student Interactions

The relevance of Hofstede's research to educational settings is "based on the assumption that role patterns and value systems in a society are carried forward from the school to the job and back" (Hofstede, 1980, p. 306).

In order to appreciate how the Four Dimensions can impact on student-teacher interactions, we will examine the extreme differences between the dimensions while recognizing that in many countries the situation may be closer to the center. However, by looking at extreme cases we can best identify situations that can create cross-cultural difficulties. For each dimension one extreme will be described, such as *High* Power Distance, and the opposite extreme can be extrapolated from the former (*Low* Power Distance).

Power Distance

High Power Distance societies are characterized by teacher-centered education, in which the teacher transfers wisdom to students. Information flow is from the teacher to the student and students are not expected to initiate communication or speak up unless called upon to do so. In such societies, teachers are respected in and out of class and are not to be publicly contradicted. Age is respected and formal presentations are appreciated. The status of the school is also an important factor in determining the status of a person.

Individualism-Collectivism

In societies that are strong on Collectivism, there is a strong sense of respect for tradition and the group. Individuals will find more satisfaction working with a group for a collective goal rather than working individually for their own achievement. Students are not expected to call attention to themselves by calling out answers. Thus, group work is preferred when giving assignments. Neither the teacher nor the student should be put into a situation where they might "lose face." The acquisition of diplomas and certificates (even through questionable means) is very highly prized.

Uncertainty Avoidance

Societies that are high in Uncertainty Avoidance have learning environments characterized by structure. Both the student and the teacher prefer structured learning situations with precise objectives, detailed assignments, and adherence to a schedule set up well in advance. In such an environment, lecturing is most common and there are no interruptions or disagreements with the "all-knowing" teacher. Learning the subject as precisely as possible is more important than learning how to learn.

Masculinity

In a society characterized as being Masculine, teachers encourage competition and openly praise the success of the "winners." Failure, however, is detrimental to success and leads to low self-esteem. In order to prove themselves, students try to make themselves visible and they choose academic subjects that have clear career paths. In highly masculine societies, there is more gender segregation in careers, so males tend to avoid feminine academic subjects.

National Differences and Correlations Between the Dimensions

The research findings show that there is a very strong correlation between Power Distance and Individualism/Collectivism (Hofstede, 1980). Societies that are high in Power Distance also tend to be high in Collectivism. This association may be due to the fact that both Low Power Distance and High Individualism correlate with national wealth. When national wealth is controlled for, the correlation disappears.

Countries that are high on Individualism and low in Power Distance include the United States, Australia, Great Britain, The Netherlands, Canada, and New Zealand. These are joined by Denmark, Sweden, Switzerland, Germany, Ireland, Norway, and Finland, with Israel and Austria both having scores less individualistic but with less Power Distance.

Countries that are relatively high in Power Distance *and* high in Individualism are Italy, Belgium, France, South Africa, and Spain (though the latter is less individualistic than the others). Costa Rica was the only country in the study that had low Power Distance and low Individualism.

The countries that were the *highest* in Power Distance and Collectivism were mostly in South America (Guatemala, Panama, Venezuela, Ecuador). These are followed by countries that were a little less collectivist or that had slightly lower Power Distance scores: Colombia, Indonesia, Pakistan, Peru, Taiwan, Singapore, El Salvador, Korea, Thailand, Chile, The West African Region, Hong Kong, Portugal, Yugoslavia, and Mexico. Malaysia and the Philippines were each very high in Power Distance but only moderately high in Collectivism.

Several countries scored moderately high in both Collectivism and Power Distance. These included Greece, Turkey, Brazil, Arab countries (Egypt, Lebanon, Libya, Kuwait, Iraq, Saudi Arabia, UAE), India, Japan, Argentina, Jamaica, and Uruguay.

Uncertainty Avoidance and Masculinity did not correlate as strongly. Listed are a sample of the countries that scored the highest in Uncertainty Avoidance: Greece, Portugal, Guatemala, Uruguay, El Salvador, Belgium, Peru, Japan, Korea, Panama, Argentina.

Weak Uncertainty Avoidance was found among the following countries (in descending order): Singapore, Jamaica, Denmark, Sweden, Hong Kong, Ireland, Great Britain, Malaysia, India, the United States, Canada, Norway, and The Netherlands.

Countries that were distinctively feminine included Sweden, Norway, Denmark, The Netherlands, Costa Rica, Finland, Yugoslavia, and Chile. Countries that were at the high end of the Masculinity scale include Japan, Austria, Venezuela, Mexico, Switzerland, Ireland, Jamaica, Germany, and Italy.

The Fifth Dimension: Confucian Dynamism

A fifth dimension called *Confucian Dynamism* was developed after the first four factors (Chinese Culture Connection, 1987; Hofstede, 1991; Hofstede & Bond, 1988). This dimension was developed as part of an effort to explain the rather sudden economic growth among some Asian countries, notably Japan, South Korea, Taiwan, Hong Kong, and Singapore.

Michael Bond and a group of researchers who refer to themselves as The Chinese Culture Connection set out to examine whether there was a connection between the acceptance of Confucian teachings within a society and the degree of economic growth (Chinese Culture Connection, 1987; Hofstede, 1991; Hofstede & Bond, 1988). The research, which was carried out in 22 countries, showed that rapid economic growth was found in societies that valued and practiced certain significant Confucian values. The "dynamism" aspect of the concept comes from the findings that not all Confucian values were correlated to economic growth to the same degree. Rather, some values were emphasized while others were followed less rigorously.

Confucian values that were emphasized in the societies that experienced economic growth included the following:

a. Persistence and perseverance (if at first you don't succeed, try, try, try again)
b. Observing adherence to status relationships in which there were mutual obligations between the junior and senior members (father-son, older brother-younger brother, manager-subordinate)
c. Thrift: saving, saving, and more saving
d. Having a sense of shame

The researchers found that although the following Confucian values exist in the economically successful societies, they were de-emphasized:

e. Personal stability
f. Protecting face
g. Adherence to tradition
h. Reciprocal giving of favors and gifts

An analysis of Confucian Dynamism shows that "those countries which emphasize the dynamic aspects involving the future and the importance of hard work have experienced economic growth within recent years" (Brislin, 1993, p. 264).

The de-emphasized values can be seen as factors that could retard growth if practiced too rigidly. For example, too much adherence to tradition would subvert the need for change. Similarly, too much personal stability would reduce the likelihood of taking risks necessary for entrepreneurship and business growth. However, do not be misled into thinking that these values are dismissed; they are simply not emphasized to the same degree as the others. The implications for university educators is that professors will appreciate persistent students (Value a above) who stick to their assigned tasks and who respect status relationships, as in the professor-student relationship (Value b above). Professors will also report students who experience shame (Value d) if they do not take their assignments seriously.

Applications

Using the Inventory

Now turn to the answer sheet from the Self-Assessment Exercise in Part I and look at the scores. Survey your students/trainees to see where they scored. It is best to have students place an X on a large flip chart page or on an overhead transparency so the "norm" for the class can be determined. This can then lead to a discussion of the reason for any differences and/or similarities found in the class. Although it is not a good idea to *require* those outside the norm to try to provide an explanation, it would certainly be a good idea to invite people to discuss their scores. This exercise could also be done in small group discussions with each group reporting to the entire class. Members of groups can ask: How similar or different are we from our national norms, and why? (The United States, for example, would be found in the quadrant featuring High Individualism and moderately Low Power Distance.)

Group Exercise

Arrange the students into small groups (3-5). Ask some groups to assume they are from a High Power Distance culture and going abroad to teach students in a Low Power Distance culture. Have the group come up with potential problems, in and out of class, that might be encountered (see Hofstede, 1986, for further guidance in applying these concepts). Have the group come up with possible strategies that might be adopted to avoid the potential problems in and out of class. Have the group discuss any actual similar situations like this that they know about or have experienced.

Have a second set of groups assume they are from a Low Power Distance culture and are going abroad to teach in a High Power Distance culture. Have them conduct the same exercise described above.

Assign additional groups similar tasks reversing High and Low Individualism, High and Low Uncertainty Avoidance, and High and Low Masculinity. Have each group report on the following:

a. The potential problems anticipated in and out of class

b. Strategies they adopted for behaviors in and out of class to allow them to fit in to their new environment
c. Any actual cases like this on their campus

One way to make this exercise more realistic for your students is to invite someone from the office that is responsible for international students on your campus to sit in on the class and address the issues as they relate to experiences at your school. One note of caution: First brief the person you are going to invite in order to be sure they understand what you will be doing and what you expect of them. Make sure they understand the assessment tool, the Four Dimensions of Culture, and the way they will be applied.

Using the Case Studies

Have your students read the case studies in the second part of this chapter. Ask your students to try to explain what had happened. Next, have the students fill out the self-assessment. Deliver a brief lecture explaining Hofstede's Four Dimensions. After describing the Dimensions, have the students return to the cases and offer alternative explanations using Hofstede's research. An analysis of each of the cases using Hofstede's model is provided below.

Discussion of Japan Case Study

American society is characterized by a strong sense of individualism. In fact, in Hofstede's research (1980), the United States scored highest in Individualism of all the countries studied. In societies high in Individualism, students are expected to work on their own initiative for their personal achievement, which will be rewarded by the society. Inducements to compete and succeed *as individuals* permeate the educational systems and the society. American children are taught that individual achievement, hard work, and fair play will lead to success.

In highly Collectivist societies such as Japan, group work is idealized as the preferred method to achieve success. Calling attention to oneself through individual initiative for individual rewards is not the ideal. Working within the group context, whether at home, school, or work, is rewarded and leads to success.

Although teachers are honored for their knowledge, the social order of society is preserved by learning how to be an effective group member. In such societies, it is common for students to collaborate before and sometimes during tests. A student who did not cooperate by not engaging in group preparation for exams or by not letting his or her paper be seen by others would become an outcast and could not succeed within the context of the group. The future assistance of the others would be withdrawn and the stigma of not being a team player would have dramatic consequences. There have been hundreds of recorded incidents of Americans going abroad to study and being shocked by the apparent "cheating/cooperating" found in other more Collectivist societies. Likewise, there have been many cases in which international students coming to the United States to study found themselves quickly ostracized from their American peers because they anticipated greater sharing of information during tests and exams and were labeled as cheaters when they acted on their expectations.

In the description here, the Japanese students were acting in a perfectly appropriate manner for success in Japan. Likewise, the American students were acting as Americans do. The Japanese students had no way of knowing that they had created such a serious violation of trust in the eyes of the Americans.

The American professor should have been prepared for this situation. Granted, he is part of an American institution, but he is operating in Japan and the honor code form is not going to change a custom that the students have been socialized to perform throughout their lives. The American students were outraged by the actions of their Japanese "friends." A deep sense of betrayal destroyed much of the trust that had been developed. Such deep wounds do not heal quickly, if at all.

The educational issue here was not what or whether the students learned but how they learned and how their learning was evaluated. Obviously, in this situation the underlying cultural values of the importance of group versus the importance of the individual destroyed the educational process and the promise of successful intercultural interaction.

Discussion of Nigerian Case Study

One of the most significant differences between cultures is the degree to which the society views the distribution and display of personal power (Brislin, 1991). There are vast differences in how people are expected to demonstrate power differences in society. Hofstede's research (1986) examines how differences in Power Distance can impact on student-teacher interaction. In Low Power Distance societies, open displays of power are avoided, academic titles are sometimes exchanged for first names, and the give and take of a good intellectual debate in class between the professor and students is often seen as a very desirable outcome. In such societies, class time is often extended into after-class discussions, sometimes over coffee, soft drinks, or beer.

In High Power Distance societies such as Nigeria, there is an expectation that the professor is the expert who deserves significant deference. Academic titles are always used in public and private conversation and communication is mostly in one direction, from the professor to the student. In classroom settings, the students are expected to sit dutifully and respectfully at their desks as they take notes, which they will be expected to repeat back as close as possible to the original. In such societies, students only speak up when invited to do so by the teacher and teachers are *never* corrected, contradicted, or criticized in public.

The offense of public correction is in effect the public humiliation of a person deserving the utmost of respect for his privileged position. Such an act does more than cause the professor to "lose face;" it violates the shared cultural expectations regarding the distribution and use of power in the society.

In this situation, Charles had made an inexcusable mistake for which he was going to suffer. Charles's attempt to smooth things over immediately after the insulting incident was based on how he might have acted in the United States. In this case, it is entirely likely that Charles is not even aware of the offense. In such situations, it is advisable to consult with a cultural informant, someone who understands the culture and who can interpret the situation for the novice. Because Charles had already established some friendships at the school, his best tactic would be to seek the help and advice of a cultural informant who could explain the situation and provide some guidance as to how to resolve his predicament. In societies in which High Power Distance is common, it is often advisable to use a mutually respected intermediary to help resolve conflicts. In this case, if Charles barges into the administrative offices demanding "fair" treatment, his appeal will fall on deaf ears. The professor has and deserves all the power according to the norms in his country. His authority cannot be questioned. However, if Charles appeals for help from a respected intermediary, there is a good chance of ameliorating the situation.

Discussion of Korean Case Study

The application of Hofstede's research (1986) to Harold's predicament is multifaceted. The distinction between Individualism and Collectivism is again helpful. In highly Individualistic societies, students are expected to speak up in class in response to a general invitation to do so. There is a great emphasis on learning how to learn, teachers are supposed to be fair and impartial, and the need to prevent someone from losing face is weak. In this situation, Harold was approaching his students as if they were Americans. He called out for answers in a situation that might cause someone to lose face if they had a "wrong" answer. More important, Harold expected the trainees to respond as individuals rather than asking them to come up with a group response.

Hofstede's Dimension of Power Distance also helps to explain part of Harold's problem. In High Power Distance societies such as Korea, there is a strong belief in the authority and wisdom of the instructor. The focus of all teaching is from teacher to student. The teacher is there to teach and the students are there to learn. The notion that the students could somehow come up with the objectives of the program is absurd in this context. The instructor must know the objectives and be prepared to dictate these to the students. More important, the very content of the course "The Qualities of a Master Instructor" is something that the American had come thousands of miles to tell the Korean students. In the eyes of the Korean students, this instructor, who asks them to tell him what the qualities are, must be some sort of a fool. He has certainly lost credibility. When Harold finally gets around to providing the students with his "wisdom" by writing the qualities on the board, he becomes even less credible, because many of the qualities of a good instructor that he lists are clearly negative qualities in the Korean context and many of the bad qualities he lists are in fact good qualities in the Korean context.

In addition to the cultural contradictions discussed above, Harold began the class by making two additional mistakes. First, he began the class by telling everyone to call him by his first name. Although this may be the norm in the United States, where an egalitarian situation is preferred, in Korea, Harold should have started with formal titles until he developed a closer relationship with his students.

In addition, Harold followed up his introduction with a joke about the company. Again, although this may work in Chicago, where the clever ridiculing of everyone and everything may earn one some respect, it has the opposite impact in Korea. By beginning the class with a joke about the company, Harold was developing a sense of mistrust among his students. How could someone who is so disloyal to the employer in front of the class be a good teacher?

A final problem for Harold regarding Power Distance was Harold's insensitivity to the distribution of power that existed among his students. In many cases similar to Harold's, there is a senior member of the group to whom the group defers and shows respect. To Harold, all the students were equal. Achievement is based on performance and merit. In the case here, there was a senior person to whom Harold should have shown special attention and respect. However, Harold was not aware of this. Had Harold shown special attention to the senior person, Harold would have earned respect. When Harold asked the group for a response, he was slighting the senior member of the group who would otherwise perform the role of a spokesperson for the group, especially in the early stages of the relationship. By ignoring the importance of the role of power within the group, Harold had fallen through yet another hidden cross-cultural trap door.

One mistake instructors who work with international students often make is to gravitate to those students who have the best command of English. Although it may seem perfectly normal to want to communicate with those who appear to have the best ability to do so, such actions will often ignore the hidden power relationship that permeates the situation. In most cases, it is advisable to seek out the senior person, brief him or her before the program, show them proper respect, and *never* put them in a situation that might cause them to lose face in front of their group. Be sensitive to the fact that the second-language proficiency of the senior person may not be as good as others in the group.

Uncertainty Avoidance is a third Dimension of Hofstede's research that comes into play here. Compared to the United States, South Korea ranks very high in Uncertainty Avoidance. In the learning environment, the level of Uncertainty Avoidance can clearly shape the nature of student-teacher interactions.

In Low Uncertainty Avoidance environments, students feel comfortable in unstructured learning situations and teachers reward students for their innovative contributions to the class. In Korea, Harold's attempt to engage his students by asking them to supply the objectives for the course created a serious violation of the role he was expected to play. He was supposed to provide a structured course with clear and precise objectives. *He* was supposed to supply the answers, not them! Harold had created a situation full of uncertainty and ambiguity. This was not a comfortable learning environment for the students.

All organizations that attempt to take intact educational systems or prepackaged courses overseas are bound to be undermined by cultural differences. In many cases, the instructors may not even know that they have failed; in other cases, the failure will be all too obvious. In either event, there is no excuse for organizations to be so blatantly ethnocentric as to expect that what works at home will fit neatly into another corner of the world. All course materials and teaching methods are culture bound. It takes very little effort to review course content and instruction style to make courses more culturally sensitive and therefore effective. All instructors who are going to teach overseas would significantly benefit from cross-cultural training prior to going abroad. As the cases above illustrate, the cost of ignorance and insensitivity can be disastrous.

Role Plays

An interesting way to use Hofstede's research is to have students/trainees design a role play based on the findings. For example, you could ask one of your participants to prepare a presentation on a topic and employ a style characteristic of Low Power Distance and High Individualism (similar to the United States). You could then have a group of participants play the role of students in a culture that is High Power Distance and High Collectivism. Similarly, you could make assignments based on any set of combinations of the Dimensions, for example, teacher who is Low Power Distance, Highly Individualistic, Low Uncertainty Avoidance, and Masculine.

Additional Activities

There are many ways to promote cross-cultural understanding in the classroom. One approach is to use a textbook published in another country. This allows students to learn the subject matter and gain an appreciation of what is important from the perspective of that country. You as the instructor can point out any differences from the standard text you use.

Another idea is to invite an international student or a visiting international scholar to your class to make a presentation on a cross-cultural topic such as differences in education, dating, family relations, and the like. It is important that you select someone who is comfortable with making such a presentation and not make someone feel obligated to do so. In the event that you have no resource people on your campus, the Council for International Exchange of Scholars (CIES), which sponsors the Senior Fulbright Program, prepares a directory of all Fulbright scholars arranged by discipline. CIES will assist in making short-term visits or lectures possible. The address for CIES is 11 Dupont Circle, Suite 300, Washington, DC 20036.

Another resource on campus is the students who have returned from studying overseas. Many of these students are very willing to share their experiences. In addition, there may be teachers or others in the community who have taught abroad.

For faculty who are conducting training programs for other faculty, you may wish to have the faculty create their own critical incidents based on their own experiences. They might then try to apply Hofstede's concepts to explain the incident.

References

Brislin, R. (1991). *The art of getting things done: A practical guide to the use of power*. New York: Praeger.

Brislin, R. (1993). *Understanding culture's influence on behavior*. Fort Worth, TX: Harcourt, Brace, Jovanovich.

Chinese Culture Connection. (1987). Chinese values and the search for culture-free dimensions of culture. *Journal of Cross-Cultural Psychology, 18*, 143-164.

Hofstede, G. (1980). *Culture's consequences: International differences in work-related values*. Beverly Hills, CA: Sage.

Hofstede, G. (1986). Cultural differences in teaching and learning. *International Journal of Intercultural Relations, 10*, 301-320.

Hofstede, G. (1991). *Cultures and organizations: Software of the mind*. London: McGraw-Hill.

Hofstede, G., & Bond, M. H. (1988). Confucius and economic growth: New trends in culture's consequences. *Organizational Dynamics, 16*(4), 4-21.

9 International Students and International Student Advisers

PAUL PEDERSEN

Every admission and/or assignment of a student to a course of higher education in a foreign country, and thus to an extended sojourn and exposure abroad, represents a major assumption of responsibility, a considerable investment in funds, and a significant opportunity to contribute both to the individual concerned and to articulated or implied broader common goals, national and international.

Seth Spaulding
and Michael Flack (1976)

Often our knowledge regarding international students is at best fragmented and incomplete. Through this module readers will gain a more complete perspective of the actual demographics of international students in the United States as well as the problems and challenges they face. Through the use of resource people and role plays, participants in this module will gain a stronger feeling of empathy toward the often overlooked plight of the international student.

Contents

I. Self-Assessment Exercise

II. Case Studies: Critical Incidents

III. Skill Concepts

IV. Skill Applications

V. Field Exercises

Self-Assessment Exercise

Read the following list of questions regarding international students and international student advising. Grade yourself according to how well you think you could answer the question, given the opportunity. An A grade assumes you would be able to write a truly excellent, accurate, and comprehensive answer. An F grade indicates that you would not know where to start and have no idea how to answer the question. A B indicates that you would be able to write a good answer. A C means you would be able to write an adequate answer. A D means you would write an inadequate answer. Please write your grade after each question.

Questions

1. How many international students are there in the United States and what are the four largest contributing countries?
2. What are the four academic fields most frequently chosen by international students in the United States?
3. What are the four colleges or universities in the United States with the largest numbers of international students?
4. Approximately what percentage of international students in the United States are female?
5. Why do international students come to the United States to study, according to the research data available?
6. Why is the term *international student* becoming more popular than the term *foreign student*?
7. What are some of the psychological theories most frequently used to describe the dynamics of an international student's adjustment or accommodation?
8. What are the five stages of the *U Curve* in describing culture shock of international students and are these stages supported by research?
9. How might international students deal with stress differently than U.S. nationals?
10. Should international students be allowed to create co-national subcultures on campus? Why or why not?
11. Which characteristics of international students are most likely to change and which characteristics are least likely to change?
12. Do international students experience more problems than students in general?
13. What are five or six reasons that an international student might not seek counseling?
14. When international students seek counseling, whom are they most likely to contact for help on personal problems and why?
15. What are the personal problems that international students are most likely to encounter?
16. What are the characteristics most likely to determine an international student's ability to cope?
17. What style of counseling is most likely to succeed in working with international students and why?
18. What are some areas requiring research with regard to international students?

19. What countries outside the United States have the largest concentrations of international students?
20. What are the trends regarding international educational exchange?

Scoring

Score your own paper according to the grades you gave yourself on each item. Each A grade counts 3 points, B grade counts 2 points, C grade counts 1 point, D grade counts 0 points, and F grade counts –1 point. Divide your final score by 20 to get your grade point average.

You may have noticed that this is a very difficult set of questions and you should not be surprised if you are forced to give yourself a lower grade than you would like. The remaining sections of this unit should make it possible for you to raise your grade.

Case Studies: Critical Incidents

The objective of the following critical incident case examples (Brislin, Cushner, Cherrie, & Yong, 1986) is to encourage a group to identify and discuss the consequences of alternatives faced by international students. You will be presented with a series of situations that have actually happened to international students. You or a resource person should "take on the role" of the international student in each situation as though you or the resource person were experiencing the situation. A discussion guide will be provided for each critical incident to help you judge responses "in role." You may choose to role play the situation in front of a group with yourself in the role of the international student and others in the group seeking to "help you" to make the situation more realistic. If international students can be brought into the group as resource persons, your analysis and discussion is likely to be much more useful.

The international student resource person should be allowed to select an incident with which he or she is already familiar and comfortable. The more time the resource person has to consider the incident, the more realistic the student will be in projecting her- or himself into the role. The facilitator might ask the student to come to the front of the room while the facilitator briefly reads or summarizes the situation. Then the student is invited to speak for 1 or 2 minutes about how he or she feels in that dilemma. Then the audience is invited to ask questions, give advice, comment, or respond to the student in some helpful way. After about 8 or 10 minutes, the facilitator ends the discussion. The resource person then goes out of role and highlights those comments from the audience that seemed particularly helpful. Then the resource person is applauded and the next resource person is introduced.

The Faculty Adviser

You came to the international student counselor for help on academic problems. It soon became apparent that you are having a difficult time communicating with your academic faculty adviser. You described the adviser as always busy and as impatient with your questions when you did ask for clarification. As a result, you often agreed to decisions you did not really understand because you felt your adviser wanted you to answer that way. You are terrified of the academic adviser. The adviser is totally unaware of your feeling and since you seldom sought him out for help, he assumed you are doing fine. You are your academic adviser's only international student advisee. Usually international students are advised by two other faculty members in the department who are already overloaded with advisees. You want to change advisers to one of these other two faculty members who are too busy to accept new advisees.

Background

There is probably no relationship as important to the academic success of an international student as the relationship with his or her academic adviser. The adviser helps any student make the necessary decisions and adjustments, but this resource is particularly important for an international student who lacks the support system available to other students who have grown up in this country. Advisers often perceive international students as more time-consuming than U.S. nationals because international students are perceived to have greater difficulty in making adjustments. There are no extrinsic rewards in most university systems for faculty advisers who spend a lot of time and take their responsibility for working with international students seriously. Some faculty seem to enjoy working with international students, however, and tend to accumulate more foreign students among their advisees than others. When a student has an unsatisfactory relationship with his or her faculty adviser, there is a formal procedure for changing advisers, but frequently the international student is unfamiliar with the procedure and embarrassed to make the change. Asking the student to change advisers can also be perceived as dangerous, in view of the academic adviser's fairly arbitrary authority and informal influence over other faculty members in the department.

The Actual Decision

The student was not forced to reject her academic adviser but was assigned one of the other faculty as a co-adviser along with her previous academic adviser. The previous academic adviser was able to learn more about the special problems in advising international students from his colleague who was more familiar with international students. The new co-advising faculty member was able to accept a share of the advising responsibility with a minimum of additional effort. The problem was solved without creating stereotyped "international student experts" among the faculty while at the same time training other faculty in the department for working with international students. Because all persons were spared an embarrassing confrontation, the student felt more confident that none of the faculty would be angry at her and prejudice her academic future.

Discussion Questions

1. Should some faculty specialize in advising international students?
2. Does advising international students require more effort than advising U.S. nationals?
3. When a student asks his or her adviser permission to change to another adviser, does the old adviser take this as a personal insult?
4. What are some of the special problems that come up in advising international students?
5. Why does the academic system not provide rewards for good advising as it does for good teaching and research?

Working Without Permission

You were caught working illegally by the Immigration and Naturalization Service (INS) and called to a deportation hearing. You claimed that you applied for work permission during the academic year but did not hear from the INS for 2 months. When summer came, you thought that international students were allowed to work without permission since they do not need to be in school. However, the INS claimed that you knew accepting the job was illegal, or you would not have applied for permission to work. Since you had never received a denial letter you felt INS was being unfair. The procedure was lengthy and humiliating for you. You felt whatever offense might have been committed did not justify the expense of time and effort by either the INS or yourself. The job you took was in a nursing home for a small amount of pay after they had tried desperately but unsuccessfully to find someone else to work there. Finally, the INS relented and let you stay, but they gave you a scolding about the problems this country is facing with unemployment and made it plain that international students should never displace U.S. nationals. You listened to the lecture but felt bitter about it.

Background

The INS has tended to interpret regulations more strictly in recent years, particularly relating to an international student's financial support. The international student is subject to INS regulations, which are interpreted administratively without the due protection afforded under the law. From the student's point of view, INS seems to be arbitrary in interpreting these regulations according to their feelings about particular students from particular countries. International students are easily intimidated by the INS, and even routine inquiries are often perceived as harassment. The INS officers are not trained in cross-cultural communication beyond what they learn on the job. Consequently, their way of dealing with international students is not always sensitive to cultural variables. The regulations for international students staying temporarily in this country are both necessary and complicated. For exactly those reasons, it is especially important that INS staff have the benefit of some cross-cultural training. Many of their encounters with international students leave the student feeling as if he or she is suspected of committing a crime. Some of the students come from countries in which the "routine investigations" by government officials are perceived as police surveillance. There is probably no single aspect of an international student's U.S. experience as typically anxiety provoking as staying in status with the INS. This puts a great burden of responsibility on the international student adviser both to know the regulations and develop trusting relationships with INS agents and to help train INS staff where that opportunity is available.

The Actual Decision

Not all INS agents are insensitive. Most international student advisers have cultivated a relationship with at least one or two INS agents who are sensitive to international students' special circumstances and who take extra time to help international students through the system. In this case, the student was reassigned to a different and more sympathetic INS agent who helped the student understand the procedures for keeping the job and staying in status.

Discussion Questions

1. What are some reasons an international student might fear the INS?
2. Who would the INS describe as a "good" international student?
3. Under what conditions should international students be allowed to work while they are in the United States?
4. How will the student describe the INS to other international students?
5. How could trust between the INS and international students be encouraged?

Fail Grading

You asked the international student adviser to "talk to" your instructor to see if there was any way your grade in a particular course could be raised to a C. You believed you knew the material even though you did badly on the exam. You are already on probation, so a failing grade would cause the university to drop you. As a consequence, the INS would require you to return home or transfer to another program of study. Because it is in the middle of the year, no other university or program would be likely to accept transfers, especially from a failing student. After seeing both the faculty member and you, the adviser arranged a meeting for the three of you in the faculty member's office to identify alternatives. From your point of view the issue should be whether or not you knew the material rather than how well adjusted you are to the U.S. environment. The adviser seemed intimidated by the system and unable to advocate your case as you would have liked.

Background

International students are at a disadvantage when competing with U.S. students for higher grades. U.S. students are accustomed to the grading system, familiar with the test format and questions, more fluent in English, not confronting the multitude of cultural adjustments, and not subject to INS requirements that complicate an international student's life. Although these factors are not directly related to the student's academic performance, they certainly have an effect. Some well-meaning faculty who are aware of this inequity attempt to compensate for it by giving the international student higher grades than their work would ordinarily merit. Other international students sometimes use this argument in trying to get their grades changed. Other faculty feel they have no choice but to hold all their students accountable for the same level of academic achievement. The international student adviser is often asked to intervene on behalf of an international student when extenuating circumstances may have contributed to the student's failure. Not only the student but the university has a considerable investment to protect in helping the student succeed.

The Actual Decision

Ideally, the student should have been helped before he was put on probation, but frequently the student will avoid counseling except as a last resort. After some discussion, the faculty member agreed to let the student withdraw from the course retroactively, providing that the student would take more courses in English as a Second Language before continuing in the graduate program. The international student adviser met with the student to arrange a contract indicating in detail what the student had to do to stay in school, including regular meetings with the academic adviser. Being able to influence a policy decision also gave the international student adviser more confidence in his ability to work with the system.

Discussion Questions

1. Did this international student get more help than a U.S. student might have received under similar circumstances?
2. Should international students receive "special treatment" in helping them adjust to university requirements?
3. What were the other alternatives that could have resulted from this incident and what were their consequences?
4. Why do you suppose the student didn't seek out help earlier than he did?
5. Will the academic adviser get a reputation of being "soft" on international students for what he did?

The International Student Office

You are a U.S. student who wrote a letter to the campus newspaper suggesting that the International Student Office be eliminated. You wrote: "If we have to save money and cut budgets in the university, the least painful way is to abolish the position of the International Student Adviser and the supporting budget. For one thing, we cannot really maintain a separate office for a relatively small group of students. The time has come that we must treat all students alike and not have services for any 'special' group. Secondly, we really will not hurt anybody by this decision, because international students are just students like any other students and thus can enjoy the same services as are available to any other student. This action might actually work better for international students because having a special international student adviser probably isolates international students from other students. International students will be more integrated with other students on campus. The great majority of international students on our large campus reportedly don't visit the ISO office anyway unless they have to. It is only a small minority of international students that have difficulties and they are often marginal students who possibly should not have been brought here to begin with. We must make sure that these students make a realistic decision about leaving here if they can't make it on their own. The International Student Adviser's office often protects these students, asking for more and more exceptions when in fact these extensions only delay a decision to terminate them eventually. The money we save by eliminating the ISO can be redirected to important programs related to the special problems of our own society."

Background

The International Student Office was organized on most university campuses because of specialized problems arising among international students requiring specialized knowledge. To some extent, each campus office is designed as its own "Office of Student Affairs" for international students, with financial aid, housing, counseling, and other services being available. Problems of special immigration forms, difficulties in cross-cultural adjustment, and special requirements international students need to meet prompted setting up this special office. The task of this office is loosely defined according to the needs of the international student population. Other special populations, such as ethnic minorities, have objected to the idea of an International Student Office as favoring one special group at the expense of other groups. If the office were eliminated, many of its services would be eliminated or shifted to other offices where staff would need to be retrained to perform them.

The Actual Decision

Eliminating the International Student Office was considered as a possibility for streamlining student services but the office was retained. The objectives of the office were clarified, redefined, and specified in such a way that its contribution to the educational mission of the university was both obvious and necessary. The office responsibilities were changed from being a "service station" to a formal unit of academic affairs, helping to internationalize the formal and non-formal university curriculum. Support groups were established for international students and U.S. nationals to work together in a structured setting. International students were invited to speak on the campus radio station about world events. International students were also assigned to speak at high schools throughout the community as resource persons. The role of the office was judged to be fundamental to the university mission.

Discussion Questions

1. Should there be a separate office on campus for international students?
2. Would our offices be able to assume the responsibilities of working with international students if the ISO office were eliminated?
3. What are the weaknesses in the assumptions made by the letter author to the university newspaper?
4. How would you respond to international students who read this letter and came in to talk about it?
5. What parts of the letter are true?

Financial Aid

You were refused financial aid and made an appointment with the Director of Financial Aid to learn why. You were told there was barely enough money to meet the needs of U.S. minorities such as blacks, Native Americans, and Hispanics, whose needs came first. You became angry because international students were being evaluated by a more strictly defined need criteria than other students. You came to the international student adviser and said the reason minorities were getting aid was their militancy and organizational pressure. You described this policy as part of an anti-foreign bias in admissions, awarding teaching or research assistantships, and at every other point where international students always came last. You threatened to organize international students to demonstrate against the university. You complained that international students are being treated unfairly and inequitably. You asked the international student adviser to decide which side he is on, the students' or the institution's.

Background

Financial aid is usually allocated according to need rather than as a reward of academic excellence. It is, however, difficult to measure need across different individuals applying for assistance and even more difficult to compare the need of a U.S. national with that of an international student from another country. International students are not eligible for federal aid and are excluded from other programs available to U.S. nationals. Consequently, there is more pressure on those funds that are available to international students as well as other students generally. Financial problems have increased because of rising tuition and a diminished opportunity to work on campus or off campus. As a result, there are fewer funds but increased need for financial aid among students generally and among international students in particular. International students do not have local family resources, are often hampered by currency regulations against getting money from home, cannot drop out and work for a term without endangering their legal status, and are often unaware of those financial resources available to them. It is important that the international student adviser be somehow independent, even from the university he or she represents, to best serve the university. At the same time, the adviser must be *more* than an advocate of international student interests.

The Actual Decision

The international student adviser offered to help the student document the student's arguments with as many specific incidents of inequity as possible. They prepared a detailed plan on how specific policies could be made more equitable and requested that the report be placed on the agenda for the next Board of Regents meeting. The adviser suggested to the student that a public demonstration should only be a last resort after all normal channels for grievance had failed to produce results.

Discussion Questions

1. Is financial assistance distributed equitably to international students in comparison with other student populations?
2. Should the international student adviser take the side of the university or that of the international student?
3. Is the office of the international student adviser fairly described as a buffer between students and the institution?
4. Would a demonstration be more effective than a report to the regents in changing policy?
5. Were the students being unreasonable in their demands for a review of the financial aid policy?

Understanding the Experiences of International Students

International students are expected to learn a new language, new rules for interpersonal behavior, and a new set of roles that all the other students on campus have spent their whole life learning. International students come from a wide diversity of national, ethnic, and cultural backgrounds, but they are expected to "adjust" to a relatively narrowly defined set of behaviors in order for them to succeed. Colleges and universities in the United States have become increasingly dependent on the tuition and teaching assistance of international students, particularly in the sciences. However, international students also create problems relating to language, culture, political loyalties, and financial need, with Barber and Morgan (1988) suggesting that when the proportion of international students is half or more the disadvantages outweigh advantages. This is especially true in universities where the positive educational internationalizing advantages of their presence are neglected.

There are many facts about international students that are not generally known. According to the Institute of International Education (Zikopoulos, 1991), there were 386,851 international students enrolled in U.S. colleges and universities for 1989-1990, representing a 5.3% increase over the previous year. These male (65.8%) and female (34.2%) students come mostly from China (33,390), Taiwan (30,960), Japan (29,840), India (26,240), or The Republic of Korea (21,710). The most popular fields of study are business/management (75,570), engineering (73,420), math/computer science (36,210), physical/life science (32,910), and social sciences (28,580). The universities with the largest populations of international students include Miami-Dade Community College (5,518), U.S.C. (3,705), University of Texas/Austin (3,568), University of Wisconsin-Madison (3,295), and Boston University (3,248). The IIE suggests that as of October 1991, each student should expect to pay $832 per month in the Northeast and slightly less in other regions of the country. This cost does not include books, tuition (nearly two-thirds pay "out of state" tuition at public universities), and direct university costs. It should be no surprise, therefore, that international students spent $3.3 billion more in the United States in 1986 than U.S. students spent abroad. In 1990, the U.S. education trade *surplus* hit $4.3 billion and is running at about $4.7 billion in 1991. Next to military equipment and agricultural goods, education is the most important generator of foreign exchange. Next to the United States, other countries with large populations of international students include France (124,000), West Germany (82,000), England (57,000), and Japan (31,000), although Japan's average yearly rate of increase has been 21.5% from 1984 to 1989 (Hirai, 1990).

Reasons for Encouraging International Exchange

The motive for international educational exchange with the United States has evolved from the 1950s and 1960s emphasizing a humanitarian motive, to the 1970s and 1980s emphasizing competition with Communism, to the 1980s and 1990s indicating the need for Americans to understand other cultures. A new rationale gaining importance argues from the economic advantage of international students to the U.S. university (Chandler, 1989). The danger of emphasizing economic advantages of international students is to de-emphasize the infrastructure and staff required to work with those students.

Reichard (1990) cites a recent survey of 6,200 (or about 50%) of the members of the National Association for Foreign Student Affairs (NAFSA) that indicated that 70% have degrees beyond the BA, 22% have earned doctorates, 44% are planning to undertake further academic study, 41% have studied outside the United States, 40% have spent at least 2 years outside the United States, 34% have worked for the U.S. government abroad, 31% have taught in foreign universities, 10% have been Fulbright scholars, and 7% have served in the Peace

Corps. Their academic background ranges from education (27%), social sciences (21%), to the humanities or the arts (18%). Foreign student advisers come from a wide range of backgrounds and are not a homogeneous group.

There are many reasons for sending students to a foreign country for their education. Eide (1970) suggested that contact with international students will (1) improve international relations, (2) increase our tolerance of other cultures, (3) lead toward a more homogeneous world through a refined synthesis, (4) teach interdependence on an international scale, and (5) clarify our knowledge of ourselves.

Bochner (1972) analyzes the arguments against exchange. Critics of sending students abroad suggest that they will (1) refuse to return home after graduation, resulting in a "brain drain," (2) learn skills that are inappropriate back home, (3) learn skills too advanced for back home, (4) be selected because of family or political influence irrespective of their ability, (5) return home angry because of real or imagined injustices in the host country, and (6) return home to further widen the gap between rich and poor, inviting political instability.

Student Adjustment

There are many theories grounded in cross-cultural research generally, but a lack of grounded theory about international students has seriously inhibited research on that population. The research has usually emphasized adjustment problems or successful outcomes without looking at the developmental process experienced by international students. There has also been a minimal effort to relate other cross-cultural theories to the dynamics of sojourner adjustment (Church, 1982). Traditional student development theories—such as Perry, Chickering, and Minority Ethnic Identity models—have not been successful in explaining international students' behavior (Pedersen, 1991). Most studies have been situation specific, with nonrandom populations of convenience, and unrelated to other research on international students, relating to almost no comprehensive theory building through research (Klineberg, 1982). Some research has focused on "person" variables. Berry (1984) advocates a cognitive approach to international students focused on psychological adaptation to "acculturative stress." The international student must choose from these options: assimilation, which means giving up the student's cultural identity; integration, which means fitting into the larger social framework; rejection, requiring withdrawal from the larger society; or deculturation, resulting in alienation and a loss of identity. The acculturation process is described by Adler (1985) as developing through five stages of a U-curve: from (1) the "honeymoon stage," when the student feels like a tourist; to (2) depression, when the student is overwhelmed by personal inadequacy in the new culture; to (3) hostility, when the student blames the host culture; to (4) autonomy, when the student sees both good and bad aspects in the host culture; and finally to (5) biculturalism, when the student is as comfortable in the host culture as back home. Research has not clearly supported the U-curve hypothesis because (1) it oversimplifies the many dependent variables, (2) adjustment seldom follows a neatly defined U-shape, with students starting out at different points and adjusting at different rates, (3) students seldom achieve real biculturalism, and (4) adjustment outcome criteria are vague.

Research has failed to show a clear relationship between personality variables and successful adjustment. Kealey and Ruben (1983) reviewed research on Peace Corps staff, overseas businesspersons, technical assistance personnel, and military and religious workers and were unable to predict who would be successful. However, characteristics of empathy, interest in local cultures, flexibility, tolerance, and technical skill were all found to be important among those persons judged to be successful. Studies of physiological aspects as a person variable in acculturative stress have demonstrated a tendency of international students to somatize stress through headaches, stomach problems, and other non-organic symptoms (Thomas & Althen, 1989).

Beyond the Personalities of Students

Other research has focused on "situation" variables. Training and social support have proven more important than selection in facilitation of adaptation abroad (Furnham & Bochner, 1986). Behavioral approaches involving modeling, reinforcement management, self-reinforcement, and desensitization have also proven their value (Tanaka-Matsumi & Higginbotham, 1989). The literature on social role theory is very promising in researching intercultural adaptation given its focus on constructivism and interactional contact in a contextualist notion of development (Steenbarger, 1991). The greater the cultural difference between the international student and the host culture, the greater likelihood for misunderstanding. Perhaps, for that reason, international students frequently isolate themselves in co-countryperson groups. Many foreign student advisers advocate interaction between international students and American students as an important part of the educational exchange experience. However, relationships with co-nationals is highly correlated with other measures of success (Alexander, Klein, Workneh, & Miller, 1981; Pedersen, 1975; Torrey, Van Rheenan, & Katchadourian, 1970).

Spaulding and Flack (1976) provided the last comprehensive review of research about the situational effect on international students. Their conclusions still apply: that (1) students' basic cultural or religious attitudes, career goals, and attitudes toward their home country change very little, whereas (2) attitudes about open-mindedness, gender relations, knowledge, and freedom change a great deal following study abroad. Although international students reported depression as the third most frequent problem they faced in the United States (Klineberg & Hull, 1979), there has been too much emphasis on pathology in studying international students. Because international students seldom seek out professional counseling, it is difficult to measure the seriousness of their problems. We can be reasonably sure that international students experience more problems than students in general and have fewer resources to help them solve those problems. Taft (1977) relates the magnitude of an international student's coping task with (1) the size of the cultural gap, (2) the abruptness of discontinuity, (3) the salience of necessary changes, and (4) the goodness of fit between the host culture and the back home culture.

Other research has examined the importance of counseling to international students. International students are more likely to seek counseling on educational, vocational, or medical problems than other "personal" problems. They are more likely to drop out after their initial contact. They are more likely to seek help from a close friend or co-national than from a professional counselor. They prefer direct to indirect counseling methods. They may prefer receiving counseling in informal settings rather than formal settings (Pedersen, 1991). We are still not sure how to define "success" in counseling international students, without inadvertently imposing our own cultural values.

In addition to research, much emphasis has been given to training in the literature about international students. Mestenhauser (1983) has written extensively on how to learn from sojourners on the university campus. Brislin and Pedersen (1976) describe the Intercultural Communication Workshop (ICW) as a popular and well-established training model. Miller (1989) and Westwood, Lawrence, and Paul (1986) discuss the importance of peer counselor training in working with international students. Pedersen (1990) documents the importance of training to prepare international students for their back-home reentry experiences after completing their study abroad.

Although international students are likely to be assessed by the same tests as other students generally, the accuracy of these test measurements is being widely challenged (Thomas, 1985; Tompkins & Mehring, 1989). The Graduate Record Exam (GRE), for example, has been found to be inappropriate for international students (Wilson, 1986). Data from clinical and psychological measures have also proven difficult to interpret (Worchel & Goethals, 1989). Descriptive checklists such as the Michigan International Student Problem Inventory (Crano & Crano, 1990) have proven the most useful measures and the easiest to interpret.

University Policy

Most universities take their international students for granted. The National Association for Foreign Student Affairs (NAFSA) has therefore provided guidelines to help institutions evaluate their international student programs (Althen, 1983). The adequate program should (1) have a clearly stated institutional policy, (2) relate to the academic programs and academic staff, (3) relate to the basic purpose and strength of the institution, (4) demonstrate sensitivity to the students' cultural needs, (5) provide special services by trained personnel, (6) demonstrate respect and sensitivity for cultural differences, and (7) be periodically evaluated. Much future research is needed to strengthen and articulate the importance of international students for the basic mission of the U.S. university and educational system. Although cultural and language barriers are very important to international students, another, perhaps even greater, problem is being unable to make friends with Americans. This is especially difficult for students whose lack of English language fluency requires them to take courses different than those in which other Americans are enrolled. Because many international students come to America expecting to make American friends, they are often disappointed in the number and the quality of their friendships. A typical comment might be: "Americans are very friendly . . . but they are not friends." American students, however, frequently describe international students as staying in their nationality groups, speaking their native language in public, and otherwise isolating themselves from other Americans. There is some misattribution in both of these stereotyped perspectives. More activities should be created to foster interaction between international students and Americans both on and off campus.

Skill Applications

The five case studies presented and discussed in Part II of this module provide valuable exercises for use in a variety of ways: (1) Role playing the incident with students and discussing the issues *in role* is likely to be insightful. (2) Asking students to "spot the concept" in each critical incident will sharpen their ability to identify significant issues in context. (3) Identifying reasonable alternative responses to each situation and the consequences of each alternative would provide a measure of expertise for developing an "intercultural sensitizer" (Leong & Kim, 1991). (4) Inviting international students to join the group as resource persons will certainly increase the usefulness of these situations. Eleven additional situations are presented and discussed in Pedersen (1991) as a supplement to these five situations. Mestenhauser (1983) suggests many ways in which international students provide valuable educational resources in the classroom. It would be very useful for a group studying international students to include international students in the membership.

To warm up a group and to demonstrate to them their need to learn more about international topics it is useful to use the "World Picture Test." This process involves giving each participant a large sheet of paper, a table or area on which to draw, and a pencil with an eraser. The participants are given 5 minutes in which to draw a map of the world on the paper. If more than 5 minutes is allowed, participants are likely to be too embarrassed by the inadequacy of their drawing, and usually 5 minutes is enough to gather the data for discussion. Participants then are matched with partners in dyads with their drawings and asked to discuss the following questions: (1) Does a person's awareness of the shape of a country reveal that person's awareness of that country's culture? (2) When a country is left out what does it mean? (3) When a continent is left out what does it mean? (4) What country is in the center of the person's map and what does that mean? (5) When a country is drawn out of place or scale in relation to other countries what does that mean? (6) Were students better acquainted with countries they had visited? (7) Was either partner surprised by the results of this exercise?

When the group has completed this exercise a longer exercise may be introduced involving the design of a simulation called "Multipoly." The objective of this simulation is to identify significant aspects of an international student's experience in terms of (1) the events all students encounter, (2) the alternatives available to different groups encountering each event, and (3) the different consequences for different groups that follow from each alternative. The gameboard on which this simulation will be designed resembles the gameboard for Monopoly, although the rules are entirely different.

1. Divide the larger group into small groups of six persons each, attempting to include as many international students as U.S. nationals in each group.
2. Within each group of six, each student will be asked to select a role of U.S. student, U.S. faculty, U.S. staff, or international student, international faculty, and/ or international staff member. Students need to identify a particular faculty or staff position with which they are already familiar. Those choosing international student roles need to select countries with which they are already familiar. Each participant selecting a student role needs to decide whether the person in role is "wealthy" or "poor," thus determining the socioeconomic level of the student.
3. Students will fill in the 20 to 40 blanks around the perimeter of the gameboard indicating the 20 to 40 different events likely to occur on a college campus. It may be useful for the facilitator to identify these events ahead of time to speed the process.
4. Students will identify the three most likely alternatives available to persons encountering each event. These alternatives need to be selected so that each alternative will be available to all players in their role.
5. Students will then discuss and identify the likely consequences of each alternative for each student *in role*, being as realistic and authentic as possible. The net result will be a gameboard with 20 to 40 events identified around the perimeter, with three alternative responses to each event, and positive or negative consequences identified for each alternative. Essentially you now have one game with six sets of rules.
6. While designing the simulation it will be important to discuss the ultimate goal of playing the game in terms of money, influence, popularity, power, or some other reward. Tokens or a score can be derived by awarding or taking away points according to the positive or negative consequences attached to each alternative for each event.
7. It will also be important to discuss whether all players begin the simulation with the same amount of resources. Presumably, the more wealthy students would begin with more resources than the less wealthy students.

8. The group may want to design "Chance" or "Community Chest" type cards to further complicate the simulation.

9. The group may want to include a skill-variable in the play. For example, if a player can name all three (or more) alternatives available for each event and/or the positive/negative consequences of each alternative, then the student earns a higher score than someone unable to identify the alternatives and/or consequences.

10. The game should be designed in such a way that players will increase their understanding of the events encountered on campus, the realistic alternatives available in response to each event, and the positive or negative consequences of each alternative for each of the six roles of the players.

The emphasis in this orientation exercise is on the *design* of a simulation for teaching about the role of international students. However, the different teams may want to exchange their final products and attempt to play one another's simulation according to the other group's rules. The facilitator should help the groups to be realistic in their identification of consequences and to keep the rules simple enough to be easily understood by someone outside the group.

Field Exercises

The last section of this module suggests field experiences by which members of the group might increase their learning about international students by going outside the classroom. Just about any opportunity to spend time with international students in either formal or informal activities is likely to result in learning and should be encouraged. The facilitator should make sure that the intergroup contact occurs under "favorable" conditions, where everyone enjoys the contact and looks forward to more contact in the future, where the issues bringing them together are important and not frivolous, where neither side loses status by coming together, and where persons coming together are of approximately equal status (Amir, 1969). Some of those structures may include the following:

1. Visiting faculty from other countries can be invited to the campus to give courses, guest lectures, or provide a resource on campus to internationalize the courses in that person's area.

2. U.S. faculty could be funded to visit the home countries of their international students to learn more about that country's problems in the faculty members' area of study.

3. An ongoing comprehensive assessment or research project could be designed and distributed among international students to evaluate their educational experience. A similar project may survey U.S. students to evaluate their opinions about the importance of having international students on campus.

4. The university "policy statement" indicating the role of international students on campus (direct or implied) can be brought to the group for discussion and evaluation in terms of underlying assumptions, strengths, and weaknesses. The group may choose to draft a policy statement for submission to the university if no such statement exists.

5. Recruiting teams can be assembled by appropriate fields and programs to target promising countries and regions of the world for bringing additional students to the university.

6. Alumni from other countries could be surveyed for suggestions and assistance in recruiting international students.

7. The procedure by which an international student gets admitted once the university and field of study have been determined can be discussed. The group may suggest ways that this process can be streamlined.

8. The group may initiate contact with international secondary schools around the country to identify the ways in which a university and field of study are determined.

9. The group may want to build a special relationship with another university in another country for the exchange of ideas and information as well as the possible exchange of persons.

10. Programs in specific fields of study can be surveyed regarding their experiences with international students. Those with large numbers of international students can be interviewed regarding the positive and negative consequences of that situation. Those with smaller numbers of international students can be interviewed about the positive and negative consequences of their recruiting more international students.

References

Adler, P. (1985). The multicultural man. In L. Samovar & L. Porter (Eds.), *Intercultural communication* (2nd ed., pp. 410-426). Belmont, CA: Wadsworth.

Alexander, A., Klein, M., Workneh, F., & Miller, M. (1981). Psychotherapy and the foreign student. In P. Pedersen, J. Draguns, W. Lonner, & J. Trimble (Eds.), *Counseling across cultures* (2nd ed., pp. 227-243). Honolulu, HI: University of Hawaii Press.

Althen, G. (1983). *The handbook of foreign student advising*. Yarmouth, ME: Intercultural Press.

Amir, Y. (1969). Contact hypothesis in ethnic relations. *Psychological Bulletin, 71*, 319-342.

Barber, E. G., & Morgan, R. P. (1988). *Boon or bane: Foreign graduate students in U.S. engineering programs*. Research Rep. Series No. 15. New York: Institute of International Education.

Berry, J. W. (1984). Psychological adaptation of foreign students. In R. Samuda & A. Wolfgang (Eds.), *Intercultural counseling and assessment* (pp. 235-248). Toronto, Canada: Hogrefe.

Bochner, S. (1972). Problems in culture learning. In S. Bochner & P. Wicks (Eds.), *Overseas students in Australia*. Auburn: New South Wales University Press.

Brislin, R., & Pedersen, P. B. (1976). *Cross-cultural orientation programs*. New York: Gardner.

Brislin, R., Cushner, K., Cherrie, C., & Yong, M. (1986). *Intercultural interactions: A practical guide*. Newbury Park, CA: Sage.

Chandler, A. (1989). *Obligation or opportunity: Foreign student policy in six major receiving countries.* New York: Institute of International Education.

Church, A. T. (1982). Sojourner adjustment. *Psychological Bulletin, 91,* 540-572.

Crano, S., & Crano, W. (1990). *Development of a measure of international student adjustment.* Unpublished manuscript, Department of Psychology, Texas A&M University, College Station.

Eide, I. (Ed). (1970). *Students as links between cultures.* Oslo: Universiteit Forlaget.

Furnham, A., & Bochner, S. (1986). *Culture shock: Psychological reactions to unfamiliar environments.* London: Methuen.

Hirai, K. (1990). Motivation and purpose of symposium: Problems on foreign students in Japan. In K. Hirai (Ed.), *International symposium on internationalization and foreign student problems* (pp. 17-21). International Conference Center, Kobe, Japan, October 29-30. Unpublished final report.

Kealey, D., & Ruben, B. (1983). Cross-cultural personnel selection criteria, issues and methods. In D. Landis & R. Brislin (Eds.), *Handbook of international training* (vol. 1, pp. 155-175). New York: Pergamon.

Klineberg, O. (1982). Contact between ethnic groups: A historical perspective of some aspects of theory and research. In S. Bochner (Ed.), *Cultures in contact: Studies in cross-cultural interaction* (pp. 320-335). Oxford: Pergamon.

Klineberg, O., & Hull, W. (1979). *At a foreign university: An international study of adaptation and coping.* New York: Praeger.

Leong, F., & Kim, H. (1991). Going beyond cultural sensitivity on the road to multiculturalism: Using the Intercultural Sensitizer as a counselor training tool. *Journal of Counseling and Development, 70*(1), 112-119.

Mestenhauser, J. (1983). Learning from sojourners. In D. Landis & R. Brislin (Eds.), *Handbook of intercultural training* (vol. 2, pp. 153-185). New York: Pergamon.

Miller, K. (1989). Training peer counselors to work on a multi-cultural campus. *Journal of College Student Development, 30*(6), 561-562.

Pedersen, P. (1975). Personal problem solving resources used by University of Minnesota foreign students. In R. Brislin (Ed.), *Topics in cultural learning* (No. 3, pp. 55-65). Honolulu, HI: East West Center.

Pedersen, P. (1990). Social and psychological factors of brain drain and reentry among international students. *McGill Journal of Education, 25*(2), 229-243.

Pedersen, P. (1991). Counseling international students. *The Counseling Psychologist, 19*(1), 10-58.

Reichard, J. F. (1990). The policy and practice of accepting foreign students in the United States of America. In K. Hirai (Ed.), *International symposium on internationalization and foreign student problems* (pp. 48-54). International Conference Center, Kobe, Japan, October 29-30. Unpublished conference report.

Spaulding, S., & Flack, M. (1976). *The world's students in the United States: A review and evaluation of research on foreign students.* New York: Praeger.

Steenbarger, B. N. (1991). All the world is not a stage: Emerging contextualist themes in counseling and development. *Journal of Counseling and Development, 70*(2), 288-296.

Taft, R. (1977). Coping with unfamiliar cultures. In N. Warren (Ed.), *Studies in cross-cultural psychology* (pp. 120-135). London: Academic Press.

Tanaka-Matsumi, J., & Higginbotham, H. (1989). Behavioral approaches to counseling across cultures. In P. Pedersen, J. Draguns, W. Lonner, & J. Trimble (Eds.), *Counseling across cultures* (3rd ed., pp. 269-298). Honolulu, HI: University of Hawaii Press.

Thomas, K. A. (1985). *A comparison of counseling strategies reflective of cultural value orientations on perceptions of counselors in cross-national dyads.* Unpublished doctoral dissertation, University of Minnesota, Minneapolis.

Thomas, K., & Althen, G. (1989).Counseling foreign students. In P. Pedersen, J. Draguns, W. Lonner, & J. Trimble (Eds.), *Counseling across cultures* (3rd ed., pp. 205-242). Honolulu, HI: University of Hawaii Press.

Tompkins, L., & Mehring, T. (1989). Competency testing and the international student: A commonsense approach to detecting cultural bias in testing instruments. *Journal of Multicultural Counseling and Development, 17*(2), 72-78.

Torrey, E. F., Van Rheenan, R., & Katchadourian, H. (1970). Problems of foreign students: An overview. *Journal of the American College Health Association, 19,* 83-86.

Westwood, M., Lawrence, W., & Paul, D. (1986). Preparing for reentry: A program for the sojourning student. *International Journal for the Advancement of Counseling, 9,* 221-230.

Wilson, K. (1986). *The relationship of GRE General Test scores to first year grades for foreign students: Report of a cooperative study.* Research Rep. No. 82. Englewood Cliffs, NJ: Graduate Record Examination Board.

Worchel, S., & Goethals, G. (1989). *Adjustment: Pathways to personal growth* (2nd ed.). Englewood Cliffs, NJ: Prentice Hall.

Zikopoulos, M. (Ed.). (1991). *Open doors: 1990-1991 report on international education exchange.* New York: Institute of International Education.

Social and
Health Services

10 Intercultural Communication for Health Care Professionals

COLLEEN MULLAVEY-O'BYRNE

Beliefs regarding the cause of an illness are directly related to perceptions about the necessities for a cure. For example, if people believe that they are suffering from a retribution for a past deed, no amount of medication is likely to cure their illness. This module aims at increasing cultural sensitivity toward different illness beliefs and practices of people from different ethnic and cultural backgrounds. Specific frameworks and models of illness are discussed, commonly encountered problems are introduced, and exercises aimed at developing culturally sensitive skills are provided.

Contents

I. Introductory Exercise: Explanatory Models of Illness

II. Self-Assessment Exercise

III. Case Studies

IV. Skill Concepts

V. Skill Applications

VI. Field Exercises

Introductory Exercise: Explanatory Models of Illness

We all have ideas about what makes us sick. These include beliefs about the cause of an illness we experience, what kind of illness it is, the natural course we expect it to take, and how it should be treated. We also have particular ways of thinking about and describing the symptoms we have and our personal experience of being in a state of ill health.

The sources we draw on to inform us about our state of ill health and to explain it to others are popular, professional, and traditional. Families, peers, and other members of the local lay community are the usual sources of popular information about illness. This is especially so for seasonal illnesses, illnesses that are prevalent in a local community, and those that are relatively common, for example colds and fevers. Professional ideas and practices relating to ill health come from doctors trained in the biomedical model, physicians trained in often formal systems (e.g., Chinese medicine), nurses, and other profession-ally trained and qualified health care providers. The sources of traditional infor-mation are specialists in healing who are generally not recognized as qualified professionals. Included among these are herbalists, iridologists, reflexologists, and the charismatic or sacred healers (Parsons, 1990, pp. 131-132).

Kleinman (1980, pp. 104-118) used the term *explanatory models* (EMs) to describe the explanations for illness and disability given by health practition-ers and their clients/patients. He distinguished between lay explanatory models and the clinical models used by health practitioners. Parsons (1990, p. 131) indicated that it is often difficult to match the doctor's perception of a particu-lar illness and/or disability with the patient's understanding of their experi-ence of it. The disparity is likely to be even greater when the patient and the doctor (or other health professional) come from different cultural backgrounds.

Exercise: Beliefs About Illness

This exercise has three main goals:

1. To help you explore the different ideas and beliefs people have about illness and to recognize the different sources they draw on to inform them about this matter.
2. To encourage you to explore attitudes toward ideas and beliefs about illness that are significantly different from your own.
3. To generate material that can provide the basis for a field exercise to be presented later in the module.

Individual Tasks

1. Draw on your own experience to generate a list of explanations you and others you associate with on a regular basis use to explain specific instances of illness and disability. In your list include the perceived cause and a generally accepted

way of managing it. Try to use the words people actually use to talk about their illnesses, for example:

"I have the flu [nature or diagnosis]. I think it's a bug I caught because I'm run down [causes]. I need to go to the doctor to get an antibiotic, then I think I'll put myself on a course of vitamins to build myself up again [treatment/ management]."

2. Are you aware of explanations other people outside your immediate social group (for example, people from other cultural groups) use to describe illness and disability? Do they differ significantly from the explanations you have already provided? If there are significant differences make a second list of explanations. Again try as far as possible to use the actual words you have heard people use to describe illness and/or disability.
3. What are the main differences between the explanations in your two lists?

Small Group Tasks

4. Form a small group with other members of your training group to discuss the lists you have each made. Prepare a combined list in which you allocate the explanatory statements to categories that appear to have some common bases for the explanations given.

Large Group Tasks

5. Present the list generated by your small group to the larger group. Draw attention to difficult and/or unresolved issues in the discussion.
6. At this stage the trainer/group leader should assist the group to summarize the exercise. Summarizing focuses on reaching some level of agreement about which explanations appear to have some common features; which explanations participants feel most comfortable with; which they are least comfortable with; and the possible reasons for this being so.

On completing the exercise the trainer/group leader should remind participants to retain their individual and group lists. They will need to refer to them at a later stage in the training module.

Self-Assessment Exercise

This exercise is designed to help you focus on your experience of situations in which you find yourself providing your particular type of health care service to a client or clients from a cultural background that is different from your own.

Please read each statement carefully and answer in relation to your perception of the extent to which the statement is true for you. If the statement is true

for you sometimes, place a + in Column 1 opposite the particular statement; if
it is almost always true for you, place a + in Column 2; if never true, place a +
in Column 3; if it depends on the situation, place a + in Column 4.

This is not a test; there are no right or wrong answers!

When I am providing health care services to a client from a cultural background that is different from my own, I am able to identify when:				
	1	2	3	4
1. their concept of the inner structure of the body may be different from mine.				
2. their ideas about the way the body works may be different from mine.				
3. the intervention I use to improve their health/functional ability may not be consistent with what they believe will improve their condition.				
4. their ideas about their role as a sick or disabled person may be different from mine.				
5. problems that arise are not culturally based.				
6. problems that occur do have a cultural basis.				
7. misunderstanding is due to intercultural communication breakdown.				

Write down specific examples from your clinical work to support your
response to each statement. Discuss your responses and the examples you have
provided with other members of your training group. The trainer/group leader
should encourage participants to identify the attributes and skills that support
positive responses to each or all of the items.

Case Studies

Her First Job in Singapore

Background

Judy Evans recently graduated from an Australian university with a degree
in physiotherapy. She traveled to Singapore to take up her first appointment
as a physiotherapist at a large general hospital. Judy has always wanted to
travel and to work in different cultural settings. She has prepared for this particular position by reading books on Singaporean history and culture and recent
journal articles about health problems and health care services in Singapore.

She has some knowledge about the different cultural groups she will be treating, a commitment to gaining more knowledge and understanding of the people, and the intent to learn a local language.

In the account that follows, Judy describes a clinical incident that she believes had a cultural basis.

The Story of Judy Evans and Mrs. Mamoud

It was my first day at the hospital. The morning had gone well and I had been involved in all the things I had anticipated that I would do on my first day: meeting the staff, going on a tour of the outpatient clinic, seeing some of the treatments used frequently in the clinic, and getting a general idea of the organization of the physiotherapy part of the service. I was very impressed with what I saw. The staff were using up-to-date techniques and state-of-the-art technology. I had not expected to find quite the level of sophisticated technology I was seeing. The clinic appeared very like the large outpatient clinics where I had done some of my clinical placements back home.

The staff came from a variety of countries and cultural groups, which included Hong Kong, China, Malaysia, and India as well as Singapore, Australia, Canada, and England. The senior physiotherapist, a Singaporean Chinese who had completed her physiotherapy course in England, referred to her staff as "her international family of physiotherapists." Everyone was very eager to find out about me, my interests, my family, and why I had come to Singapore.

After lunch I was feeling reasonably comfortable in my new environment and eager to start treating my patients. I was very aware of the numbers of people who were arriving to have treatments and of the large caseloads carried by individual staff. I was determined not to increase their workload by asking for assistance. I had listened attentively to the senior physiotherapist when she had been orienting me to the clinic. As well as taking note of the routines in the clinic, I had also formed a good idea about the location of equipment and supplies.

When the senior physiotherapist informed me that another staff member would be assisting me with my afternoon caseload, I was quick to reply that this would not be necessary. I was sure I could manage. She did not respond directly to me, but smiled and wished me a successful afternoon. She added that she would be in a clinical meeting for 1 hour and would speak to me again after she returned to her office.

I was full of confidence and excitement when I collected the referral card for my first patient from the reception desk. As I walked into the main treatment area I read the referral to myself: "Mamoud, Alya. Female, 32 years, married two children. Diagnosis: Painful right knee, restricted movement following car accident. Treatment: assess, mobilize."

As I called her name I tried to guess who Mrs. Mamoud might be from among the large number of people in the room. I waited a few seconds before calling her name again. This time one of the physiotherapists who was collecting her patient for treatment said, "I think Mrs. Mamoud is one of the two women in black seated on the bench behind you. I suspect that she does not understand English. You will need to go up to her and indicate that you will be treating her."

I was still feeling confident as I turned to walk over to the two women. It was then that I saw that they were totally dressed in black, with only their eyes and hands visible. An article I had read, which reported that health professionals were often culturally insensitive to the needs of Muslim women, flashed before me and I panicked. I couldn't think what to do, which is very unusual for me. I am sure that Mrs. Mamoud and her companion saw the panic written all over my face and wondered what had happened. I kept saying to myself, "How am I going to communicate to Mrs. Mamoud that I need to examine her knee, in a way that is culturally sensitive, when she and I don't even speak the same language?"

Discussion Questions

1. What are the main issues raised in Judy's story? Which appear most likely to have a cultural basis? Why?
2. Would you say that Judy's behavior indicates that she was culturally sensitive? Do you believe the senior physiotherapist was culturally sensitive to Judy's needs? What instances from the story support your answers? Why do you see these as culturally sensitive or culturally insensitive behaviors?
3. Discuss the alternatives available to Judy when she realizes that language is a barrier to communicating with Mrs. Mamoud. Generate a list of options Judy might explore to help her carry out an initial assessment of Mrs. Mamoud's knee, options that are both culturally sensitive and clinically correct.
4. How do you think the other staff would respond if Judy asked them for assistance? Do you think they would see her as an additional burden to their workload? What conceptual basis do you have for your response?
5. What are Mrs. Mamoud's possible expectations for treatment? What might be her needs, when thinking about culturally sensitive approaches to treatment? In what ways might her needs differ from those of other clients? In what ways are they similar?

Home Therapy

Background

This case study was reported by Kate Lewis, an occupational therapist who provided home care therapy programs to patients after discharge from the hospital.

The Story of Joe Camilleri

Joe Camilleri is a 65-year-old man who had a cerebrovascular accident (CVA) and as a result has a left hemiplegia. Joe emigrated to America from Calabria in Southern Italy when he was 25. He established a small but successful delicatessen business with a cousin. After 5 years he returned to Calabria for a short visit and to marry Antonia, a woman from his village. They returned to America and worked to build an even bigger and more successful business. Joe has gone back to the old country every 2 years for a holiday, sometimes with Antonia, sometimes alone. They have five children, all of whom are married, and nine grandchildren. Their oldest son and his wife live with Joe and Antonia in a comfortable two-story apartment behind the delicatessen. They are directly involved in running the business with Joe and Antonia. The other children live close by with their families and are involved in related businesses, for example, importing, wholesale foods, shop fittings, and accounting. They are a very close-knit family in which Joe is clearly the patriarch.

Joe is a well-known identity in the local community and an active member of the local Italian Social Club. Prior to the CVA he enjoyed arguing about politics, playing cards, entertaining family and friends, and going to the opera. Joe has been overweight for some time and has high blood pressure. He takes tablets to control the blood pressure, has a diet plan to follow, and has a light exercise program.

After 1 week in the hospital to stabilize his condition, Joe was transferred to a rehabilitation center where he was very unhappy. He insisted that he must go home to his family, so he was discharged early on a home rehabilitation program. At discharge Joe had good return in his left arm and hand but was experiencing some residual problems associated with grasp and release. He was able to attend to his personal care needs but required some assistance with tasks requiring fine motor coordination. His ambulation was functional, he was able to make transfers with minimal supervision, and his cognitive and perceptual functions were intact. However, the family noticed a big difference in his mood. His son Paolo commented that his father was "a changed man since the stroke. It is as if he has given up on living."

Two days after Joe was discharged from the rehabilitation center, the home care occupational therapist visited him. The purpose of the visit was to assess what might be required to help him function independently at home and to start a home therapy program. Her duties also included checking that Joe was continuing to take his medication and adhering to his diet and exercise program.

When she arrived, Kate was greeted by a woman nursing a small baby, who introduced herself as Anna, Mr. Camilleri's daughter-in-law. Anna explained that her husband and mother-in-law were serving in the shop, but that she was available to assist and answer any questions. Anna led Kate through to the sitting room, where Joe Camilleri was lying in bed propped up on pillows. Before they entered the room, Anna told Kate that her father-in-law refused to get out of bed and insisted that since his life was over, he had best just lie there and wait to die.

"He refuses to get dressed and insists that Mama take him to the toilet and bathe him. Paolo has to shave him. I am worried about Mama; she has not been well and is working so hard. While the baby is small I try to give her a break from attending to him during the day. But he insists that she must take him to the toilet."

She explained that the bed was in the sitting room because Papa could not manage the stairs to go to the bedroom. She added, "Besides, Papa always likes to be in the center of things, so he knows what is going on and can tell us all what to do."

Anna introduced Kate to her father-in-law and Kate quickly explained the reason for her visit. Joe's answer was to shake his head and tell her that there was no point in her coming to see him. He was a sick old man, who was no good to anyone and must now be looked after by his wife and family until he died. Kate reminded him that only a few days ago when he was discharged he was able to dress himself and could walk quite well using a cane.

Joe replied loudly, "I would rather be dead than let people see me, Joe Camilleri, use a walking stick!" He added, "So, and what is the point of walking when any time I might be struck down again and die, eh? You think I should get up? I think it is better to stay in bed and wait to see if this arm gets better."

Kate asked Joe if any of his friends or customers had been to visit him since he had been home. Joe replied that he was ashamed to let any of his friends see what a weak apology for a man he now was. He would wait to see if he got better before seeing anyone. Meantime he would rest in bed. If he did not get better, then the family must all pray that God would be merciful and take him.

He continued to resist any attempts Kate made to persuade him to get up and dress. However, he showed some interest when she asked to test the strength and movement in his arm. He allowed her to test grip and release in his left hand but complained that it was very painful when she moved his arm and hand. He agreed to her visiting him again that week, to work on his arm to make it strong again.

When Kate reminded him that he would also have to do some work to make the arm stronger, Joe replied, "What do you mean ? I am a sick man. I will let you work on this arm to make it better. I must bear the pain while you exercise my arm. That is enough."

Discussion Questions

1. What are some of the cultural beliefs that underpin Joe's response to his illness and disability?
2. What effect might these beliefs have on the home therapy program? What issues will need to be resolved?
3. What issues will Kate need to approach with great sensitivity?
4. Given the cultural background of the family do you see any way of reducing the stress and demands on Antonia?
5. Joe complained about pain in his arm when Kate was testing for grasp and release. What advice do you have for Kate about how she might deal with this while she is treating him?

Some Issues in Health Care in Culturally Diverse Societies

During the latter part of the 20th century the populations of many nations have become increasingly culturally diverse. A number of factors have been linked to this phenomenon. Included among these are large-scale human migrations, rapid advances in the technologies associated with communication and transportation, expansions in the internationalization of business, and multinational government projects. A consequence of this phenomenon is greater contact among people whose ways of perceiving and thinking about the world differ significantly, people who have different values, beliefs, lifestyles, languages, customs, and practices. The contexts in which such contact occurs are many and varied and include travel, business, work, recreation, and the education, welfare, and health services.

Increased contact among people from different ethnic and cultural backgrounds brings intercultural differences into sharp focus and may also highlight intracultural differences within a single culture group. Brislin, Cushner, Cherrie, and Yong (1986, p. 13) suggested that differences in values and in perceptions of what constitutes socially appropriate behavior are typical problem areas for people moving across cultures.

In cross-cultural situations, in which people are confronted by values and guidelines for living, interacting, and establishing relationships with others that are very different from their own, contact can be a source of frustration, irritation, and even conflict. Negative experiences of this kind, if they remain unresolved, can lead to prejudice, stereotyping, and discriminatory behavior toward people who are perceived as culturally different.

Interactions between people from different cultures are further complicated when people are not able to communicate across cultures. This is especially so when they have little knowledge and understanding of each other's culture and have not developed the intercultural skill of respect for differences (Hodge, 1988, p. 21).

Issues that have their basis in cultural differences are especially problematic in health care. If unresolved they can lead to a client receiving inappropriate or poor quality care. The increased cultural diversity of the health care work force itself also creates the potential for culturally based problems to surface in the workplace between staff who have different ethnic and cultural backgrounds. Problems that are unresolved at this level have the potential to disrupt services on a broader scale.

Recently published research and government reports have drawn attention to cultural issues in health, health care management and treatment, and disability (Helman,1990; Mitchell,1988; Palmer & Short, 1989; Parsons,1990). The problems experienced by migrants and other ethnic minorities in obtaining satisfactory health care continue to be reported (Bates & Linder-Pelz, 1990; Quesada & Heller, 1977; Thiederman, 1986).

Investigators in the field have identified lack of knowledge among health professionals about the health beliefs, practices, and needs of different cultural groups and intercultural communication difficulties as major issues in health care provision (Barnett, 1988; Bates & Linder-Pelz, 1990; Eliandis, Colanero, & Roussos, 1988). However, sources of information about skills and strategies that will assist health professionals provide services that are culturally sensitive and appropriate have not been easy to access. Notable exceptions are contained in the work of Helman (1990); Galanti (1991); Reid & Trompf (1990); and Kinebanian & Stomph (1990).

Key Concepts

A number of key concepts in the literature concerned with culture provide useful guidelines for understanding culturally based differences in beliefs about illness and disability, which may emerge in health care contexts (Fitzgerald, 1992; Schofield, 1990). Some of these concepts have developed through investigations of health, illness, and healing beliefs and practices in different cultures. Others are strongly based in theoretical approaches to cross-cultural comparisons of medical systems. Those that are most relevant to this module are sociocultural frameworks for analyzing medical systems (disease etiologies, Foster, 1976; dual systems, Young, 1976; "indigenous" medical systems, Kleinman, 1978, 1984; medical pluralism, Parsons, 1990; Helman, 1990) and explanatory models of illness (Helman, 1990; Kleinman, 1984; Parsons,1990).

Sociocultural Frameworks for Analyzing Medical Systems

Macro-level analysis of medical systems informs us about the relationship between health and illness in the population and the political and economic structures and processes in the society. Micro-level analysis addresses questions we may have about the relationship between the sick person, his or her personal support system, and the healer; and the particular sickness, the treatment, and the healing process (Parsons, 1990, p. 135).

The medical system in a society provides us with information about how that society views illness and disability. It is also the mechanism that transmits to members of the society the dominant model that has evolved to explain these phenomena in their society. This model includes information about what is regarded as illness and disability and what is not; the causes of different illnesses and how they are best treated; and how the sick person is expected to behave. It also provides information about the skills of the healers and their status and roles in the society, as well as the roles family members and friends are expected to take in an illness episode (Parsons, 1990, p. 134).

Knowledge that health care beliefs and practices may be different within and across cultural groups can help health care providers develop greater sensitivity to the way people from diverse cultural groups express their health care needs. An understanding of medical systems in other cultures should assist health service providers to be more attuned to the culturally based expectations for health care held by people from cultural backgrounds that are different from their own.

The framework developed by Foster (1976, pp. 773-782) uses disease etiologies as the focus for cross-cultural analysis of medical systems. It addresses questions relating to beliefs about the causes of diseases, whether they are attributed to the act of a supernatural being, another human being, or naturalistic causes. The framework also addresses the consequences for treatment, management, and future prevention when the cause of a particular disease is attributed to one of these alternate sources. In personalistic systems, where the disease is attributed to supernatural forces or to the act of another human being, the healer seeks to establish *who* caused the disease to occur in this particular person(s) and *why*. In naturalistic systems, where disease is attributed to natural causes, the questions asked by the healer are concerned with *how* the person got the disease and *what* it is. In the latter system, explanations for illness are impersonal and include natural forces, the environment, and disturbances of equilibrium within the human system. A knowledge of the predominant disease causation beliefs in a particular cultural group can provide guidelines to assist health professionals develop an understanding of the client's responses. Such knowledge can also provide a basis on which to build communication strategies that are sensitive to the cultural needs of the client and take account of the client's expectations for the healing process.

Another framework, developed by Young (1976, pp. 147-156), classified medical systems according to whether they located the cause of illness within the body or outside the body. Systems that use physiological or biological explanations for disease causation are described as *internalizing*, whereas those that identify the cause of disease as something external to the person and outside their control are called *externalizing*. Clients bring their culturally based beliefs about the cause of their illness and expectations for its management to the clinical setting. The level of sensitivity the health professional has to these beliefs and expectations can have an impact on the professional's relationship with the client, on the therapeutic process, and on the intervention outcomes for the client.

A more complex sociocultural framework has been developed by Kleinman (1978), which permits relationships between popular, folk, and professional arenas in a particular medical system to be analyzed. The purpose of this is to provide a better understanding of the dynamics that are operating within the system. The model places family decisions about health issues, family health care practices, social networks associated with health care, and community support agencies in the popular arena. The folk arena is composed of nonprofessional healers, traditional healers, herbalists, and faith healers; qualified health professionals trained in their professional speciality fit within the professional arena.

Although the dominant medical system in Western society is the biomedical model, other alternate systems of medical care are used by many people. In Australia many older migrants, especially those from Asian countries who do not speak English, prefer to visit traditional healers to have their health care needs met (Galanti, 1991). Included among these alternate healers are Chinese herbalists and naturopaths. The Kleinman model provides for analysis of the interface between the different approaches people take to seek relief from illness and the competing contexts in which care is provided. It also allows conflict between different models to be identified, cultural changes to be followed, and major influences on health and health care to be identified and analyzed. This flexibility and adaptability means that it is a particularly useful framework to use in attempting to understand the varied healing beliefs and practices evident in pluralistic societies.

Medical Pluralism

In the 1990s, most medical systems could be described as *pluralistic*. This means that while one system may be dominant in a society, alternate systems are also available to people. The level of acceptance for these alternate systems varies greatly within and across cultural groups. In some instances pluralism is also used to describe a medical system in which different approaches to healing have been incorporated into the dominant model (Parsons, 1990, pp. 136-138), for example in Chinese medicine.

In Australia, the biomedical model of medical and health care is dominant. However, other systems operate and are relatively widely used, for example, traditional healing. The beliefs and practices associated with traditional healing are sometimes a source of conflict, when these practices come into contact with the mainstream biomedically dominated health care system (Parsons, 1990). Lay people are sometimes hesitant to inform healers from different systems, especially those who are based in the biomedical model, that they have been seeking relief from their ailments through an alternate system of medical care.

In a pluralist society the sources people turn to in seeking relief from illness or assistance in managing disability may be located in one or more of the discrete systems available to them. Parsons (1990, p. 137) nominated five popular factors that influence people's choice of a preferred system of healing/health care in pluralist societies. These are the following:

1. Past or current advice from family and friends about the nature of the illness and the way it should be managed.
2. Exposure to different healing practices including biomedicine.
3. Location of the service (includes considerations about transport and access).
4. Cost involved.
5. The quality of care (perceived skill of the particular healer).

Increasingly, assistance to manage the functional aspects of disability is seen to be more appropriately located outside the biomedical model of healing in the broader arena of community health.

Explanatory Models of Illness

Helman (1992, p. 86) suggested that patients and doctors have different views about ill health, even when they come from the same cultural background. A similar situation also exists for other health professionals and their clients/

patients. These differences frequently lead to communication difficulties in clinical situations, which are heightened when the parties involved in the encounter come from different cultural groups.

In attempting to overcome this problem, Kleinman (1980, p. 105) developed lay and clinical explanatory models (EMs) to provide a framework for understanding the different explanations for illness given by health professionals and their clients. Although lay and clinical explanations may be different, both are concerned with the same five main dimensions of illness: (1) what caused it (etiology); (2) what the symptoms are, when and how they commenced (timing and mode of onset of symptoms); (3) what changes have occurred in the body since the onset (pathophysiological processes); (4) what type of illness it is and the course it will take (natural history and severity); and (5) how it should be treated (appropriate treatment).

In Kleinman's view, the explanatory models used by lay people to describe illness are concerned with the most pressing aspects of a particular bout of illness, its impact on them and significant others in their life, and their expectations for treatment and recovery. Although health practitioners would cover all dimensions in developing the explanatory model for a patient's illness, they may choose not to provide a full and detailed explanation to the patient and/or their significant others (Parsons,1990, p. 132).

Explanatory models are related to a specific illness event and influenced by multiple factors in addition to those that are based in culture (Helman, 1990; Kleinman,1980). For example, the personality of the patient and her or his particular life circumstances at the time also influence the explanations health professionals give.

Parsons (1990, pp. 132-133) discussed a number of advantages and shortcomings associated with adopting the explanatory models approach to improve the process and outcome of clinical encounters. Eliciting the client's explanation of the illness or disability can provide the health professional with useful knowledge about its significance and meaning to the client, the client's expectations about treatment, and the outcomes the client anticipates. When the client's EM is compared with the EM of the health professional it is usually possible to discern some areas of commonality in the two models. These provide a good starting point from which negotiations to resolve major differences can be initiated. The goals for such negotiations are to develop strategies that are sensitive to the client's needs, nonjudgmental and sufficiently flexible to accommodate alternate points of view, while at the same time ensuring that high quality appropriate care is being delivered to the client.

Eliciting EMs is problematic in situations in which the health professional and the client do not speak a common language. Strategies to overcome the language barrier in such situations include the use of bilingual health professionals and/or interpreter services. Another shortcoming associated with EMs is the likelihood that clinical explanations that are based in the biomedical disease model will not be subjected to the same scrutiny as the explanatory models of lay people.This potentially increases the likelihood that clinical bias could go unnoticed.

Parsons also raised the issues of power and social distance in relation to the use of EMs. She questioned whether the health professional really engaged in negotiating power issues with the client or whether in many instances the professional's interests were in seeking to make the client comply with therapy or treatment regimes. Issues of power in helping relationships are compounded when sociocultural differences between the provider and the client are compounded by cultural differences.

Cassell (1976, pp. 47-83) made an interesting distinction between *illness* and *disease*. He described illness as something human beings have—their subjective experience of a bout of ill health. In this approach, illness also includes the way people are affected by ill health, what they do to get better, the causes they attribute to the particular episode, and what it means to them and those with whom they associate.

Alternatively, disease appears to be what the doctor says the patient has. In determining a diagnosis, the doctor engages in a scientific process in which he or she seeks to establish the cause of illness through using objective numerical measures preferably of physiochemical data within a framework that separates the mind and the body (mind-body dualism). Diseases are viewed as entities, and in the treatment process emphasis is placed on the patient (especially on organs or systems in the patient's body) rather than on factors in the physical and social environment (Helman, 1990, p. 86). The patient's description of the illness may bear little resemblance to the doctor's diagnosis of the disease. This is perhaps to be expected because they each experience the event from different perspectives. This analysis can also be extended to include comparisons of the explanatory models offered by other health professionals and their clients. This is especially so for those health professionals who are most closely aligned with the biomedical disease model.

Helman (1990, pp. 90-91) suggested that the way people explain their ill health is part of a wider model common to a particular society, which the members of that society draw on to explain other phenomena that also have adverse outcomes. Health professionals who are engaged in direct service provision in a culturally diverse society come into contact with people who have varied explanations for illnesses and different ideas about appropriate therapeutic management. The same can be said for beliefs about the cause of disability and the views different cultural groups hold about the appropriateness of intervention to develop functional ability and independence in a person who has a disability.

Attributing Causes to Ill Health

Helman (1990, pp. 102-103) suggested that lay people attribute ill health to sources that lie within the person, in the natural world, in the social world, and in the supernatural world. However, the causes of ill health are not necessarily restricted to one source; they may be attributed to multiple sources. Helman also suggested that illness etiologies linked to social and supernatural causes are the more likely explanations given for illness in non-industrialized societies, whereas natural and patient-centered explanations tend to be associated with Western society. He cites Chrisman (1977) as the source for a list of causes of illness commonly given by lay people in the United States. The eight causes are: debilitation, degeneration, invasion, imbalance, stress, mechanical causes, environmental irritants, and heredity (Helman, 1990, p. 103).

Parsons (1990, pp. 135-136) discussed causes of illness that are attributed to the supernatural. These are associated with two main sources. First, they may be mystical, such as fate, retribution for bad deeds, or the activities of hostile spirits that may take possession of the person's body and cause them to become ill. Second, they may be linked to the work of a sorcerer, who deliberately sets out to make the person ill, or witchcraft, in which some intended or unintended action by a person makes another person ill.

Galanti (1991) also included object intrusion as another causal explanation for illness that is linked to the supernatural. In this situation, a foreign magical object that has entered the body is perceived as the cause of illness. She suggests that many health professionals, who have been educated in the Western biomedical model of health care, experience problems in providing culturally sensitive care to people who give supernatural reasons for their illnesses. Causal explanations that are attributed to the supernatural fit more comfortably with traditional models of healing.

The literature supports a variety of explanations for illness that have their roots in different cultural systems and that people draw on to construct explanations of a particular illness they are experiencing. Landy (1983, pp. 211-213) indicated that people who come from Anglo-Celtic origins are comfortable with natural explanations that attribute the cause of illness to infection, stress, organic deterioration, accidents, and human aggression. Galanti (1991, p. 11) provided an explanation firmly based in the biomedical model when she reported that most Americans believe that germs cause disease. Still other explanations for illness can be found in Chinese medical lore and in the humeral theory of the ancient Greeks, both of which attribute the cause of illness to an imbalance in the body.

Chinese medical theory, which is part of a larger belief system, is concerned with the balance of yin (cold) and yang (hot) in the body, whereas the Greek theory is focused on the balance of body fluids (blood, phlegm, black bile, and yellow bile). The physiological theory that supports these classifications equates health with balance. Factors that are believed to upset the body in Chinese medical theory include strong emotional states and an imbalance in the type of foods eaten. Treatment in both systems is directed toward restoring balance and may involve eating specific types and combinations of foods and/or abstaining from others. Used in this way, food becomes medicine and is a significant component in the therapeutic management process.

Helman (1990, pp. 34-37) discussed the dual system adopted by some cultural groups in India, the Islamic nations, Latin American countries, and China to organize "items" relevant to the theory of health and balance into classifications of *hot* and *cold*. The classificatory system includes foods, medicines, various types of illnesses, physical and mental states, and forces within the natural and the supernatural world. Although many similar items are included in the lists generated by different cultures, there are many variations in the way items are classified. A basic treatment principle appears to be that illnesses that are classified as "hot" are treated with "cold" foods, whereas those that are classified as "cold" are treated with "hot" foods. This is done to restore the balance to the body system.

The image people develop of their bodies is influenced by the views their cultural group holds about the physical properties and functions of the body and its psychological and social significance. These images tend to be focused around four main areas of concerns: body size, shape, and surface; clothing and adornments; the internal structure of the body; and the way the body functions. Social gender is derived from the particular culture's definition of what is acceptable maleness and appropriate femaleness in the society. The definitions give attention to appearance, behaviors, and feelings, and these features influence visible dimensions such as body size and shape. Self perceptions of one's body are influenced by the dominant view of what constitutes an acceptable male or female body. These perceptions, in turn, influence people's perception of their roles in their society and the way they behave under certain conditions. In societies which emphasize masculine values (see Chapter 8 by N. Goodman), men in particular seek to present an image that is strong, effective, and tough. In such cultures, illness is often viewed as an event which strikes those who are weak. If the illness is lengthy or results in disability, it is likely to have a devastating effect on the man's psychological and social image of himself. This negative image, in turn, will have an impact on any treatment or rehabilitation program that might be introduced.

Clothing serves social purposes beyond that of protecting the body's surface. People's clothing and adornment may convey information about their social standing in their community, their economic status, their group membership, changes in their status, and their religious affiliation. The type and color of the clothing, the body parts that are covered, and the extent of the covering may be associated with cultural taboos. For example, Muslim women wear a black garment known as a *chador*. It is loose fitting and covers all parts of the body except for the eyes and hands. It is meant to reduce women's attractiveness to men and is worn as a symbol of their status in their society.

Metaphors of Illness

Understanding the metaphors of illness that are commonly used in different cultures and learning to use these appropriately in communicating with clients about their illnesses can contribute toward more effective communication, when an interpreter is available or the client and the health professional share a common language. Good (1977, pp. 25-58) reported that "heart distress" is often used by Iranians, especially the women, to describe physical and mental symptoms of illness that are not necessarily related to heart disease as it is understood in the United States, Australia, and other Western countries. Still other metaphors people use, perhaps more in Western society, are drawn from the images and practices of war, for example, "zap the germs," "battle outbreaks of disease," "fight cancer," "fend off a cold."

The extent to which these specific metaphors are used by clients from non-industrialized societies is probably limited. It is likely that they have a similar system of metaphors they use to communicate about illness, which draws on elements in their cultural background, for example, local environmental factors or the spirit world. Treatment processes and outcome are greatly enhanced when the health professional appreciates the significance of the client's metaphorical communications about the particular illness.

Communication Style

The Western medical model uses a direct question/answer mode to elicit and communicate information in clinical situations. This mode of communication is considered to be impolite and even rude in cultures where interpersonal communication is indirect. In these cultures, the parties engaged in an interpersonal exchange learn much of what is being communicated from inference and nonverbal communication (for example in the Thai culture).

Health professionals from English-speaking backgrounds often use negative and double negative questions when seeking information from their clients. For example, "You don't want to be dependent on your family, do you?" "Do you want the pills or the mixture?" People for whom English is a second language often experience difficulty in responding to such questions and may be judged by native English-language speakers as having poor language skills when they appear uncertain about how to respond. Communication breakdown in such situations could be described as *cross-cultural pragmatic failure* (Thomas, 1983).

Cross-Cultural Pragmatic Failure

Thomas (1983, pp. 91-110) discussed two types of pragmatic failure that potentially occur in cross-cultural contexts, *pragmalinguistic failure* and *sociopragmatic failure*. She suggests that pragmalinguistic failure can occur at two levels. First, when the person receiving the information understands the nature of the communication (e.g., they are being asked a question) but not the intended sense (e.g., what the person actually wants to know): "Do you want the pills or the mixture?" Second, when the person receiving the communication does not understand the intended pragmatic force behind the communication (e.g., what they believe is a compliment is really a disguised sarcastic comment): "You don't want to be dependent on your family, do you?"

Sociopragmatic failure occurs when people have different perceptions about the appropriateness of language behavior in a given situation. Thomas (1983, p. 104) gives three examples of sociopragmatic failure that may occur in cross-cultural communication:

1. Requests that may be considered an imposition in one of the cultures involved in the communication.
2. Topics that are considered inappropriate in a specific context.
3. Failure of the parties engaged in a communication event to accurately assess the power relationship involved, adopt the culturally acceptable social distance, or use the required form and sequence of address.

Nonverbal Communication

There are many cultural groups that make extensive use of the nonverbal aspects of communication to convey meaning in interacting with others. These nonverbal aspects include posturing, gesturing, and the use of facial expression. They can be difficult for someone outside the culture to interpret accurately unless the outsider is familiar with communication conventions in the particular culture. For example, whereas forward head nodding is usually taken for agreement or "Yes"in cultures that have an Anglo-Celtic background, in Cambodia forward head nodding usually signifies a negative response.

The eyes are also used to convey meaning, but the meaning attached to different communication conventions in which the eyes are important may vary quite markedly between cultural groups. This can be a source of embarrassment and confusion. For example, people from Anglo-Celtic backgrounds generally believe that it is appropriate to gaze at a person directly when talking to the person. However, in many Asian cultures it is considered impolite to engage in direct eye contact. Lowered eyes and averted gaze signify respect for superiors in some Asian and Pacific Island cultures, whereas in Australia, the United States, and other similar cultures, using the eyes in this way is frequently taken to mean the person has something to hide and may even be considered untrustworthy. This attitude is reflected in statements such as, "He couldn't even look me in the eye" and "Look at me when I am speaking to you."

In health care situations that involve people from different cultural backgrounds, the potential for miscommunication and misinterpretation of nonverbal communications is high, even when those involved are sincerely seeking to understand each other. Misunderstanding in such situations can take on critical dimensions when health care is involved, especially when the situation involves making critical decisions.

Nonverbal communication across cultures is treated in greater depth in Chapter 14 in this book by Theodore Singelis.

Cultural Brokerage

Awareness of the need to provide health services that are both culturally sensitive and relevant to the recipient of the particular service is gaining momentum throughout the world, especially in culturally diverse societies. To deal effectively with the diversity which is evident within, as well as across cultures, health service providers must learn to develop strategies that are adaptable and flexible (Fitzgerald, 1992, pp. 1-5). Cultural brokerage is a concept which appears to provide strategies which meet these criteria.

Weidman (1982, p. 211) used the term *cultural brokerage* to describe strategies that have been adopted to reduce the disparity between cultures and to develop more open and effective communication links. Applied to the health care services, culture brokerage means resourcing both the care provider and the recipient of care with information about each other's cultures, especially those aspects that are concerned with health care. Fitzgerald (1992) extended the concept of cultural brokerage to include training community-based health and rehabilitation workers from specific ethnic groups to assist in providing health and rehabilitation services to their communities. Two other strategies that have been adopted to reduce disparities in cross-cultural health care contexts are the use of interpreter services and the involvement of bilingual health workers in treatment sessions (see Chapter 16 in this book by Carolina Freimanis).

Still other strategies that can be useful in health care situations involving cross-cultural interactions have been identified. Included among these are the following:

1. Seeking the advice of other health care workers in the same environment.
2. Networking to develop awareness of various members of one's community who can be called upon for assistance.
3. Becoming familiar with support resources that are available.
4. Deliberately working at developing a heightened awareness of the verbal and nonverbal responses of other people in health care contexts so as to develop a higher level of skill in making accurate attributions about behavior.

Although these strategies are being used more frequently within health care systems, the supports and resources necessary to implement them are not always immediately or readily available to those providing direct services to clients. However, they are more likely to be adopted and used to their best effect in situations in which health care providers are interculturally sensitive and have the capacity to accept the relativity of their own views. Health care providers in such situations will also have an understanding of the multiple cultural dimensions inherent in any situation that involves an encounter between a health care provider and a client. They will recognize the presence of diversity within as well as across cultures and will have a commitment to developing effective intercultural communication skills. These attitudes and skills provide a basis from which culturally sensitive and relevant health care services can be developed in culturally diverse societies.

Skill Applications

There are a number of ways in which the concepts reviewed earlier in this chapter can be applied in skill training. Suggestions for implementing some of these, using the case studies from Part III of this chapter as a focus, are presented below.

Exercise 1: Exploring Respect for Diversity

One of the themes woven into the case study "Home Therapy" is respect for diversity. The purpose of this exercise is to identify and explore the personal requisites that are necessary to effectively communicate respect for diversity.

Instructions

1. Ask participants to team up in small groups (3 to 5 members). Each group should seek to ensure that its membership is as diverse as possible. Suitable criteria for establishing diversity might include gender, culture, first language, occupation, and leisure interests. Once the groups have formed, ask each to appoint a spokesperson to report back to the large group on the outcomes of their deliberations and someone to take notes during the small group discussions.

2. Ask individuals in each group to read the story "Home Therapy" again and (a) to write down instances where they believe individuals in the story showed or did not show respect for each other's differences and (b) to state why they believe the particular instance indicated a respect for or indifference toward diversity. It is important that this part of the exercise is completed without consultation with other members of the group.

3. When all members have completed Item 2, ask them to share what they have written with their small group, using the following ground rules for any discussion that may follow the information shared by a group member:
   - Group members must give positive verbal feedback to each other about the information they present.
   - Different perceptions of instances in the case study should be spoken about, but only in positive statements. For example:

Person A: I thought that . . . was an excellent example of showing respect
for other people's customs, because. . . .

Person B: That's an interesting point. I had not thought about that instance
in quite that way. I was thinking that . . . because. . . .

The group should make a list of the different views members express in
their responses to Item 2 for the spokesperson to feed back in the large group.

4. Report back to the large group, using the same ground rules. After the feedback
   session, the group leader/trainer should direct discussion toward exploring how
   participants felt about the process. Did they find it was difficult/easy to accept
   other's views without arguing or trying to change their opinions? What feelings
   did they become aware of during the process?
5 Ask participants to return to their small groups to complete the next step in the
   exercise.
6. Ask each small group to develop a list of personal requisites that they believe are
   necessary to be able to communicate respect for diversity.
7. Report back to the large group.

Exercise 2: Communicating Sensitivity to Cultural Needs in Clinical Settings

There are a number of themes that run through the case study "Her First
Job in Singapore." One is concerned with culturally sensitive communication.
This exercise provides participants with an opportunity to explore strategies
for providing treatment that is both culturally sensitive and clinically appropriate. Participants in the training group will need to reread "The Story of Judy
and Mrs. Mamoud" to prepare for the exercise.

The goal for the end of the role play is for Mrs. Mamoud to be seated in a
cubicle accompanied by her sister-in-law with Judy commencing the assessment.

Instructions

This exercise uses role-play techniques. Instructions for using these techniques are provided in Chapter 11 in this book by Mullavey-O'Byrne.

Setting

The role play picks up from the end of the case study where Judy is saying,
"How am I going to communicate to Mrs. Mamoud that I need to examine her
knee in a way that is culturally sensitive, when she and I don't even speak the
same language?" The setting is the busy outpatient department where patients
are waiting for physiotherapy treatment.

Role Card: Mrs. Mamoud

Recently your knee was injured in a motor vehicle accident. Since the accident your knee has become increasingly painful and stiff, so your doctor has recommended physiotherapy treatment and referred you to the outpatient department of a large hospital near to where you now live. You have recently arrived from Bangladesh with your husband and two small children. You do not speak English, so your sister-in-law (who speaks a little English and is familiar with the city) has accompanied you to the hospital. You are relieved to be receiving physiotherapy treatment, as you were told by your doctor that it would relieve the pain and stop your knee becoming stiff. Your expectations are that you will receive your treatment from a woman physiotherapist in an area that offers you privacy and that your sister-in-law will be in attendance while you are receiving treatment. You know that physiotherapy involves exercise and probably massage and realize that your leg will need to be bare for the treatment. You also expect you will learn exercises you must practice at home and will probably have to come for several treatments.

In playing the role, your task is to make sure that you are treated in private, by a woman physiotherapist, and that your sister-in-law remains with you. You do not understand what Judy says to you but can understand her nonverbal communication. You sense that she is upset about something and wonder if it is that she does not want to treat you. You become very worried when you think she is asking a male physiotherapist to take you for treatment, but apart from communicating this to your sister-in-law you remain calm. You are disappointed that the physiotherapist who is allocated to treat you does not speak your language, but more than that you are concerned that she does not understand your cultural needs when you are receiving treatment. Your sister-in-law tries to assist, but she speaks and understands only a little English.

You should be smiling and wanting to cooperate at the beginning, moving toward being frustrated because of the language problem and quite concerned when you think a male physiotherapist is going to treat you.

How you respond after this depends on whether you believe Judy understands your cultural needs.

Role Card: Judy Evans

After the initial difficulty you experience when you see Mrs. Mamoud and her companion, you to go up to them and speak to see if Mrs. Mamoud's companion speaks English. You discover very quickly that her English is very limited and that she understands very little of what you are saying. You gesture towards the small treatment cubicle and indicate to Mrs. Mamoud that she should follow you. Her companion moves to follow you. You motion her to sit down and explain that the treatment cubicle is too small for you all to fit. She does not seem to understand. One of the male physiotherapists walks by with a patient, so you ask him if he would be able to explain to her. He says he cannot speak the language either. Mrs. Mamoud and her companions seem to be becoming upset and are talking more loudly to each other. Other people in the waiting room are starting to take an interest in what is going on. You feel that everyone is looking at you.

Your task for the role play is to arrive at a situation where Mrs. Mamoud will allow you to examine her leg. She will do so when (and if) you have convinced her that you understand her cultural needs. For this to happen you will need to understand Mrs. Mamoud's particular needs and communicate understanding of these to her.

Role Card: Mrs. Mamoud's Sister-in-Law

You were pleased to accompany your sister-in-law to the outpatient department but are very anxious because your English language skills are very limited. The physiotherapist who comes to treat Mrs. Mamoud does not speak your language, nor does she appear to understand your cultural needs. You try to understand, but she talks very quickly, so you miss a lot of what she says.

Your goals for the role play are to ensure that you remain with Mrs. Mamoud during the treatment session and to ensure that she receives treatment from a woman.

Role Card: Male Physiotherapist

When Judy Evans asks you if you are able to communicate with Mrs. Mamoud, you reply that you are sorry, but you do not speak or understand Mrs. Mamoud's language. Because she does not ask you for any other advice, you do not embarrass her by offering further information.

Special Instructions

In the discussion that follows the role play, encourage participants to share their feelings about similar situations they have experienced and to explore a range of possible strategies that could be used to bridge the gap between Mrs. Mamoud and Judy.

Field Exercises

Journal of Metaphors of Body-Mind and Illness

This exercise is designed to complement and build on the Introductory Exercise in this module, Explanatory Models of Illness. The exercise is intended to help you develop greater sensitivity to the way people express the meaning of illness and/or disability within the context of their lives and to enhance your ability to respond to the diverse ways in which your clients express their culturally based health care needs.

The exercise is ongoing and could form the basis for a staff development project over a period of weeks.

Instructions

1. This exercise requires you to keep a daily journal in which you enter statements you hear people use to describe states of good health or ill health. Take note of the way you choose to describe your own state of health/bouts of illness you may experience, as well as that of other people in your home, work, and leisure environments. Think about your response to the expressions other people use to describe their states of health/illness.

2. As your collection develops review it from time to time. In your review look for metaphorical themes you may be able to associate with different groups of people. For example, from examining the entries in your journal you may see a pattern emerging in the way members of your family describe their health or bouts of illness, or you may notice similarities in the metaphors people from certain other cultural groups use to talk about health and illness.

3. If the exercise is a part of a staff development project, it would be helpful for members of the training group to review their journal entries in pairs or as a group, to clarify issues that may have emerged for individuals.

Self-Assessment

The second exercise in this module is a self-assessment that was designed to help you examine your ability to identify cultural differences that are present in your own areas of health care practice.

1. As you have now completed the module, it would be useful (and interesting) for you to complete the form again (without referring to your previous responses).

2. When you have completed the assessment form for the second time, compare your two sets of responses to see if there are any differences between them.

3. At this stage the trainer should draw the attention of participants to the list of attributes and skills that they had previously identified as supporting positive responses to the items in the Self-Assessment.

4. The last part of the exercise requires each participant (a) to quietly reflect on any changes the participant is aware have taken place in her- or himself over the period of the training program and (b) to note the direction of the change and set personal goals for the future.

The self-assessment can provide a basis for ongoing review of the cultural dimension of your treatment programs and could be a useful stimulus for peer review.

References

Barnett, K. (1988). *Aged care policy for a multicultural society.* Policy Options Paper, Department of the Prime Minister and Cabinet. Canberra, Australia.

Bates, E., & Linder-Pelz, S. (1990). *Health care issues.* Sydney: Allen & Unwin.

Brislin, R., Cushner, K., Cherrie, C., & Yong, M. (1986). *Intercultural interactions: A practical guide.* Newbury Park, CA: Sage.

Cassell, E. J. (1976). *The healer's art: A new approach to the doctor-patient relationship.* New York: Lippincott.

Chrisman, N. J. (1977). The health seeking process: An approach to the natural history of illness. *Culture, Medicine, and Psychiatry, 1,* 351- 357.

Eliandis, M., Colanero, R., & Roussos, P. (1988). *Issues for non-English speaking background women of Australia.* Policy Options Paper, Department of the Prime Minister and Cabinet. Canberra, Australia.

Fitzgerald, M. (1992, April/May/June). Multicultural clinical interactions. *Journal of Rehabilitation,* pp. 1-5.

Foster, G. (1976). Disease etiologies in non-Western medical systems. *American Anthropology, 78,* 773-782.

Galanti, G. (1991). *Caring for patients from different cultures: Case studies from American hospitals.* Philadelphia, PA: University of Pennsylvania Press.

Good, B. (1977). The heart of what's the matter: The semantics of illness in Iran. *Culture, Medicine and Society, 1,* 25-28.

Helman, C. (1990). *Culture, health and illness: An introduction for health professionals.* Jordan Hill, Oxford, UK: Butterworth Heinemann.

Hodge, A. (1988). *Australian identity in a multicultural society.* Policy Options Paper, Department of the Prime Minister and Cabinet. Canberra, Australia.

Kinebanian, A., & Stomph, M. (1990). Developing a program for occupational therapy students concerning cross-cultural occupational therapy care. *Abstracts. World Federation of Occupational Therapists, 10th International Congress.* Melbourne, Australia.

Kleinman, A. (1978). Concepts and a model for the comparison of medical systems as cultural systems. *Social Science and Medicine, 12,* 85-93.

Kleinman, A. (1980). *Patients and healers in the context of culture.* Berkeley, CA: University of California Press.

Kleinman, A. (1984). Indigenous systems of healing: Questions for professional, popular and folk care. In W. Salmon (Ed.), *Alternative medicine: Popular policy and perspectives.* London: Tavistock.

Landy, P. (1983). Medical anthropology. A critical appraisal. In J. Ruffine (Ed.), *Advances in Medical Social Science* (vol. 1, pp. 185-314).

Mitchell, G. (1988). *Health policy for a multucultural Australia.* Policy Options Paper, Department of the Prime Minister and Cabinet. Canberra, Australia.

Palmer, G., & Short, S. (1989). *Health care & public policy: An Australian analysis.* Melbourne, Australia: Macmillan.

Parsons, C. (1990). Cross-cultural issues in health care. In J. Reid & P. Trompf (Eds.), *The health of immigrant Australia: A social perspective* (pp. 108-148). Sydney, Australia: Harcourt, Brace, Jovanovich.

Quesada, G. M., & Heller, P. L. (1977). Sociocultural barriers to medical care among Mexican Americans in Texas: A summary report of research conducted by the Southwest Medical Sociology Ad Hoc Committee. *Medical Care, 15*(5 Suppl), 93-105.

Reid, J., & Trompf, P. (Eds.) (1990). *The health of immigrant Australia: A social perspective.* Sydney, Australia: Harcourt, Brace, Jovanovich.

Schofield, T. (1990). Living with disability. In J. Reid & P. Trompf (Eds.), *The health of immigrant Australia: A social perspective.* Sydney, Australia: Harcourt, Brace, Jovanovich.

Thiederman, S. B. (1986). Ethnocentrism: A barrier to effective health care. *Nursing Practice, 11*(8), 52- 59.

Thomas, J. (1983). Cross-cultural pragmatic failure. *Applied Linguistics, 4,* 91-112.

Weidman, H. H. (1982). Research strategies, structural alterations and clinically applied anthropology. In N. J. Chrisman & T. W. Maretzki (Eds), *Clinically applied anthropology. Anthropologists in health science settings* (pp. 201-241). Dordrecht, The Netherlands: D. Reidel.

Young, A. (1976). Internalising and externalising medical belief systems: An Ethiopian example. *Social Science and Medicine, 10,* 147-156.

11 Intercultural Interactions in Welfare Work

COLLEEN MULLAVEY-O'BYRNE

In addition to the ever-persistent communication barriers between people of different cultures, professionals in welfare often face an added challenge of dealing with people who did not necessarily choose to move across cultures. These include religious and political refugees, as well as people forced to emigrate for economic reasons. This module familiarizes readers with a variety of commonly encountered problems faced by social services workers. Relevant theories and frameworks are introduced that should help people organize their thinking about their intercultural interactions. Role plays aimed at developing culturally sensitive skills are provided along with a thorough explanation of how they should be conducted.

Contents

Self-Assessment Exercise:
Satisfaction in Intercultural Interactions in Welfare Work

Self-Assessment

This exercise has been designed to assist you in developing your personal goals for this training module.

1. Take a few moments to reflect on recent situations at work in which you were in some way involved in providing services to clients whose cultural/ethnic background was different from your own.
2. Identify three specific instances in which you were aware of being particularly (a) satisfied and/or (b) dissatisfied with your contribution to these situations. Make brief notes about what happened that caused you to feel this way.
3. Ask yourself the following questions in relation to each of the three instances. Make notes of your responses to each question, as you will refer to them again later in the module.
   a. In what way was the satisfaction or dissatisfaction I experienced related to my *knowledge* or *lack of knowledge* about:
      * the client's particular needs and cultural background?
      * the resources available to assist them/help me assist them?
      * culturally appropriate strategies to assist the client?
      * the client's language?
      * alternate methods of communicating with people from different language speaking groups?
   b. In what way was the satisfaction or dissatisfaction I experienced with my contribution related to my *skill* or *lack of skill* in:
      * accurately perceiving and understanding the client's needs within the particular situation?
      * accurately communicating understanding of the client's needs and the particular situation to the client?
      * communicating the client's needs and situation to those involved in assisting the client?
      * selecting and implementing the appropriate action?
      * communicating with the client in his or her own language?
   c. In what way was the satisfaction or dissatisfaction with my contribution related to:
      * my sensitivity to the client's needs and cultural background?
      * my beliefs about other cultures and ethnic groups?
      * my beliefs about who should receive welfare assistance?
      * my beliefs about people who seek welfare assistance?
      * my beliefs about the way people should/should not behave toward others in specific situations?

When you have completed your self-assessment you will see that one set of responses relate to knowledge, one to skills, and the last to attitudes, beliefs, and values. Each of these influences the way we interact with people from cultural backgrounds that are different from our own.

4. Select someone from the group to be your partner. Discuss and compare your responses. Using the three groupings as a framework, discuss insights you each may have had about your strengths and weaknesses in providing welfare services to clients from different cultural and ethnic backgrounds.

In consultation with your partner identify *specific areas* where you believe training would increase your ability to provide appropriate services to your clients. *Make a list* of them to refer to while you are participating in the training module. The examples that follow provide a guide to making your list.

Examples

- Knowing what to do when I can see the client has a problem but am unable to identify what it is or why there is a problem.
- Dealing with a client who insists on speaking to someone who has higher authority, when I am the staff expert on the particular matter.

Case Studies

The Escribanos

The informant for this case study was a welfare worker at a Portuguese Welfare Center in an inner-city suburb of Sydney. The center employs three part-time Portuguese-speaking welfare workers. Their role is to assist Portuguese-speaking migrants and refugees deal with problems they encounter settling into their new environment. This role covers assisting with completing forms, advising on appropriate services, assisting with locating resources, interpreting and translating information, and helping the newcomers to establish networks in the local community. It does not include long-term counseling; clients in need of this type of service are referred to the appropriate counseling service.

The center receives financial support from the Portuguese community and some government funding through the Department of Immigration. The migrants and refugees served by the center have come from Portugal and other Portuguese-speaking countries such as Brazil, Angola, Timor, and Goa. Although the three welfare workers all speak fluent Portuguese, they do not necessarily come from the same cultural background as their clients; for example, Mercedes, who was the informant for this case, is second-generation Portuguese Australian.

Maria and Jesus Escribano's Story

Maria and Jesus migrated to Australia from Brazil 8 months ago. Jesus is an accountant, Maria a hairdresser. Maria resigned from her job when she and Jesus married 18 months ago, as Jesus did not want his wife to go out to work. Both speak some English but are not fluent.

The couple were persuaded to come to Australia by a Brazilian friend, who told them about opportunities available to do well if you worked hard. He agreed to help Jesus find work as an accountant. However, for family reasons, the friend returned to Brazil 2 weeks after Jesus and Maria arrived. Since then they have been alone, with no support system. Jesus found that his accountancy qualification was not recognized in Australia. To qualify to practice, he would have to complete additional requirements, improve his English-language skills, and pass a qualifying exam. Maria missed her family and wanted to go back to Brazil. However, Jesus disagreed, pointing out that he would be ashamed to return "looking like a failure." They must stay and show they are successful. Jesus began to look for some other kind of work.

After 2 months, Jesus obtained work as a cleaner. Over the next 2 months the Escribanos managed to save enough money to allow them to move out of the boarding house where they had been living and lease a modest apartment. At the time they were signing the lease contract, they sought advice from the local Portuguese Welfare Center. They were assisted by a young welfare worker, a recent graduate from a 2-year diploma program in social welfare. Mercedes, a second-generation Portuguese Australian, also spoke fluent Portuguese.

When they moved into their apartment, Maria discovered that their next-door neighbors owned a hairdressing salon and that they had a staff vacancy. They offered Maria the position. Jesus was adamant that his wife would not go to work, so Maria refused the offer and settled into full-time homemaking activities.

Life was looking good for Jesus and Maria until 1 month ago when the company that employed Jesus filed for bankruptcy and laid off all its staff at 1 day's notice. Since then, Jesus's attempts to find work have not met with success.

He has become increasingly depressed and anxious, has difficulty sleeping at night, and paces around the apartment smoking. When Maria was again asked to work in the salon, she tried to persuade Jesus to let her take the position but only until he found a job. This seemed to make him more depressed and he remained adamant that his wife would not go out to work.

Maria became very worried about her husband's health and about their ability to continue meeting their financial commitments, when they had no source of income. The little savings they had were almost gone. She telephoned the Portuguese Welfare Center and spoke to Mercedes, who made an appointment for them to see her. After confirming a time, Maria asked if there was a man at the center who would help Jesus find a job. When Mercedes replied no, that she would meet with them but would then refer Jesus to the Commonwealth Employment Service for help in getting a job, Maria expressed doubt that Jesus would come to the interview.

However, Jesus does arrive with Maria for the interview. Although they both look tired and anxious, Jesus also appears dishevelled.

Mercedes commences the interview by saying that she understands that these are difficult times for them and attempts to reassure them that she is available to help in whatever way she can. She suggests that the first step they should take is to apply for unemployment benefits to help pay the bills while Jesus is looking for work. She adds that assistance with groceries and foodstuffs, if necessary, could be arranged for a short period of time. She also adds that it is not an easy time to be looking for work, as many people are unemployed.

Jesus says, "Can you find me a job? I want work, not money and food for nothing! Maybe your boss can find a job for me?"

Mercedes explains that she does not have a boss who will help him find work, that he must go to the Commonwealth Employment Service to look for work, and that he is eligible for unemployment benefits while looking for a job. This seems to make Jesus angry, and he starts speaking loudly saying, "I am telling you that I want a job, not money for nothing. I am an accountant, my friend says there is plenty of work for accountants in Australia, so we come. Now I find no work for accountants, but plenty of work for a hairdresser. What is this country where a man cannot get work, but they ask his wife to work? I am feeling sick in this country, it is not a good place to be. When I was deciding that we would come I was told that there is plenty of opportunity if you are willing to work hard. Now I am here, there is no work for a man; there is no opportunity; this is a big lie they have told me."

Discussion Questions

1. What are the main themes in this case study? Do they have a cultural basis? If so, what is this, and how is it affecting the Escribanos' situation? What other issues are there?

2. What are the main problems that have to be resolved, from Jesus's perspective? from Maria's perspective? from Mercedes's perspective? from your reading of the case study?

3. Is the influence of culture evident in the exchange between Mercedes and Jesus? If so, why, and in what way does this affect the interaction?

4. What is your response to the information Mercedes gives Jesus? Why did he become upset? Could Mercedes have been more effective in the way she communicated to Jesus and Maria?

5. What experience do you have of similar situations? How did you react? How did you cope with the immediate situation?

Brigitta

This account was provided by a volunteer community welfare worker with a church group that sponsors and supports refugees. The group works closely with official refugee organizations. Several people in the group hold professional positions; others are retired.

Brigitta's Story

Janet, a volunteer community welfare worker with a refugee support group, tells a story about some aspects of assisting a Romanian family to settle in the community. The family consisted of a middle-aged man, Lazlo; his younger sister,

Zita, and her 5-year-old daughter, Brigitta; and their elderly mother, Mrs. Szabas. Janet was very involved with the family, helping them find reasonably priced accommodation, getting donations of furniture and household items to help them set up a home, and generally introducing them to the community and the way of life. This also included enrolling the daughter, Brigitta, at the local school, taking the women shopping to the local supermarket, and organizing for Zita and Lazlo to attend English language classes. Mrs. Szabas did not wish to learn English, saying she was too old.

On the first day Brigitta was to attend school, Janet arrived to accompany Brigitta, her mother, and grandmother to the school. Brigitta had on her very best dress, her black patent shoes, and patterned socks. Her hair was elaborately curled and tied up with ribbons. She was also wearing a coat even though it was summer and quite hot. The grandmother and mother were beaming and looking very pleased with Brigitta. Zita said, "My little girl looks so beautiful. I am so proud that I send her to school looking so fine."

Janet was very surprised at the way Brigitta was dressed, because the previous week she had taken Zita and Brigitta shopping to buy the cotton uniform dress, lace-up shoes, and socks all girls wore at the local school. She also noticed that Zita and her mother were dressed in their best clothes and that Mrs. Szabas was looking with disapproval at the way she was dressed in an open-necked blouse, jeans, and sandals.

She said to Zita, "Brigitta does look beautiful, but she is much too well dressed to go to school. This is not suitable. It will be better if she wears the school dress we bought last week." Zita looked very distressed and replied, "My mother will not be pleased. She was not pleased with the dress for school."

Janet explained that none of the children would be dressed in their best clothes. When Zita conveyed this to her mother, she smiled broadly, nodded, and said to Zita that is how it should be, her daughter would be the best dressed. When Zita told Janet this, she tried to convince them that Brigitta would not be able to run around and play with the other children because she would have to keep her clothes clean. Again the grandmother had an answer— children go to school to learn, not to play. It is only Janet's last argument, that it is "a school rule," that changes the grandmother's mind. Reluctantly she allowed Brigitta to put on the school clothes but insisted that she wear the coat in case it turned cool.

Janet did not hear from the family during the week but on the Friday received a phone call from the class teacher who told her that Brigitta has not been at school since the day she enrolled. When Janet asked if there were any problems, the teacher replied that there were no real problems, only a little one about Brigitta not washing her face and hands. She explained the incident to Janet.

"On the Tuesday morning Brigitta's mother came to see me. She seemed overly upset that Brigitta had not used the soap and hand towel in her bag to wash her face and hands before and after eating. Brigitta's mother seemed very angry with Brigitta and had expected me to punish her. Poor thing, she seemed to be embarrassed that this had happened. I reassured her that other children often forgot to wash their face and hands and that I wasn't particularly worried about Brigitta forgetting, especially on her first day."

"Of course," she added, "I planned to check on all the children each day after that. It was the first day back after the long holiday, so we were busy attending to all sorts of matters, and I didn't check that the children had actually done what they had been told to do."

They both agreed that this was probably not the problem, but that maybe Brigitta was sick or did not want to go to school.

Janet had planned to visit the family at the weekend but decided to bring her visit forward to the Friday evening. Zita opened the door to her and invited her in. After exchanging greetings, Janet told Zita that the teacher was concerned that Brigitta may be sick since she had not been back to school since the Monday.

Zita replied, "Brigitta is not going back to that school. It is not a good school. The teachers do not know how to make children behave. Brigitta was very naughty, the teacher did not punish her. She will stay at home with her grandmother."

Janet was again very surprised and asked what was it that Brigitta had done that was so bad.

Zita replied, "We gave Brigitta soap and a cloth to wash her face and hands before and after eating. She did not use them. This is very unclean and not correct. When I tell the teacher, and ask did she punish Brigitta for this, she said no, she did not know that she had not used the soap and cloth. Then she said not to worry, washing was not important, did not matter, many children did not wash before and after taking their lunch. This is a very bad thing for the teacher to say. It would not happen in Romania, when I was at school. My daughter must learn better ways. We will teach her at home."

Janet continued to see the family, and from time to time tried to get them to reconsider sending Brigitta to school, even if only to make friends with other children. Zita replies that Brigitta would be sent to school when she was certain her daughter would behave in a proper manner, even if others did not know how to. Brigitta eventually started school when she was 7.

Discussion Questions

1. Is culture an issue in this account? What reasons can you give to support your response? In relation to Janet? In relation to the Romanian family?
2. What values are highlighted in the story that could have a cultural basis? Why is it so important to the family for Brigitta to be the best dressed child at the school? Is it likely that cultural values influenced the way Brigitta was dressed to go to school, or were other factors more influential?
3. Does washing the face and hands before and after eating have particular cultural significance to Romanians? Is it the face and hand washing that is important or is something else behind this? Why are the family so upset by what happened at the school?
4. Why do you think the family eventually sent Brigitta to school when she was 7? Was it because she had learned to behave in a proper manner, or could there have been some other reason(s)?
5. Why do you think Janet continued to mention sending Brigitta to school when she went to visit the family? What would you have done if you had been in Janet's situation?

Skill Concepts: Social and Welfare Work

Introduction

Social welfare in one form or another has become a global phenomenon. In recent times countries throughout most parts of the world provide varying levels of training for welfare workers. The challenges faced by workers in this field are many and varied. One such challenge is associated with providing services that are accessible to those who most need them in societies that are becoming more and more structurally complex; another derives from the cultural and ethnic diversity evident in the populations of many societies. It is within this context that welfare workers must address what is probably their most immediate and professionally confronting challenge—delivering services that are culturally sensitive and appropriate to the needs of individuals and groups within their environment (Anagnostou & Cox, 1988).

Although the concept of welfare may mean different things to different people, a traditional view is that it means services provided for disadvantaged individuals and groups. Where such services exist they are provided by government instrumentalities, nongovernment charitable organizations, or a combination of both.

In a discussion of the "welfare state," Jamrozik and Boland (1988, p. ii) suggested that welfare has two distinct but interrelated functions. First, there is a maintenance function that ensures that dependent populations receive a minimum level of income (for example, those who are unemployed, supporting mothers, people whose level of disability precludes them from earning an income, and the aged). Second, there is a facilitative function, which provides such services as education, health, child care, and low-income housing. Jamrozik and Boland (1988), writing in the Australian context, indicated that problems of access and equity for migrants and minority groups in this country have been associated with the latter function.

However, the type and level of welfare provided are not the same in all societies. Both intra- and inter-society variations are evident in the nature and extent of such services, how they are provided, who or which organizations are responsible for delivering them, and how and by whom the services are funded. One factor that does appear to transcend societal variations is that human contact and human communication are essential elements in the process. Effectiveness in helping people from different cultural backgrounds, including migrants, refugees, and minority groups, to access welfare assistance appropriate to their needs requires an extensive knowledge of the system, interpersonal and intercultural communication competence, and networking skills to tap into community resources.

Shoroszewski (1984, p. 19) saw the greatest barrier to providing effective welfare services to these groups as the lack of confidence and feelings of inadequacy experienced by the service providers. Jamrozik and Boland (1988, p. 32) presented a somewhat different view of obstacles to effective service provision. Included in their list are language difficulties, insufficient information available in community languages, inadequate design of public contact areas, the complexity of the system, and in some instances, the low level of skill and authority among front-line service providers.

Clearly, some of these problems are structural and need to be addressed at the policy level. However, problems associated with the attitudes of staff and their levels of competence and confidence in dealing with individuals and groups whose culture is different from their own is best addressed through education and training. This training needs to be focused on intercultural sensitivity and intercultural communication skills relevant to welfare contexts.

Sanders (1977, p. 79) advocated adopting an international perspective "which is cross-cultural and involves a comparative approach" in professional training programs to prepare social workers to work in multicultural society. He and others who support this approach suggest that graduates from such programs would have an enhanced sensitivity and understanding of cultural differences within their own society, as well as in other societies. They would also be able to apply knowledge and skills differentially to resolve social welfare problems in different cultural contexts (Hokenstadt, 1984).

Key Concepts

A number of key concepts have been identified in cross-cultural and intercultural research that provide useful frameworks for understanding culturally based miscommunications and misunderstandings that give rise to difficulties in social welfare situations. Those that are most relevant to the exercises and case studies in this module are the culture-general framework (Brislin, Cushner, Cherrie, & Yong, 1986); theories of culture transition in migration (Cox, 1980; Huntington, 1981; Kovacs & Cropley, 1975; Oleszkiewicz & Foster, 1979); and acculturation (Berry, 1990).

The concept of cultural variability, in particular the individualism-collectivism dimension (Hofstede, 1980; see also R. Brislin's Chapter 5 on individualism and collectivism, this volume), high and low context communication (Gudykunst & Ting-Toomey, 1990; Hall, 1976), and variations in facework (Ting-Toomey, 1988) also provides useful insights.

Culture-General Framework

Brislin et al. (1986, p. 39) proposed that people who interact with others who have been socialized into a different culture are likely to have many common experiences, especially when that interaction takes place over an extended period of time. Based on an extensive review of the relevant literature, they identified core experiences reported in intercultural interactions. These they organized into three broad categories of themes that are concerned with: intense feelings or emotional responses people have to culturally different situations; misunderstanding and possible conflict due to differences in commonly discussed areas of knowledge; and culturally based differences in ways of organizing, responding to, and communicating information and in ascribing causes to events, human behaviors, and interpersonal interactions.

The three categories and their related 18 themes are listed below:

1. *Intense Feelings or Emotional Responses:* Anxiety; Disconfirmed expectancies; Belonging; Level of tolerance for ambiguity; Confrontation of one's own prejudices.

2. *Knowledge Areas:* Work; Time and space; Language; Roles; Individual vs. group allegiances; Rituals and superstitions; Hierarchies, class, and status; Values.

3. *Bases of Cultural Differences:* Categorization; Differentiation; Ingroup-outgroup distinction; Learning style; Attribution.

Although the 18 themes did not emerge from the welfare literature in particular, they encapsulate experiences common to the welfare context and provide a framework for developing a better understanding of culturally based issues in this field. The full range of themes cannot be discussed in this module (see Brislin et al., 1986), but those that are particularly relevant to the exercises and case studies will be described more fully.

Disconfirmed Expectancies

Looking ahead and generating ideas about what they will be doing in the future and how life will be for them is an activity all people engage in from time to time. In this way they set up expectancies about how things will be. If the reality matches or is better than the expectation, positive feelings are generated. However, often these expectancies are not met. When the time comes, "Things are not how they were meant to be." Brislin et al. (1986, p. 249) use the term *disconfirmed expectancies* to describe this phenomenon and suggest that when an individual has a very strong expectation about "how things will be," the individual is likely to see any deviation that occurs as greater than it is. Strong emotional reactions, for example, frustration, are often associated with disconfirmed expectancies.

Confronting One's Own Prejudices

Confronting one's own prejudices frequently elicits feelings of anxiety and negativity. Part of the process of being socialized into our cultural group involves learning to relate to those who are different from us with some degree of caution. In some instances we may have been strongly cautioned against, even punished for associating with, others who were very different. In welfare work it is possible that the client or the welfare worker may be confronted with their prejudices toward the other's cultural background, ethnicity, or religious affiliation. This interferes with their ability to deliver effective services. Participating in structured self-awareness exercises to explore attitudes toward others and the basis for these can provide a useful and relatively nonthreatening way of confronting one's prejudices.

Language

Language differences are an important consideration when attempting to engage in cross-cultural communication. These differences are often a major source of miscommunication and misunderstanding in welfare situations, where interpreters are not readily available. This theme also includes knowledge about government policy on languages and the attitude of government and private organizations toward other-language-speaking groups, toward making information available in the major community languages, and toward recruiting staff who are bilingual.

Pollak and McCarthy (1984, p. 8), writing from the Australian experience, cautioned that a person's ability to speak a second language does not mean that they necessarily are competent to translate or interpret. Competence in the skills required to fulfil these roles is a function of training and experience. Bates and Linder-Pelz (1990, p. 39), also writing in the Australian context, reported that prior to interpreter services being introduced into the health services, other migrants from the same-language-speaking group (for example, family members, hospital cleaning staff) were often asked to interpret. This practice frequently led to a breakdown in communication, with instructions being misinterpreted, misunderstood, and not carried out.

Roles

An individual's experience in his or her own culture allows the individual to make generalizations about role expectations, functions, and performances within that particular culture with a reasonable degree of accuracy. In another culture, all or many of the dimensions associated with a particular role or roles may be different. Differences in roles and role expectations can also be a cause of anxiety and may have a negative impact on the individual's sense of self-worth (Brislin et al., 1986, p. 281).

When people cross over into another culture, different expectation about role relationships can cause problems in family relationships, marital relationships, and relationships at work. Dimensions of role relationships (personalness, formality, hierarchy, and permitted deviation from role) have been identified. These appear useful ways of understanding the differences in role relationships across cultures (Gudykunst & Ting-Toomey, 1990).

Values

The values or internalized views people hold about areas of human interest —such as relationships, lifestyle, politics, and child rearing among others—are also a product of their socialization. Such views are taken as proper, appropriate, and not to be questioned in the particular cultural group. For the welfare worker, learning to understand the values deemed to be important by a particular cultural group is an essential step toward providing culturally sensitive and appropriate services to that group of people.

Attribution

People try to understand the world and the behavior of others by examining, exploring, and making causal connections between events in their lives and the interactions they have had with others (Esdaile & Madill, 1993). They base these causal connections on observations of others' behaviors and reflections about their own behavior. Judgments about the causes of behavior are called *attributions* (Brislin et al.,1986, p. 42). The information people draw on to make these attributions is arrived at within the context of a specific culture. It is less likely to provide an accurate basis for making judgments about behavior in another cultural context. Understanding the part played by culture in shaping the attributions people make and appreciating the different perceptions people may have of the same event or behavior are important aspects of effective intercultural communication.

Culture Transition in Migration

In the literature dealing with change, a number of risk factors have been linked to change associated with culture transition. Cox (1980) suggested that three main approaches have been adopted to the study of this phenomenon: psychological, sociological, and process-oriented. The psychological approach focuses on the way the person making the transition experiences adjusting to a new culture. Some of the risks identified by Cox are nostalgia, culture shock, marginality, culture tension, and culture strain.

Social environment also plays an important part in helping migrants make the transition to a new culture. The way migrants and refugees are received by members of the host society and the services available to assist them in making the transition are significant factors in their adjustment and resettlement. Another important factor appears to be linked to involvement in the local ethnic community and the attitudes that community has toward the host culture (Pollak & McCarthy, 1984, p. 21).

Research reported by a number of other investigators points to still other factors that are important considerations in the process of adaptation and resettlement. Huntington (1981) discussed loss and grief as major risk factors in culture transition and emphasized the need for migrants and refugees to work through the grieving process. The need to make a gradual separation from the past, and the potential for strategies based on multicultural concepts to be used to assist this process has been discussed in Kovacs and Cropley (1975). Loss of self-image has also been identified as a major risk factor that migrants and refugees experience (Oleszkiewicz & Foster, 1979).

Clearly, those working in the field of social welfare need to be sensitive to these factors and to develop culturally appropriate ways to assist their migrant and refugee clients to minimize the threat these factors pose to their successful adaptation.

Acculturation

Berry (1990, pp. 242-252) used the term "psychological acculturation" as the framework for discussing the adaptations individuals make when they move across cultures. He distinguishes between acculturation, which denotes culture change at the societal level, and psychological acculturation, which describes change at the level of the individual.

Certain key elements in the framework presented by Berry provide useful ways to gain further understanding of intercultural interactions that occur in situations that involve culture contact and culture change. The concepts from this framework that are most applicable to the content of this module are: voluntariness of contact, acculturation attitudes, and acculturative stress. Within this module it is possible to give only a brief explanation of these concepts.

Voluntariness of Contact

Berry distinguishes between five groups who experience acculturation: ethnic groups, native peoples, immigrants, refugees, and sojourners. The distinction is based on the degree to which the culture contact is voluntary, the amount of movement involved, and the degree of permanence. He proposes that people who voluntarily choose to move across cultures (migrants) are less likely to experience difficulties in adjusting than people who have been coerced or forced into the acculturation process (refugees, native peoples). He also suggests that temporary residents (sojourners) may experience more health problems than permanent residents (ethnic groups) as they do not have the same supports.

Acculturation Attitudes

This refers to the attitudes individuals and groups within a particular culture hold toward individuals and groups from another culture and the effect of such attitudes on the ways they choose to relate to each other. Berry uses a "dominant culture–acculturating culture" scenario to develop a conceptual framework that illustrates the relationship between acculturation attitudes and acculturation strategies.

He proposes that a central issue for the individual crossing over into another culture is the degree to which the individual wants to hold on to the old culture or to relinquish it and become part of the host culture. Other factors that come into play are: the extent of contact the individual wants to retain with the individual's own group and the extent to which the individual wants to seek out new contacts in the dominant culture, and the degree of freedom the acculturating group has to make its own decisions on these matters.

The conceptual framework suggests that an individual who strives to hold onto the old culture and seeks social contact only with members of that culture has adopted a separationist strategy to cope with contact with the other culture. Alternatively, the person who relinquishes his or her old identity and cultural ways and seeks interaction only with members of the dominant culture is described as "following the assimilation track."

Should the individual choose to hold on to aspects of the old culture and to interact with members of the dominant culture, the individual is said to be "using an integrationist strategy." Marginalization occurs when the individual has little or no interest in maintaining connections with either culture.

However, the degree of freedom individuals or groups have to select their own strategy is moderated by the current government's political ideology and policy decisions. These also reflect commitment to specific attitudes and strategies that may or may not be in concert with the individual's attitudes and preferred strategy.

Acculturative Stress

This term is used to describe behaviors associated with stress that are known to relate to the individual's experience of the acculturation process. Berry emphasizes that culture change does not always generate stress and in many instances can be a positive experience. However, research suggests that there is a relationship between mode of acculturation and level of stress; for example, people who feel marginalized or who pursue a separationist track report higher levels of stress than those who adopt integrationist and assimilationist strategies (Berry & Kim, cited in Berry, 1990, p. 249).

Among other factors that have been linked to acculturative stress in the research are the attitudes and policies relating to culture that prevail in the dominant society and the extent to which existing policies exclude or provide only reduced access to resources and limited participation; the availability of social supports and social networks; and the level of acceptance shown toward the acculturating group by the dominant group (Berry, 1990, p. 250).

Cultural Variability

The Individualism-Collectivism Dimension. Only those aspects of individualism-collectivism that are specifically relevant to the case studies in this module will be discussed in this section. The topic is covered in greater depth in the module authored by Goodman, Chapter 3 in this book.

The term *individualism-collectivism* incorporates a "cluster of attitudes, beliefs and behaviors toward a wide variety of people" (Hui & Triandis, 1986, p. 240). This cluster contributes to an explanation of some of the major differences across cultures.

At the level of generality this dimension refers to the extent to which the goals of the individual or the collective goals of the group take precedence in a cultural group (Gudykunst & Ting-Toomey, 1990, p. 40). Within this general framework, specific aspects have been identified that provide useful guidelines for recognizing and understanding the basis of some culturally based differences that occur in situations involving contact between people from different cultural groups (Brislin, Chapter 5, in this book; Hofstede,1980).

Facework and Saving Face. Although "saving face" has been linked mainly to the behavior of people from Eastern cultures, the concept of *facework* is common to all cultures (Gudykunst & Ting-Toomey, 1990, p. 84). Face is the public "self-image" people present when relating to others. Symbolically it represents the self the individual wants others to see. Although people in all societies engage in facework to present a particular image of themselves in public, the values that support these particular behaviors, the rules that govern facework, and the meanings ascribed to various patterns of facework may differ across cultures. This leads to misinterpretation and misunderstandings in intercultural communications.

Gudykunst and Ting-Toomey refer to "the authentic self" and the "social self" and suggest that cultural values and beliefs about the concept of self influence the image of self a person chooses to present in public. The individualism-collectivism dimension provides insights into some aspects of facework in the public presentation of self in different cultures.

In individualist cultures, such as Australia and the United States, value is placed on maintaining consistency between the public self and the inner private self (Gudykunst & Ting-Toomey, 1990, p. 85). Greater value is placed on the inner self with an emphasis on bringing one's feelings and beliefs to the attention of others. Within these and other individualist cultures, this is sometimes referred to as being "authentic and straightforward" or "putting your real self forward."

Alternatively, the self in collectivist cultures (Indonesia and Thailand, for example) is relationship based and intricately connected to other members of the group. It could be said that the self is defined in relation to others and that the public presentation of self is shaped by established patterns and sets of prescribed mutual obligations.

In collectivist cultures, one of the functions of facework is to assist others to maintain the appropriate public image of self while at the same time ensuring that one's own public self does not lose in the process. To suffer a loss of face is a serious matter that brings shame to oneself and to one's family in many collectivist cultures.

In societies that include both collectivists and individualists, welfare workers need to be attuned to the underpinning values that support the presentation of the public self from both individualist and collectivist perspectives. Effective welfare work requires a sensitivity to possible situations that could cause a client to lose face and an awareness of the cultural basis for the strategies and processes the client uses to present and maintain face. Within collectivist cultures, an indirect mode of communication is more likely to be the preferred mode. It is considered more polite and less likely to lead to confrontation and embarrassment. In cultures based on individualistic values, the preferred mode of communication is direct. Communications that are indirect or require the recipient to infer what is meant may be regarded with suspicion or considered to be a waste of time.

Low- and High-Context Communication. Low-context communication describes a communication mode in which the message to be communicated is contained primarily within the explicit statement and/or behavior of the person or persons sending the message. This mode of communication tends to be more closely linked to individualistic cultures, whereas high-context communication more accurately describes the communication mode adopted in collectivist cultures (Gudykunst & Ting-Toomey, 1990, p. 44). High-context communication requires much more of the person receiving the message. Much of the information the person is seeking to transmit lies in the physical context or within the person themselves. Very little is communicated directly and much is inferred and ambiguous (Hall, 1976).

A comparative analysis of key constructs of face across individualistic low-context cultures and collectivist high-context cultures has been undertaken by Ting-Toomey (1988). The summary table (Gudykunst & Ting-Toomey, 1990, p. 93) provides an excellent reference for exploring constructs associated with the concept of face in the case studies in this module.

Skill Applications

The three case studies and their related discussion questions present many opportunities for the application of skills related to the concepts discussed in

Part III. One way of implementing skill training is to use some techniques borrowed from psychodrama. One of these is role play.

Role Play

Role play is a derivative of psychodrama (Moreno, 1977) that has been used extensively in education and training as well as in therapy. As an education and training tool, role play is problem-oriented and focused on working out alternate and more effective approaches to a general problem. The technique has been used successfully to teach interpersonal communication skills, to explore themes common to particular groups, to develop alternate strategies for resolving problems, and to attempt to bring about attitude change (Mullavey-O'Byrne, 1987).

Role Play in Training for Intercultural Skills. All human beings have role-taking ability. They use this ability to interact with others in daily life situations. However, it must be remembered that the patterned sequence of interactions associated with different roles in societies and the behaviors considered appropriate to those roles in various situations vary within and across cultures. What may be appropriate in one cultural context may be inappropriate in another. This has both advantages and disadvantages for using the technique to train for intercultural skills. Trainers who are sensitive to these differences and appreciate the diversity that may be present in a training group should find role play a very useful strategy, if they adopt a few basic guidelines.

Basic Guidelines for Using Role Play in Training. The group leader (trainer) is responsible for keeping the role play and the discussion that follows focused on aspects of the situation that would be common to most similar situations. It is counterproductive to the goals of the training session to allow the discussion to move to a deep emotional level or to focus on a particular person in the group.

Participants in a training group need some preparation prior to taking on a part in a role play. This may take the form of *role cards* with specific instructions about the character they will play and the behaviors expected of them in the role. The trainer or the person who prepared the role play scenario may also choose to model the role(s) and/or coach the players in their roles to ensure that the roles they play reflect the goals of the training session.

The amount of time required for a role play will vary in relation to the degree of enthusiasm and confidence the trainer has with using the method, the skill of the players and their level of involvement in playing the roles, and the level of interest shown by the other members of the group.

At the end of the role play and before the discussion, the trainer or group leader should ensure that those who were involved in playing roles are debriefed. Debriefing is an integral part of these techniques and the responsibility of the trainer/group leader. Debriefing involves addressing the person by her or his name in real life and asking the person to talk about the following:

- Their experience in the role they played
- Insights they may have had about the problem from the perspective of the role they were playing
- Skills they became aware of using
- Skills they saw others using
- Problems that evolved during the role play/sociodrama
- Alternate strategies they could have adopted

Instructions and Suggestions for Trainers

- Begin the preparations for the role play by checking whether participants recall the particular case from the earlier discussions. They may need to be reminded about the key concepts and the themes, if the role play is not scheduled for the same day.
- Provide all participants with information about the setting. This could be as an overhead or given to each participant as a handout.
- Encourage participants to nominate members of the group to play the designated roles. Alternatively ask for volunteers.
- When the two players have been identified, give each the role card that describes the appropriate role. Do not allow them to see each other's role card. Members of the audience should not view the role cards either.
- Allow about 5 minutes for the players to prepare their roles, without consulting each other.
- Consult the players about the way they want to set up the scene (table, chairs, etc.).
- Signal when to start the role play.
- Prompt the players if they are having difficulty staying in role or keeping the action going until there is some substance for discussion. Watch for the appropriate time to make a closure.
- After the role play has finished, invite the people who played the roles to comment on their experience before opening up the discussion to the group.
- At all times, guide the discussion toward the main themes and issues associated with contact between cultures that are likely to be found in similar situations in social welfare.

Applying the Skill Concepts Through Role Play

Each of the three case studies contains themes that can form the basis for role plays focused on developing intercultural sensitivity and acquiring some of the skills associated with effective intercultural communication.

In this section, suggestions are made about possible scenarios that could provide the situational and relational contexts in which participants acquire and develop these skills.

Suggestions Relevant to Case Study 1: The Escribanos

The main themes touched on in this case study are aspects of culture transition in migration (for example, culture shock and culture tension), disconfirmed expectancies, and cultural differences in values and attitudes toward roles and role relationships.

The outline for the role play that follows is an example of one way to organize a role play using the themes in the Escribanos' story. The role play focuses on (1) developing sensitivity to the risk factors associated with the early stages of adapting to a new culture, (2) developing an understanding of the impact differences in cultural values can have on interactions and relationships in welfare situations, and (3) exploring ways of communicating with sensitivity.

Setting

The dialogue takes place in a meeting between Mercedes and Juanita, one of the other welfare workers at the center. It is the day after Mercedes' interview with the Escribanos. Mercedes is concerned about the Escribanos and has decided she needs to clarify some aspects of yesterday's interview and seek advice about future management of the Escribanos' problems. She has asked one of her colleagues, Juanita, to meet with her to discuss her concerns about the case.

Role Card: Mercedes

You are feeling concerned about the Escribanos and believe that you did not have a satisfactory interview with them. You were surprised that Jesus responded in the way he did when you spoke about applying for unemployment benefits. You find it difficult to understand why he seemed so offended and rejected something he is entitled to since he is out of work. You understand that he is angry because he cannot work as an accountant unless he completes further studies. Although you understand that he was upset that Maria was offered work when he couldn't get a job, you feel that it would be sensible if she did go to work, even if only until Jesus found a job. You also think about the "skills she is wasting," which she could be using to reduce the stressful situation they are in.

Your goal in talking with Juanita is to gain some insights into the reasons for your unease about the interview and to discuss strategies you could use to be more effective in helping the Escribanos.

Role Card: Juanita

You arrived from Brazil 3 years ago with your husband and 4-year-old son. The family had planned to emigrate and you had managed to save a little money to help you get started. In Brazil you had been an English teacher before you married. Since your arrival you have completed a certificate course in welfare on a part-time basis. You feel you have gained a great deal of knowledge from the welfare course and now have a much better understanding of the process you went through as a migrant and thus are well qualified to help your clients.

Your husband owns a one-third share in a taxi cab and is happy that he is in a business, as he had a small business in Brazil. He regards the part-time work you do as "good" because it is helping others, not real work. He is the breadwinner in the family and you support him in that role.

You enjoy your work and have good working relationships with Mercedes and the other welfare worker. However, you feel that sometimes Mercedes could be more sensitive to her clients, attentive to what they are not saying as well as what they are saying. Although she comes from a Portuguese family, you feel she is impatient with some of the old ways and beliefs, although she takes pride in identifying herself as Portuguese Australian.

Your goals for the discussion are to help Mercedes identify the source of her unease and to encourage her to explore her own attitudes and their possible impact on the situation with the Escribanos.

Suggestions Relevant to Case Study 2: Brigitta

The main themes that are addressed in this case study are roles and role expectations, child rearing practices, and attribution.

The outline for the role play that follows focuses primarily, although not exclusively, on the part played by the attribution in the miscommunication and misunderstanding between Zita Szabas and the teacher.

Background Notes

Brigitta and her family are refugees from Romania. They escaped at the time of the overthrow of the Communist regime in that country. They spent several months in a refugee camp before they were granted asylum in Australia. We know little about their lives except that their country of origin is believed to have operated under a corrupt and oppressive regime. Life in refugee camps also has its problems. People living in these circumstances face all the health problems associated with overcrowding, for example, poor sanitation and hygiene. Factors such as fear of violence, involuntary repatriation, and anxieties about the uncertain future contribute to the mental stresses they must cope with on a day-to-day basis.

Setting

The setting for this role play is the school on the day after Brigitta enrolled. Brigitta's class teacher, Catherine Blair, is in the classroom setting up for today's class. Zita Szabas knocks at the door. Catherine welcomes her and invites her to come in and sit down. She does so. Catherine decides that there must be a problem because Brigitta is not with her mother. She enquires if Brigitta is ill or is unhappy about coming to school.

From here on the role play follows the conversations reported to Janet by Zita Szabas and the teacher in the case study. Additional information for those playing the roles is supplied in the role cards.

Special Instructions

The group members who take the roles should be comfortable with role playing and well briefed on the expectations for the roles they will take. It would be appropriate for the players to prepare their roles in advance and to consult with each other about the conversation they will have. However, it would detract from the learning experience if they were to share the inner thoughts associated with their respective roles.

Role Card: Catherine

You are surprised to see Mrs. Szabas Junior, as Brigitta appeared well and happy at school yesterday. You are aware that the Szabas family are refugees from Romania and have great admiration and respect for them because of the hardships they have lived through.

Your initial impressions of Brigitta are that she is very well behaved, pleasant, and attentive, but maybe a little scared about the new environment. You feel that is quite natural, because many children are scared on their first day. You expect this would be more so for Brigitta, because this must all be very strange to her and she does not know many words in the English language.

When Brigitta's mother tells you about the face cloth and soap and asks whether you punished Brigitta, your initial response is to think that Zita Szabas is upset because she believes you punished Brigitta. You hasten to reassure her that you did not punish her. However, Zita's reply to you causes you to decide that she believes that you should have punished Brigitta. At this stage you wonder if Zita is embarrassed because she believes you may think she has not trained her daughter properly. You decide to ease her embarrassment by telling her that other children also forget, that you are not really bothered by what happened, and that she should not fuss about it.

The bell rings for school to start. You explain you must go to collect your class. You thank Zita for coming to see you and invite her to come again. Zita still appears a little upset, but you feel you have done your best to explain and believe that she will think about what you said and understand. You have given her the option to come to see you at any time. You tell her that you expect to see Brigitta in class later in the morning. She says Brigitta will not be coming later as she has a chill. You feel a little uneasy and uncertain about what is really going on but believe that Zita is reasonably satisfied with your explanations and that Brigitta will be back at school, if not that day, then the next day. You think it must be difficult for the family to be separated after all they have been through and decide to let them take their time.

Your goal in the role play is to try to show Zita Szabas that you understand, to reassure her that this is not a big problem and that she should not be worried that it happened.

Role Card: Zita Szabas

You are very distressed about Brigitta's lack of hygiene—you have carefully explained to her the importance of washing hands after going to the toilet and before and after eating. Brigitta knows that if you do not do this you will get sick. She has disobeyed you. This disobedience is a serious matter; if she does not obey at school, the family will also have problems.

You go to see the teacher to talk about this matter. You are very surprised when the teacher says she did not punish Brigitta and amazed when she tells you it does not matter that Brigitta did not wash her hands. You do not understand this way of thinking. There is something quite wrong when there are no rules to prevent the children becoming sick. You decide that you must protect your daughter by first teaching her to be obedient at home. This is how she will learn not to be in trouble at the school and to keep from being sick. However you feel you must think about how you can do this, so you are cautious and tell the teacher that Brigitta has a chill.

Your goal in the role play is to check out whether this school has good hygiene and whether the teachers make the children obey the school rules. You are very concerned about cleanliness and obedience and expect the teachers to check that the children wash their hands and to punish the children if they disobey. You want the teacher to know this. However, your goal is also to maintain a cordial relationship and not put yourself in a vulnerable situation.

Field Exercise

Self Assessment Follow-Up

In the Self-Assessment Exercise in Part I, you asked yourself questions about satisfaction with your contribution to providing services to clients whose cultural/ethnic background was different from yours. You also formulated a set of personal goals you were hoping to achieve through participating in the module. The exercise has a number of useful applications.

First, to assist you review the extent to which you perceive you achieved the goals you set for yourself at the outset of the module.

- Review your goals and estimate your percentage of achievement—80%? 95%? 40%? What were the positives in the experience ? What were the negatives?

Second, to help you refocus your attention on the reason you have participated in the training module. This is, of course, to enhance your ability to provide culturally sensitive and appropriate welfare services to your clients.

- Review the notes you made when you completed the self-assessment form initially. Do you have any perception of positive changes in your level of knowledge? level of skill? attitudes? If your response is affirmative, note the changes you perceive. If you are not aware of any changes, indicate why you think this is so.

Third, and most important, to provide you with a tool to use in your everyday work situation that will contribute to your ongoing personal and professional development.

- Use the self-assessment form as a tool for regular ongoing review of your work with clients. The questions will help you identify areas of strength you may wish to enhance and areas of weakness you will want to address. The form provides a basis for peer review sessions, for mentor relationships, and for determining staff development needs.

References

Anagnostou, P., & Cox, D. (1988). *The education and training of social and welfare workers for a multicultural society*. Policy Options Paper, Department of the Prime Minister and Cabinet. Canberra , Australia.

Bates, E., & Linder-Pelz, S. (1990). *Health care issues* (2nd ed.). Sydney: Allen & Unwin.

Berry, J. W. (1990). Psychology of acculturation: Understanding individuals moving between cultures. In R. Brislin (Ed.), *Applied cross-cultural psychology* (pp. 232-253). Newbury Park, CA: Sage.

Berry, J. W., & Kim, U. (1988). Acculturation and mental health. In P. Dansen, J. W. Berry, & N. Sartorious (Eds.), *Health and cross-cultural psychology* (pp. 207-236). London: Sage.

Brislin, R., Cushner, K., Cherrie, C., & Yong, M. (1986). *Intercultural interactions: A practical guide*. Newbury Park, CA: Sage.

Cox, D. (1980). *Migration and integration in the Australian context*. Melbourne: University of Melbourne, Department of Legal Studies.

Esdaile, S. A., & Madill, H. D. (1993, March). L'attribution de causes aux evenements considerations theoriques et leurs applications theoriques et leurs applications a l'enseignment et a la pratique de l'ergotherapie. *Acta Ergotherapeutic Belgica*.

Gudykunst, W., & Ting-Toomey, S. (1990). *Culture and interpersonal communication*. Newbury Park, CA: Sage.

Hall, E. T. (1976). *Beyond culture*. New York: Doubleday.

Hofstede, G. (1980). *Culture's consequences: International differences in work related values*. Beverly Hills, CA: Sage.

Hokenstadt, C. M. (1984). Curriculum directions in the 1980's: Implications of the new policy statement. *Journal of Education for Social Work, 20*, 15-22.

Hui, C., & Triandis, H. (1986). Individualism-collectivism: A study of cross-cultural researchers. *Journal of Cross-Cultural Psychology, 17*, 225-248.

Huntington, J. (1981). *Migration as part of life experience*. Paper presented at the Seminar in Cross Cultural Therapy, N.S.W. Institute of Psychiatry, Sydney, Australia.

Jamrozik, A., & Boland, C. (1988). *Social welfare policy for a multicultural society*. Policy Options Paper, Department of the Prime Minister and Cabinet. Canberra, Australia.

Kovacs, M., & Cropley, A. (1975). *Immigrants and society: Alienation and the assimilation of immigrants*. Sydney: McGraw-Hill.

Moreno, J. L. (1977). *Psychodrama* (vol. 1, 4th ed.). New York: Beacon House.

Mullavey-O'Byrne, C. (1987). *A study of empathy training with occupational therapy students*. Unpublished master's honors thesis, Macquarie University, Sydney, Australia.

Oleszkiewicz, E., & Foster, S. (1979). *The emigration process: Why immigrants and the majority population so seldom meet*. Fourth Seminar on Adaptation and Integration of Permanent Immigrants. Paper No. INF/HQ20634/79. Geneva: Intergovernmental Committee for European Migration.

Pollak, L., & McCarthy, M. (Eds.). (1984). *Options for practice: A book of readings in migrant health*. Sydney, Australia: Department of Health, N.S.W.

Sanders, D. S. (1977). Developing a graduate social work curriculum with an international cross-cultural perspective. *Journal of Education for Social Work, 13*, 76-83.

Shoroszewski, N. (1984). A model for social welfare practice—Interpreting the migration process. In L. Pollak & M. McCarthy (Eds.), *Options for practice: A book of readings in migrant health*. Sydney, Australia: Department of Health, N.S.W.

Ting-Toomey, S. (1988). A face negotiating theory. In Y. Kim & W. Gudykunst (Eds.), *Theory in intercultural communication*. Newbury Park, CA: Sage.

12 Multicultural Counseling

PAUL PEDERSEN

If counseling, as a profession, is to receive acceptance from the culturally different, it must demonstrate, in no uncertain terms, its good faith and ability to contribute to the betterment of the group's quality of life.
Derald Wing Sue and David Sue (1990)

In addition to providing a broad definition of multicultural counseling, this module provides readers with an opportunity to examine the nature of counseling along with the various controversies surrounding the necessity or appropriateness of counseling culturally different others. When counseling someone from a different culture, one of the biggest barriers we face is that we are unable to make accurate attributions. Many counselors dream of being able to read into the client's mind. The Triad Model approach enables that dream to partially come true. One of the most important points Pedersen makes is the need to examine our biases as well as the biases that are inherent to counseling as a field of study. He emphasizes the need for us to recognize that it is sometimes the system that needs to change, not the client.

Contents

Self-Assessment Exercise

To assess your own current comprehension of multicultural counseling, review the following list of essay test questions. Grade yourself according to how well you think you could answer each question if required to do so. An A grade means you believe you could give an accurate, comprehensive, and complete answer to the question. A B grade means you could give a fairly good answer to the question. A C means you could give an adequate answer to the question. A D means your answer would be inadequate. An F means you would not know where to begin in trying to answer the question. Read each question carefully and then write your grade after each question.

1. What are the ways that cultural differences between a counselor and a counselee affect counseling?
2. How serious is the implicit cultural bias among counselors and counselor training programs?
3. How can counselors evaluate their own implicit cultural bias?
4. How could counselors be better trained to work in a multicultural population?
5. How do psychological problems vary with the culture of the clients?
6. Why are some methods better than others in working with persons from other cultures?
7. How can we learn from other cultures in sharpening our own skills as counselors?
8. Is *counseling* itself, as a product of Westernized, developed cultures, culturally encapsulated?
9. Can we assume that all counseling is to some extent "multicultural?"
10. What are the dangers of cultural encapsulation for a counselor?
11. To what extent is counseling a means of social control and oppression by the comfortable over the distressed?
12. To what extent is a counselor committed to "changing" the environment and not merely helping a client adjust?
13. What is the evidence that professional counselors are culturally conditioned in their responses?
14. What are the characteristics of "cultural encapsulation" among counselors?
15. What are some of the barriers to accurate communication across cultures?
16. What are some of the ways that Westernized systems of counseling might be biased or irrelevant elsewhere?
17. What are some of the ways Western psychology and non-Western cultures might view counseling differently?
18. Is the person who claims to be "healthy" to be considered healthy by his or her own definition?
19. What are some ways a counselor education program could become more sensitive to multicultural client populations?
20. When you are counseling in an unfamiliar culture, do you use your own or the host culture methods?

Be sure that you have graded each question according to how well you think you could answer it. For every A grade give yourself 3 points, B grade 2 points, C grade 1 point, D grade 0 points, and F grade –1 point. Add up your score for the self-assessment test and divide that total score by 30 to get your grade point average.

You will have noticed that some of these questions are very difficult to answer. Although some questions could be answered with a yes or no, the choice of answer would require considerable explanation. You should not feel embarrassed by finding your score lower than you had expected. Some of the above questions will be answered later in this unit.

Case Study Transcripts: The Triad Model

When counseling clients who are culturally different, you may not understand why the client is behaving in one way or another. The counselor may perceive accurately that something is wrong and yet be unable to grasp the precise problem. At that time, the counselor may well wish that he or she could read the client's mind to really hear what the client is thinking but not saying. This *Triad Model* is an attempt to train counselors to hear the positive (procounselor) and negative (anticounselor) internal dialogue of a culturally different client in a four-way role-played interview. The objective of this role play is for counselors to obtain direct and immediate feedback about the culturally different client's internal dialogue in response to the counseling experience.

The task of the procounselor is to articulate the positive messages a client might be thinking but not saying. The task of the anticounselor is to articulate the negative messages a client might be thinking but not saying. The procounselor and anticounselor may be speaking at the same time that the counselor or client is speaking, to simulate the client's ongoing internal dialogue.

The Triad Model is a training tool and should not be used in an actual counseling session. The simulation is intended to help counselors make culturally appropriate attributions about the culturally different client in a safe setting. Practice with different sets of culturally different clients-procounselors-anticounselors are intended to sharpen the counselor's perception of her or his own biases in culturally different situations.

It is important to include both a procounselor and an anticounselor so that both positive and negative messages in the client's internal dialogue are attended to. If only an anticounselor is used, the counselor may feel "ganged up" on and respond defensively and inappropriately.

The following case examples will be presented in the form of a brief introduction followed by a counseling transcript. These transcripts can be useful in training by dividing counselor trainees into groups of four persons and assigning each person one of the four roles: counselor, client, anticounselor, or procounselor. Each person will read his or her part exactly as scripted on a first reading. In a second reading, the four persons will be encouraged to expand on the script for their roles and include some of their own comments. In a third reading, the four persons will be encouraged to discard the script entirely and follow the same general interview format using their own words entirely. Following the reading of the transcript, you will be asked to write in (1) the positive thoughts you think the client might have been thinking regarding the interview and (2) the negative thoughts you think the client might have been thinking regarding the interview.

In our attempt to understand the complexity of multiculturalism, we develop simplified models that can be explained and understood but that use only selected aspects of reality. It is easier to construct these simplified models of complex reality than to deal with the complexity of a real world. The danger is that we confuse the models or labels with reality and become "encapsulated" in our own private reality.

An alternative perspective is to treat complexity as our friend rather than our enemy. Complexity protects us from our own reductionistic assumptions. People who can manage more complexity will be able to see many different dimensions, classifications, theories, or alternatives to explain a situation. Because multicultural reality is inherently complex, those who are multidimensional will be more likely to identify appropriate responses. This model of multicultural counseling will seek to preserve the complexity of culture through a simulation of the complicating factors.

Incident 1: An "Independent" Mother's Career Choice

In this interview, a black male counselor interviews a Caucasian female client. The *salient* culture relates more to gender than to ethnicity, however. She has come to the counselor complaining of physical symptoms following the birth of her baby, her dissatisfaction with the help she has received from medical doctors, and lack of support from her husband. The problem unfolds to include more than just her physical health. The interview includes four persons: the counselor, the client, the anticounselor, and the procounselor. The anticounselor's task is to articulate the negative aspect of the client's internal dialogue. The procounselor's task is to articulate the positive aspect of the client's internal dialogue. The counselor and client are actually able to hear everything the anticounselor and procounselors say in the interview and are free to respond accordingly.

Counselor: Maybe I can help you out?
Client: Well, you know, I don't know. I really don't know.
Anticounselor: I doubt it. I don't think so.
Client: I went and saw my doctor and he said, you see, I've had all these terrible headaches and my stomach's been hurting me and I've just been

bleeding. But I guess you don't understand about that, I had a baby and I've been bleeding since then. And I just feel lousy and he said there's no . . .

Procounselor: Focus on her feelings.

Anticounselor: How can he understand you? He can't understand you. He's a man first of all. He's not going to support you. He's not going to understand what you're going through. He'll just side with your husband.

Counselor: O.K. I think it's pretty evident that I'm a man and I'm a male counselor, but possibly I've had some experience working with women and, well, first of all, how long ago did you have the baby?

Procounselor: He understands your concern about seeing a male counselor.

Client: Well, the baby's 6 months old and I've just been really feeling rotten. And I want to get back to work is what I want to do. And I've told my husband. I used to work down the street, you know, in that interior design shop.

Counselor: Ummm.

Client: And he says no, you know, your job is to be home with your baby. And I've just been feeling terrible and I just can't do anything at home and the bleeding doesn't stop and the doctor tells me there's nothing wrong with me. Now, how can there not be anything wrong with me, if I've been bleeding for 6 months?

Procounselor: The counselor's on your side not the doctor's side.

Counselor: I agree with you. I would think that there's some type of problem.

Client: (Sigh)

Anticounselor: It's so frustrating!

Counselor: Is he choosing just to ignore that physical problem that you have . . . the doctor?

Procounselor: The counselor's on your side.

Client: Well, he says I'm all up tight and I'm nervous and . . . and . . . I just don't feel good. Every day when I get up and I get these terrible headaches.

Anticounselor: It's so terrible when every man you go to keeps telling you it's your problem, it's your fault, you know? There's something wrong with you. They don't understand the issues.

Counselor: Has the doctor offered any type of advice concerning the bleeding or relationship with your husband?

Client: No. He just told me that I should go see a shrink and I didn't want to see a shrink. I used to volunteer down here at your Community Center and I knew there were counselors around so I thought I'd at least start with you. I don't know if anyone can help me or not.

Procounselor: He's going to help you, not patronize you.

Counselor: What do you feel is your main problem; containing, what is it, the bleeding or your relationship with your husband or you want to go back to work right now . . .

Anticounselor: You can't separate the problems. It's everything. Everything's interrelated. How can you just separate one from the other?

Client: That's right. They're all there. I just don't feel good and I want to go back to work. I think if I go back to work, that I'll feel better. I'll have more energy. If I'm so nervous at home around the baby, and then you know, maybe I should go back to work.

Counselor: Let's say if you did go back to work, what would happen with the child? Have you made arrangements for a day care center?

Anticounselor: See, right away just like what your husband said. What would happen to the child? What would happen to the child? But nobody asks you how it feels to be home all day long by yourself, caring for the child and letting your career go down the drain.

Procounselor: Give him some time to learn more background so he can really help you do the right thing.

Client: You know, I know we can . . . If I go back to work then I could take the baby to the baby-sitter, you know. I just feel so lousy (starts to cry).

Counselor: Is this your first child?

Client: No. I have one that's 11 and he's in school.

Counselor: O.K. Ummm (pause). Is there any more information you'd like to relate? Maybe something else that's . . .

Client: What am I going to say to my husband? You know, I need to go back. I want to go back to work. Maybe I'll feel better if I go back to work. Maybe the bleeding will stop.

Counselor: You said this already to your husband. What has . . . what has he said to that?

Procounselor: Focus more on her feelings and less on content.

Client: He says my job is to be at home. You know? Here's his . . . I wanted this little baby, and I should be at home.

Counselor: O.K. Do you have arguments about this all the time? Or is this the first one?

Client: Well, I brought it up about 6 weeks ago and he said absolutely not. So then . . . then I just really feel lousier and so I finally went to a doctor and then he told me there was really nothing wrong with me, you know? Except for nerves and that I should talk to somebody.

Procounselor: You must trust this counselor a lot to be so open with him about your feelings.

Counselor: So you feel like you should be going . . . You would like to go back to work. You feel that you're able to. Um . . . You've expressed to your husband that you can get a baby-sitter. So there's no problem there. Am I correct? I'm just trying to feedback what . . .

Client: Yes. Yes.

Counselor: O.K. So you're ready to go back to work. You feel like you're physically able to go back to work. Your husband doesn't feel like you're able to go back to work.

Client: He says that I shouldn't be working. That isn't my role. That I should be at home taking care of my child.

Counselor: And your response to that is . . .

Anticounselor: Listen to him? He's just asking question after question and trying to put it in ah, you know, put this in one pigeon hole and something else in another pigeon hole. He's missing the feeling. He doesn't know what you're feeling.

Counselor: Well, the feeling I have so far . . .

Anticounselor: Ask him what he would say to his wife!

Procounselor: Focus on her problem. Give her some specific suggestions.

Counselor: The feeling that I have so far is that you desire to have some type of occupation outside of the house. You've been in the house for awhile and you want to get out into the working world. Your husband is against that move and you're for it. So there's some kind of an impasse right there. You're for it and he's against it. So you feel like maybe you're caught in the middle? And the doctor, he's not giving you much help either with the bleeding and all. So you feel like you're caught in the middle.

Discussion Questions

1. What positive thoughts is the client thinking but not saying?
2. What negative thoughts is the client thinking but not saying?
3. What would you have done differently if you had been the counselor?

Critical Incident 2: An Indochinese Refugee

Refugees present very special problems and complications for multicultural counseling. In addition to the many differences in cultural patterns there is frequently much trauma and stress attached to previous experiences. It is difficult to identify the complex and dynamic cultural salience as the topic changes from one aspect to another. This interview includes four persons, a Caucasian male counselor, an Asian-American male anticounselor, an Asian-American male procounselor, and an Asian-American male client. Each of the four persons is able to hear and respond to the others during the interview.

Counselor: Well, good afternoon, Bruce. What can I do for you today?

Procounselor: Just relax and tell him what's troubling you.

Client: Well, ah . . . Lately . . . First of all, let me tell you, I am a refugee from Indochina, and I have been here for quite a while. Now, when I was back in my country I had a good job in the government and I was a head of household. But, due to the political situation, changes, I fled to the United States. When I got here, I was very happy. I was ready to start my life all over again. But, very soon after my arrival, I found out that I was not able to do anything that I was thinking about. And, this due to the lack of knowledge of language and I think that is the main thing. I cannot communicate with other people, so, but I look for job, you know, nobody will hire me. Not only that, but I came here alone, and I left all my . . . ah . . . member of my families back in my country, and once in a while I will receive some letters or . . . Very sad, and I very worried about them, and at the same time I am very worried about myself. I really do not know what to do. I don't know where to start.

Counselor: O.K., so you have two problems. One of them is your family. Is all your family still back . . .

Client: Yes, they are still back there.

Anticounselor: I don't know if he can help you. He's not from our culture.

Client: Well, I . . .

Counselor: How's your family doing?

Procounselor: See, he understands how important your family is to you.

Client: Well, all the news that I got from them is terrible. Anytime I heard from them they are crying, they are telling me that they do not have food to eat, they don't have clothes to wear, and just terrible.

Anticounselor: You get very upset anytime you hear from them or think about them, like right now.

Client: Yes, that's right.

Anticounselor: You don't hear from them very often, do you?

Client: Ah . . . Sometimes once a month, sometimes once every 3 months or so, depending.

Counselor: Are you able to help them in any way?

Procounselor: He understands how helpless you feel.

Client: I was thinking that I would be, but I really cannot because I cannot even help myself here.

Counselor: I see.

Anticounselor: You feel very hopeless now, don't you?

Client: Yes, that's how I feel . . . Yes.

Anticounselor: No more any hope for you to get reunited with them or for you to have a start over here.

Client: Well, that's why I come here, to see you today, to see if there would ever be any possible way.

Anticounselor: I don't know if they are really listening to us now. You only start with the two problems and then they don't know where we are already.

Counselor: What work did you do before you came here?

Client: I worked for the government.

Counselor: What kind of work?

Anticounselor: You see? I told you. You told them once already.

Procounselor: Let him get to know you so that he can help you better.

Client: I work in the Department of Health.

Counselor: And exactly what were your jobs?

Client: Well, I was a Public Health Officer, and I was working in a hospital as an administrator.

Counselor: I see, you were an administrator? And you've applied for that sort of work?

Client: I have gone around to all the hospitals here, including the Health Department, but nobody would take me, because they told me that I cannot understand English so I cannot work.

Counselor: What are you living on right now?

Procounselor: He doesn't mean to pry into your personal life. He just wants
    to help you.

Client: Well, I work as a part-time, as a dishwasher . . . Yes.

Anticounselor: I'm not sure whether he's asking that question to find out if
    you have money to pay him. I don't know if they know anything about
    our situation.

Counselor: You're not able to make it on the money you get dishwashing.

Procounselor: Maybe this counselor has some new ideas that will help you
    get a better job?

Client: I make very little. Just enough for me to live on.

Anticounselor: Do you really think that they can help us?

Discussion Questions

1. What positive thoughts is the client thinking but not saying?
2. What negative thoughts is the client thinking but not saying?
3. What would you have done differently if you had been the counselor?

Review the two case examples in their interview format to discuss the
counseling style being used, the alternative styles that might have been used,
the changing and dynamic cultural salience, the authenticity of the anticounselor or procounselor, and the way in which culture determined the behaviors
of both the counselor and the client.

Skill Components and
Constructs for Multicultural Counseling

Multicultural counseling is based on an assumption that each client, counselor, presenting problem, and counseling environment is shaped by many different culturally defined relationships. In this broad definition of culture all
counseling is to some extent multicultural. Approaches to counseling that disre-
gard the culture factor are not likely to be appropriate and accurate. If individual differences are those characteristics we were born with, then culture includes
everything that has happened to us since birth. One's skin color, for example,
was determined before birth, but the "meaning" that one's skin color has taken
on was shaped through culturally defined relationships.

This broad definition of culture includes *ethnographic* variables such as ethnicity, nationality, religion, and language; *demographic* variables such as age,
gender, and place of residence; *status* variables such as social, educational, and
economic; and *affiliations* including both formal affiliations to family or organizations and informal affiliations to ideas and a lifestyle. In this broad definition
each person has perhaps a thousand or more different cultures or cultural iden-
tities, with each identity becoming *salient* at different times and places.

Multiculturalism also emphasizes the ways in which one is *different* from other people and the way one is *similar* to other people. Those who have overemphasized similarity across persons, groups, and cultures have imposed a "melting pot" metaphor on society that presumes differences don't really matter. Those who have overemphasized differences across persons, groups, and cultures have imposed stereotypes and an exclusionary isolation of groups from one another. Multiculturalism emphasizes both culture-specific characteristics that differentiate and culture-general characteristics that unite at the same time. In a sense, you must become "cross-eyed," by keeping one eye focused on similarities and the other on differences, to see clearly through this multicultural lens (Pedersen, 1991).

Potential Biases

Multicultural counseling grew out of the civil rights movement and the feminist movement as special interest groups became more outspoken against a white, middle-class, urban, male-dominant culture as the single standard for normality. The multicultural counseling literature points out examples of cultural bias that needed attention.

1. There is no single concept of "normal" that applies across all persons, situations, and cultures.
2. Individualism is not the only way to view human behavior and must be supplemented with collectivism in some settings.
3. We are trapped by boundaries of status, academic discipline, and perceived area of expertise that inhibit our usefulness in a complicated multicultural setting.
4. The abstractions of a low-context perspective will not be understood in a high-context culture where examples are required.
5. Dependency is not a bad characteristic in all cultures and must be understood in context.
6. Natural support systems are important to the individual.
7. Linear thinking must sometimes be supplemented by skills in nonlinear thinking.
8. When the individual is right and the system is wrong we need to know how to change the system to fit the individual rather than force the individual to "adjust."
9. We dare not ignore history in our assessment of individuals and groups.
10. We each must assume that our own view is to some extent culturally biased. (Pedersen, 1988)

The counseling profession generally has assumed that the status quo values of a dominant culture apply universally across cultures. Wrenn (1962, 1985) pointed out the "cultural encapsulation" of counselors and counseling through ethnocentrism (my way is the best way) or through relativism (every person for him- or herself). Encapsulation results from depending on the dominant culture to define normal behavior, being insensitive to cultural differences, protecting the status quo against change, and depending on a technique-oriented job definition. Multiculturalism grew out of work by those counselors who recognized and opposed cultural encapsulation.

Lee and Richardson (1991) point out some dangers in the multicultural perspective, however.

1. Multiculturalism can be defined so broadly and vaguely that it has no meaning.
2. Cultural groups can end up being stereotyped if within-group differences are ignored.
3. If similarities across cultures are overemphasized a new form of racism can emerge.
4. It is not necessary to "throw out" everything we learned about traditional counseling in favor of the multicultural perspective.
5. All forms of counseling may be rejected by minorities because of their past oppression by the dominant culture.

There is a need for multicultural counseling to protect the accuracy of judgment. Ridley (1989) describes examples of unintentional racism that reduce accuracy in counseling.

1. "Color blindness" in counselors usually indicates discomfort with cultural issues and unexamined biases.
2. Attributing problems to the client's cultural background in a "deficit hypothesis" is an attempt to blame the victim.
3. Transference of positive or negative feeling to the counselor from previous relationships may result in misinterpretation by the counselor.
4. Transference of positive or negative feeling to the client from previous relationships may also result in misinterpretation by the counselor.
5. Some counselors dedicated to "helping" the oppressed actually have a need for power and paternalistic dominance.
6. Counselors might respond inappropriately when clients accurately identify cultural bias in the counselor.
7. Culturally appropriate nondisclosure may be misinterpreted by the counselor.

People can think of their cultures as "teachers" who have taught them when and how to do what they do. These cultural patterns were waiting for them even before they were born to guide their thinking and actions. Culture is important because it teaches people what to do and say. It teaches people the rules of the game, what to do, and what things really mean. For that reason it is important to look beyond the behaviors of a culturally different person and focus on the expectations or values behind that person's behavior. If two persons come toward a person and both of them are smiling—same behavior—but only one of them wants to be your friend—different expectations—the person may want to respond to each one differently.

It is only when you learn the culturally defined expectations and values behind another person's behavior that you can hope to be accurate in your assessment of that behavior. Even persons who behave differently may have the same expectation and value. For example, think of your best friend in all the world. Would you accept behavior from strangers that you do from your friend in the same way? You almost certainly would not. Why do you accept those behaviors from your friend? Each person shares the same expectation of "friendship" with our best friends, and even bizarre behaviors by your friend are interpreted as expressions of that friendship. Multiculturalism is the search for "common ground" or shared expectations across populations who behave very differently.

Controversies

Multiculturalism is a term that is not always viewed positively and there is a great deal of controversy about this construct. One positive way of describing multiculturalism is that it represents the search for "common ground" or shared expectations across populations who have different world views and behave very differently. Even among people whose behavior is apparently hostile and contentious there may be some shared values such as fairness, hope for their children, or desire for personal safety. These elements of common ground demonstrate areas of similarity in the midst of diversity called *multiculturalism*.

Multicultural counseling grew in part from anthropology and ethnographic studies of exotic population (Draguns, 1989). Sue and Sue (1990) document a parallel source in the long tradition of minority authors writing on multicultural issues who have been neglected for decades. Casas (1984) credits the new interest in multicultural counseling to (1) demographic changes, (2) increased visibility and pressure by minority groups, (3) profit incentives for working with minorities, (4) heightened group consciousness, (5) legally mandated affirmative action in employment and education, (6) the transportation of school children by bus from one area to another to guarantee the integration of socioeconomic classes in every school, and (7) demands for bilingual education. This interest grew out of the militant civil rights movement of the 1950s, the community mental health movement and the antiwar movement of the 1960s, the emphasis on minority issues in the 1970s, the refugee problems of the 1980s, and the rapidly increasing demographic proportion of non-whites in the 1990s.

Counseling itself is foreign to many cultural groups who depend more on support from family and close friends or who prefer to go inside themselves for support in times of psychological stress. Going to a stranger to discuss a personal, confidential, and potentially embarrassing problem may be seen to threaten the welfare of the social unit rather than help the person. With the increase in modernization and Westernization, counseling by professional strangers is, however, becoming a more frequently sought out resource.

The research on multicultural counseling has frequently been flawed, however. Ponterotto and Casas (1991) point out 10 weaknesses in the research.

1. There is no unified conceptual framework.
2. The counselor-client process variable is overemphasized and psychosocial variables are underemphasized.
3. Too much research is based on analogues outside the real world.
4. Intracultural within-group differences are disregarded.
5. There is an overdependence on samples of convenience.
6. There is continued reliance on culturally biased measures.
7. The subject's cultural background is inadequately described.
8. The limits of generalizability are not defined.
9. There is inadequate minority input.
10. There is a failure of responsibility toward minority subject pools.

Competencies

The American Psychological Association commissioned a paper on education and training to define competencies of multicultural counseling. This paper by Sue et al. (1982) provided guidelines for much of the later work on multicultural counseling. The competencies were divided into those emphasizing awareness, those emphasizing knowledge, and those emphasizing skill. This three-level developmental continuum grew out of the 1978–1981 National Institute of Mental Health training project in Hawaii called "Developing Interculturally Skilled Counselors" (DISC) (Pedersen, 1981). The four awareness competencies included (1) to become aware of one's own culture, (2) to become aware of how one's values might affect clients, (3) to become comfortable with cultural differences, and (4) to know when a culturally different person should be referred. The four knowledge competencies included (1) to understand the sociopolitical dynamics between majority and minority cultures, (2) to have knowledge about a client's culture, (3) to have knowledge about traditional and generic counseling theory and practice, and (4) to know institutional barriers to multicultural counseling. The three skill competencies included (1) to generate a wide variety of verbal and nonverbal responses for different cultural settings, (2) to send and receive verbal and nonverbal messages accurately across cultures, and (3) to advocate for change of the system when necessary.

Multicultural counseling is more than a fad. It is more than a good-hearted humanitarianism toward other people. It is more than a necessary evil in an imperfect world. It is more than a method for communicating with exotic people. Multicultural counseling is a generic approach to counseling that provides a *Fourth Force* to supplement psychodynamic, behavioral, and humanistic theories in a future society characterized by multicultural values (Pedersen, 1991).

Multicultural counseling will bring about several changes to the field of counseling generally. (1) All counselors will need to become more aware of culturally learned assumptions being made by themselves and their clients. (2) The argument for multiculturalism from an ethical imperative of "doing good" will be supplemented by the argument for "being accurate." (3) The pre-service training of counselors will emphasize multicultural dynamics and include a higher proportion of minorities. (4) Research will need to report cultural differences in its sample populations and will temper generalizability of its findings to those populations. (5) A more complete repertoire of skills, strategies, and techniques that can be appropriately matched to culturally different clients will appear.

Skill Applications

Multicultural counselors need to understand (1) the explicit verbal exchange between the counselor and the client, (2) the counselor's own internal dialogue, and (3) the client's internal dialogue. The more culturally different the counselor and client are from one another the more difficult it will be to understand the client's internal dialogue. It is a fair assumption, however, that part of the client's internal dialogue will be negative and part will be positive.

One approach to training multicultural counselors (Pedersen, 1988) is to match a coached client with two other culturally similar persons—one as a procounselor emphasizing the positive and one as an anticounselor emphasizing the negative side of what the client is thinking but not saying. The culturally different counselor can hear both the positive and the negative side of the client's internal dialogue in a role-played interview by listening to all three of the other participants. The two case examples presented earlier in this chapter demonstrate how an anticounselor and a procounselor might function in an interview.

Review the brief transcript excerpts that follow and write in what you believe an anticounselor and a procounselor might say in the blanks provided; or you may role-play the dialogue in a training session.

Part 1

The first set of statements is transcribed from an interview between a white male counselor and a black female client discussing relationship problems the black female is having at the university.

1. Identity

Client: O.K., my problem is that I don't seem to be able to trust the white people here on campus. Being black, I seem to have sort of a problem with this sort of thing and I don't know what to do about it and somebody recommended you. Said that you were a good counselor, so I decided to come, and get some help from you.

Counselor: Do you have any problems relating to the black students on campus, Terry?

Client: No, not really. You know, there are people everywhere. Some you don't like, some you do like.

Anticounselor:

Procounselor:

2. Relationship

Counselor: How do you feel in terms of our relationship now? You came here and we have been talking for about 2-3 minutes. How do you feel about the way we've been talking?

Client: Well, you haven't helped me for one thing. I mean you just . . .

Anticounselor:

Procounselor:

3. Comfort Evaluation

Counselor: Do you feel uncomfortable with me?

Client: Um, not now, not yet.

Counselor: I um . . . I, ah, . . . (pause) I don't feel any discomfort with you at all.

Client: Oh, well, cuz I'm a friendly person I suppose. (laugh)

Anticounselor:

Procounselor:

4. Counselor's Culture

Counselor: Are you getting a little uncomfortable, Terry? . . . Perhaps because I'm white? In sharing some of these things with me?

Client: Um . . . Not really, and it's like I said, you know, I try to be pretty open-minded about what I'm talking about. But the thing I want to know is can you really understand where I'm coming from? What kind of things I'm really dealing with?

Anticounselor:

Procounselor:

Part 2

The second set of statements is transcribed from an interview between a white male counselor and a Latin-American female client discussing relationship problems the Latin-American female is having at the university.

1. Identity

Client: Yeah, they treat me like dirt, that's it, you know? And I feel divided inside. Like they don't care for me as a whole person.
Counselor: Ummm . . . You said divided. What is the division?
Client: The division is that they just want sex. They don't want to see me as a whole person.
Anticounselor:
Procounselor:

2. Relationship

Counselor: Could you tell me what you would rather have from them? How you would like a man to treat you when you go out with him?
Client: Well, its just that, especially the first time . . . for some time . . .
Counselor: Um mmm . . .
Client: I like to get to know the person in a different way.
Anticounselor:
Procounselor:

3. Comfort Level

Counselor: O.K., I better ask you another question then. How comfortable are you with me? Should . . . maybe I'm not the right person to work with you . . . because I'm an American man.
Client: So far you're O.K. . . . because you are far enough . . .
Anticounselor:
Procounselor:

4. Counselor's Culture

Client: Yeah, you see this thing, these things for me are very intense for me right now because I just came. I've been here for only about a month.
Counselor: Would you feel better if I got back behind the desk and we sort of had that between us?
Client: No, then you remind me of my father.
Anticounselor:
Procounselor:

Review the statements you made as a procounselor or as an anticounselor in dyads or small groups. Pay attention to how your response was similar or different from the response of others in the group. Consider the following questions in your discussion:

1. Were the statements of the anticounselor and procounselor accurate? Why or why not?
2. How might the counselor respond on hearing the anticounselor or procounselor statements?

3. How might the client respond on hearing the anticounselor or procounselor statements?

4. How might it be useful for multicultural counselors to monitor the anticounselor and procounselor messages in a client's internal dialogue?

The Triad Model Exercise

The following exercise will require several steps and its use assumes familiarity with all the exercises presented previously in this module. The purpose of this exercise is to familiarize trainees with how the Triad Model works when participants interact *without* prepared scripts. Practice with trained client-procounselor-anticounselor teams will result in culture-specific counseling skills.

1. Divide the class into four-person groups with any leftover persons acting as observers.

2. Within each small group each person will have the opportunity to role-play a counselor, client, procounselor, and anticounselor. As each person's turn to be the counselor comes up, the other three persons will identify an area of "shared cultural identity" among them *that is not shared by the person in the counselor role*. This area of cultural similarity may relate to ethnicity, nationality, religion, language, age, gender, place of residence, social status, educational status, economic status, formal affiliations to a group or informal affiliations to an idea, perspective, or familiarity with a special problem or population.

3. The three-person team of client-procounselor-anticounselor will create a presenting problem based on their area of shared similarity with a shallow (more obvious/overt) and a deeper (less obvious/covert) level to the problem.

4. The counselor will work with the three-person team for 5 or 10 minutes attempting to help the client manage the problem while getting feedback from the anticounselor and procounselor. The client will genuinely seek help on the problem. The anticounselor will articulate the client's negative internal dialogue. The procounselor will articulate the client's positive dialogue. *There should always be at least two or three persons speaking at the same time to adequately simulate the dynamics of internal dialogue*. Anyone may speak with anyone during the interview, but physical violence is discouraged.

5. After the interview, the participants will go out of role to discuss the interview process and content for about 5 or 10 minutes.

6. At the end of the discussion, the participants will change roles and repeat the process until everyone has had an opportunity to play each role.

Field Experiences

Any opportunity for participants to experience the counseling process in a culturally unfamiliar setting is likely to result in learning about multicultural counseling in the field. As the participants become aware of how culture is broadly defined, they will discover that each counseling interview is to some extent multicultural even though that cultural factor is frequently overlooked. The following field experiences have proven useful for learning about multicultural counseling.

1. Multicultural counseling frequently occurs outside the formal setting and formal methods of an office interview. Take careful notes of your interactions with each person or group of persons outside the office during the day, making notes at least hourly. Define to your own satisfaction the "function" of counseling. Review your notes and identify as many informal methods and settings as possible where you facilitated the counseling function even though you and/or the other person may not have previously viewed that exchange as having anything to do with counseling.

2. Volunteer for work in an agency populated by persons culturally different (broadly defined) from yourself. Select an agency or organization with which you are unfamiliar. As you volunteer for a specific function within that organization, listen to and observe the interaction between persons in that setting for evidence of helping, supporting, facilitating, and other characteristics associated with counseling. Keep a journal on your observations. At the end of 6 or 8 visits as a volunteer to the unfamiliar organization or agency, review your journal to identify recurring cultural patterns both among the participants and in your own response to the situation.

3. Invite resource persons from populations generally unfamiliar to you and your group to join you as a resource person. There should be one resource person for about every five participants. Meet with the resource person in small groups to discuss the meaning and function of "counseling" as seen in that resource person's cultural setting.

4. Review back issues of a counseling journal looking at the description of samples in empirical articles. Record the extent to which the sample's salient cultures have been reported and what difference it might make to the research's conclusions if the many different other cultures in the sample had been reported more comprehensively.

5. Review the ethical guidelines of any professional counseling association and look for examples of cultural bias within each ethical guideline as it is now written. Discuss how the guidelines might be revised to present a less culturally biased framework (see Pedersen, 1988, pp. 175-182 for examples of bias).

6. Develop a study group to identify examples of cultural bias in the other courses being taken by students in the group. Work together as a group to identify and articulate the difficult questions that multiculturalism requires. Introduce these questions later in classroom discussions when group members attend their *other* classes. Report back to the study group on the results of raising the multicultural questions in classrooms.

7. Organize support groups for international students attending the universities in your region. Keep each support group small (4 to 5 persons plus one counselor/facilitator) and without a specific agenda so that the students can bring up any issue they like. Continue regular weekly meetings of the support groups over a period of a term. At the end of the term evaluate the learning both by group members and the facilitator regarding multicultural counseling.

8. Organize intercultural communication workshops of larger groups (15 to 25 persons) either as an intensive weekend workshop or as a regular credit-bearing class for a term. Recruit members so that half the participants will be U.S. nationals and half will be non-U.S. nationals. Keep the agenda open for discussion but try to introspect on how participants from different cultures are communicating with one another. Discuss guidelines for communicating with and helping persons from other cultures based on the group experience.

9. Keep a written daily journal identifying insights regarding your own cultural identity, assumptions, and culturally influenced behaviors during the day. Look for patterns in your own behaviors that relate to culturally learned expectations and values. Try to identify where you learned those cultural expectations and values.

10. Identify examples of cultural conflict within a person, between persons, or between groups. You may find examples in the newspaper, the broadcast media, other publications, or from your own life experiences. Identify the behaviors that lead to conflict either within the person or between persons. Identify the expectations and values behind those behaviors as they may be similar or different across roles, persons, or groups. Identify areas of common ground or shared expectations/values that could become the basis for mediating multicultural conflict. Develop a plan for how you would proceed to help culturally different people mediate their conflict with one another by emphasizing their shared expectations and values rather than their differing behaviors.

Conclusions

This chapter has attempted to provide a measure for self-assessment, case examples of multicultural counseling, some background on the components and concepts behind multicultural counseling, a design for skill development and training, and some examples of field experiences for enhancing multicultural counseling skill. You will no doubt discover additional resources, methods, and approaches that build on or adapt these suggestions. Hopefully, you will develop approaches that are superior to those suggested here. In any case, allow yourself to consider the many ways in which multicultural counseling can make your job easier rather than harder and more rather than less satisfying for the future.

References

Casas, J. (1984). Policy, training, and research in counseling psychology: The racial/ethnic minority perspective. In S. D. Brown & R. W. Lent (Eds.), *Handbook of counseling psychology* (pp. 785-831). New York: John Wiley.

Draguns, J. G. (1989). Dilemmas and choices in cross-cultural counseling: The universal versus the culturally distinctive. In P. Pedersen, J. Draguns, W. Lonner, & J. Trimble (Eds.), *Counseling across cultures* (pp. 3-22). Honolulu, HI: University of Hawaii Press.

Lee, C. C., & Richardson B. L. (1991). *Multicultural issues in counseling: New approaches to diversity.* Alexandria, VA: American Association for Counseling and Development.

Pedersen, P. (1981). *Developing interculturally skilled counselors.* Final report to the National Institute of Mental Health (Rep. No. 1-T24, MH 15552). Honolulu, HI: The Institute of Behavioral Sciences.

Pedersen, P. (1988). *A handbook for developing multicultural awareness.* Alexandria, VA: American Association for Counseling and Development.

Pedersen, P. (1991). Multiculturalism as a generic approach to counseling. *Journal of Counseling and Development, 70*(1), 6-12.

Ponterotto, J. G., & Casas, J. M. (1991). *Handbook of racial/ethnic minority counseling research.* Springfield, IL: Charles C Thomas.

Ridley, C. (1989). Racism in counseling as an aversive behavioral process. In P. Pedersen, J. Draguns, W. Lonner, & J. Trimble (Eds.), *Counseling across cultures* (pp. 55-79). Honolulu, HI: The University of Hawaii Press.

Sue, D. W., Bernier, J. E., Durran, A., Feinberg, L., Pedersen, P., Smith, C. J., & Vasquez-Nuttall, G. (1982). Cross-cultural counseling competencies. *The Counseling Psychologist, 19*(2), 45-52.

Sue, D. W., & Sue, D. (1990). *Counseling the culturally different: Theory and practice.* New York: John Wiley.

Wrenn, C. G. (1962). The culturally encapsulated counselor. *Harvard Educational Review, 32,* 444-449.

Wrenn, C. G. (1985). Afterward: The culturally encapsulated counselor revisited. In P. Pedersen (Ed.), *Handbook of cross-cultural counseling and therapy* (pp. 323-329). Westport, CT: Greenwood Press.

Communication Across Cultural Boundaries

13 Interpersonal Versus Non-Interpersonal Realities: An Effective Tool Individualists Can Use to Better Understand Collectivists

TOMOKO YOSHIDA

We often use the phrase "he/she is an intelligent person." However, a truly intelligent person does not simply use his/her brain, but also uses his/her "ki" (heart, mind, attention). In fact, the person who is the most intelligent is the one who uses his/her "ki" towards other people.

Suzuki (1986, p. 144, translation by author)

We often hear people make such statements as "you really need to face reality," or "why don't you try to be more logical?" The assumption here is that there is one reality that we all see and that logic is the same for everyone. The author of this module argues that social values affect people's perceptions of reality, and this then affects their perception of logic. A society that values collectivism will obviously place a higher value on harmony and good interpersonal relationships while an individualistic society is likely to encourage behavior that brings merit to specific people. This module is aimed at individualists who seek to better understand collectivists. It provides people with an opportunity to examine the extent to which they emphasize a particular reality. At the same time, it provides people with opportunities to learn specific behaviors aimed at facilitating communication with collectivists.

Contents

Inventory

During their sojourns, many people find themselves in situations where no amount of logic seems to explain the behavior of the people in the host culture. Similarly, many individuals find themselves in situations where host country nationals cannot understand *their* logic no matter how many times it is explained to them. I have compiled below a set of commonly experienced "puzzling situations," some of which you may have personally encountered. You will also notice that some of these situations can occur *in your own home* or community. If you find yourself empathizing with any of the people in the following situations, you will most likely gain some insights from this module.

1.   As a tourist in a certain country (e.g., Mexico, Portugal) you have repeatedly found yourself in situations in which the directions you received from the locals got you nowhere. The people seemed to be extremely friendly and helpful so you know that their intentions were good. What puzzles you is why they did not simply admit to the fact that they did not know the directions.

2.   When interacting with people from certain countries (e.g., Japan, Korea) you have found yourself in various situations where you have misinterpreted their "No" for a "Yes," or vice versa. You are slightly frustrated and not sure *why* they are not more direct and forthright with you.

3.   Either through personal experience or through the media you have heard that Japanese businessmen spend most of their time either at work or socializing with colleagues from work. You wonder why it is necessary for them to involve themselves so intensely and personally with their coworkers and their organizations.

4.   Either through anecdotes or through actual experience you have learned that in doing business with many non-Americans (i.e., Mexicans, Filipinos, Japanese) you need to spend a significant amount of time engaging in "small talk" and pleasantries instead of getting down to business. Some sources recommend spending the whole first day getting to know the person and not to attempt bringing up business issues. This seems to be an extremely inefficient use of time and you are puzzled by it.

5.   A friend of yours has a difficult time being punctual. She often gets distracted by friends or acquaintances she meets on the way to her appointments. Sometimes you have a hard time understanding why she does not simply tell them that she has prior commitments.

How to Use This Inventory

The main purpose of the inventory is to pique people's interest. There are many ways in which the inventory can be used. The following are a few suggestions:

1. *Guided imagery:* Trainees are instructed to close their eyes while the trainer describes one or more of the scenes from the inventory as realistically as possible. Although not as "real" as an actual situation or a role play, this can be a time-saving approach that can help trainees vicariously experience some puzzling cross-cultural situations.

2. *Role play:* Some of the scenarios can be role-played by trainees or by invited guests. If the role plays are videotaped they can then be used later on for further discussion.

3. *Movie sections:* Some of the items in the inventory (i.e., Items 1 & 2) can be found enacted in popular movies or TV series. Using an excerpt demonstrating these behaviors might be an interesting opener for a workshop.

4. *Articles:* Bringing in statistics or articles related to certain items (such as Items 3 and 4) can generate interesting discussion.

5. Another usage of the inventory is discussed in the "Skill Applications" section of this module.

Self-Assessment Exercise

Please read the following statements and circle the option in the scale that best represents the way you would behave in the following scenarios. If you are bicultural or multicultural, you may want to take the inventory more than once. Bicultural or multicultural people are (among many features) those who either consciously or unconsciously adjust the way they act or talk according to the community or the country in which they find themselves. If you are able to interact successfully in distinctly different cultures or subcultures, you may want to take the inventory more than once, each time visualizing how you would behave in a particular country or community (similar to the way the inventory was taken twice for the individualism-collectivism module, Chapter 5). You will notice that the Likert-type scale has a set of numbers on top as well as under the descriptors (i.e., strongly agree, disagree). You can circle the numbers on top while envisioning yourself in one culture and circle the numbers at the bottom with a different culture in mind. For a more extensive use of this assessment, please jot down the reasons for your decision in the blanks that follow the items.

1. If I were walking down a street and someone accidentally bumped into me (it was most likely their fault), I would probably mumble an apology.

5	4	3	2	1
strongly agree	agree	depends	disagree	strongly disagree
5	4	3	2	1

Why did you choose this answer? _____

_____

_____

2. If I were discussing a matter with a friend and we disagreed entirely, I would try to change the subject or make an ambiguous remark so that we do not end up in a disagreement.

5	4	3	2	1
strongly agree	agree	depends	disagree	strongly disagree
5	4	3	2	1

Why? _____

_____

3. If an acquaintance of mine had spent a lot of money on a new dress (which I think looks awful) and asked my opinion on it, I would tell her that it looked good.

5	4	3	2	1
strongly agree	agree	depends	disagree	strongly disagree
5	4	3	2	1

Why? _____

_____

_____

4. A close friend of mine had an intense argument with his or her spouse and came to me in tears. I listened to what he or she had to say and felt that the spouse might have a point. I would still sympathize with my friend and keep my comments to myself.

5	4	3	2	1
strongly agree	agree	depends	disagree	strongly disagree
5	4	3	2	1

Why? _____

_____

_____

5. I respect those who are very attuned to other people feelings.

5	4	3	2	1
strongly agree	agree	depends	disagree	strongly disagree
5	4	3	2	1

Why? _____

_____

_____

6. I believe that joining my colleagues for regular lunches or some other form of informal activity helps improve our performance as a group and therefore facilitates job efficiency.

5	4	3	2	1
strongly agree	agree	depends	disagree	strongly disagree
5	4	3	2	1

Why? _____

_____

7. When looking for a job or trying to collect information (such as where to get the best deal on cars or computers), I often call friends or acquaintances for their help or suggestions.

5	4	3	2	1
strongly agree	agree	depends	disagree	strongly disagree
5	4	3	2	1

Why? _____

_____

8. I did some extra work last Saturday for my boss. I had assumed that I would be paid for the extra hours I worked. On Monday, however, my boss thanked me for a job well done but also stated that he or she would not be able to pay me for those hours because of logistical reasons. Even though I feel that it is unfair I would refrain from confronting my boss.

5	4	3	2	1
strongly agree	agree	depends	disagree	strongly disagree
5	4	3	2	1

Why? _____

_____

9. An acquaintance of mine has returned one of my books. The book now looks quite decrepit. He or she apologizes profusely and offers to buy me a new one. Instead of accepting his or her offer, I simply smile and say something to the effect of "Don't worry about it, it's just going to sit on my shelf anyway."

5	4	3	2	1
strongly agree	agree	depends	disagree	strongly disagree
5	4	3	2	1

Why? _____

_____

10. As a supervisor, if I have to give negative feedback to an employee, I worry about its effects on our (work) relationship.

5	4	3	2	1
strongly agree	agree	depends	disagree	strongly disagree
5	4	3	2	1

Why? _____

_____

Understanding the Results of the Assessment

If your answers were largely on the left side of the continuum (higher score), you probably have a tendency to emphasize *interpersonal reality.* In other words, during an interaction with others you believe that making them feel good is extremely important. However, if most of your responses were on the right-hand of the continuum (lower score), you might have a tendency to emphasize *external reality.* Instead of concentrating on the other party's feelings, you believe that "business is business" and like to focus on factors such as rules and regulations, verifiable information, and other tangible elements in life (more on interpersonal and external reality in the following chapter).

Some of you may have found the inventory frustrating because your answers would depend largely on the specifics that were not included in the scenarios. For example, in Question 3, your reaction might depend largely on how close you are to that particular friend. Many people do not operate on only one "reality" but more often use a mixture of the two. If you experienced a large amount of frustration or tended to mark "depends" for many of the questions, you are probably very context-sensitive and use the two forms of reality equally as often. If you are bicultural or multicultural and took the inventory more than once, you might have noticed a marked difference in your scores depending on which culture you were visualizing. However, you might have noticed that on certain items your scores were identical or at least very close whereas on other items they varied quite drastically. What does this tell you about the importance you place on certain values?

As you read the rest of this chapter, the two concepts (i.e., interpersonal reality and external reality) should become clearer to you. An explicit understanding of the terms should help people recognize why it is easier to get along with certain people than with others and why many unnecessary arguments take place. These concepts should also help elucidate many of the "puzzling situations" introduced in the inventory (Part I). This chapter will emphasize cases or social situations when the distinction is most impactful on people's feelings about each other. These situations involve contact and possible clashes among people who differ in the most frequent and preferred orientation.

One of the main goals of this assessment exercise as well as the module itself is to increase awareness. As a result, you might start "catching" yourself analyzing your everyday behaviors. You might even notice some discrepancies between your answers to the inventory and your actual behaviors. As you start consciously analyzing many of these behaviors you will probably encounter many pleasant surprises. Good luck!

Case Studies: Critical Incidents and Explanations

Critical Incident 1: The Job Interview

George is an American exchange student studying at a Japanese university as part of a 1-year-abroad program. It has been 2 months into the school year and George feels settled into the routine life of a college student and feels ready to start a part-time job teaching English for extra money. For the past few weeks he has been looking at various English-language newspapers and responding to job advertisements. After going to several interviews, however, George has experienced a growing sense of frustration with his prospective employers. Interview after interview, George would leave the building feeling confident that he would get the job. The interviewers would not only seem extremely responsive but would also comment on his excellent qualifications. Each interview would end with something to the effect of: "George, we are very impressed by your qualifications; we will think about it and let you know."

Infallibly, however, George would never hear from them. After waiting a couple of weeks, he would try calling the companies to see if any progress was made. Each time he would hear a rather baffled answer and would be told that they would have to think about it some more and call him back. Again he would wait to no avail. Angry and frustrated, George mentioned this to two American friends he had met at the university. Their conversation went as follows.

George: I can't believe it's been 3 weeks since I started interviewing and all of the places are "still thinking"! What's taking them so long???

Mary: You know what, George? If I were you I'd give up and try looking some more . . .

George: But there's still the possibility that I'll get one of the jobs I interviewed for . . . right?

Frank: Not necessarily . . . the Japanese can be really two-faced, you know . . . they tell you one thing and mean another. I have been through 20 different interviews myself and the only time they actually called me back was when I got the job! Even though all the other places told me how qualified I was during the interviews, none of them had the decency to keep their promise of notifying me later.

Mary: That's the same for me! When I got my job they called me back almost immediately after the interview. The other places didn't even bother writing or calling me. It's *so* frustrating, because if they would tell us "Yes" or "No," at least we would know whether we should keep looking some more or not!

George: Yeah! Personally, I think it's really rude that they don't call us back after saying that they would!

Why do you think these English language schools did not call or write the interviewees back to inform them that they did not get the job? Please choose an alternative and then look at the commentaries that follow. Since this is not a test, there is no right answer. There is, however, an answer that is more plausible than the others. To maximize learning, we recommend that you read through *all* the alternatives as well as *all* the accompanying commentaries instead of simply reading the material related to just one of the options.

1. The companies were probably conducting many interviews at the same time and were, therefore, too busy to reply.

2. Since the companies did not want to embarrass George and make him "lose face," they tried to relay their message through nonverbal cues such as delaying the answer and simply not replying.

3. The interviewers were being insincere. Instead of being up front with George, they led him to believe that he would get the job even though he didn't have a chance. They were trying to be nice to him because he was a foreigner.

Rationales for the Alternative Explanations

1. Although this is possible, it is unlikely. If this was, in fact, the case they would have given George a straight answer when he called them to see how things were going. Remember that the interviewers seemed rather baffled by George's phone call and told him that they would have to think about it some more. Please choose again.

2. This seems the most likely answer. The Japanese avoid saying "No" outright in order to save the other party's "face" and to preserve interpersonal harmony. Since receiving a direct rejection is extremely humiliating for many Japanese, people often employ various tactics such as delaying answers, using silence, and making tangential responses instead of saying "No" directly (Imai, 1981; Ueda, 1974). This is not a unique phenomenon but is often used by people from many other cultures such as the Filipinos, Hawaiians, and Arabs (Rubin, 1980). This will be discussed in more detail later.

3. Although many Americans interpret the Japanese use of *honne* ("real meaning") and *tatemae* ("one's public facade") as being devious or insincere, from a Japanese perspective it is an important social courtesy. In a culture in which the collective is revered over the individual, people must constantly strive at maintaining good interpersonal relationships. Avoiding unpleasant messages such as saying "No" is therefore an essential part of being a socially responsible member of society. Indirectness and the use of *honne* and *tatemae* make it possible for people to give negative responses without actually saying "No". The use of these behaviors, however, necessitates a more active role on the part of the listener. Sojourners in Japan must be careful not to take messages as they appear but should practice reading between the lines and understanding the nonverbal behaviors of the people with whom they are interacting (more on nonverbals in Chapter 14 in this book by Singelis). The interviewers were *not* being insincere. Please try again.

Critical Incident 2: The Promise

Phil, the president of the student government at a large private American university on the East Coast, was having problems with Nestor, a foreign student from the Philippines. During their last meeting, Phil asked Nestor if he could take on an extra project, to which Nestor agreed very graciously. It has been a month, however, and Nestor has not even organized a subcommittee. Phil has had similar problems in the past where Nestor would pleasantly agree to help out with a project yet only provide minimal participation because of his many other commitments. Nestor is involved in over 10 student organizations, occupying a significant role in each. Considering this, it is no wonder that he is unable to spare much time to any one organization. Phil, however, feels that if Nestor has committed to something he should by all means take on full responsibility. If he cannot fulfill what is expected of him he should simply say "No." Nestor, however, is angry at Phil for accusing him of irresponsibility.

Amy, who is close to Nestor as well as Phil, receives a phone call from Phil.

"Amy, I don't know what to do! Nestor has done it again! He promised to head that project we talked about at our last meeting a month ago and he *still* hasn't done anything about it! Now it's too late for me to find anyone else to do it . . . I just don't know *why* he's so irresponsible! I've given him so many chances and he keeps on letting me down. The worst part of it is that even though it's all his fault, he's mad at me for some reason and refuses to talk to me anymore. This is getting ridiculous!"

Later on, she hears from Nestor.

"Amy, I'm really disappointed with Phil. I thought we were friends so I've been agreeing to do all these projects he's been pushing my way even though I don't have the time to do it. He knows that. But he still gets upset when I don't get it done on time! What does he think? Does he *really* think that it would be logically feasible for me to do all that considering my tight schedule? I'm really frustrated because he keeps on making unreasonable demands on my time even though he knows how swamped I am! You know, Amy, I've really had enough . . ."

What do you think lies at the root of this problem?

1. This is not a cross-cultural problem. Responsibility is a universal concept and Nestor simply needs to learn to take responsibility for his own actions.

2. This is a communication problem. Both parties are responsible for not confronting each other about their behaviors. Phil should have voiced his unhappiness with Nestor's previous behaviors and Nestor should have done likewise.

3. The two parties seem to differ in their assumption of what a responsible individual is expected to do. According to Nestor's definition, it is the leader's responsibility to determine and assign only what his or her subordinate can reasonably handle. According to Phil's definition, however, each individual is responsible for determining how much he or she should undertake.

Rationales for the Alternative Explanations

1. Although responsibility is a universal concept, what defines it varies across cultures. Is the responsible individual the person who effectively maintains harmony between people? Or is the responsible individual one who is capable of asserting his or her needs or opinions despite its possible consequences to the group? According to the Filipino culture, Nestor was being a responsible adult by doing his best to preserve harmony and save Phil's "face." Knowing

how busy Nestor was, Phil should not have asked Nestor to take on the extra job, at least not in front of the whole group. Please try again.

2. From a Western perspective this might seem to be the best answer. We tend to believe that when problems arise, confronting the other party is much better than keeping the problem to ourselves. In many other cultures, however, confronting someone directly is only used prior to the termination of a relationship. One's unhappiness might instead be relayed indirectly through someone. Please try again.

3. This is the best choice. Responsibility, the role of the leader, as well as other values are often culturally defined. Because of the importance placed on maintaining harmony, the Filipinos will often do all they can to avoid saying "No." In addition, they will also be careful not to put others in a situation where they would have to give a direct refusal. Therefore, when a leader asks someone to perform a task it is assumed that the person will willingly accept. This also means that the leader is responsible in making sure that the person has enough time and resources to perform the job well. From an American perspective, however, refusing to take on a job is perceived as having adequate responsibility and assertiveness. The job of the leader is to find someone to get the job done. The subordinates' responsibility is to decide for themselves if they have the time and energy to accommodate to the leader's requests.

Skill Concepts: Interpersonal, External, and Internal Reality

In her book *You Just Don't Understand*, Deborah Tannen (1990) received much attention from the media as well as the general public by introducing the concept that "talking about it" is not necessarily the answer to our problems. She proposed that because men and women seek to fulfill different goals through communication, talking about a problem can often aggravate a situation instead of smoothing it out. Tannen and many researchers in the field of gender differences (i.e., Carol Gilligan, 1982; Nancy Chodorow, 1974) have stated that because of differences in socialization women are much more interdependent than men. Communication for women is a means of establishing intimacy, whereas men tend to see communication as a means to assert their independence. Both feel that *they* are being logical. Hence, conflict results.

Those who are familiar with the above-mentioned literature will undoubtedly see many parallels in the following discussion. In the same way that gender differences exist in communication styles, so do cultural differences. There is a clear relationship in that the traditional role of women in the American culture is more collectivist than individualist. Although knowledge and acceptance do not necessarily go hand in hand, the former is usually necessary for the latter to take place. With this assumption, we will discuss the following skill concepts in hopes that it will take some of the mysticism out of collectivist behaviors.

Independence Versus Interdependence

The definition of maturity came up during a conversation I recently had with an American colleague concerning a mutual acquaintance. The person in question was a man from Taiwan who was working on his master's degree at our university. Although this man was close to 30 years old, this was his first time away from his parents. He was still financially dependent on them and intended to return to Taiwan after acquiring his degree. He often called his family in Taiwan for long periods of time and hence had an exorbitant telephone bill. As we were talking about him, my colleague pointed out his seeming immaturity. I was aghast at this thought for several reasons. First of all, it seemed very reasonable for the oldest son to continue living with his parents and to spend much time with them on the telephone. Second, I viewed his willingness to accept money from his parents not as *dependence* but as *interdependence*. By accepting financial support from his parents he was in return making a commitment to take care of them during their old age. Third, during group outings or parties, our Taiwanese colleague never ceased to amaze me by exhibiting a remarkable amount of restraint and patience. Unlike the individualists in the group, this man consistently strove to accommodate to all of our needs, maintaining harmony within our group.

In their discussion of the *independent self* versus the *interdependent self*, Markus and Kitayama (1991) propose that in many collectivist societies (see Chapter 5 in this book by Brislin for more on collectivism and individualism), mature adults are those who are able to think of their own personal needs as being secondary to the needs of the group. Unlike in the West, giving in to another person's decision is not a passive or weak gesture but is a sign of tolerance, self-control, flexibility, and maturity (Kumagai, 1981; Markus & Kitayama, 1991). Our colleague from Taiwan, therefore, would merit much respect as an extremely responsible member of society. However, our American colleagues who take pride in their initiative and independence would be perceived as lacking maturity. For many individualists, autonomy, independence, and assertiveness are signs of good movement toward career success. Therefore, finding himself in an individualist society, our colleague from Taiwan was perceived as not being "a candidate for the fast track" because of his apparent lack of autonomy and overall passivity.

In discussing the fundamental differences between individualists and collectivists, Hsu points out that the character used for *people* in Chinese as well as Japanese literally means "individual's interactions with his fellow human beings" (Hsu, 1985, p. 33). In addition, the character for *person* is made up of two strokes, one supporting the other. In short, **collectivists** see people as interdependent beings that exist only in conjunction with others. An individual is not an entity of his or her own but is, rather, an integral component of a larger structure called society. According to Ho (Ho, in press), there are five common themes that emerge from a review of the literature on Asian cultures. They are: (1) collectivism, (2) reciprocity, (3) other-directedness, (4) maintenance of harmony and avoidance of open conflicts, and (5) conformity.

A natural outgrowth of this interdependence is **reciprocity**. Because people must continuously depend on others, when summoned they are naturally more willing to accommodate. Gift giving is considered an essential part of many collectivist societies, serving the need to affirm and reaffirm one's connections with others. Reciprocity also establishes a clear boundary differentiating those in the ingroup from those in the outgroup. For example, the Japanese customarily engage in the semiannual (i.e., *oseibo* in the winter and *ochugen* in the summer) practice of presenting gifts to people in their ingroups. The process is a reciprocal one with the amount spent on the gifts determined by one's status and the type of relationship maintained with the other party. Although ingroup members carry mutual obligations and indebtedness toward each other, this by no means extends to persons outside their group. Foreign visitors are sometimes surprised and disappointed at the lack of congeniality or politeness displayed toward them without realizing that it is only when they are perceived either as an ingroup member or a potential ingroup member that they are entitled to many of these privileges.

Another phenomenon that comes as a result of interdependence is the need to be **other-directed**. People can display this trait through extreme sensitivity to others' feelings and desires while viewing their own preferences as being secondary to that of the group. An interesting example that reflects this difference comes from comparing Western psychotherapy with *Naikan therapy*, which derives its roots from Japanese Buddhism. Naikan therapy consists of structured meditation conducted in solitude for 1 week. Customarily, the *sensei* (teacher) assigns one topic per day to the client. Most of the "topics" are relevant people in the client's life, such as his or her mother, father, siblings, spouse, and friends (Reynolds, 1980). During the course of the day, the *sensei* enters the room at various intervals asking the client to reflect on the various gestures of kindness and sacrifices the person has made for them, as well as the multitude of inconveniences and problems the client has caused in return.

> Initial difficulties in concentration and a rather bitter view toward significant others is replaced by "the emergence of the real self" with accompanying feelings of regret, guilt, and sorrow over the way the client has treated his loved ones. The client may want to die; he may even voice thoughts of suicide. The next stage is prompted by the sensei's reminder that in spite of his own insensitivity and unkindness to others they loved and cared for him. When he recognizes this, the client feels repentance accompanied by a strong desire to serve and repay others. His motivation develops out of the wellspring of gratitude that erupts from within. Then comes joy, new purpose, and new meaning in life (Reynolds, 1980, p. 48, male pronouns in original).

As a result of this treatment, most clients' sense of interdependence is renewed. It fosters a strong sense of humility and gratitude toward others, moving clients away from a self-oriented existence. This stands in sharp contrast to Western methods of psychotherapy, which focuses primarily on the individual's own trauma, rarely acknowledging the sacrifices or acts of kindness exhibited by significant others. When and if others are introduced into therapy sessions, their negative rather than positive effects on the client's life often tends to be the focus.

Maintenance of harmony and avoidance of open conflicts is another characteristic that is found in many collectivist societies. Again, in a society in which people must constantly depend on each other, respecting the feelings of others (especially those in their ingroup) becomes an all-important factor. According to Lynch (1973), smoothness of interpersonal relations is so important to the Filipinos that people will do all they can to

> avoid outward signs of conflict: glum or sour looks, harsh words, open disagreement, or physical violence. It connotes the smile, the friendly lift of the eyebrow, the pat on the back, the squeeze of the arm, the word of praise or friendly concern. It means being agreeable even under difficult circumstances. . . . It means a sensitivity to what people feel at any given moment, and a willingness and ability to change tack (if not direction) to catch the slightest favoring breeze. (p. 10)

With this in mind, Critical Incident 2 should make more sense. Being the mature adult he was in his cultural terms, Nestor was trying his best to maintain harmony and to avoid overt conflict. When asked to help out, therefore, he would always smile and agree enthusiastically. Knowing of Nestor's other commitments, Phil should have taken one of two choices: (1) not put Nestor "on the spot" in the first place, or (2) if he had already imposed the project on him, at least do his part in maintaining harmony and avoiding overt conflict by not blaming Nestor for being irresponsible. If he were more interculturally sophisticated, Phil would have undoubtedly recognized nonverbal signals emitted by Nestor that would translate to "I really don't have the time to do this, Phil."

This tendency holds true for many of the other Asian cultures as well. When people are in situations in which they must convey an unpleasant message, they do so *very* indirectly. Much too often, individualists are unable to understand what is being said to them even when the Asian person feels that he or she is being *extremely* direct. Simply stated, directness in the Asian sense would still be considered indirect from an American perspective. An indirect message in the Asian sense, therefore, inevitably goes unnoticed most of the time. An example would be the practice of saying "No" without doing so directly. In response to the great deal of confusion expressed by many Americans, various researchers have discussed this phenomenon quite extensively. Ueda (Ueda, 1974) and Imai (Imai, 1981) discuss 16 ways in which the Japanese avoid saying

"No." Rubin (1980) extends the discussion further to incorporate examples from other cultures such as Taiwan, Korea, Poland, the Marshall Islands, and Indonesia, providing concrete suggestions on how to tell when someone from these cultures is trying to say "No." In sum, it should be of no surprise that in these societies where interdependence and group harmony are highly valued, **conformity**, instead of self-assertion, is a prevalent characteristic. This does *not* imply that individuals in these cultures do not experience discrepancies between their inner feelings and their outward role demands but merely demonstrates that they perceive the latter as more important (Smith, 1985).

Many of these traits, however, are not limited only to Asian cultures but hold true for many other cultures, especially those with an agricultural history (i.e., some African, Latin American, and South European cultures; Markus & Kitayama, 1991). Even in the United States, members of Quaker communities, as well as people in many small towns and rural communities, often display similar characteristics. As mentioned earlier, it has also been argued that many women in the United States demonstrate these behaviors and values that are associated with collectivism (Gilligan, 1982; Tannen, 1990).

External (Objective) Versus Interpersonal Reality

If conceptions of the "self" do in fact vary across cultures, it follows that people's understanding of "reality" must also differ. It is common knowledge that individuals' perceptions are selective in that they pick and choose what is relevant to themselves. Although people often believe that they see reality as it exists, everybody sees "reality" differently from each other. Despite individual variances, it is proposed that there are even larger cultural differences in the perception of reality. Diaz-Guerrero (1975) suggests that reality can be broken up into two general categories: *interpersonal reality* and *external (objective) reality*.

Interpersonal reality refers to the feelings and impressions created during interactions between two or more people. Good interpersonal reality is characterized by the generation of pleasant feelings, and bad interpersonal reality is reflected through disagreement or conflict. Although many interactions enable the simultaneous consideration of both realities, certain situations force people to choose or to emphasize one over the other. Culture is often the guiding force in making such decisions. Diaz-Guerrero (1975) suggests that interpersonal reality is often perceived as more important than external reality for many Mexicans.

> Ask a Mexican for street directions. He will often go into a complex series of explanations and gestures, frequently grinning; he will make you feel good. But you may get nowhere with his directions! Simply because he cannot answer your question, the Mexican would never let the real thing, the pleasant interpersonal encounter, go to waste. (p. 19)

Some of the readers may notice that after a conversation with certain people they feel "good" for no apparent reason. In contrast, they may notice that conversations with certain others, more often than not, tend to end with unpleasant feelings. People who are *interpersonal reality* oriented focus on creating good feelings during encounters, avoiding overt conflict as much as possible. This may mean telling white lies, bending the truth, skirting the issue, pretending to agree, or simply sticking to pleasant conversational topics. Although within a given culture there are always people who are more adept at creating good *interpersonal reality* than others, it is also clear that some cultures attach a greater value to this characteristic than others. As mentioned earlier, people who live in societies that ascribe to the *interdependent* view of the self need to constantly pay attention to ingroup members' feelings and opinions. In their societies, the creation and maintenance of good interpersonal reality often determines the success or failure of a person's career and other lifelong goals. For example, according to Miller (in press), the "Hindu Indian view of interpersonal responsibilities" is seen as "obligatory rather than voluntarily assumed."

An interesting discussion can be found in a Japanese book entitled *Kikubari no susume* (Suzuki, 1985), which literally means "advocating the act of giving out your heart." *Kikubari* figuratively means putting yourself in another person's place and providing them with whatever they need most. Kikubari can range from small but meaningful gestures such as presenting your business card using two hands instead of one to more extensive acts such as helping out during times of crisis. The main characteristic of *kikubari* is that the person is sensitive enough to offer help or kindness *without* being asked. *Kikubari* is the personal touch that helps foster relationships. For example, it might mean providing your guest with their favorite cool drink on a hot day (without being asked), avoiding conversational topics that you know makes them uncomfortable, and in general, behaving in a manner that makes the other party feel special. In short, *kikubari* is something that makes other people feel good, thus fostering good interpersonal reality. What makes this book extremely interesting is that during the first 9 months that it was on the market, over 2,700,000 copies were sold. One of the reasons underlying its apparent success was that various schools distributed the book at graduation ceremonies and some companies gave it out to newly employed college graduates. Because of its success, the sequel to the book was published the following year (Suzuki, 1986).

This phenomenon demonstrates that the Japanese openly acknowledge that small interpersonal behaviors can make or break a contract. This is not to say that these same behaviors are of no consequence to individualists. In fact, they often play a large role in various settings. The difference is that collectivist societies *openly* acknowledge and treat interpersonal reality as relevant even in business settings, whereas individualist societies will often, on the surface, frown on mixing subjective feelings with business. American companies, for example, would be much less likely to distribute a book of this nature to their employees and would not openly admit such statements as the ones made below by Suzuki, the author of the book and a renowned host of various educational television shows in Japan.

> I receive several phone calls daily inviting me to deliver a speech or asking me to write a manuscript. Often times, I decide whether I will take it or not after the first few seconds on the phone with them. . . . When I am making a business call and no one answers after five or six rings I find it safe to assume that their company does not amount to much . . . (pp. 51-52, translation by author)

Because interpersonal reality is acknowledged as part of the Japanese societal norm, many companies conduct various training programs for newly entering employees dealing with topics that create and maintain good feelings between people. Behaviors such as the proper way to bow, present a business card, serve tea, answer phones, as well as other behaviors that create a good impression on the other party are covered. If American companies were to conduct such training sessions, two possible arguments would be likely to arise. One would be "you are insulting my well-developed social skills" and the other would be the irrelevance of "personal" factors in business relationships. In general, it is safe to say that a stronger personal dimension is involved in conducting business with collectivists. The amount of time spent getting to know one's business partners *prior* to negotiations as well as the amount of time spent with colleagues after hours both reflect the importance attached to interpersonal reality (Items 3 and 4 in the inventory, Part I).

External reality refers to measurable, verifiable phenomena that exist in nature. These are often what people accept as "facts." For example, if one were to find a stray animal on the street, it would be fairly easy to find out various external realities, such as the type of animal it is (e.g., dog, cat, rabbit), its breed (e.g., cocker spaniel, dachshund), its sex, how much it weighs, how healthy it is, as well as other tangibles. Additional factors that are often classified as "external reality" are ideas and widely accepted societal norms such as "you should not slurp when you drink your soup" or "honesty is the best policy."

From a Western perspective, behaviors such as telephone manners would be classified as being "interpersonal" and therefore less important. It would be considered unprofessional to determine which jobs to take based on the other party's telephone manners. Instead, people would be expected to stick to *external reality* factors such as the amount of pay involved, the reputation of the organization, the qualifications of their agent, and the type of publicity that would be given in return. This is not to say that the interpersonal factors do not influence the decision at all. The difference would be that the *salient* factors determining the decision would be those related to external reality. For example, if one were interviewing two equally qualified candidates for a job, it is more than likely that the person who is able to create a better interpersonal reality will get the job. Once the decision is made, however, chances that the American interviewer will credit the candidate's ability to make the interviewer *feel good* (interpersonal reality) are very unlikely. If asked, the interviewer will more likely attribute his or her decision on the candidate's "professional attitude," "better communication skills," and the like. In other words, external reality factors are perceived as being more socially acceptable in making business decisions.

At this point a few words of precaution must be made. As mentioned earlier, these two concepts are not mutually exclusive. Most people see both realities and can often accommodate to both. However, when they must make a choice one reality takes precedence over the other. As with other cultural differences, there will naturally be exceptions to the rule with various contextual factors affecting each situation. Readers must also be advised that since the concepts are based on an American framework they are best used in explaining the logic behind collectivists' actions as interpreted by individualists rather than vice versa. For collectivists, many of the factors that have thus far been classified under "interpersonal reality" are significant and *real* to them and are hence likely to be classified under "external reality." If individualists are able to understand the distinction with the additional knowledge that collectivists see interpersonal reality as carrying as much or more importance than external reality, many "puzzling aspects" of collectivist behavior might be resolved.

For example, Critical Incident 1 can be analyzed using the two concepts. In this incident, George confused the behaviors (i.e., compliments and positive tone) that were meant to create good interpersonal reality as being indicative of external reality (i.e., whether he would get the job or not). For many collectivists good interpersonal reality is often a goal in itself. Commenting on George's high credentials, therefore, accomplished this very goal. The external reality task, which was to tell George that he did not get the job, was done indirectly through avoiding the topic and postponing the decision. George, however, assumed that there was one goal (i.e., deciding whether he would get the job or not) and that good interpersonal reality would be dependent on the outcome of this goal. He, therefore, misread the interviewer's attempt at fostering good interpersonal reality as an indirect sign that he would be hired for the position. By understanding that for many Japanese creating good interpersonal reality can be a goal in itself, George might be able to avoid making erroneous attributions in the future.

Here are a few patterns that should be noted when presenting these concepts:

1. *There is often a clear overlap between the two realities*. For example, if Mary is supposed to meet John at 2:00 p.m. for a business meeting and he is on time (external reality) she will most likely be pleasant to him (interpersonal reality). Since there is no clash or disagreement, both realities coexist and there is little reason to think about them.

2. *The two realities become clear when there is a clash*. If John had been 30 minutes late, however, Mary would have had to decide whether she should cut his appointment short or at least say something regarding his tardiness (emphasizing

external reality) or whether she would benefit more by being extremely pleasant to him (emphasizing interpersonal reality).

3. *The concepts are not necessarily black or white—there are many gray areas.* If Mary decided to be nice and cordial to John (interpersonal reality) because she was planning to ask him for a favor (external reality) and also because she likes to avoid overt conflict when possible (interpersonal reality), there is clearly a mix of the two concepts.

4. *Interpersonal reality can affect people's perception of external reality.* For example, if two different people had been 30 minutes late (external reality) to see Mary but she clearly liked one person over the other (interpersonal reality), her reaction to the two's tardiness is likely to differ quite significantly.

5. *External reality can affect people's perceptions of interpersonal reality.* Sometimes we notice that certain traits in people we have known for a while are less irritating or may even be pleasing after we find out that they have a hidden talent (i.e., plays a musical instrument, won a speech contest, organized a major charity event in the community), of which we were not previously aware. The colleague who was once considered "moody" now has an "artistic temperament" and the neighbor who was once considered "incessantly talkative" is now considered an "amazing orator."

6. *Different people and cultures classify the world differently.* As mentioned earlier, collectivists are likely to classify as "external reality" any factors that individualists place under "interpersonal reality." This is obviously related to the overwhelming importance of interpersonal relations in collectivist societies as opposed to individualist societies. Most well-meaning clashes occur when both parties believe that *they* are the ones dealing with external reality and are therefore being rational. By understanding the distinction between the two realities trainees should have the advantage of knowing that many disagreements occur not because one person is being more rational than the other but because both people feel that the reality they are dealing with is more important.

Interpersonal Versus External Versus Internal Reality

When we make decisions regarding how to behave, in addition to considering the "facts" (external reality) and how people might react to our decision (interpersonal reality), one more factor is usually involved. This is the *internal* or *personal reality* that reflects our personal preferences and desires. Imagine that your friend Sally is wearing a brand new red dress that looks expensively tailored. She asks how you like the dress. You know that Sally has been analyzed by several beauty consultants and has been advised not to wear red because it makes her complexion look dull (external reality). However, you want her to feel good about the new dress she bought (interpersonal reality). Whether you decide to emphasize external over interpersonal reality or vice versa would be the manifestation of your *internal reality* or your personal inclinations.

Another example of *internal reality* can be observed in the following scenario. You are going to dinner with a group of friends and are now in the process of deciding where to go. There are usually several factors that people consider when making this decision. What you want to eat (internal reality), how much you can afford (external reality), what restaurants are in the vicinity (external reality), and what other people want to eat (agreement or disagreement can affect interpersonal reality) are usually considered. The major difference between collectivists and individualists is that when placed in a situation in which one reality must be chosen over the other, collectivists have a stronger tendency to choose interpersonal over non-interpersonal reality (i.e., external and internal reality), whereas the opposite is true for individualists. A typical situation when a group of Japanese decide to go out for dinner is to have a circle of people asking each other "What do *you* want to have for dinner?" only getting the answer "It doesn't matter, what do *you* want?" until someone finally hints *very* subtly that he or she has a possible suggestion. Usually this is accepted immediately with much enthusiasm and rarely with any opposition. Because people are worried that their internal reality may clash with someone else's (possibly leading to bad interpersonal reality), often a significant amount of probing is conducted before a concrete suggestion is made. Even though the individuals inevitably have varied preferences (internal reality), they only see it as being of secondary importance to maintaining harmonious relations with the other group members (interpersonal reality).

If a group of Americans had congregated, however, the typical reaction is for everyone to state what they want (internal reality), talk about the pluses and the minuses, and finally settle down to a "majority rules" (quantifiable, thus external reality) conclusion. The individuals are less likely to worry about offending someone by disagreeing with their choice (interpersonal reality) and, therefore, place more emphasis on external as well as internal reality. In fact, many Americans find the situation irritating (bad interpersonal reality for them) when a group of people spend close to 30 minutes feeling each other out and being indecisive. What defines good interpersonal reality is, therefore, culturally as well as personally defined.

Suggestions for Individualists

The first step to interacting more effectively with collectivists is to develop an ongoing commitment to *attempt* to understand the reasons behind their behaviors. Instead of dismissing them as inscrutable or illogical this framework clarifies to individualists that collectivists are simply placing more emphasis on a different reality. Often, like George in Critical Incident 1, we misattribute behaviors that were meant to be in one reality as being in another. As discussed earlier, in George's case, he misattributed the interviewer's compliments, which were intended to foster good interpersonal reality, as cues that meant that he would be hired (external reality). His confusion and frustration would not have occurred if George had understood that creating good interpersonal reality is often a goal in itself for many collectivists. The following are some suggestions that individualists can follow to facilitate understanding of the behaviors of collectivists.

1. Remind yourself that in many circumstances collectivists perceive interpersonal reality as being much more important than external or internal reality.

2. Be familiar with some of the behaviors collectivists display to avoid creating bad interpersonal reality. Some of these are: being very indirect (so they can change their position in an argument at any time if necessary), avoiding the word *no* if possible (Imai, 1981; Rubin, 1980; Ueda, 1974), making it a point to ask others what they think, spending a lot of time "feeling each other out," and apologizing constantly and profusely.

3. If you are in a situation in which you are puzzled by their actions, ask yourself what the interpersonal, internal, and external realities are for the other person as well as for yourself. Then, try to evaluate which reality the other person is giving priority to in contrast to the reality you feel is important.

4. Pay attention to other people's nonverbals more (more on this in Chapter 14 by Singelis).

At this point, many individualists need to evaluate their alternatives. People naturally find it easiest to communicate with others who give priority to the same reality as they do. When communicating with collectivists, individualists may find themselves in situations in which the clash between interpersonal reality and the non-interpersonal realities (internal and external) are too extreme for comfort. This is where careful judgment is called for. Sometimes compromises can be made. Some people will decide to take the "when in Rome, do as the Romans" approach, whereas others will prefer to be understanding of other people's actions without changing their own behaviors, and still others will make their decisions on a case-by-case approach. The following are suggestions for those who seek to modify their behaviors to match those of collectivists.

1. When communicating with collectivists, practice saying things that will make them feel good.

2. Learn to use apologies as a social lubricant (Sakamoto, 1982). In collectivist societies, apologies are usually reciprocated, with both parties "taking the blame." What individualists need to remember is that "taking the blame" is mainly a social front and does not necessarily put a person "at fault" from an external reality perspective. The key is to remember that it is very hard to be angry at an apologetic person. Apologies usually soften whatever negative feelings may be building between people.

3. When you have a choice, always give due consideration to the alternative that fosters interpersonal reality before making a decision. Many Americans

are socialized to believe that if they know what is "right" (external reality) it is their obligation to persuade and convince others. Try challenging this assumption. Consider the various consequences of bad interpersonal reality. For example, breaking a consensus could lead to someone losing face and possible exclusion from the group. Confronting a boss can also cause loss of face and lead to negative outcomes at work. Another interesting phenomenon to note is that after arguments, we often do not remember what we argued about but we do remember the negative feelings that were generated through the encounter.

4. When communicating with collectivists, practice a more indirect style of communication. Avoid saying "No" as much as possible. A few of the ways in which the Japanese say "No" are: using silence, counter questioning, making tangential responses, leaving, lying, and making "Yes, but . . . " responses (Ueda, 1974).

5. When making requests or invitations, form your statements so that the other party can easily back out without saying "No." A strategy that the Japanese often use is saying "if you don't mind . . . " (*moshi yoroshikereba . . .*) followed by an offer or a request. The statement should be made very tentatively, using extensive periods of silence during which they can read into the other party's nonverbals. For example, someone might say "If you don't mind, I was planning on cooking shabu shabu for dinner . . ." (look at the other party's reactions) . . . and (a) if he or she seems eager, proceed with the invitation, or (b) if he or she looks tentative, say something like "You must be busy, right?" By phrasing your questions in this manner, negative answers require affirmation rather than negation. The key often lies in understanding the nonverbal messages they are sending you.

In sum, it can be said that although knowledge and understanding may not immediately change our behaviors, they provide us with a different perception of "reality." Familiarity with this conceptual framework should not only provide trainees with a tool that can facilitate understanding of otherwise puzzling behaviors manifested by collectivists but should also provide them with a basis from which behavioral changes can evolve. The following sections provide exercises that should familiarize trainees with these concepts. As a result, trainees should be able to internalize the process of analyzing everyday situations using these concepts. Strategies can then be discussed and implemented when necessary.

Skill Applications

Understanding and *reframing* are key concepts in this module. Instead of viewing cultural differences as problems, they can be looked at as a puzzle or a game that can stimulate intellectual discussion.

Exercise 1: Using the Self-Assessment Exercise

The main goal of this exercise is to foster empathy between people who give primary consideration to interpersonal reality and those who give primary consideration to external reality. This exercise will take place as a large group discussion. The trainer should do the following:

1. Ask the participants to fill out the self-assessment at the beginning of this chapter (approximately 5 minutes), if they have not already.

2. Ask the participants whose answers were more on the right side of the continuum to raise their hands, followed by those who tended to mark those options on the left side. If a clear pattern cannot be seen for the inventory in general, the trainer might want to go item by item to see if there are at least one or two that bring out opposing viewpoints among the participants present. If there are at least one or two where there are significant numbers of people representing both sides of the continuum, alternative *a* in Step 3 can be taken.

3. Either one of two formats can be taken: (a) if there seems to be enough trainees who marked opposing ends of the continuum, they should be broken up into groups of four with both extremes represented; (b) if the trainees seem to have marked mainly toward the middle of the continuum, the trainer can divide them into groups of four while randomly assigning half the group to take on the "strongly agree" perspective and the other half the "strongly disagree" perspective.

4. The trainer should make it clear that the purpose of this exercise is to develop *empathy* toward a different way of seeing reality. Most trainees will not change their way of seeing things but will at least learn that there is a logic behind other people's behaviors. As the discussion becomes more intense, trainees may need to be reminded that the main goal is *not* to convince others that their way is the best but to understand that other people's way of thinking makes sense as well.

5. Participants should then go through the self-assessment exercise items one by one, explaining to each other *why* they chose a particular answer. (If they were randomly assigned to take on a certain perspective, they should still try their best to explain why to the rest of the group regardless of what they really believe.) The participants can either go through the items chronologically or pick and choose which ones interest them most.

6. Reconvene as a large group. Ask participants for any insights or comments they would like to make. *Note:* There is no reason to cover *all* the items in the assessment exercise because they are ultimately based on the same two concepts (i.e., external and interpersonal reality). If a stimulating discussion is generated through Item 1, it might be a better idea to let the groups spend the whole session on this particular item rather than rushing through the others.

Exercise 2: Using the Inventory

This exercise has two main goals: (1) to familiarize trainees with the practice of using the three realities to analyze various situations, and (2) to give trainees an opportunity to examine which of the three realities they tend to value most. Trainers should distribute five copies each of the questionnaire on the following page to all the participants. Participants should at their leisure fill out the questionnaire for each item in the inventory at the beginning of this module. After they have completed the questionnaires, trainees should spend a moment or two reflecting on what they learned about themselves through the exercise.

The following is an example of how the questionnaire can be filled out. This one is based on Item 1 of the inventory.

1. What were your initial reactions when you first encountered this phenomenon (either in real life, via the media, or through this inventory)? *The Mexicans are lying. I'm not sure why, but it might be a game they play with foreigners.*
2. What type of behavior or response would you feel more comfortable with? *To get a straight answer. If they know it, that's great. If they don't, then that's fine, too.*
3. Which reality (or realities) would you classify these expectations (i.e., your answer to Question 2) under? *Mainly external. I want to know the facts!*
4. Why do you think he or she or they acted in the way he or she or they did? *Because they did not want to say "No, I don't know" and disappoint us.*
5. Which reality (or realties) would you classify their expectations (i.e., answer to Question 2) under? *Interpersonal reality.*
6. What bothers you most about this practice? *I'm never sure whether to believe them or not.*
7. Which of your values feels violated? *Honesty, time.*
8. Why do you think this person (or these people) prefer this mode of interaction? *It shows people's sincere desire to please others.*
9. What type of "social skills" do you think people in this society have to accommodate to these practices? *They probably have a way of knowing (perhaps through their nonverbal behaviors) when people are telling "the truth" from an external reality perspective and when they are simply saying something to create good interpersonal reality.*
10. What do you think are some of the advantages of this system? *People do not have to worry about being rejected openly. There is a lot of caring and sincerity involved.*

Inventory Questionnaire

Please fill out one sheet for every item on the inventory.

1. What were your initial reactions when you first encountered this phenomenon (either in real life, via the media, or through this inventory)?

_____

_____

2. With what type of behavior or response would you feel more comfortable?

_____

_____

3. Which reality (or realities) would you classify these expectations (i.e., your answer to Question 2) under?

_____

_____

4. Why do you think he or she or they acted in the way he or she or they did?

_____

_____

5. Which reality (or realities) would you classify their expectations (i.e., answer to Question 2) under?

_____

_____

6. What bothers you most about this practice?

_____

_____

7. Which of your values feels violated?

_____

_____

8. Why do you think this person (or these people) prefer this mode of interaction?

_____

_____

9. What type of "social skills" do you think people in this society have to accommodate to these practices?

_____

_____

10. What do you think are some of the advantages of this system?

_____

_____

References

Chodorow, N. (1974). Family structure and feminine personality. In M. Z. Rosaldo & L. Lamphere (Eds.), *Woman, culture, and society.* Stanford, CA: Stanford University Press.

Diaz-Guerrero, R. (1975). *Psychology of the Mexican: Culture and personality.* Austin: University of Texas Press.

Gilligan, C. (1982). *In a different voice.* Cambridge, MA: Harvard University Press.

Ho, D. Y. F. (1993). Relational orientation in Asian social psychology. In U. Kim & J. W. Berry (Eds.), *Indigenous psychologies: Research and experience in cultural context* (pp. 240-259). Newbury Park, CA: Sage.

Hsu, F. L. K. (1985). The self in cross-cultural perspective. In A. J. Marsella, G. DeVos, & F. L. K. Hsu (Eds.), *Culture and self: Asian and Western perspectives* (pp. 24-55). New York: Tavistock.

Imai, M. (1981). *16 ways to avoid saying no.* Tokyo: The Nihon Keizai Shimbun.

Kumagai, H. A. (1981). A dissection of intimacy: A study of "bipolar posturing" in Japanese social interaction—*amaeru* and *amayakasu*, indulgence and deference. *Culture, Medicine, and Psychiatry, 5,* 249-272.

Lynch, F. (1973). Social acceptance reconsidered. In F. Lynch & A. d. G. II (Eds.), *Four readings on Philippine values* (pp. 1-68). Quezon City, Philippines: Ateneo de Manila University Press.

Markus, H. R., & Kitayama, S. (1991). Culture and the self: Implications for cognition, emotion, and motivation. *Psychological Review, 98*(2), 224-253.

Miller, J. G. (in press). Cultural diversity in the morality of caring: Individually-oriented versus duty-based interpersonal moral codes. *Behavior Science Research,* Special issue: Moral reasoning in cross-cultural perspective.

Reynolds, D. K. (1980). *The quiet therapies.* Honolulu: University Press of Hawaii.

Rubin, J. (1980). How to tell when someone is saying "no"! In M. P. Hamnett & R. W. Brislin (Eds.), *Research in culture learning: Language and conceptual studies.* Honolulu, HI: The East-West Center.

Sakamoto, N. (1982). *Polite fictions: Why Japanese and Americans seem rude to each other.* Tokyo: Kinseido.

Smith, R. J. (1985). A pattern of Japanese society: In society or knowledge of interdependence? *Journal of Japanese Studies, 11,* 29-45.

Suzuki, K. (1985). *Kikubari no susume.* Tokyo: Kodansha.

Suzuki, K. (1986). *Kikubari no susume, part 2.* Tokyo: Kodansha.

Tannen, D. (1990). *You just don't understand.* New York: Ballantine.

Ueda, K. (1974). Sixteen ways to avoid saying "no." In J. C. Condon & M. Saito (Eds.), *Intercultural encounters with Japan: Communication—contact and conflict.* Tokyo: The Simul Press.

14 Nonverbal Communication in Intercultural Interactions

TED SINGELIS

Nobility and dignity, self-abasement and servility, prudence and understanding, insolence and vulgarity, are reflected in the face and in the attitudes of body whether still or in motion.

Socrates (Xenophon, *Memorabilia III*)

The unspoken dialogue between two people can never be put right by anything they say.

United Nations Secretary-General Dag Hammarskjöld

Too often, nonverbal communication is neglected during intercultural communication training workshops. At best, a few culture-specific gestures are covered. Nonverbal communication is much more extensive; some researchers claim that up to 93% of the social meaning of a message is carried via nonverbal channels. This module not only examines the nature of nonverbal communication but familiarizes readers with a variety of possible pitfalls that can occur when communicating with culturally different others. Readers are also given an opportunity to explore, in detail, nonverbal behaviors that are both familiar (from their own culture) and unfamiliar (necessary for communication in other cultures).

Contents

III. Skill Concepts: The Importance, Functions, and Pitfalls of Nonverbal Communication in Intercultural Interactions

IV. Skill Development Exercises

V. Field Exercise

Self-Assessment Exercise:
Nonverbal Communication Knowledge

This exercise is intended to assist participants develop an awareness of (1) their own nonverbal communication in intercultural interactions and (2) cultural differences in nonverbal communication.

Instructions: Assume that you are living and working in a country other than your own, or that in your work you deal with many people from cultures other than your own. Respond to the statements as best you can, agreeing and disagreeing if possible. For some statements you may feel that the response depends heavily on information that is not given (such as the culture of the other person). In that case, mark the "it depends" response but make a note as to what specific information would enable you to respond more definitely. Circle a number to indicate your choice.

1. I can usually tell when there is something bothering the people I interact with because they will usually display a sad or depressed manner.

1	2	3	4	5
strongly disagree	disagree	it depends	agree	strongly agree

2. The best way to get along with others and avoid misunderstandings is to express my thoughts and feelings clearly and directly via verbal communication.

1	2	3	4	5
strongly disagree	disagree	it depends	agree	strongly agree

3. I can usually tell when others are displeased with my work because they tell me how I can do better.

1	2	3	4	5
strongly disagree	disagree	it depends	agree	strongly agree

4. Since people from all cultures use the same facial expressions to show their emotions, I can usually tell how others are reacting to me.

1	2	3	4	5
strongly disagree	disagree	it depends	agree	strongly agree

5. I use direct eye contact with my superiors to show that I respect them and am paying attention to what they say.

1	2	3	4	5
strongly disagree	disagree	it depends	agree	strongly agree

6. When meeting people for the first time, I always act in a relaxed and confident manner in order to make a good first impression.

1	2	3	4	5
strongly disagree	disagree	it depends	agree	strongly agree

7. When a person responds to my question with silence, it usually indicates that the person has not understood what I said but does not want to cause embarrassment to me or him- or herself by asking me to repeat the question.

1	2	3	4	5
strongly disagree	disagree	it depends	agree	strongly agree

8. What is not said in a conversation is often more important than what is expressed directly.

1	2	3	4	5
strongly disagree	disagree	it depends	agree	strongly agree

9. Laughter always indicates that a person is happy and comfortable.

1	2	3	4	5
strongly disagree	disagree	it depends	agree	strongly agree

10. People who have strong body odor are offensive and should be taught proper personal hygiene habits for their own good.

1	2	3	4	5
strongly disagree	disagree	it depends	agree	strongly agree

11. I use a lot of gestures and emphasis in my voice to make points because my foreign language skills are not very good and these nonverbal clues will help me to be understood by people who do not speak my language.

1	2	3	4	5
strongly disagree	disagree	it depends	agree	strongly agree

12. I usually try to keep a conversation active and lively because people will think I am not intelligent, or my language ability is very poor, if I am silent.

1	2	3	4	5
strongly disagree	disagree	it depends	agree	strongly agree

13. Since people know I am from a different culture, my appearance is not an important factor in how they think about me.

1	2	3	4	5
strongly disagree	disagree	it depends	agree	strongly agree

14. When I get conflicting messages from people's verbal and nonverbal communications, it is better to consider only the verbal communication because the nonverbal messages are ambiguous and I am not familiar with the meaning of nonverbal communications in other cultures.

1	2	3	4	5
strongly disagree	disagree	it depends	agree	strongly agree

15. The best way to establish good relations with others is to demonstrate my friendliness and goodwill by smiling, laughing, and generally treating others as equals.

1	2	3	4	5
strongly disagree	disagree	it depends	agree	strongly agree

To workshop leaders: The purpose of this self-assessment exercise is to generate discussions and so there is no "scoring" of the instrument and there are no "right and wrong" answers. If you choose to discuss these items in a group format, keep in mind that people may disagree about the proper response to a given item because they have different cultures in mind. This is precisely the point of the exercise! Nonverbal communication varies across cultures; for example, what is common behavior in the United States may not be common elsewhere.

Case Studies: Critical Incidents

Critical Incident: I Think She Likes Me

Jim Deveneu was a systems analyst for an international consulting firm based in New York City. Having studied Spanish as well as computers while in college, he was attracted to this particular consulting firm because of the possibilities for overseas assignments. Jim was still single and felt he had the freedom to relocate at this point in his career. He enjoyed meeting people from different cultures and felt that he was especially sensitive to their feelings and attitudes. He had dated women from several different cultures when he was in college.

After 2 years in the home office, Jim's chance for an overseas assignment came when he was offered a position as an assistant manager in San Jose, Costa Rica. Jim jumped at the opportunity and soon found himself at work in the San Jose office. His work went well and Jim was impressed by the cosmopolitan sophistication of his coworkers. Even though most of them spoke English quite well, they were appreciative of Jim's willingness to speak in Spanish and many helped him improve his language ability. After several weeks at his new job, Jim was feeling quite comfortable. Although being occasionally upset that people in Costa Rica kept him waiting without giving him reasonable excuses, Jim had established good relations with his coworkers and his clients.

Jim took it as a sign of his success in establishing good rapport with the host nationals when he was invited to a party to celebrate the first communion of his coworker's son. He happily accepted and queried other coworkers as to what would be an appropriate gift. Because he had not socialized much since arriving in San Jose, Jim looked forward to the appointed day as an opportunity to meet people outside his office and to make some social contacts.

Jim arrived at the party and found a larger than expected gathering of adults and children. He was warmly received by the host and hostess and thanked for his kind gift. Jim was enjoying the pleasant atmosphere of the party and was talking with one of his coworkers when their conversation was joined by an attractive young woman who was introduced as Gabriella Herrera. Jim was immediately attracted to her warm smile and attentive eyes. When his coworker excused himself, Gabriella did not follow, but continued talking with Jim. She stood close to Jim and occasionally touched his arm or shoulder as she asked many questions about his background and his work. When Jim reciprocated these casual touches, Gabriella did not pull away or seem bothered by his intimacy. Jim was getting the distinct impression that she was as attracted to him as he was to her. He was about to ask her for a date when the host joined them and said, "I see you have met Senora Herrera." Jim tried to mask his surprise at learning that she was married but wondered how good a job he had done. He breathed a sigh of relief that he had not embarrassed himself by asking her out but was left wondering if he had been purposely misled or had misread her feelings about him.

Discussion Questions

1. Do you think Jim was purposefully misled?
2. Why did he have the impression that Gabriella was attracted to him?
3. What are some cultural explanations for this misunderstanding?
4. What individual differences may have contributed to the cultural differences that were behind the misunderstanding?

Critical Incident: Just Trying to Be Friendly

Glen Saito is a third-generation Japanese-American. He was born and raised in an upper-middle-class suburb of Los Angeles. His father was a dentist and his mother taught elementary school. Glen has always been especially outgoing and personable. He was well liked by his classmates and was even voted "Mr. Congenial" by his high school senior class. It seemed natural for him to become a student adviser on finishing his MA degree in educational administration.

Glen had been a student adviser at a small Midwestern college for 2 years when the college decided to recruit a number of Japanese students to increase the school's diversity, as well as its enrollment. Given that the limited resources of the college precluded hiring a specialist, Glen was asked to become the foreign student adviser. "Besides," the dean said, "since you are Japanese, they will be more comfortable and see how easy it is to be successful here." Although he had some reservations about the new responsibility, Glen accepted the challenge.

Glen had always been successful in dealing with American students by conveying to them a feeling of equality and openness. He tried hard not to put himself above them. He dressed casually and requested that students call him by his first name. By establishing a warm and friendly relationship with students he was able to gain their trust and respect. He found that students reacted better when they were allowed to take the initiative in seeking his help rather than being coerced into following his advice. His "open door" policy was well received and well used by American students. Because he was young, Glen felt that he could make students comfortable by showing that he was similar to them in his attitudes and behaviors. For example, he sometimes made jokes about the president of the college. Although Glen realized that the Japanese students would require some special attention, he saw no reason to change his basic style to accommodate the Japanese students. After all, he thought, "everyone deserves to be treated the same way." But in order to show he was sensitive to the Japanese problems, Glen began to study the Japanese language. He felt that it would help him to identify with the difficulties of functioning in a second language.

When the 12 Japanese students arrived, Glen hosted an orientation session for them that involved a campus tour, a lecture from the dean about academic requirements, and a picnic with American students. During the orientation Glen explained his "open door" policy and said he hoped the Japanese would feel free to visit him anytime. At the picnic Glen made it a point to introduce himself to each of the Japanese students personally and to make them feel comfortable. He told students to call him by his first name and joked with them about the difficulties of learning a new language. He even tried out a few of the Japanese phrases he had learned. The Japanese seemed amused by his joking and were surprised that he could not speak Japanese well. They also seemed a bit "uptight," but Glen thought they were just nervous about communicating in English. All in all, Glen had the impression that the orientation had gone quite well. The students had gotten a lot of useful information about their school life and he had done his best to convey to them that he was approachable and friendly. He looked forward to helping them with the problems he knew would arise during the semester.

Glen was surprised that none of the Japanese came to see him during the first week of classes. He had thought that they might have some difficulties with determining course requirements and the general logistics of dropping or adding classes. Then, during the second week, he received a call from the dean's office asking why the Japanese students were coming to the dean to ask routine questions about changing classes. Glen thought that he had made clear his role as adviser to the Japanese, but he sent out a letter explaining again that the students should come to him with their problems before approaching the dean. After that, a few students came to see him with questions about their classes, but when he asked them how they were getting along, they seemed to hesitate and just answer "OK." Glen thought that they were still having some trouble with their English, but since no problems were expressed he assumed that things were going well enough.

Glen did not discover how mistaken he was until after the Christmas break. About half of the Japanese students did not return to school after the break! When inquiries were made, it was learned that many students had transferred to other U.S. universities because they felt they had not been given adequate guidance. It was also discovered that several incidents of Japan-bashing had occurred and some students felt unwelcome on campus. Glen was quite surprised by all of this. He could not figure out what had gone wrong.

Discussion Questions

Why did the Japanese go to the dean before going to Glen? What nonverbal cues contributed to this tendency? Do you think that Glen's age or appearance had anything to do with the Japanese reluctance to consult him? How do you think the Japanese viewed the "open door" policy? Why didn't the Japanese let

Glen know there were problems—or did they? How could Glen have altered his approach to be more successful with the Japanese? What nonverbal behaviors should he have changed?

Skill Concepts: The Importance, Functions, and Pitfalls of Nonverbal Communication in Intercultural Interactions

Introduction

Nonverbal communication is a fundamental part of intercultural interactions. Sometimes this aspect of communication is overlooked in training or it is treated as a kind of vocabulary problem, with different gestures having different meanings in different cultures. However, the range of nonverbal behavior goes well beyond gestures. This chapter approaches nonverbal communication from a consideration of meaning across a variety of functions, recognizing that shared meaning, both verbal and nonverbal, is a necessity for successful communication. An implicit assumption here is that successful communication across cultural lines involves not only language but also culturally sensitive social skills as embodied, in part, in nonverbal behavior. As Michael Argyle observes, "Social skill requires correctly producing and receiving nonverbal messages. Moreover, we [Argyle and colleagues] came to believe that social skills, like motor skills, can be trained" (in Myers, 1990, p. 170).

The purpose of this module is threefold. First, it hopes to raise the reader's awareness of why nonverbal communication is important but difficult in intercultural interactions. Second, its goal is to increase knowledge about the functions of nonverbal behavior and how these functions give rise to opportunities for misunderstanding. Finally, this chapter will make suggestions to help improve skills for successful nonverbal communication in intercultural interactions.

Let's begin with a definition. The simplest definition of nonverbal communication is "communication without words" (DeVito, 1989, p. 3). This includes how we look, how we move, how we sound, and how we smell. Touching, eye contact, and the use of space and time are also facets of nonverbal communication. Everything we do that can be given meaning by others is included. Although the words themselves are not a part of nonverbal communication, the other aspects of speaking, such as tone,[1] loudness, and speed are an important part of nonverbal communication called *vocalics*. Notice that we do not have to intend to send nonverbal messages; meaning is dependent on the receiver's interpretation. Even doing nothing can carry meaning when interpreted by another person. It has been said that we cannot not communicate nonverbally (Watzlawick, Beavin, & Jackson, 1967). The wide range of behaviors that can carry meaning and the fact that these behaviors can be interpreted by another without our intention to communicate make nonverbal communication especially tricky business when more than one culture is involved.

Importance of Nonverbal Communication

Nonverbal communication is an important part of any interaction, but cultural differences make it crucial, though often difficult, in intercultural interactions. Research among Westerners has shown that nonverbal communication is more powerful than verbal. Although estimates vary from 65% (Birdwhistell, 1955) to 93% (Mehrabian & Ferris, 1967), most researchers would agree that a substantial part of the social meaning of a message is carried via nonverbal channels. Although this may seem astonishing, if you stop to think about your own experience, you may well agree with these estimates. For example, almost never do we ask, "Do you like me?" But almost always we know when someone does. We know because we've gotten the message through nonverbal channels. Often we are not aware exactly how or when the message was received, but we are usually quite sure of the content.

The power of nonverbal over verbal communication is especially apparent when there is a contradiction between the two modes (Argyle, Alkema, & Gilmour, 1971; Mehrabian & Weiner, 1967). How many times have we received the verbal message, "No, I'm not mad at you," with the accompanying facial expressions, body postures, and tone of voice that made us more than aware that the person actually was *very* mad at us?

In intercultural interactions, nonverbal communication may become even more important because of difficulties with language. The fact that at least one communicator is working in a second language means the verbal content may not be as clear as it would be in an intracultural interaction. Consequently, the reliance on nonverbal communication may be even greater than normal. Regardless of language difficulties, some characteristics of nonverbal communication help explain why it is more powerful than verbal communication.

Characteristics of Nonverbal Communication

Multichannel

There are several reasons nonverbal communication affects us so deeply. First, nonverbal communication is multichanneled. That is, nonverbal communication can come from visual, auditory, olfactory, or tactile channels. These various channels tend to work together rather than being isolated. Facial expression, tone of voice, and body posture can all combine to convey a message of happiness, or well-being, which is far stronger than the simple verbal message, "I feel happy." Verbal communication, in contrast, comes from only one channel—auditory for spoken language or visual for the written form.

Primacy

A second source of the power of nonverbal communication comes from its ontogenic and phylogenic primacy. Put simply, this means that as a species and as individuals, we developed nonverbal communication abilities before we developed verbal communication skills. Animals are capable of communicating nonverbally. They organized their societies and their relationships quite well. Although they cannot clearly communicate future or past events nonverbally, neither can we. As individuals, we develop nonverbal communication skills long before we can talk (see Woods, 1981). Research has shown that even at birth babies are capable of changing their vocalizations to reflect psychological needs (i.e., hunger vs. pain). Further, Roberts (1987) showed that mothers (better than fathers) could determine the meaning of their baby's cry (e.g., "I'm hungry" or "I'm wet"). In this case, the nonverbal message was decoded by the mother to determine the meaning. However, often nonverbal messages are not consciously decoded.

Unmediated

The final, and perhaps most important, source of nonverbal communication's power is the fact that it's often unmediated communication. By this I mean that, unlike verbal communication, nonverbal communication does not necessarily have an intervening process between the message and its source (in the case of sending) or interpretation (in the case of reception). There is evidence (discussed below) that indicates certain (not all) emotions are expressed by the same physical displays in all cultures. This leads us to believe that there is a direct physical ("hardwired") connection between the experience and expression of some emotions. The intuitive knowledge of this direct connection between inner feelings and outer expressions may contribute to the fact that nonverbal expressions are (sometimes naively) more trusted than verbal expressions (Burgoon, Buller, & Woodall, 1989). However, as DePaulo (1992) points out, "perhaps one of the most interesting aspects of nonverbal behavior is that it is only rarely totally unregulated" (p. 203). In social interactions people tend to exert a conscious or unconscious control over their nonverbal expressions. These attempts to regulate nonverbal expressions may not always be successful, but they are pervasive (DePaulo, 1992). I shall return to this point in the discussion of culture-general and culture-specific nonverbal behaviors.

In the reception of nonverbal messages, one is not normally required to process a symbolic code and therefore be consciously aware of the meaning. When we see someone smile with joy or wince with pain, we do not have to decipher this message. The meaning of many familiar nonverbal behaviors is directly interpreted from the image itself rather than being mediated by a symbolic system (i.e., language). Because it is unmediated, many times a nonverbal message affects us directly and emotionally. Without a conscious effort, we may mirror another's joy with a smile or reflect another's pain with our own wince (Dimberg, 1982; Vaughan & Lanzetta, 1980). At other times, *unexpected* nonverbal behaviors may cause us to actively contemplate their meaning (Burgoon, 1978; Burgoon & Hale, 1988). The stranger who sits too close to us in a public place causes us to consciously wonder what is intended by this behavior. In an intercultural context, we may observe unexpected nonverbal behaviors that make us pause and consider their meaning. In any case, nonverbal behaviors often have ambiguous meanings.

Ambiguous

The very nature of nonverbal communication makes it ambiguous. It is continuous, changing constantly, and some specific behaviors, such as facial expressions, may last for only a fraction of a second (Cacioppo & Petty, 1983). Behaviors are not discrete and usually have more than one possible cause and interpretation. For instance, laughter may be elicited by humor or embarrassment. Sometimes a behavior may have no meaning at all for the person producing it. The meaning of nonverbal behavior is determined by the receiver, who seldom confirms it with the sender. We never say to someone, "Would you mind repeating that expression, I didn't quite catch the meaning." A smile could mean happiness, satisfaction, or embarrassment. Touch can be especially ambiguous, and the intention of the person touching may be quite different than the message received. This can be a source of misunderstanding between the sexes.

Unlike verbal communication, which has relatively clear, agreed-upon meaning (and is verifiable), nonverbal communication usually can be interpreted in different ways. Even under the best circumstances, nonverbal communication can be difficult to interpret. Added to this inherent ambiguity are variations in individuals, contexts, and cultures.

Differences in Nonverbal Communication

Three additional factors also contribute to the difficulties in successfully interpreting nonverbal messages.

Individual Differences

Individuals differ in the expressiveness of their nonverbal communication. Perhaps you know people who are very bubbly and outgoing. If on a given day, you ask them how they are doing and they say "I'm doing well" with a modicum of enthusiasm in their face and voice, you may suspect that there is some problem. In contrast, a person who is normally very quiet and understated, who gives an equally enthusiastic answer of "I'm doing well," may be conveying a message of great joy. People have a kind of baseline for their nonverbal communication. We have to judge any given message against the normal level of expressiveness and style for that person.

Context Differences

Context can have a profound effect on the meaning of nonverbal messages. A whisper between acquaintances in a church may be the result of the norm that requires us to avoid disturbing others who are worshipping. This whisper probably has no special meaning beyond conveying a respect for those nearby. But whispering in a lover's ear in a public place where normal levels of conversation are expected may convey a sense of intimacy. We cannot consider the meaning of nonverbal communications without considering the context that surrounds the message. Learning the proper combinations of behavior and context is admittedly difficult but is essential to the success of long-term relations with culturally different others.

Cultural Differences

The third factor that contributes to the difficulty in interpreting nonverbal communication is cultural differences. Some theorists (Birdwhistell, 1970; Effron, 1941; Hall, 1959) contend that nonverbal behaviors are learned behaviors governed by cultural guidelines learned in the socialization process. Other theorists (e.g., Darwin, 1872/1965; Ekman, 1971; Izard, 1971) approach nonverbal behaviors as biologically determined and therefore invariant from culture to culture. I have mentioned a little of the evidence on both sides of this debate, but the following section will examine the ways cultures are alike and different in their use of nonverbal communication to express emotions.

Culture-General Aspects of Nonverbal Behavior

Some aspects of nonverbal communication have pan-cultural meanings, especially if they involve the display of emotions. Since Darwin's 1872 study, "The Expression of Emotion in Man and Animals," some researchers have sought to demonstrate that nonverbal communication has universal meanings. Research using facial expressions has shown that six emotions are recognizable in all cultures: anger, fear, happiness, sadness, surprise, and disgust (Ekman, 1971, 1975; Izard, 1971). Another piece of research that contributes to the contention that emotions are universally recognizable was a comparison of American and Japanese identifications of emotions (Sogon & Masutani, 1989). In this study, actors portraying various emotions were videotaped from behind. Both Americans and Japanese who viewed the videotape were able to identify the emotions correctly. Despite this evidence, which demonstrates that some emotions are universally recognizable, emotions can be difficult to recognize, even within cultures. The problem, mentioned previously, is that nonverbal displays of emotion are seldom unregulated. When we *want* others to recognize our emotion we can display it in a way that will be generally recognized across cultures. However, often we try to control (regulate) our emotional displays in order to present ourselves in a certain light or to follow norms that govern what emotions are proper to display at that time (DePaulo, 1992).

Display Rules

Cultures differ in the specific rules governing the display of emotions. Each culture guides its members as to when, where, and with whom the display of specific emotions is permissible (Ekman & Friesen, 1975). The runner-up in a beauty pageant smiles broadly as her rival is crowned the winner because the display rules forbid her to show the disappointment that she is experiencing. Evidence for the existence of these display rules was reported by Ekman, Friesen, and Ellsworth (1972). Comparing Japanese and Americans, they reported equal degrees of facial expression in the two groups when participants were shown disgusting movies in private. However, when the experimenter was present, the Japanese showed less amounts of facial expression in response to disgusting movies than Americans. The conclusion is that the presence of the experimenter invoked the Japanese social norm prohibiting the display of emotion (especially negative), which resulted in the Japanese controlling the expression of their disgust.

So far I have focused on nonverbal behavior as it functions in the expression of emotion. As such, we have seen that the universal aspects of emotional expression are affected by the imposition of culture-specific display rules. However, nonverbal behavior also serves a number of other communicative functions (to be discussed). Some researchers have sought to show that nonverbal behaviors are learned and culturally patterned (e.g., Birdwhistell, 1970; Hall, 1959).

Culture-Specific Nonverbal Communication

Just as languages assign different words to carry the same meaning, cultures assign different nonverbal behaviors to carry the same meaning. In Sri Lanka, moving the head from side to side like a metronome signifies agreement. In America, nodding the head up and down is the signal for agreement. Similarly, in some cultures the same attitudes are conveyed by different behaviors. Direct eye contact is a sign of respect and attention in America; whereas in Laos, downcast eyes are a sign of respect and attention. The American father says to his child when scolding him, "Look at me when I talk to you." The Laotian father may say, "Don't look at me when I talk to you." Thus, the same nonverbal behavior can carry different meanings for members of different cultures. These culture-specific uses and interpretations of nonverbal communication, as well as the display rules described previously, can lead to misunderstanding when people from different cultures communicate.

Four Pitfalls of Nonverbal Communication

There are four types of pitfalls that one must avoid to successfully communicate nonverbally across cultures.

Misattribution

One form of misattribution is the incorrect assigning of meaning to a nonverbal behavior. For example, American teachers of Asian students often misinterpret silence on the part of their students. Asian students may not speak out in class as much as their American counterparts. American teachers are used to students who willingly answer questions and speak up in front of others. Therefore, the American teachers may interpret the silence of the Asian students as a lack of interest or dullness when, in fact, their silence is really a result of respect for the teacher and a reluctance to stand apart from their classmates. When students are placed in small groups and asked to discuss the material among themselves, the interest and competence of the Asian students is evident.[2]

In the critical incident "I think she likes me," Jim wrongly attributed Gabriella's close conversation distance and touching to an attraction to him. However, for her these behaviors are the cultural norm and were not meant to send him a signal of affection or special liking.

Sending the Wrong Signal

The second pitfall for nonverbal communication in intercultural interactions is sending the wrong signal. In the example above, this was Gabriella's error; it is really the other side of misattributions. An individual intends to send a message; however, the nonverbal behavior used to convey the message has a different meaning in the counterpart's culture. Therefore, the individual inadvertently sends the wrong message. Richard Nixon fell into this pitfall when visiting Latin America. On arriving, Nixon gave the A-Okay sign. However, this gesture has a very different meaning in Latin America. Putting the thumb and forefinger together in a circle and extending the other fingers is an obscene gesture (indicating the female genitalia) in Latin America. Richard Nixon was very embarrassed and the Latin Americans were very offended. This type of misunderstanding is not uncommon.

Recall the critical incident in which Glen Saito wanted to send a message of confidence and trust to his Japanese students by allowing them to come to him if they needed guidance. His friendly and casual behaviors were meant to make the Japanese comfortable. The Japanese students, however, interpreted these behaviors as showing a lack of authority and concern.

Context Confusion

Sometimes we can send the right message at the wrong time and this can result in misunderstanding. This is the third pitfall, called context confusion. Often people may recognize and emulate the nonverbal behavior of a different culture, but they do not have enough experience to know in what context this nonverbal behavior is appropriate. The American businessman who is entertained at nightclubs in Japan may feel that he has finally broken through the "inscrutable" Japanese front. The Japanese are very relaxed. They laugh, make jokes and generally feel very comfortable. The next day when the American goes to a meeting in the Japanese offices, he feels that this same behavior can be carried over into the office setting. However, when making jokes and laughing at the office, he is met with a very different reaction than the night before. His relaxed behaviors are met with stiff and seemingly cold reactions. He is confused about the proper context for these behaviors and the results can be disastrous.

Missing Signals

The final pitfall in communicating nonverbally interculturally is missing signals. Sometimes signals are unfamiliar or too subtle to be recognized by a person from a different culture. Slight differences in tone or emphasis may go unrecognized by second speakers of languages. Often irony or sarcasm that completely changes the meaning of a verbal message is completely missed in intercultural interactions because one of the members does not perceive the subtle differences of voice quality that signified the modification.

Other types of nonverbal behaviors may also be overlooked because of their subtlety. Display rules that limit the expression of emotion or negative affect may cause members of one culture to control these expressions to an extent that they become very subtle. Although members of their own culture are well aware of these subtleties and have little problem recognizing them, in intercultural interactions the subtle cues are often lost on those who expect a clearer display. A classic example of this pitfall is the misunderstanding that often accompanies the Japanese use of a slight sucking of air and tilt of the head to indicate a negative response. These behaviors will often accompany a verbal reply that only hints at the negative such as, "That may be difficult." The overall meaning is perceived as an unambiguous "No" by most Japanese. But for an American, the nonverbal cues are not interpreted and the matter may be pursued to the embarrassment of both parties.

These four pitfalls are typical of nonverbal communication difficulties in intercultural interactions. To get a better idea of how and when these difficulties arise, I shall next discuss the functions of nonverbal communications, pointing to cases of misunderstanding that can occur around each.

Functions of Nonverbal Communication

Nonverbal communication functions similarly across cultures, but often cultures use different behaviors to fulfill the same function. These differences contribute to the pitfalls described above.

Replaces Verbal Communication

The first function of nonverbal behavior is to replace verbal communication. Instead of saying, "Come here," sometimes we may use a gesture to replace those words. This type of gesture is called an *emblem*. Of course, the problem is that emblems vary from culture to culture, with each culture having its own lexicon of emblems to replace words (Morain, 1978). For example, in Korea, "come here" is signified by a gesture using the hand. The hand is held about eye level with palm down. The fingers are curved slightly downward and wiggled. This gesture is easily confused with a good-bye wave in American culture and is often a source of confusion for Western visitors in Korea.

Modifies Verbal Communication

The second way nonverbal communication functions is to modify verbal communication. Loudness and tone of voice can modify the meaning of the words we use. Often in America loudness is used to emphasize words; however, in Japan there is a saying, "He who raises his voice first has lost the argument." One can easily see how using the voice for emphasis can be misunderstood in Japan. In addition, the general restraint in the expansiveness of nonverbal behaviors in Japan and the accompanying sensitivity to nonverbal cues may make the larger and louder gestures of an American irritating to Japanese. As mentioned previously, nonverbal communication can modify verbal communication so as to contradict the verbal message. Clearly, if this nonverbal contradiction is not understood, there will be a large misunderstanding.

Regulates Social Interaction

The third way nonverbal communication functions is to regulate social interaction. Turn taking is largely governed by nonverbal behaviors. In America, if one wants the next speaking turn, one may gaze directly at the speaker, lean forward, and perhaps make some head nods to signal one's readiness to speak. An inhalation of breath coupled with the straightening of the back, as if ready to speak, also contribute to the signals indicating a desire for a turn (Wiemann & Knapp, 1975). In passing a turn, eye contact is very important. Although I know of no empirical research that has addressed cultural differences in the effect of turn-taking cues in intercultural interactions, it has been shown that the inability of blind people to send and receive appropriate visual cues is a source of conversational difficulties with the sighted (Kemp, 1980, 1981; Sharkey & Stafford, 1990). The implication, of course, is that culturally different turn-taking rules and cues may have a straining effect in intercultural interactions. In the absence of empirical data, one must rely on the anecdotal reports of experienced culture observers such as John Condon.

Condon (1984) reports one area of intercultural turn-taking difficulty associated with the different perceptions of silence in Japan and America. Japanese are more comfortable with silence than Americans. Americans feel that more than a brief silence signifies that one has given up one's turn at speaking; whereas in Japan, longer pauses are allowable within one's speaking turn.[3] As a consequence, Japanese often feel that Americans interrupt them. Similar confusion also occurs when questions are asked. Often, a second-language speaker will take time to process the question and formulate an answer. Americans who are impatient with this silence will feel that the question has not been understood and either repeat the question, sometimes more loudly so as to be better understood, or they may just change the topic. Clearly, this type of behavior does not facilitate intercultural interactions.

Another function of nonverbal behavior that falls under the general rubric of regulating social interaction is that of synchronizing conversants. Kendon (1970) carefully analyzed videotapes of British conversations at a London pub. He found that a speaker's words are typically coordinated with his or her own body movements. Further, he found that speakers' and listeners' movements were also coordinated such that they were mirror images. Kendon commented that this type of synchrony conveys interest and approval. Again, there is little evidence that this type of synchrony, or lack of it, exists in intercultural interactions. But given other differences in nonverbal behaviors, it is not unreasonable to assume that synchrony can be a problem in intercultural interactions. Hall (1976) suggests that members of some cultures (high-context) value more and are more aware of syncing than are members of other (low-context) cultures. He proposes that those who rely more heavily on syncing "do not know how to deal with people who are out of phase" (p. 79).

Carries Emotional Messages

The fourth function of nonverbal communication is to carry emotional messages. As discussed above, these messages may be universally recognizable, although differences in culture-specific display rules and sensitivity to subtle cues can be sources of confusion. Another example of the difficulties that can arise in this area is contained in the critical incident "Just Trying to Be Friendly." Here the Japanese students who came to see Glen were unable to express their unhappiness directly but gave nonverbal cues such as hesitations and brief answers when asked how they were doing. The Japanese expected that Glen would be sensitive to these cues and understand that there were some problems. Unfortunately, although Glen did notice these nonverbal cues, he attributed the behaviors to language difficulties and expected the Japanese to be more direct in expressing their problems and emotions. The resulting lack of communication contributed to the loss of students.

Conveys Attitudes

The final way that nonverbal communication functions is in the presentation of attitudes. Attitudes about one's self, one's communication partner, and the relationship of self and other are critical messages that are carried primarily on nonverbal channels. These attitudes are a substantial part of the social messages that were reportedly 93% carried by nonverbal communication. Self-presentation is a major area that falls into this category. Because self-presentation, attitudes, and the relationship of self and other are crucial to intercultural interaction, the next section is devoted to an analysis of this function of nonverbal communication.

Attitudes and Nonverbal Communication

One of the most difficult but also most important tasks for successful intercultural nonverbal communication is sending and receiving messages about one's attitudes towards self and others that are understood in the same way by both parties. These attitudes are especially critical in establishing relations between people from different cultures. Of course, there is a wide range of attitudes that can be conveyed. The present discussion will limit itself to four of these attitudes.

Liking and Affection

Proximity and touching behavior are often used to convey attitudes of liking and affection. As we saw in the critical incident, close proximity and frequent touching convey an attitude of affection. Some cultures (e.g., Latin American and Southern European), known as high-contact cultures, use touching behavior frequently and tend to have a closer distance for conversation. An individual from a low-contact culture (e.g., Britain and North America) can frequently misinterpret these behaviors as liking and affection, as we saw in the first critical incident "I Think She Likes Me." Of course, even in high-contact cultures touching and close proximity can convey liking and affection. But just as individuals may have a baseline that must be considered when interpreting their nonverbal messages, so too do cultures. In Costa Rica, there is a different baseline for the amount of touching and distance that conveys liking. Because Jim was guided by his own perception of what was a normal amount of touching, he mistakenly attributed the degree of touching and closeness of conversation distance shown by Gabriella to be intimacy. Clearly, this can be a difficult distinction to make when one is not familiar with habits in a specific culture. Likewise, a lack of familiarity about touching taboos in a culture may result in bad feelings.

In Thailand, patting an adult on the head is not well received. This seemingly innocent gesture of affection is offensive to Thais because the head is thought to be the seat of the soul and touching the head may allow the soul to escape through the top of the head. Although one can never hope to become familiar with all of the taboos for every culture, knowing the types of attitudes that can be conveyed nonverbally is a useful starting place for successful communication.

Involvement and Attention

Cultures vary in the methods used to convey involvement and attention to one's conversation partner. In America, a slight forward lean and direct eye contact convey an attitude of involvement and attention. In contrast, Japanese may use very different means to convey these attitudes. An American full professor who was making a speech to a large group of Japanese professors and students was concerned during his speech because many in the audience that filled the auditorium were sitting with their eyes closed. He thought, "My speech is dying. They're all falling asleep." After his speech was finished, a number of the Japanese approached him enthusiastically telling him how much they enjoyed his speech and making comments that showed they had heard every word he said. In Japan, closing the eyes while listening to another, especially a higher status person giving a speech to a large audience, indicates one is giving one's complete attention to the words of the speaker, not a disinterest in the speaker. Clearly, the American had misinterpreted the closed eyes of the Japanese. Americans, however, frequently send the wrong message to their Asian counterparts in trying to convey an attitude of confidence and competence.

Confidence

In America, confidence and competence are associated with relaxed postures. These same attitudes are more closely associated with slightly tense postures in Korea. This is especially true when one of lower status is dealing with an individual of higher status. For example, when interviewing for a job in America, one will make a good impression if he or she is relaxed, direct, and displays a confident attitude with a firm tone of voice and no hesitation in answering questions. However, in Japan an interviewee may make a better impression with a slightly tense posture and by conveying a more modest attitude through pauses and tone of voice.

Although appearance is also an important indicator of confidence and competence, it tends to be less emphasized in America than in many other countries. Americans are willing to make allowances for individual preferences in style of dress, length of hair, and general appearance. In many other countries, deviations from the norm in appearance may have detrimental effects on one's impression. Appearance is one contributor to the impression formed about an individual's status.

Status and Respect

Status and respect are key attitudes that must be conveyed in order to establish successful intercultural relationships. Americans may not place as much emphasis on dressing the part as Asians do. Americans tend to minimize status differences; therefore, they may not pay as close attention to the nonverbal cues that signify status and respect. Although they may realize that bowing is a signal of respect, the subtleties involved in proper bowing will probably escape most Americans. Because of their emphasis on egalitarianism, Americans may not use many nonverbal behaviors associated with status in other cultures. Thus in the critical incident, Glen's friendly and relaxed behavior was interpreted as a lack of status and the Japanese students went to the dean with their questions. Status and respect are also conveyed through eye contact. As described earlier, there are cultural differences in the type of eye contact signifying respect that can cause miscommunication.

Status and respect can also be conveyed through the use of time. Cultures vary in the emphasis placed on promptness and the meaning conveyed by making a visitor wait. Being kept waiting is often offensive to people in the West who value promptness, whereas in South American countries waiting for an appointment may be the normal course of events. From these examples, it is clear that to successfully communicate nonverbally across cultures requires an adjustment in how one sees others' nonverbal behaviors and how one communicates nonverbally.

Suggestions for Successful Nonverbal Communication

Changing how one behaves and how one understands others' nonverbal communication is the key to successful nonverbal communication across cultures. Nonverbal communication methods are, in part, habits closely allied to self-image (see DePaulo, 1992). Just as our self-image is tied to a culturally consistent system of beliefs and values, so our nonverbal communication is tied to our cultural background. Changing these fundamental ways in which we behave and view the world is not an easy task.

Complicating the adjustment to nonverbal behaviors in other cultures is the fact that there is little correlation between cultural dimensions such as individualism-collectivism and types of nonverbal behavior that are used in those cultures. Therefore, it is difficult to make predictions about what type of behaviors can be expected without having specific information about that culture. There are, however, a few generalizations that may help.

As mentioned previously, a distinction can be made between high-contact and low-contact cultures. Knowing where a culture is on this continuum will help to explain differences in proxemic and touching behaviors. Had Jim known that Costa Rica was a high-contact culture, he probably could have avoided his misattribution. Another generalization that may be useful is that members of collectivist cultures will generally be more sensitive to nonverbal behaviors than those from individualist cultures (although the British may be a notable exception, among others). The emphasis on harmony and relationships in collectivist cultures tends to make the nonverbal channels a more important source of information, especially concerning negative messages. Members of these cultures are socialized to be more sensitive to nonverbal expressions and expect others to be equally sensitive to their nonverbal cues, especially when the other is higher status (Roland, 1989).

Despite the fact that there is no substitute for culture-specific knowledge about nonverbal communication, I would like to offer some suggestions that may be useful in improving nonverbal communication skills interculturally. These suggestions refer to the process of coping in a new culture, while one gains specific knowledge, rather than trying to propose specific behaviors that should be employed. The point is to try to avoid the pitfalls that were described earlier.

Be Aware and Delay Attributions

First, be aware of others' behaviors and how they affect you. Often, we are not aware of the source of our impressions about others. Subtle cues below the level of consciousness, or familiar behaviors that are not consciously processed, may nonetheless affect us strongly. Misattributions may be avoided if we can become aware of the basis of our impressions. Other nonverbal behaviors (especially when unexpected) may be very noticeable, even striking, and affect us at an emotional level. Body odor in some cultures is an acceptable, even desirable, personal characteristic. In other cultures, body odor may be so offensive that a reaction is almost unavoidable. In this case, it is suggested that we do not make evaluations of these behaviors. We must delay attributions until we are confident we know the meaning of these behaviors. Sometimes nonverbal behaviors may cause very strong, even emotional reactions because of our cultural programming. For example, a Hindu Indian may have a very emotional reaction of disgust at seeing another person eating with the left hand. Because tradition reserves the left hand for the toilet, Indian culture has conditioned its members to react in this way. Overcoming this type of conditioning is a difficult task. But at least if the Indian is aware that the intention is not to offend, it may be easier to tolerate this type of behavior. Sometimes we may not know the meaning of others' nonverbal behaviors; but if we have an awareness that those behaviors are different and that they affect us, we can seek out an informant to help us understand specific nonverbal behaviors in another culture. Again, there is no substitute for culture-specific knowledge, but an awareness and sensitivity of others' behavior can prevent us from making misattributions based on our own cultural assumptions. Just as being aware of others' nonverbal communications helps us avoid misunderstandings, being aware of our own behaviors makes it possible to avoid sending unintended messages.

Be Aware of One's Own Nonverbal Communication

We must endeavor to be aware of our own behaviors and how they affect others. This is a difficult task because we cannot see our own image as we interact and many nonverbal cues are emitted visually (DePaulo, 1992). Even our vocalic cues are difficult to monitor because physically we do not hear in the same way that others hear us. But noticing our own behaviors is not impossible, and especially noticing how our behavior affects others may give us valuable clues to the success or failure of our nonverbal communication. For instance, the American who is used to speaking in a loud and forceful voice will probably not be aware of this behavior. Unless he or she pays attention to the reactions of others, there is little chance that this behavior will be modified to fit the more subdued voice patterns found in some other cultures. An awareness of one's own behavior will also allow one to determine the differences between those behaviors and the ones used by one's cultural counterpart.

Match Your Communication Behaviors to the New Culture

Finally, I would like to suggest that, as much as possible, we match our nonverbal behaviors to those of our cultural counterparts.[4] Although this may be difficult for a variety of reasons, if this is successfully done, it will pay handsome rewards. A 1971 study by Peter Collett illustrated this point very well. Collett trained a number of British citizens in the nonverbal behaviors of Arabs. In a 30-minute training session, he taught the British to sit closer than normal, to make continuous and direct eye contact, to use frequent touching behavior, and to avoid showing the sole of one's foot to the Arabs. Collett then allowed the trained and untrained British to interact on a one-to-one basis with Arabs. After the interaction, the Arabs were asked their impressions of their British counterparts. The Arabs who had interacted with British trained in the Arab nonverbal behaviors had significantly better impressions of their counterparts than the Arabs who had interacted with untrained British. If these simple behaviors made a difference in the success of intercultural interactions between Arabs and British, I am certain that you and I will be more successful if we are able to match even a few of our behaviors with our cultural counterparts.

A Final Note

By now many people may be discouraged. Perhaps they are overwhelmed by the subtlety and complexity of nonverbal communication that has been highlighted here. They probably think that they will never be successful in intercultural interactions because there are simply too many things to consider. Many trainers are aware that the increased knowledge gained through training may have an immediate adverse effect on one's ability to interact successfully with culturally different others. This is because the trainee's increased anxiety and self-consciousness may interfere with the social skills normally employed (see Weldon, Carlston, Rissman, Slobodin, & Triandis, 1975). However, after some time has passed and with increased contact, the training becomes integrated and its benefits are implemented. In addition, one should not let the fear of making mistakes become too great.

Many people experienced in intercultural contacts agree that there is a general tolerance and forgiveness extended to culturally different others during initial interactions. A few mistakes will usually not sabotage future relationships, so long as one gains understanding through the mistakes and becomes increasingly sensitive to cultural differences. It is hoped that the process of understanding mistakes, refraining from repeating them, and gaining from this experience will be aided by the knowledge presented here. The process was captured in the movie *Dancing with Wolves*. After his first few encounters with the Sioux medicine man Kicking Bird, John Dunbar writes in his journal, "Real communication is slow . . . most of our progress has been built on the basis of failure rather than success." Just as Dunbar succeeded through persistence, perception, and genuineness, so too can anyone be successful in intercultural communication.

Skill Development Exercises

Developing Culture-Specific Awareness

The purpose of this exercise is to identify the types of nonverbal communication that are necessary to interact successfully in one's own culture or another culture with which one is familiar. Many behaviors identified in this exercise will be instrumental in successful intercultural interactions within the specified culture. Admittedly, some will be difficult or irritating to incorporate into one's repertoire of behaviors, but without them troubles may arise.

Instructions. Break the participants into small groups (2 to 4) that are as culturally homogeneous as possible. Have the participants discuss and list the nonverbal skills and communication behaviors that would be necessary for a visitor to their culture to master in order to successfully interact. If participants are familiar with another culture, they may identify the skills necessary in that culture. If time permits, participants may be asked to identify contexts in which different or specific skills will be needed. Participants should determine what messages are conveyed by the behaviors they list.

For example, a group of Americans might list expressing emotions through vocalic variation and gestures as necessary for successful communication in the United States. These behaviors would be necessary to communicate one's opinions effectively in a work setting. A group of Japanese might identify the ability to express (and perceive) disagreement in subtle nonverbal ways as essential for success in the workplace.

After each group has listed the skills, behaviors, and contexts, they will designate one person to share their list with the whole group. A general discussion and comparison of the various behaviors could conclude the exercise.

Communicative Greetings

The purposes of this exercise (adapted from DeVito, 1989) are (1) to identify how different feeling states are expressed through greetings in different cultures (handshakes or bows), (2) to develop observational skills, and (3) to practice modifying behaviors to convey the desired messages. This exercise is most useful for students who have become familiar with the nonverbal behaviors used in a target culture. It might also be adapted to demonstrate some behaviors used in a target culture by using members of that culture to enact the greetings and feeling states.

Instructions. Participants are divided into groups of 4. Let's call the members of one group A, B, C, and D. Initially, A and B are performers while C and D are observers. A will serve as principal subject or "actor" while B serves as the "recipient" of the greeting message. The two observers should watch the interaction carefully and record their observations on the form provided.

The procedures are as follows: Performer A should read silently the list of feeling states provided and greet Performer B while role-playing each of these feeling states as though they were in the *United States.* Performer B should mentally note how he or she felt about the greeting. The observers should make notes on the specific behaviors observed and how they interpreted them.

A and B then switch roles and follow the same procedure imagining that the performers are in China (or any culture that is appropriate). After both A and B have had a chance to enact greeting behaviors, members C and D become the actor and recipient while A and B are the observers. The procedure is repeated using any cultures the participants are familiar with.

After all interactions have been completed, the observers' forms should be analyzed and the feedback from the recipients should be discussed.

Feeling States

1. I'm feeling nervous and uncomfortable.

2. I'm totally in control of myself and of the situation; I feel confident and perfectly at ease.

3. I like you and want you to like me.

Observation Form Instructions: Observers should pay special attention to the following four areas of nonverbal behavior and should record what they observe during these several greetings. Observers may confer with each other (but should not let the performers hear) and complete one form jointly or they may complete their forms independently and then confer with each other and compile a composite form. These forms will then be given to the performers and discussed with them after the entire exercise is completed.

A sample form is presented below.

Interaction 1

Facial expressions:

Eye movements and contact:

Body posture and orientation:

Physical closeness and touching:

What attitudes do you think were displayed through these behaviors?

Interaction 2

Facial expressions:

Eye movements and contact:

Body posture and orientation:

Physical closeness and touching:

What attitudes do you think were displayed through these behaviors?

Interaction 3

Facial expressions:

Eye movements and contact:

Body posture and orientation:

Physical closeness and touching:

What attitudes do you think were displayed through these behaviors?

Field Exercise

Increasing Awareness of Nonverbal Behaviors in Natural Settings

The purpose of this exercise is to increase the awareness and observational skill of the participants. It involves keeping a journal or taking notes of nonverbal behaviors observed in social interactions. Depending on the makeup and circumstances of the participants, the interactions could involve those seen in the movies or soap operas (from their own or other cultures), those involving people considered to be socially adept, or their own intercultural interactions. The notes should contain a description of the behaviors involved, the context of the interaction, and its outcome.

The discussion of these observations could focus on cultural similarities and differences observed, the ambiguity involved in the interaction, the contexts of the behaviors, the affective dimensions of the behaviors, and the outcomes produced. Pitfalls avoided or encountered may also be useful discussion topics.

Notes

1. It should be noted that in a number of languages (e.g., Mandarin), tone has lexical function and will be less available to carry paralinguistic meaning.

2. A videotape titled *There's Got to be a Better Way* that explores this and other issues important to the multicultural classroom is available from the Center for Study of Multicultural Higher Education, University of Hawaii, Honolulu, Hawaii 96822.

3. For a perceptive and nontechnical discussion of Japanese and American turn-taking and conversation styles, see Sakamoto and Naotsuka, 1982.

4. There is a danger here of falling into the context pitfall by choosing an inappropriate model after whom to pattern our behavior. For example, a teacher should probably not match his or her behavior to that of students.

References

Argyle, M., Alkema, F., & Gilmour, R. (1971). The communication of friendly and hostile attitudes by verbal and nonverbal signals. *European Journal of Social Psychology, 1,* 385-402.

Birdwhistell, R. (1955). Background to kinesics. *ETC., 13,* 10-18.

Birdwhistell, R. (1970). *Kinesics and context.* Philadelphia: University of Pennsylvania Press.

Burgoon, J. K. (1978). A communication model of personal space violations: Explication and initial test. *Human Communication Research, 4,* 129-142.

Burgoon, J. K., Buller, D. B., & Woodall, W. G. (1989). *Nonverbal communication: The unspoken dialogue.* New York: Harper & Row.

Burgoon, J. K., & Hale, J. L. (1988). Nonverbal expectancy violations: Model elaboration and application to immediacy behaviors. *Communication Monographs, 55,* 58-79.

Cacioppo, J. T., & Petty, R. E. (1983). *Social psychophysiology: A sourcebook.* New York: Guilford Press.

Collett, P. (1971). Training Englishmen in the non-verbal behaviour of Arabs. *International Journal of Psychology, 6,* 209-215.

Condon, J. C. (1984). *With respect to the Japanese.* Yarmouth, ME: Intercultural Press.

Darwin, C. (1965). *The expression of emotions in man and animals.* Chicago: University of Chicago Press. (Originally published in 1872).

DePaulo, B. M. (1992). Nonverbal behavior and self-presentation. *Psychological Bulletin, 111,* 203-243.

DeVito, J. A. (1989). *The nonverbal communication workbook.* Prospect Heights, IL: Waveland Press.

Dimberg, U. (1982). Facial reactions to facial expressions. *Psychophysiology, 19,* 643-647.

Efron, D. (1941). *Gesture and environment.* Morningside Heights, NY: King's Crown Press.

Ekman, P. (1971). Universal and cultural differences in facial expressions of emotion. In J. K. Cole (Ed.), *Nebraska symposium on motivation* (pp. 201-283). Lincoln, NE: University of Nebraska Press.

Ekman, P. (1975, September). The universal smile: Face muscles talk every language. *Psychology Today, 9,* 35-39.

Ekman, P., & Friesen, W. V. (1975). *Unmasking the face.* Englewood Cliffs, NJ: Prentice Hall.

Ekman, P., Friesen, W. V., & Ellsworth, P. (1972). *Emotion in the human face.* New York: Pergamon.

Hall, E. T. (1959). *The slient language.* Greenwich, CT: Fawcett Premier.

Hall, E. T. (1976). *Beyond culture.* New York: Anchor.

Izard, C. E., (1971). *The face of emotion.* Englewood Cliffs, NJ: Prentice Hall.

Kemp, N. J. (1980). Social interaction in the blind. *International Journal of Rehabilitation Research, 3,* 87-88.

Kemp, N. J. (1981). *An experimental analysis of visual communication and social interaction.* Unpublished doctoral dissertation. University of Kent, Canterbury, England.

Kendon, A. (1970). Movement coordination in social interaction: Some examples described. *Acta Psychologica, 32,* 1-25.

Mehrabian, A., & Ferris, S. (1967). Inference of attitudes from nonverbal communication in two channels. *Journal of Consulting Psychology, 31,* 248-252.

Mehrabian, A., & Weiner, M. (1967). Decoding of inconsistent communications. *Journal of Personality and Social Psychology, 6,* 109-114.

Morain, G. G. (1978). *Language in education: Theory and practice no. 7, Kinesics and cross-cultural understanding.* Arlington, VA: Center for Applied Linguistics.

Myers, D. G. (1990). *Social psychology* (3rd ed.). New York: McGraw Hill.

Roberts, M. (1987, June). No language but a cry. *Psychology Today, 21,* 57-58.

Roland, A. (1989). *In search of self in India and Japan: Toward a cross-cultural psychology.* Princeton, NJ: Princeton University Press.

Sakamoto, N., & Naotsuka, R. (1982). *Polite fictions: Why Japanese and Americans seem rude to each other.* Tokyo: Kinseido.

Sharkey, W. F., & Stafford, L. (1990). Turn-taking resources employed by congenitally blind conversers. *Communication Studies, 41,* 161-182.

Sogon, S., & Masutani, M. (1989). Identification of emotion from body movements: A cross-cultural study of Americans and Japanese. *Psychological Reports, 65*, 35-46.

Vaughan, K. B., & Lanzetta, J. T. (1980). Vicarious instigation and conditioning of facial expressiveness and autonomic responses to a model's expressive display of pain. *Journal of Personality and Social Psychology, 38*, 909-923.

Watzlawick, P., Beavin, J. H., & Jackson, D.D. (1967). *Pragmatics of human communication.* New York: Norton.

Weldon, D. E, Carlston, D. E., Rissman, A. K, Slobodin, L., & Triandis, H. C. (1975). A laboratory test of effects of culture assimilator training. *Journal of Personality and Social Psychology, 32*, 300-310.

Wiemann, J. M., & Knapp, M. L. (1975). Turn-taking in conversations. *Journal of Communication, 25*, 75-92.

Woods, B. S. (1981). *Children and communication: Verbal and nonverbal language development* (2nd ed.). Englewood Cliffs, NJ: Prentice Hall.

15 Approaching Cultural Crossover in Language Learning

M A R K   S A W Y E R

L A R R Y   E .   S M I T H

> *I am not a good mimic and I have worked now in many different cultures. I am a very poor speaker of any language, but I always know whose pig is dead, and, when I work in a native society, I know what people are talking about and I treat it seriously and I respect them, and this in itself establishes a great deal more rapport, very often, than the correct accent. I have worked with other field workers who were far, far better linguists than I, and the natives kept on saying they couldn't speak the language, although they said I could! Now, if you had a recording it would be proof positive I couldn't, but nobody knew it! You see, we don't need to teach people to speak like natives, you need to make the other people believe they can.*
>
> Margaret Mead
> Discussion Session on Language Teaching,
> in Sebeok et al. (1964, p. 189)

"Language and culture are inextricably tied together." If this assumption is in fact true, then the teaching of language must also be linked with the teaching of culture. This module not only covers the importance of cultural understanding, it also alerts students to a second language with specific language functions (e.g., addressing people, expressing emotions, interrupting conversations for various reasons) that often lead to cultural misunderstandings. Various strategies that will increase the probability of success in cross-cultural interactions are provided, along with exercises aimed at improving those skills.

Contents

Self-Assessment Exercise: Language and Culture Issues

The following statements are designed to elicit your judgments on issues that language learners in cross-cultural situations must face all the time. Circle the option that best reflects your opinion. Base your response on your immediate reaction to the statement. Then, if you begin to feel that "It depends . . . ," try to specify the factors your response depends on.

1. Language and culture are inextricably tied together.

1	2	3	4	5
strongly disagree	disagree	don't know	agree	strongly agree

2. Genuine communication across cultures is impossible.

1	2	3	4	5
strongly disagree	disagree	don't know	agree	strongly agree

3. Becoming a successful cross-cultural communicator involves confronting your own values and beliefs.

1	2	3	4	5
strongly disagree	disagree	don't know	agree	strongly agree

4. Becoming a successful cross-cultural communicator involves confronting the values and beliefs of your conversational partners.

1	2	3	4	5
strongly disagree	disagree	don't know	agree	strongly agree

5. In any language, greetings reveal important social information, such as the relative age and status of the speakers.

1	2	3	4	5
strongly disagree	disagree	don't know	agree	strongly agree

6. Cultures vary greatly in the functions of their greetings.

1	2	3	4	5
strongly disagree	disagree	don't know	agree	strongly agree

7. Smiling is a universal lubricant for cross-cultural interactions.

1	2	3	4	5
strongly disagree	disagree	don't know	agree	strongly agree

8. It is generally advisable to withhold expressions of anger outside of one's own culture.

1	2	3	4	5
strongly disagree	disagree	don't know	agree	strongly agree

9. Language learners should interrupt their conversational partners to ask for repetition whenever they have not completely understood what has been said.

1	2	3	4	5
strongly disagree	disagree	don't know	agree	strongly agree

10. The best strategy for a language learner to keep a cross-cultural conversation going is to give frequent short responses to encourage the conversational partner to continue speaking.

1	2	3	4	5
strongly disagree	disagree	don't know	agree	strongly agree

11. To interrupt frequently to summarize or rephrase what your partner has said is a good way to confirm your understanding.

1	2	3	4	5
strongly disagree	disagree	don't know	agree	strongly agree

12. Commonly used ways of interrupting are very useful for students of a second language to learn.

1	2	3	4	5
strongly disagree	disagree	don't know	agree	strongly agree

13. Open-ended questions are better than yes/no questions for stimulating conversation.

1	2	3	4	5
strongly disagree	disagree	don't know	agree	strongly agree

14. When you don't want to answer a question or discuss a certain topic, it is best to say so directly.

1	2	3	4	5
strongly disagree	disagree	don't know	agree	strongly agree

15. A vague invitation should be interpreted by a language learner as no invitation at all.

1	2	3	4	5
strongly disagree	disagree	don't know	agree	strongly agree

16. To develop a friendship, it is useful to refer to your conversational partner by name more than once during a conversation.

1	2	3	4	5
strongly disagree	disagree	don't know	agree	strongly agree

17. Language learners should use every possible opportunity to speak the language of their cross-cultural communication partners.

1	2	3	4	5
strongly disagree	disagree	don't know	agree	strongly agree

Case Studies: Critical Incidents

The following three critical incidents depict typical situations in which the communication between speakers from different cultures is not as successful as the speakers had hoped it would be. In each case, at least one of the speakers is speaking a second language, but problems of actual comprehension and expression are only secondary. Discuss the kinds of behavior and/or strategies that would have made these conversations more successful, keeping in mind that any failed communication has at least two possible basic sources—the two partners in the communication.

Incident 1

Ben Robinson had felt on top of the world his first week in Lyons. His diligence in keeping up with his advanced French-language courses while completing his MBA seemed to have paid off: He had no trouble communicating with anyone he met; he had even been successful in striking up conversations in sidewalk cafes. Now, however, on his first day at work in the French subsidiary of a reputable American company, something was going wrong. While waiting in the reception area for his appointment to meet the vice president under whom he would be working, he started a conversation with Jacques Tanner, a young French executive who was also waiting there. After exchanging greetings and pleasantries, Ben told Jacques how excited he was about being in France and said he was sure that his family, who would be arriving the next week, would love it too. He went on to ask Jacques if he was a family man. When the Frenchman replied that he had two sons, Ben started asking about them as well, since he also had two sons. As Ben was getting more enthusiastic about the similarities in their lives, Jacques seemed to be getting more distant; he certainly was not keeping up his side of the conversation.

Discussion Question

What could explain this situation?

Incident 2

Tom Spies had a great group of students in his English as a Second Language (ESL) class that fall. Among the best were Toshi and Junko, two Japanese students who seemed unlike other Asian students Tom had taught in the past in that they often volunteered to speak in class and even asked unsolicited questions. Both had also come to his office on more than one occasion to continue discussions of subjects brought up in class. Moreover, Toshi was a top player in the soccer league in which Tom also played, and Tom frequently saw Junko at the campus coffee shop. When November came around, Tom thought it would be a great idea to invite Toshi and Junko to his parents' house for Thanksgiving dinner. Both seemed pleased to be invited, and both accepted. The dinner did not go quite as expected, however. Since Tom knew that neither of his students as at all shy, he gave them only the amount and type of attention he would have given to any Thanksgiving guests from his own culture. Every once in a while, he tried to coax them into the lively good-humored conversations he was having with his parents, but both seemed reluctant to speak. Toshi and Junko left feeling disappointed because they thought Tom and his family had shown little interest in them and had not allowed them to get a word in edgewise. Tom's parents were also disappointed; they told Tom afterward that next time he should bring home students who had a little more interest in being there.

Discussion Question

What are the possible causes of this perception gap?

Incident 3

Peggy Dupont had majored in Mandarin as an undergraduate and, while teaching English to immigrants in San Francisco for 3 years, had also become reasonably fluent in Cantonese. Now she was working for an up-and-coming outdoor-gear company that was rapidly expanding and looking for new markets. When the company had made initial contact with Victor Cheng, who represented an important Asian distributor in Hong Kong, it was obvious to everyone that Peggy, with her knowledge of Chinese language and culture, was the person to send to begin negotiations with him. Peggy was in a euphoric mood when she arrived at Hong Kong Airport and took a taxi to her hotel. This was her first trip to Hong Kong, and everything was just as she had imagined, only better. In her meeting with Mr. Cheng the next morning, Peggy was amazed at how easily and quickly she seemed to be able to establish a rapport in Cantonese. Cheng complimented Peggy on her linguistic ability and praised the company for being progressive enough to send a woman. He also mentioned that he had relatives in San Francisco. However, when they got around to business, even though Peggy thought she was speaking comprehensibly enough, Cheng seemed to become more and more frustrated with the conversation.

Discussion Question

What was Peggy's and/or Cheng's problem?

Central Concepts: Culture and Language

The following are nontechnical discussions of issues that should rightly fall into the realm of what language teachers teach, although second-language curricula as currently structured rarely devote much attention to any of them. The discussions, though brief, should serve to help teachers focus on some of the language needs that are not dealt with sufficiently in language-course textbooks. Not all of the important areas of cross-cultural communication can be covered; the emphasis here is on those areas in which language teachers can be expected to make a difference and areas that do not require extensive culture-specific information. Hence, the orientation in this module is toward developing an awareness of the various ways in which languages reflect the cultures of their speakers. Much of the discussion is inspired by Kasper (1989), Platt (1989), and Hurley (1992). Trainers and teachers should refer to these sources for more extensive coverage of issues in the teaching of pragmatics (language in use, in contradistinction to language as a system).

What will be only tangentially provided in the present treatment is a systematic coverage of important underlying cultural concepts such as orientation toward space and time, social hierarchy, family and personal relationships, individualism versus collectivism, work, and play. Much of this information can be derived from other modules in this book, and in any case language teachers must recognize the limits to the amount of class time they can justifiably allocate to culture learning.

One important general theme that comes out in the critical incidents described above is that successful communication in a culture not your own involves drawing sufficient, but not too much, attention to yourself. Learners who are not completely confident of either their language ability or their cultural knowledge tend to be quiet and spend their time simply observing. In some ways this is not a bad strategy, but it tends to perpetuate itself and tends to make the learner rather invisible to the hosts. This was probably part of the plight of the two Japanese students in Critical Incident 2. However, barging your way into the culture, as Ben in Critical Incident 1 and Peggy in Critical Incident 2 may be accused of doing, may make your presence an obtrusive one. The discussion below should be of some help in learning to tread the fine line between being perceived in a new culture as either lacking initiative or lacking sensitivity.

Another important theme that should emerge is that, although knowledge and sensitivity are extremely desirable in cross-cultural communication, they do not complete the picture. The element of personal choice is also crucial. How much and in what ways a sojourner wants to become part of the culture will vary for each individual. The importance of the element of choice was neatly put into perspective by Jenny Thomas (1983) in her distinction between two kinds of cross-cultural communication breakdowns: pragmalinguistic and sociopragmatic. It is not important to remember these terms, but the basic idea is that pragmalinguistic breakdowns occur when language learners do not know the actual means by which a communicative function is implemented in the target culture, whereas sociopragmatic breakdowns occur when learners choose not to use the accepted cultural way of communicating because the learners feel that to do so would in some way violate one of their own cultural values. An example of the former type of breakdown is the use of an inappropriate term of address because the learner does not know the appropriate term. A familiar example of the latter type of breakdown is a learner's insistence on using a formal way of addressing a host culture teacher even though he or she knows that the teacher strongly prefers being addressed by given name only. The former kind of breakdown is relatively easy to minimize with increasing knowledge; the latter generally is not. By keeping this distinction in mind, teachers should be able to avoid a certain amount of frustration.

A review of factors involved in answers to the self-assessment statements given in Section I may be of assistance here.

Language and Culture (Statements 1-4)

It is clearly true that language and culture are closely intertwined. Much of culture is created, maintained, and expressed through language, and language is likewise shaped by the culture(s) that developed it. What is also important to realize, however, is that the meanings conveyed through language are influenced by all of the cultural experiences of the speaker. For example, a Japanese replying in English to a non-Japanese and wishing to give a negative response to a request may say "That will be difficult." The non-Japanese may believe that the Japanese means that the request is possible, but difficult, to grant, when in fact the Japanese is most likely saying that the request is impossible to grant. The linguistic code may be very clear, but the intended meaning may be obscured because of incongruent cultural assumptions. Aspects of any and every culture that a speaker has been exposed to can be reflected in language use. The important implication for students of a language, and their teachers, is that although it is not necessary to mimic the language use of the so-called "native speakers" of the language being studied, it is necessary to keep in mind the effects that divergent cultural norms of two speakers can have on the communication between them. On the basis of an awareness of potentially differing conversational expectations, speakers can make sound decisions about how best to facilitate communication, whether it be through accommodation, assimilation, explicit discussion of perceived differences, or some other type of solution.

Some scholars of communication have claimed that genuine cross-cultural communication is impossible, but this conclusion is based on a very strict criterion for genuine communication. There have been many cases of successful and meaningful cross-cultural communication between members of very different cultures—even, quite often, between people with limited language in common.

Communicating one's intended meanings completely across cultures is indeed problematic, but a perfect match between intended and perceived meaning is also problematic even within one's own culture. Again, the important point is that, when speaking to someone with a different cultural background, there is a need for a heightened sensitivity to the possibility of miscommunication. This heightened sensitivity will make it possible either to avoid miscommunication completely or to repair it at little cost.

For some individuals and some cultures, maintaining harmony is less important than confronting differences with the aim of achieving deeper understanding. Making one's values and beliefs quite explicit to a conversational partner can be a direct route to deeper understanding, but it may also involve a level of disclosure and/or confrontation that is culturally or personally unacceptable to that partner. Students who hope to communicate successfully across cultures must learn to evaluate these conflicting considerations, keeping in mind that the full expression of thoughts and feelings requires a certain amount of explicitness across cultures and that such explicitness generally involves some risks.

For further discussion of the fundamental language/culture issue as it relates to language teaching, refer to Valdes (1986) and Damen (1987, 1991).

Addressing People (Statements 5 and 6)

In one sense, the many types of customary greetings found in various languages all serve about the same functions: to acknowledge the presence of a person and possibly to begin a conversation. The implication of this fact is that learners should avoid thinking of the meanings of the greetings in literal terms. However, the choice of greetings often reveals much about speakers and the perceived relationships between them, whether or not such information is explicitly encoded. For example, in English, a language reputed to be quite egalitarian, there are important social differences in the uses of "How do you do?" "How are you?" "How are you doing?" and "How is it going?" Therefore, language learners must learn to perceive and express the often nonliteral social meanings of greetings in specific cultural contexts. It is also very useful for language learners to try to rid themselves of overly literal interpretations of the words used in greetings. For example, in English-speaking cultures, nonnative speakers would do well to get used to the fact that being asked "How are you?" is not normally an offer to listen to a detailed report of the addressee's health condition; likewise, the non-native speaker should feel free to use the phrase without obligation to be genuinely interested in the conversational partner's health. In similar fashion, typical nonliteral greetings in other cultural settings, such as greetings that might be translated as "Where are you going?" or "Have you eaten?" are not considered to be prying into other people's business or extending invitations for a meal.

Being able to use the expected greetings and responses to greetings is a high priority for getting conversations smoothly under way. In one's own culture, conversations often develop with the two speakers unaware that it is happening. This kind of naturalness is much less frequent in cross-cultural conversations, but by being willing to use conventionalized greeting forms and, if necessary, practicing them to the point of automatization, learners will find themselves in many more conversations with much less effort.

Expressing Emotions (Statements 7 and 8)

Although smiling can function as a nearly universal sign of goodwill, and therefore facilitate good relationships between people, there is a lot of cross-cultural variation in how much smiling is appropriate in various situations, and there are also different sorts of smiles in various cultures that have functions quite distinct from expressing goodwill. For example, certain smiles among Japanese and Thai often express contained embarrassment or anger. Learners of Japanese and Thai thus need to be made aware of the different types of smiles among Japanese and Thai, just as learners of English from cultures that are more measured in their smiling behavior need to know that Americans, for example, give and expect to receive smiles quite freely.

It is probably a useful starting assumption that outside of one's own culture verbal expression of anger should be minimized. This way of operating will be more likely to avoid than to cause trouble. But there is no guarantee: Refraining from verbally expressing anger may be taken as a sign that everything is all right, or it may even be interpreted as an indication of character weakness. Therefore, language learners need to learn and practice appropriate ways of expressing anger in the cultures they are bound for and also need to develop context knowledge about the role of the expression of anger in that culture. In Mediterranean cultures, for example, what appears to be anger is often expressed quite freely in conversations with both friends and strangers, but often it is intended primarily as a sign of enthusiasm or as a device to deepen involvement in the conversation. It is expected to be taken lightly and is soon forgotten. In other cultures, however, an outward expression of anger can often be taken as a sign that a serious interpersonal problem has developed.

Interrupting Conversations for Various Reasons (Statements 9-12)

The extent to which non-native speakers should break the flow of conversation to ask for repetition or clarification cannot be specified but should nevertheless be considered carefully by language learners. If a learner lets a conversational partner continue speaking despite an incomplete understanding of what is being said, the learner continues to receive input and the speaker's meaning may become more comprehensible. However, the speaker is likely to gain a mistaken impression of (1) the learner's level of language ability and (2) the nature of the relationship, since the learner's participation in the conversation seems minimal. However, if the learner stops the speaker whenever there is less than perfect communication, the speaker will know very well what the learner's level of comprehension is but may become frustrated because of the difficulty of sustaining the conversation. A valuable skill for a learner will thus be to learn culturally appropriate ways to ask for repetition, especially ones that allow the speaker to pinpoint what has not been understood.

Seemingly less crucial an issue but ultimately just as important is signaling the fact that the speaker has been understood. In some cultures the constant signaling of understanding is expected, whereas in others such signals would be considered distracting and annoying. They might even be mistakenly considered attempts by the listener to assume the initiative in the conversation. Since one's own style of responding is habitual and largely unconscious, the practicing of the type of response that is expected in the target culture is well worthwhile.

As a language learner, summarizing or rephrasing what your partner has said is definitely a good way to confirm your understanding; it is also a good way to stretch your speaking ability. However, in some cultural contexts this type of responding behavior may be misunderstood by the speaker as an indication that what he or she has said was unclear or was not said in the best way.

Because learners of a language tend to be slower in initiating utterances due to lack of skill or confidence, knowing how to interrupt a conversation that is moving too fast for entry can be a valuable skill. It is a skill that must be used very carefully, though, since its overuse or use in the wrong situation can easily cause offense. When learners are unsure of themselves, one potentially effective strategy is to begin the interruption with an explicit statement such as "I'm very sorry to interrupt, but . . . ," which shows clearly that you are sensitive to conversational rules and are (possibly) violating them only with great reluctance. If the other participants in the conversation are at all sensitive, they will subsequently give the non-native speaker more conventional and smoother opportunities for entry into the conversation.

Keeping the Conversation Moving (Statement 13)

As a conversational strategy for language learners, open-ended questions tend to generate much more input than yes/no questions. The conversational partner will most likely give a longer and more detailed answer, and indeed an interesting conversation may be stimulated. However, open-ended questions also diminish the amount of control the learner has over the topic of conversation. They can lead quickly to a situation in which the learner can no longer participate actively. The ability to combine both kinds of questions skillfully is another skill that is worth developing in the language classroom.

Choosing Conversation Topics (Statement 14)

With many individuals in some cultures, for example, North American and Northern European cultures, it may be best to state directly that you do not want to answer a question or discuss a certain topic. Usually, however, doing so involves the risk of making subsequent conversation very awkward. In some cultural situations, an evasive answer or a simple smile is enough to trigger a change of topic, although in a different situation such behavior may be incomprehensible and/or lead to further questioning on the undesirable topic. Although the preferred ways of avoiding and changing topics need to be learned for each cultural context, in general a good starting strategy is to give a very brief response to the undesirable question, followed immediately in the same turn with a question that leads the conversation in a related but acceptable direction.

When initiating potentially controversial or uncomfortable topics in an unfamiliar cultural context, it may be wise to preface the initiation with an expression such as "I'm not sure if this is an appropriate question or not, but . . . " or "Please let me know if this is not a good topic, but . . . ." Making explicit but non-obtrusive reference to the fact that you do not know all the rules of the conversation is likely to make your cross-cultural conversational partner more rather than less comfortable, as he or she is almost certainly in a similar position.

Extending and Responding to Invitations (Statement 15)

Because in some cultures invitations tend to be taken very seriously, sometimes even as obligations, people in cultures that are freer about invitations are often considered insincere if an invitation they make is not specific or not followed by a more specific one. Often, however, it is not a matter of sincerity but of a more interactive style of concretizing the invitation. Language learners need both the specific language expected in extending and responding to invitations in a culturally appropriate manner and a deeper understanding of the whole invitation process in which the language is used.

Maintaining Rapport (Statements 16 and 17)

Referring to your conversational partner by name at various times during a conversation is appreciated by people in some cultures. It is one of a variety of devices that display and develop affective common ground with the conversational partner. What the language learner needs to know is whether this is, in fact, an approved custom in the target culture and, if so, how much is too much or not enough. Also, the use of given names as opposed to family names, titles, and/or honorifics varies considerably from culture to culture, and misuse of names may evoke undesirable feelings in the person who has been referred to inappropriately.

A final consideration in maintaining rapport is the fundamental one of language choice. Many learners assume that members of the target culture will appreciate learners' efforts to speak the target language. This is often the case, but it can never be assumed. Sometimes the cross-cultural conversational partners are just as eager to learn your language and/or show respect to your culture. At times when communication must be precise, another problem may arise: Your partners may not wish to hurt your feelings by pointing out your inability to communicate adequately (for the purpose) in their language, but they may be distressed at your persistence in trying. An additional possibility is that some cross-cultural conversational partners may feel that your eagerness to speak their language implies a weakness on their part in speaking your language. Finally, some members of some cultures feel a very strong connection between their language and their cultural identity; among such people, outsiders' attempts to speak their language are often not welcomed. These possibilities should not discourage the language learner from attempting to use the target language as often as possible, but they should remind the learner of the need for constant interpersonal sensitivity in all cross-cultural situations.

Skill-Development Exercises (Simulations)

The following simulations are designed to develop experiential knowledge in speakers communicating across cultures. They are at a high level of difficulty; rather than focusing on specific communicative functions or specific conversational management techniques, each requires the skillful use of a range of strategies for the successful resolution of an important interpersonal crisis. The delicate negotiations designed into these simulations provide the challenge that advanced learners need in order to make the final approach to cultural crossover. However, given specific cultural contexts and small modifications to the content of the simulations, they can be adapted for a range of more particular or lower-level uses. They do not represent all the possible experiential activities involved in cross-cultural communication, but they should stimulate language teachers to begin imagining the possibilities available to them.

In using these simulations, it is important that each person receive only the description of the situation from his or her own perspective and realize that the other participant's perspective may be different. Be sure that both participants understand their goals and know that they are free to decide how to achieve these goals. Allow two people to attempt the simulation; when one of them succeeds in achieving his or her goals, stop the simulation (allow no more than 7 minutes in any case). The entire group can benefit from a discussion of the way in which and the extent to which the participants achieved their objectives and what else could have been done. Then allow another pair, maybe even two other pairs, to do the same simulation and, again, follow with a discussion by the entire group. It is important to discover that the goals can be achieved in many different ways.

For more ready-made simulations, guidance on how to design simulations, and background on the use of simulation and gaming, see Christopher and Smith (1987, 1991) and Crookall and Oxford (1990).

Simulation 1: Supervisors and Subordinates

Role A. You are a temporary intern at a research institute specializing in intercultural communication. You have been working under the direction of a researcher from a culture different from your own. This person, who is an expert in intercultural communication, will be evaluating your work at the end of the year, and his or her evaluation will surely affect not only the extension of your current position but also your entire career. The supervisor seems to be taking advantage of this circumstance and has several times made requests that seem unreasonable to you and seem to be unrelated to your work. You have acceded to all of them. This afternoon this supervisor called you into his or her office and asked you to sell, for their original price, two concert tickets that you had purchased some time ago; you thought it was even hinted in the conversation that you should *give* the tickets to this supervisor. The tickets are not available any more, and you have promised to take your spouse to the concert. You now must respond to your supervisor's request.

Your goal: To refuse, politely but firmly, to give or sell your concert tickets to your supervisor.

Role B. You are an expert on intercultural communication working as a researcher at a research institute specializing in intercultural communication. You are supervising a temporary intern who is from a culture different from your own. You must evaluate the work of the intern and make a decision about the extension of the internship. You have had long talks with the intern about many things, sometimes unrelated to work, in order to gain a better understanding of the intern's attitude toward life in general. For the most part, you are favorably impressed with the intern, but there is one aspect of the intern's personality that you feel needs to be modified: The intern seems to be overly eager to please. In the institute the intern is becoming known as a person who is afraid to say no to any request, and you believe that this situation must change if the intern is to develop as a scholar. In order to force the intern to take a stand and express a definite position, this afternoon you called the intern into your office and asked to buy from him or her the two concert tickets that you know the intern purchased several weeks ago. You know the intern has been planning to go to this concert with his or her spouse. You asked the intern to think about this and to let you know later. The intern is in your office now, looking a bit worried.

Your goals: To be firm about buying the tickets until the intern is able to refuse to sell; once the intern refuses, to explain the situation from your perspective.

Simulation 2: Late for Work

Role A. This is the second time this week you have been late to work. You were hoping no one would notice, but when you arrived at your office there was a message from your supervisor asking for an official explanation and stating that this explanation would be placed in your personnel file along with a report from the supervisor. This supervisor, who is from a culture different from yours, is new and is obviously trying to do an effective job. You do not know the supervisor personally, but you wish this situation had been handled in an unofficial way.

You are almost never late for anything. This week, however, you have out-of-town guests and have been showing them around every evening after work. You have not been getting to bed until 2:00 or 3:00 a.m., and this is the second morning you have overslept. Fortunately, today is Friday and your guests are leaving this weekend. Next week things should be back to normal.

You have decided to speak to your supervisor personally.

Your goals: To apologize and explain your reason for being late. To request that your tardiness not be officially recorded in your personnel file.

Role B. You are a new supervisor in your office. This morning one of your workers, who is from a culture different from yours, arrived late for work for the second time this week. This person's record appears to be good, but this behavior is not something you can permit to continue. You immediately sent this person a written message asking for an official explanation and stating that this explanation would be included, along with your report, in the worker's personnel file.

The worker is now in your office requesting to speak with you.

Your goals: To be firm. To insist that the explanation be in writing and that it be completed before the end of this working day. To make it clear that, if this behavior continues, the worker's job will be in jeopardy.

Simulation 3: Error in the Brochure

Role A. You work for an institute that conducts cross-cultural training courses for people in business and government. You have been working for the organization for 5 years. You do writing and editorial work, and one of your duties is to send out a brochure every 3 months listing all programs that are to be offered by your institute. A brochure was mailed out today, and you notice that it fails to announce an important workshop that was to be conducted by a relatively new employee whom you like very much. Your organization is expecting serious budget cuts, and your friend's job may be in danger if his or her program does not succeed. However, you know there has been some unfavorable talk about your work and if this error comes out it may be your job that will be in danger. Your friend, who is from a different country, is now at your office door.

Your goals: To apologize to your friend and to seek a solution to this problem.

Role B. Six months ago you came to this country and started to work for an institute that conducts cross-cultural training courses for people in business and government. Your work has been good, but you are considered to be an idea person and an aide to others. You have heard that there will be budget cuts coming in the near future, and you fear that unless you prove yourself to be a leader you may lose your job. You have designed a workshop that has received full support from your supervisors even though the cost (to the participants) is higher than that of most such workshops. This means that advertisements and promotions are of utmost importance if the workshop is to succeed. Today you received the brochure announcing all of the programs that will be offered by your organization during the next 3 months. You notice that there is no mention of your program in it. You go to the person who is responsible for the brochure's publication; this person, who is in a slightly higher position than yours, has been quite friendly with you in the past.

Your goals: To complain about the omission and to recommend a solution.

Simulation 4: Not Enough Sleep

Role A. For the last 2 weeks your administrative assistant, who is from a culture different from your own, has been late in arriving at work and is behind in some assignments. He or she appears to be tired and nervous. This assistant has been with the company for 5 years and has never behaved like this before. He or she has always been pleasant, prompt, and efficient. During the last week you have had three complaints about this assistant from coworkers. You have asked to see him or her, and the meeting is about to take place.

Your goals: To find out what the problem is. To make it clear to the administrative assistant that you are supportive but that things must improve within the next few days.

Role B. You have been an administrative assistant at the same company for the last 5 years. You like this job and your coworkers. You work here from 9:00 a.m. to 5:00 p.m., Monday through Friday. Two weeks ago you took an additional job, a job as a typist for a small business, and you work there from 7:00 to 11:00 p.m., 5 nights a week. By the time you get home it is almost midnight. You have not been getting enough sleep because of this, and you have been getting to work late in the morning. This has caused problems with fellow staff members because you have no time for taking coffee breaks or eating lunch with them. You are behind in your work, and this has made you nervous and irritable. You do not have to keep the second job, but you would like to keep it one more month in order to earn some extra money. Your boss, who is from a culture different from your own, has asked to see you; you are scheduled to see him or her now.

Your goals: To explain the situation to your boss. To convince him or her that within a month things will be back to normal.

Field Exercises

The following field exercises are designed to help language learners develop the ability to communicate effectively across cultures.

1. Find several videotaped films made in one or more of the countries where the relevant target language is spoken; some should be with and some without subtitles. Watch the films, concentrating on sections that are especially rich in culture-specific interactional features; replay such sections many times. Notice especially how the characters greet and take leave of each other, how they address each other, how topics are initiated, how those topics and the tone of the conversation differ from what you might have expected, and how language use changes with different combinations of conversational partners. In the films that do not have subtitles, your deficiencies in the language can force you to notice interactional features that viewers who process the language smoothly are likely to miss. In the films that do have subtitles, discrepancies between the subtitles and the actual dialogue can force you to notice language features that simply cannot be adequately translated; these are often the features that are most important for learners to understand.

2. Seek out acquaintances from the target cultures and ask them about their problems and frustrations in relating to members of your culture. Discuss the problem areas individually. Both of you are likely to benefit. Furthermore, you will gradually be able to begin to discriminate finely between reality and stereotype.

3. Be on the lookout for forms of humor in the target language—especially in newspapers, magazines, and television commercials—that apparently make fun of your culture. Try to figure out specifically what sort of perception of your culture makes each example seem humorous to members of the other culture. If, as is often the case, you cannot see the humor, ask a suitable cultural informant to explain it to you. You will probably still not see the humor, but you may get a better grasp of the cultural differences perceived by members of the other culture, and this knowledge can be very useful in future cross-cultural interactions.

Final Comments

All of the issues dealt with above may significantly affect the interactions between language learners and speakers of the target language. They are, however, given relatively little attention in most foreign-language curricula. Teachers generally do not teach these things and students often do not learn them very well; the cross-cultural competence students do develop most often comes slowly and painfully through trial and error. In the process, many students also learn how to avoid using the target language whenever possible and perhaps also how to avoid unnecessary cultural encounters.

A few language textbooks that focus on cross-cultural communication have appeared, and more are sure to be published soon. The last section of this module lists some of the ESL textbooks currently available. Although these books aid the teacher by providing organized knowledge and ready-made instructional materials, the language teacher will undoubtedly find that many of the principles of effective cross-cultural communication are difficult to teach explicitly. The analysis of critical incidents and related activities can serve well to focus students on the important issues, but experiential knowledge is ultimately essential. Therefore, role-playing and other experiential techniques must be major components of any language course that aspires to foster cross-cultural awareness and sensitivity. The preceding sections provide material for several experiential learning activities. Whenever possible, these activities should be videotaped so that the critical points at which a conversation takes a turn for the better or worse can be analyzed fully.

Suggestions for Further Reading

Irving, K. (1986). *Communicating in context: Intercultural communication for ESL students.* Englewood Cliffs, NJ: Prentice Hall.

Basically a reading text for intermediate-advanced ESL students, with cross-cultural communication and American culture as the content focus. A major emphasis on teaching American idioms through context and paraphrase tasks. Abundant use of cartoons to provide insights into culture differences.

Levine, D., & Adelman, M. (1982). *Beyond language: Intercultural communication for English as a second language.* Englewood Cliffs, NJ: Prentice Hall.

Pitched at a slightly lower level than Irving's book, and with somewhat more emphasis on speaking rather than reading tasks. Similar content focus, on cross-cultural communication in relation to an American context. More direct treatment of particular conventional speech acts frequently used in American conversations.

Levine, D., Baxter, J., & McNulty, P. (1987). *The culture puzzle: Cross-cultural communication for English as a second language.* Englewood Cliffs, NJ: Prentice Hall.

Of the three books, this is the one that could be adapted to the widest range of student abilities and curriculum types. Has the most attractive and easy-to-understand format, lending itself to being used as a source of supplementary tasks as needed. Focuses briefly but systematically on arguably the most important skills for cross-cultural communication, with plentiful examples of extended cross-cultural interactions, both successful and unsuccessful. Orientation to American culture is present but relatively unobtrusive; therefore, it is the best bet of the three books for students who are not already present in the United States.

References

Christopher, E., & Smith, L. (1987). *Leadership training through gaming: Power, people and problem-solving.* London: Kogan Page.

Christopher, E., & Smith, L. (1991). *Negotiation training through gaming: Strategies, tactics, and manoeuvres.* London: Kogan Page.

Crookall, D., & Oxford, R. (Eds.). (1990). *Simulation, gaming, and language learning.* New York: Newbury House.

Damen, L. (1987). *Culture learning: The fifth dimension in the language classroom.* Reading, MA: Addison-Wesley.

Damen, L. (1991). *Closing the language and culture gap: An intercultural communication perspective.* Paper delivered at the Conference on Interdisciplinary Perspectives on Culture Learning in the Second Language Curriculum, May 10-11, University of Minnesota, Minneapolis.

Hurley, D. (1992). Issues in teaching pragmatics, prosody, and non-verbal communication. *Applied Linguistics, 13*(3), 259-281.

Kasper, G. (1989). Interactive procedures in interlanguage discourse. In W. Oleksy (Ed.), *Contrastive pragmatics* (pp. 189-224). Amsterdam: John Benjamins.

Platt, J. (1989). Some types of communicative strategies across cultures: Sense and sensitivity. In O. García & R. Otheguy (Eds.), *English across cultures, cultures across English* (pp. 13-30). Berlin, New York: Mouton de Gruyter.

Sebeok, T., Hayes, A., & Bateson, M. (Eds.). (1964). *Approaches to semiotics.* The Hague: Mouton & Co.

Thomas, J. (1983). Cross-cultural pragmatic failure. *Applied Linguistics, 4*, 91-112.

Valdes, J. (Ed.). (1986). *Culture bound: Bridging the cultural gap in language teaching.* New York: Cambridge University Press.

16 Training Bilinguals to Interpret in the Community

CAROLINA FREIMANIS

"If you speak two languages you should naturally be able to translate or interpret from one language to another." This commonly held assumption often leads to unfortunate misunderstandings and problems. Although it is undoubtedly important to be skillful in both languages, this in itself is not enough to qualify someone as an interpreter. This module discusses interpreting as a skill that is independent of language competency. It familiarizes readers with specific exercises and abilities that interpreters need to be able to perform well. Through the exercises readers are able to experience, firsthand, the difficulty and complexity of the interpreting process and gain a new appreciation of skillful interpreters.

Contents

Self-Assessment Exercise:
Myths and Reality of Community Interpretation

The following statements refer to the skills and abilities of interpreters who serve non-English-speaking clients in settings such as hospitals, immigration offices, social agencies, and the like. Assume that you are in charge of selecting and/or training individuals who speak two languages, and who are not professional interpreters, to assume that role and act as communication facilitators. Please circle the option in the scale that best represents your opinion.

1. Communication is facilitated when friends and relatives serve as interpreters because of their close relationship with the client.

5	4	3	2	1
strongly agree	agree	not sure	disagree	strongly disagree

2. Knowledge of technical vocabulary in both working languages is a key element for community interpreters.

5	4	3	2	1
strongly agree	agree	not sure	disagree	strongly disagree

3. Community interpreters are instruments of communication, not participants in the task to be accomplished by the worker (counselor, social worker, doctor, etc.).

5	4	3	2	1
strongly agree	agree	not sure	disagree	strongly disagree

4. Community interpreters must acquire technical skills such as consecutive note-taking and simultaneous interpreting techniques.

5	4	3	2	1
strongly agree	agree	not sure	disagree	strongly disagree

5. Community interpreters should work only into their native language.

5	4	3	2	1
strongly agree	agree	not sure	disagree	strongly disagree

6. Community interpreters should give a word-for-word rendition to ensure accuracy and completeness.

5	4	3	2	1
strongly agree	agree	not sure	disagree	strongly disagree

7. Selecting communication facilitators from the client's culture ensures a better communication.

5	4	3	2	1
strongly agree	agree	not sure	disagree	strongly disagree

8. Community interpreters should not intervene in the exchange between the client and the worker (e.g., doctor).

5	4	3	2	1
strongly agree	agree	not sure	disagree	strongly disagree

9. Community interpreters are usually volunteers.

5	4	3	2	1
strongly agree	agree	not sure	disagree	strongly disagree

10. Most individuals who speak two languages have the skills to become good community interpreters.

5	4	3	2	1
strongly agree	agree	not sure	disagree	strongly disagree

11. Community interpreters may benefit greatly by learning conference interpreting skills.

5	4	3	2	1
strongly agree	agree	not sure	disagree	strongly disagree

12. It is unrealistic to expect a good interpretation between languages with very different grammatical structures.

5	4	3	2	1
strongly agree	agree	not sure	disagree	strongly disagree

13. Developing stamina enhances an interpreter's performance.

5	4	3	2	1
strongly agree	agree	not sure	disagree	strongly disagree

14. Ideas about interpreters and their work are associated with the setting in which they work.

5	4	3	2	1
strongly agree	agree	not sure	disagree	strongly disagree

15. Community interpreters commonly report that they are given a great deal of respect and gratitude for their work.

5	4	3	2	1
strongly agree	agree	not sure	disagree	strongly disagree

The preceding statements are designed to make you think about the skills and tasks of professional community interpreters and about the difference between professional interpreters and communication facilitators. Some of these statements have a preferable yes or no answer. Others have no right or wrong answers because in many cases the situation in which the interpreter works dictates the best action to follow. Throughout the chapter some ideas, as well as some factors that affect perceptions about interpretation in general, will be presented to assist in the analysis of these statements.

Case Study

The Naive "Facilitator"

Gabriel is a foreign graduate student from a Latin American country. He has a good command of English and has very few problems either communicating with his peers or following his classes. Like many graduate students, he would like to have some extra income so he decided to use his knowledge of two languages and offer his services as an interpreter. For that purpose, he signed up at a language services office that keeps a list of "interpreters" and farms out work according to availability and language combination.

When Gabriel received a call for his first assignment he was very happy, not only because it meant extra money, but also because he felt he was performing a "good deed": helping a person from his own cultural background communicate, thus enabling him or her to obtain a needed service, and also helping the agency perform its task, because without him, they would not be able to provide adequate services. He felt very confident of his language ability, so he was not expecting any mayor difficulties and was looking forward to the experience.

He had very little information about his assignment. The social worker who contacted him said only that the assignment would take place at a local hospital and that the patient was a middle-aged, working-class Hispanic woman. He expected the staff to help him with any questions or problems he might have and to treat him as an important element in the task to be performed by the staff. When he arrived, he informed a nurse that he was the interpreter, and she told him, in a disinterested and almost annoyed tone of voice, to take a seat and wait for the doctor handling the case. He started to feel uncomfortable. Nobody came to inform him about the case and he started feeling as though they had forgotten about him. Finally, the nurse asked him, in a dry and rough manner, to follow her. In the examining room, doctor and patient were already waiting for him.

The doctor barely looked up when he came in and didn't introduce himself or the patient. He seemed to be in a hurry and apparently did not consider it important to brief him on the case. The only background information he gave was that the woman had been having abdominal cramps for a few days. When he started the interview, he spoke very fast, never looked at either the patient or the interpreter, and used technical language. Gabriel started to feel that he was losing ground very quickly. He couldn't keep up with the speed and didn't know how or when to stop the doctor so he could start interpreting. When he finally started to interpret, he realized that he had lost quite a bit of information. By now, he was quite scared. He decided that the best way was to say what he remembered using as many similar words in Spanish as the doctor said in English, reasoning that this would at least ensure accuracy. However, looking at the patient's blank face and her responses, he realized that she was not understanding. As the interview progressed, Gabriel grew increasingly anxious and the doctor increasingly impatient. He displayed a total lack of interest in the case, staring out the window instead of looking at the interpreter or the patient, even when the latter was pointing at the part of the body that hurt. He tried to call the doctor's attention, but was rudely dismissed implying, with an air of superiority, that he was as incompetent and uneducated as the patient.

When the interview was over, Gabriel left with the sinking feeling that he had been unable to bridge the communication gap and that he had not been of any help. Even worse, he had also been insulted and mistreated. He had originally thought that he was needed by the agency and expected to be treated well, but when he left he realized that he had been more a nuisance and that the staff, especially the doctor, thought that he was uneducated and incompetent.

Discussion

Many aspiring "communication facilitators" believe that the only element they need in order to become interpreters is their knowledge of two languages. However, as the case above illustrates, there are many other aspects involved in an actual interpretation assignment, some of which have little to do with language ability. The main points in this case are these:

1. Lack of information on the part of the "facilitator" about the nature of the interpretation scene. Some of the problems that the facilitator encountered in this case could have been avoided, had he had previous knowledge of the situation and of what is required of an interpreter.
2. Lack of information on the part of the staff and the doctor about the nature of communicating through an interpreter.
3. Preconceived ideas on the part of the staff about the ethnic group of the "facilitator" and the patient, which hampered communication and labeled both as incompetent and uneducated.

Discussion Questions

1. Why did the doctor seem impatient and annoyed?
2. Why did the doctor think that the facilitator was incompetent and uneducated?
3. How can the facilitator obtain information about the case?
4. How can the worker (in this case the doctor) be informed about the nature of communicating through an interpreter?
5. What can the facilitator do in order to be better prepared for an interpretation assignment?

The Language Skills Gap

The previous scenario touched on problems that arise from a lack of knowledge about the interpretation process, many of which are due to extralinguistic factors. However, language proficiency is also an extremely important and often misunderstood element. Let us examine this same case from another perspective, namely, the problems that Gabriel, our foreign student facilitator, encountered because of linguistic factors.

From the beginning of the interview, Gabriel realized that the doctor used a great deal of technical terminology. Given that most medical terms have Spanish cognates (they have the same Latin or Greek roots), he thought he could solve the problem by using equivalent technical terms in Spanish. He reasoned that this would insure accuracy, based on the belief that repeating information "word for word" is the best method of interpretation. However, Gabriel knew that the patient was not getting the information. Her responses not only evidenced a total lack of understanding of what Gabriel had interpreted, they also disclosed a very limited and colloquial language level. At times he felt lost with her responses, because even though Spanish was his native language, he could not understand what she was saying, either because she used regionalisms that were unfamiliar to him or because her speech pattern was too colloquial. When he did not understand what the patient was trying to say, he used his "security blanket" technique of interpreting "word for word" into English, a solution that annoyed the doctor very much, because he couldn't figure out what Gabriel was saying. For example, during the interview the doctor asked the patient whether she had had any surgeries, to which the patient answered "*Si, me sacaron las anginas.*" Gabriel's word-for-word interpretation was "Yes, they took out my anginas." The doctor, totally confused and very annoyed, told Gabriel to find out what she meant, and when she pointed at her throat, both realized she referred to the tonsils. Gabriel knew that the word *angina* had a cognate in Spanish, so he didn't hesitate to use it. But in this case, it did not work. Had Gabriel known that among Chicanos the word *anginas* is used instead of the regular term *amigdalas* to refer to tonsils, the problem would have been avoided.

Another problem our facilitator faced was the fact that the doctor spoke very fast and at times Gabriel could not remember everything the doctor said in order to provide a complete interpretation. The result was total chaos: The doctor became increasingly impatient at Gabriel's incompetence and the patient became increasingly distressed, because she was not getting the help that she needed. In both cases, Gabriel was the target of the blame, since he could not bridge the communication gap.

Discussion

As we know, Gabriel finished the assignment feeling depressed and insulted. The discomfort of being unable to bridge the communication gap raised a disturbing question in his mind: He had native Spanish proficiency and had always been proud of his fluency in English. Then why was he unable to handle the language problems that arose in the interview? The main points in this case are these:

1. The language (as well as educational and cultural) disparity between the worker and the client. Our facilitator was completely unaware of this difference and was unable to switch from a high and sophisticated language register to a low and colloquial register.

2. A related issue is the use of technical terms in this setting. Our facilitator had a good command of his languages, and even knew technical equivalents in both of them. However, he lacked the flexibility and the breadth of vocabulary required to transfer the meaning of highly technical terms into everyday language. By the same token, even though Spanish was his native language, the patient had a different sociocultural background, so he could not understand some of her colloquialisms and regionalisms.

3. A lack of basic interpreting skills. For example, the facilitator did not intervene to make sure that the patient understood or to clarify concepts or terms he did not understand. He resorted to "word for word" interpretation and thus used awkward and probably nonsensical phrases and terms. Also, he did not stop the doctor when he felt he could not keep up with the amount of information; this in turn created gaps in communication, because he did not deliver a complete interpretation.

Discussion Questions

1. Why is "word for word" interpretation an inadequate solution?
2. How can the facilitator acquire the necessary language skills for an interpreting situation?
3. How can the facilitator research and prepare for an assignment?
4. What techniques could the facilitator acquire to be able to keep up with the amount of information he has to interpret?
5. What ethical issues can be raised in this case?

Not All Interpreters Are Created Alike: The Conference Interpreter Versus the Community Interpreter

Introduction

Communication is believed to be most effective between people who share a common language and culture, and even then, it can be an elusive goal. In today's world, technological advances and increased mobility have placed individuals and institutions within an intricate weave of languages and cultures where the problems of communication and understanding can seem insurmountable and often frustrating. The professionals who are called in to solve these problems include translators and interpreters, and their role as bridges for communication has become increasingly important.

For more than 40 years, the field of translation and interpretation has struggled to become a profession and yet it is still relatively unknown to the general public. This is especially true in the United States, where the need for trained professionals has only recently been addressed. There are many reasons, among them the controversies about foreign language learning, the relative lack of need for conference interpreting given that English is the most common language of negotiation, and the idea that language-related professions are poorly paid and thus of low status. It was in Europe that the field was born and that the first steps toward achieving international recognition were taken through the creation of professional associations and academic training programs. These programs have evolved through the years. Today, it is widely accepted that the highly specialized nature of the profession demands a type of instruction that can only be offered at the university level, in programs that usually last between

2 and 5 years. Programs at that level now exist in Taiwan, Korea, Japan, Australia, and Latin America, and yet, there is only one such program in the United States.

Nevertheless, these efforts towards professionalization have been geared mainly towards the interpreter working in international settings and therefore, to the layman, the term *interpreter* or *interpretation* conjures images of the United Nations and high-level meetings in great international conference halls or of the "summit meetings" where interpreters stand behind important delegates and whisper the interpretation. As we will see later on, this is a variation on simultaneous interpreting called *chuchotage* or *whispered interpretation*. Conference interpreters are better known and have acquired prestige and an aura of glamour because they move in the international scene and are very well paid. Indeed, professional conference interpreters may work 100 days a year, a maximum of 6 hours a day, and earn the equivalent of an executive on a normal 9 to 5, 50-weeks-per-year schedule.

However, these images illustrate the working environment of some interpreters and do not represent the whole picture. The *fact* is that most interpretation work is not glamorous and does not take place in international settings. It takes place within a community where individuals from various cultures are trying to communicate and function effectively, and the tasks and skills of interpreters serving these populations are different from those in the conference halls. The need for community interpreting is rapidly increasing, and it is important to understand it and recognize it as a professional activity with its own standards and requirements, given that the stakes are perhaps higher and more urgent than those in conference interpreting: the lives, well-being, and even property of individuals.

In this chapter, I will present an overview of the skills, training, and working conditions of conference interpreters and of community interpreters. I will end with a set of guidelines on how to improve the skills of nontrained bilinguals who already work as "communication facilitators" or who may be asked to take on that role in the future.

Conference Interpreting

It has been said that interpreting "is something of a schizophrenic activity requiring the interpreter to function more-or-less simultaneously in two languages" (Anderson, 1978). Indeed, to an observer, the task performed by interpreters can be quite fascinating and at times appear impossible. Conference interpreters work at international meetings where there are two or more working languages. Depending on the requirements of the job, they can perform either simultaneously or consecutively.

Simultaneous interpretation, sometimes mistakenly called simultaneous translation, is the best known and, to the lay person, the most intriguing form of interpretation. It requires special equipment to link interpreters, who are in booths usually raised above the level of the meeting room, with the speaker and the audience. Interpreters listen through earphones and interpret into microphones that are connected to receivers. Conference participants can then choose the appropriate language channel and listen to the interpretation through earphones. Most conference interpreting is done in this mode, since it is the most efficient in terms of time and flexibility of languages.

During this type of interpretation, the following tasks are performed almost simultaneously: (a) listening to the speaker (reception); (b) understanding the message (decoding); (c) translating the message (encoding); and (d) delivering the translated message (emitting). Because the speaker doesn't stop to let the interpreter do all this, the interpreter must listen, process, and store *incoming* information while processing and delivering the *previous* information. It is almost simultaneous because there is a lag time between the speaker and the interpreter, known as *decalage,* which allows them to listen and process information before speaking. This lag period can be very long if the interpreter works with languages that differ greatly in grammatical structure. For example, an interpreter working from German into English must listen to a whole sentence or a whole idea in order to get the main verb and be able to render the message.

Simultaneous interpretation is very demanding to the brain's information processing mechanisms and requires extensive training, stamina, and endurance. The techniques needed to reach an acceptable level of performance must be developed gradually because they involve mental processes that are not "natural," at least for most people. For example, the ability to do several things at the same time or *multiple tasking* in interpreting jargon, is neither "natural" nor easy to learn.

During the beginning stages of training the main goal is precisely to develop multiple tasking. This skill is developed through a technique called *shadowing,* or repeating incoming information exactly as it is heard (in the same language, no paraphrasing, and at times imitating the tone of the original). Although there are differences of opinion among professionals as to the effectiveness of shadowing in interpreter training, I believe that it is one of the best preparatory exercises, because it accomplishes several goals:

1. *Multi-Tasking:* Students learn to listen, process, and speak simultaneously in a less demanding condition, by factoring out the encoding process.

2. *Decalage:* Students learn to distance themselves from the speaker in terms of time. In the beginning, they are encouraged to start shadowing about 3 seconds (approximately 5 words) behind the speaker. The lag time is gradually increased until students feel comfortable with a distance of about 10 words. They are then encouraged to decide how much lag time is necessary, according to the speech patterns they hear, waiting for a meaning unit (the shortest sentence or utterance that has intrinsic meaning) or the main verb to start shadowing.

3. *Pacing:* I believe this is one of the by-products of decalage, since students learn to follow the speaker in a rhythmic manner, with no gaps and with a smooth

speech pattern. Good pacing is one of the elements that makes listeners forget that they are listening to an interpretation and not the original.

4. *Analytical Thinking:* Another important by-product of decalage, since waiting for a meaning unit encourages the analysis of information, a skill that will be invaluable when translation is introduced. Analytical thought is also developed by using speeches with heavy accents, because students must struggle to listen and understand the information, not merely repeat phonetic patterns.

5. *Stamina:* In the beginning, students cannot handle more than 5-10 minute exercises. The length is gradually increased until they can shadow 25-30 minutes comfortably. Stamina is an element often misunderstood even by lay people who have been exposed to conference situations. It can also become the basis for "interpreter humor," as in the experience that Jean Herbert (1978, p. 8), the Dean of the profession, recalls:

> Once, during a medical conference, a French doctor was evidently much intrigued by what we were doing, so he came and sat behind the booth where I was working with a colleague. At a time when we were silent, he seized the opportunity and asked us: "Why are there two of you doing this work?" My colleague explained: "We must. One of us listens and the other one speaks." The doctor was deeply impressed and passed on this valuable information to other delegates!

Conference interpreters, then, work in teams, alternating approximately every 30 minutes in order to avoid the exhaustion that ensues from the intense mental activity required for interpretation. These "inactive" periods are not truly resting periods, because "resting" interpreters must listen in order to help "active" interpreters, if necessary, and also to take notes of any important information and/or terminology being used. Nevertheless, the tension of "being on the spot" is released during the rest periods.

Along with shadowing, several public speaking skills are also taught, such as voice projection and modulation, breathing, pronunciation, and enunciation. After several months of these exercises, students are prepared to switch from shadowing into interpreting with relatively few technical problems. Many hours of practice are still needed to master the technique but training can now address problems such as vocabulary, text analysis, and more specific technical issues, such as what to do when the speech is too fast and the interpreter needs to "catch up" by abstracting information, or making "educated guesses."

Although some practicing interpreters believe that work should be done only into the native or "A" language, training is increasingly done in both the A language, and the second or "B" language. It is a common belief that working into the A language ensures better performance. However, this belief is being questioned because it isn't clear whether it is more important to have native proficiency in the emission stage or in the decoding stage. Another reason is that the market is severely reduced for interpreters working only into their A language, especially if the interpreter has only two working languages. Thus, more and more professionals are being trained to work in both directions.

A variation on simultaneous interpretation is the so-called whispered interpretation or *chuchotage*, used when only one or two people need interpretation. A simple way to imagine this type of interpreting comes from the media, where we see an interpreter standing behind a delegate, whispering the interpretation. It is also used in other situations such as in community interpreting, as we will see later on. This type of interpretation can be very hard on the vocal chords, because the interpreter has to consciously regulate the loudness of the voice in order not to disturb other delegates while keeping it loud enough for the client. It is also physically taxing since there is usually no backup interpreter, as in the booth.

Although simultaneous interpretation is the form that most impresses the lay person, professional interpreters regard *consecutive interpretation* as the art and trademark of a good interpreter. In this mode, the interpreter takes notes during a speech for periods up to 25 minutes long, and then interprets. This is the most refined form of interpretation and is considered higher in quality than simultaneous since professional standards demand that it be extremely accurate. This kind of interpretation is used in small meetings, usually between diplomats and high-level government officials. It is also used in the courts and other community settings and in this case it is called *short consecutive* because exchanges are shorter, are of the question-and-answer type, and do not require a highly sophisticated note-taking system, as in the longer, conference version.

Consecutive interpretation requires the development of recall and note-taking techniques, as well as public speaking skills. Training in consecutive interpretation is quite a recent development, since the main tenet of practicing professionals is that interpreters' notes are very personal and should be developed individually. Although this is true, there are basic techniques that can be taught that will help students develop their own notes following a logical system.

From the beginning, students learn that the consecutive technique is a non-language-specific, special note-taking system based on the analysis of information, using abbreviations, symbols from various alphabets and disciplines, and arrows and lines. The positioning of these elements in the paper is manipulated to indicate grammatical structure and the relationships between ideas. The result is a sort of map that serves as a mnemonic device in which the interpreter can see the logical outline of the speech and accurately recall what was said, even for lengths of 20-25 minutes.

Language is only secondary during the initial stage and for that reason techniques can be taught unilingually and transferred later on to any language combination the student may have. In the beginning, students are taught to analyze and recall information through memory exercises. Students listen to passages 25-40 seconds long and then repeat them, in the same language, as accurately as possible. The length and the complexity of the information is gradually increased until a mnemonic device is needed to recall the whole passage. At this point, students are told to write down one or two words that will trigger their memory, a task that requires deep concentration and analysis. A special system of abbreviations and a few symbols are gradually introduced, so students can write more information in less time. However, taking down too much information is discouraged because by doing that, attention is shifted from listening and processing to writing, which hampers recall. In this sense, consecutive note-taking resembles decalage, given that there is a small lag time between speech and note-taking, when interpreters analyze incoming information and decide what to take down, where to place it in the notes, and in what form to put it.

Students are gradually introduced to other note-taking techniques, such as the following: (a) *Verticalization:* writing information from up to down, rather than from left to right; in the beginning, students are encouraged to use narrow strips of paper to force them to write vertically. (b) *Subordination of ideas:* placing the main idea to the left, then the next related idea below and to the right, and so forth so that the end result is a "ladder" of information where, at a glance, the interpreter can see the main idea and the related ideas. (c) *Indentation:* the horizontal placement of ideas as a visual indication of their relationship. Several elements are related to indentation: *linkage words*, extremely important because they connect the different elements of the speech and enable interpreters to give a coherent rendition; *parentheses*, to set off elements that are not essential but that modify or explain one of the more important ideas; and *lines of agreement*, placed between two indented ideas to express their relationship.

The Conference Interpreter

Although the techniques mentioned above can be acquired through training, interpreters must have certain traits in order to become good professionals. Some of these are inherent, such as analytical ability, intellectual curiosity, intercultural sensitivity, good concentration, and a good voice. Others must be acquired and constantly updated. Of these, one that is often misunderstood is language proficiency. A sophisticated knowledge of the working languages is essential, but it is by far not the key element. The fact is that interpretation is not so much a field in languages as it is a field in communications. For an interpreter, language is necessary in order to perform, just as it is necessary for a biologist, a psychologist, or a nuclear physicist. In that respect, language is taken for granted, the only difference being that a biologist or a psychologist need only be proficient in one language, whereas the interpreter needs at least two and uses them as working tools. Thus, interpretation schools are not language schools, a fact that cannot be too often or too forcefully emphasized, given the lack of general knowledge about the profession.

Another important trait of the good interpreter is a wide range of knowledge, acquired through either college or experience. Interpreters must become avid readers of all sorts of materials in order to broaden their knowledge in many fields. Such is the nature of the profession: One conference might deal with the impact of Europe 1992 in Latin America, the next on a newly developed irrigation system, and the next on Middle Eastern asceticism. That is why my students grow tired of the advice I give them from the beginning: "Read a daily a day, a weekly a week, and a monthly a month. Then you will have a fighting chance."

Finally, it is believed that the interpreter should "blend into the woodwork" and be so effective and unobtrusive that listeners "forget that in fact they are listening, through the interpreter, to a person speaking in another language" (Weber, 1990, p. 153). For that purpose, interpreters are expected to adapt to different speakers and language levels so as to reproduce their tone and intention and provide their clients with the same experience as the audience who listens to the original.

Court Interpretation

Court interpretation is a special case of community interpretation because it is further ahead in its way toward becoming a profession, especially since the passing of the Federal Court Interpreters Act of 1978. This act defined the need for qualified interpreters in the courts and paved the way for a certification exam. However, training programs are still very rare and the existing ones are mostly designed to help future interpreters pass the certification exam. Although much is needed in order to increase the quality of court interpreters in general, the certification exam and the creation of state and national court interpreter associations are important steps toward the professionalization of the field, a fact that is unfortunately lacking in other types of community interpretation.

Community Interpretation

Throughout this chapter I have used the term *community interpretation* to refer to any interpretation that is not carried out in the international or conference setting. Yet, it is important to mention that this field is known by other names, for example, liaison, ad-hoc, or three-cornered interpretation (as it is called in Australia). Although there is no consensus as to which term to use, I decided to use the general term *community interpreter* to refer to the professional trained to assist those in the community who do not speak the "dominant" language so that they may have access to legal, health, educational, governmental, and social services (I will use the common case of English as the dominant language).

It must be very clear that the only element that differentiates community interpreting from conference interpreting is the setting in which interpreters work and that community interpreting is not, as some believe, a low, amateurish type of interpreting. In fact, in places such as Australia, conference interpreting is not as frequent, given the geographical and social determinants that have established community interpreting as the more relevant type of interpretation. Nevertheless, there still remains the idea that community interpreters are not professionals and the roots of this belief are found in the attitudes toward the problems and the populations they serve. To further clarify the distinction between professional and nonprofessional interpreters, I will use the term *community interpreter* to refer to professional interpreters and the term *communication facilitator*, for lack of a better term, to refer to individuals who speak two languages and work as interpreters in the community but who are not trained and/or qualified interpreters.

Given the increasing mobility of people around the world, and the unsuccessful attempts at quickly assimilating them into the dominant culture, there is always going to be a segment of the population whose members do not speak English, making the need for qualified interpreters unavoidable. Nevertheless, the role of these practitioners is often regarded as "humanitarian," a belief that contributes to the lack of understanding of their skills, perpetuates the notion of community interpreting as an unpaid service, and labels its practitioners as unskilled workers. In fact, "there is still confusion and disagreement among theoreticians, practitioners and the community in general as to what the role of a community interpreter is or should be. Is he [or she], for example, just a language 'facilitator' or a little bit of a welfare officer as well, and how can the two be distinguished?" (Vasilakakos, 1989, p. 5). Although I will limit myself to spoken interpretation, it is important to keep in mind that the following situations are all too familiar to other types of interpreters working in the community, particularly to interpreters for the deaf. Even though interpreters for the deaf are better organized, have a professional association (The Registry of Interpreters for the Deaf), and have recognized training programs, these professionals still have to struggle with the attitudes and perceptions affecting community interpreters.

Community interpreting is most common in developed countries such as Australia, England, and the United States, which have a large non-English-speaking population, many from underdeveloped countries. Some of these people may find themselves in need of welfare, legal, and/or medical services, all of which are difficult to access if there is a lack of communication and resources.

Although the situation is gradually changing, the attitude toward immigrants has been one of blame for their inability to communicate, and even for their problems. At the individual level, perceptions of racism, tolerance, and assimilation into the mainstream are very complex and have serious consequences. Yet, at the institutional and governmental level, these perceptions may affect the importance (and support) given to the quality of services for this minority, which include, but aren't limited to, interpretation. Indeed, "powerful institutional forces, the relative powerlessness of interpreters and migrant clients, and a changing but always confusing ideology of assimilation and integration [are] the determinants of interpreter practice" (Ozolins, 1991, p. 21).

One of the problems that arises from these perceptions is that immigrants are frequently labeled as "ignorant," when the true ignorance is on the part of the labeler for not understanding cultural and educational differences. Assume, for example, that a male immigrant is involved in a traffic accident and asked to testify in court. He is given a map to indicate the location of the collision or the route followed, but he may not be able to do so. The judge or the prosecutors might regard that as a sign of ignorance, believing that if he cannot read a map, he might not be able to read signs either. Thus he is considered an unsafe driver and an easy target for the blame. The fact is that reading a map and relating its symbols and lines to a three-dimensional reality are acquired skills and do not prove average intelligence (Jones, 1985). Even an "educated" person might encounter difficulties reading maps in other countries, given that maps and traffic symbols do not follow international norms.

Immigrants, who already carry the stigma of being foreigners and uneducated, are at times in need of welfare services, a stigma even for native recipients. The agencies offering welfare services are not in themselves well regarded by the public in general, and the resources available to them are usually limited.

Given this state of affairs, the practice of community interpreting has been irregular and inadequate. Because there is a frequent lack of resources in the agencies to have a pool of qualified, paid interpreters, these are only sporadically used. At times, well-intentioned interpreters decide to do community work and expect to be treated well because they are giving some of their time to help not only the client but also the agency that needs them to fulfill a task. However, their experience is often quite negative: the staff offers little support and makes them feel as a necessary evil, and when it comes to payment, interpreters may have to wait even months to receive a check.

The issue of remuneration is very controversial and has become a vicious circle. The interpretation market, especially for freelance interpreters, can be difficult to access and in order to get jobs, they might have to compete with nonprofessional interpreters who offer their services at a very low fee. The agencies, which regard the need for interpretation as a nuisance, are more concerned with cutting expenses than with quality and will resort to the cheaper, often unqualified alternative. This in turn perpetuates the notion of interpreters as nonprofessionals, not only for the low quality of services but also because the agencies will not stop to think that they really got what they were willing to pay for. They will erroneously confirm their idea of interpretation as a necessary evil that, at best, can only be partially met.

This "interpreter alternative" is what I have called *communication facilitator*. I will present some of the problems that may arise when a nonprofessional is used, stressing the fact that most of these problems can be avoided by using qualified interpreters.

A common solution for agencies is to ask an employee from the client's minority group to assume this role. This can cause problems not only because they lack the skills but also because they reflect the perceived social and educational level of that minority, and even if they are qualified, they are regarded as low class and undereducated. It may happen that they are aware of the stigma attached to that minority and will be reluctant to serve. For example, when my mother, a non-English speaking Hispanic, went for a checkup in Houston, there were no interpreters available and the doctor brought in a nurse who looked Hispanic. The nurse told the doctor, in English, that she couldn't help because she didn't speak Spanish. Later she went to my mother's room and explained that she did not want anybody to know that she spoke Spanish because it would affect her work and her relationships with other staff members.

Sometimes these communication facilitators harbor negative feelings toward the culture represented by the social worker (e.g., they don't like Anglo-Americans) and will make him or her look bad in the eyes of the client. The reverse could also happen, that facilitators want to make their cultural counterparts "look better" in the eyes of the worker and alter or edit any questionable information given by the client. Both these situations may affect the outcome of the interview so a facilitator who is a member of the client's culture may not always be the best interpreter alternative.

Sometimes the solution is the "BYO interpreter" situation, when clients bring a relative or a friend to be the language facilitator; but this may cause other types of problems. For example, if clients bring their child or a friend to help them communicate in a medical examination, they might feel embarrassed to talk about personal or intimate matters in front of them or fear that the information will leak into the community. Clients may avoid mentioning delicate issues altogether, and in so doing alter the information presented. This in turn can affect the chances for improving the condition for which they originally sought help.

There are concerned individuals with bilingual skills who offer their services as volunteers and in this case the quality is variable, depending on their experience. Although these well-intentioned individuals fulfill an important role given the state of the profession, it is not the solution to the problem. A variation of the volunteer scene is the case of interpretation agencies that have lists of bilinguals in many language combinations who are willing to work as communication facilitators in the community. They charge for their services, but just as in the case of volunteers, their quality is very variable. Community interpreters are not volunteers. They are paid professionals who play a key role in the task to be accomplished by the agency and should be regarded as such by the people working with them.

Although the importance of having qualified community interpreters has already been established, their skills and abilities need to be studied and recognized in order to increase public awareness and to upgrade services to a professional level. For this to become a reality, community interpreters must be trained so they can offer quality services for which they can charge a fair fee. Likewise, the agencies who work with interpreters and the public in general must be educated as to the need and the nature of the profession so that they can demand quality services and be prepared to regard the practitioners as professionals.

Through this brief description of community interpreting, it can be seen that the road paved by conference interpreters, who struggled long and hard to be recognized as bona fide professionals, still needs to be traversed by community interpreters. In this case the road will be more tortuous because they differ from conference interpreters who have acquired an aura of prestige as a result of an international and high-class working environment. Community interpreters will have to struggle with prejudice, attitudes, and preconceived ideas about the population they serve and about themselves. People with these prejudices have already bestowed on community interpreters an aura of low-class, undereducated, and, in the best of cases, humanitarian "nonprofessionals."

The Skills of Community Interpreters

The skills and abilities of community interpreters resemble those of conference interpreters, but there are important differences. I have already talked about the international and community settings and how they affect the way the profession is perceived. Yet, the setting also affects the type of interpretation rendered. In an international conference, the audience usually has everything in common except for language. The audience in a conference on computer technology, for example, is formed by programmers, engineers, systems analysts, and so forth, who gather to share ideas on a specific topic. The task of the interpreter is to help people understand what their counterparts are saying in another language. Even though there may be cultural differences, these are not as crucial as in the community setting, where cultural disparity can be a greater problem than language difference. Indeed, "Language in the strict sense of words and grammar may even be the least significant cause of misunderstanding" (Jones, 1985, p. 35).

If the interpreter is not aware of cultural differences and interprets word for word, there can be serious consequences. For example, one of my conference interpretation students was interpreting in court for a Latin-American defendant, and the judge asked him his name. He answered something like José Manuel Gómez Pérez-Marín, and the judge asked: "How come you have so many last names?" The defendant answered: "They are my first last name and my second last name." Her interpretation to the judge was: "They are my father's last name and my mother's last name." She told me that while she was doing this, she had visions of me scolding her for not following the original exactly, but I told her that she did the right thing for that situation. By profiting from her knowledge of the Latin culture she avoided a lengthy interrogation. It not only would have been useless, but also potentially harmful for the defendant, since he could have been perceived as a criminal, giving several aliases to cover his identity.

Community interpreters must also be skilled in interpersonal communication and be able to work well with others from very different backgrounds (see module in this book by R. Brislin, Chapter 2). The interpreter "is responsible for enabling professional and client, with two very different backgrounds and perceptions and in an unequal relationship of power and knowledge, to communicate to their mutual satisfaction" (Travillian-Vonesh, 1991, p. 21). To achieve this, interpreters must be aware of cultural differences and of nonverbal behaviors (see module in this book by T. Singelis, Chapter 14), and also be able to put aside their own prejudices.

Language is, of course, very important for interpreters in general, but the focus is different depending on the setting in which they work. Contrary to conference interpreters, who need to be very proficient in technical vocabulary, community interpreters must develop breadth and flexibility of vocabulary. Technical vocabulary is not as essential, for several reasons. First, community interpreters can usually talk to both parties before the actual interview and ask or look for any terminological problems that might arise. Second, even if community interpreters used technical terms, clients may not always understand them. Assume that a working-class, mature woman goes to the doctor and says: "When I come around I have a pain in the bottom of my bucket." Were the interpreter to use a word-for-word rendition, the doctor would probably not understand and be very annoyed at the interpreter's incompetence. Likewise, if the doctor says that this is a simple case of dysmenorrhea (instead of the common phrase "menstrual cramps"), this client would not understand. Therefore, community interpreters must have a wide range of vocabulary and be able to switch registers from the technical to the colloquial, if necessary. This also means that they must have a good knowledge of the agency for which they work, be it the courts, immigration, social or health services. Unfortunately, the job market does not allow for specialization and interpreters must have some knowledge of all possible work environments to be able to deal with their specific terminologies.

The working situation places community interpreters in a triangular relationship—worker-interpreter-client—that can be very complex. The relationship between each side of the triangle can have important effects on the outcome of the interview.

Worker-Interpreter Relationship

The role of each must be very clear in order to establish a good working relationship. Workers must be aware that interpreters are essential to achieve their goals and they must regard them as partners in the task at hand. Unfortunately, workers are usually not happy to work in a situation where an interpreter is necessary. Take the example of a male physician. "Since time is of essence to him, the doctor is not always happy to brief the interpreter. He is not meeting an easy patient; in fact, he is about to meet two people he'd rather not meet: the patient, whom he may have met before and had trouble under-standing, and the interpreter. The interpreter's presence will mean a loss of his precious time as everything will have to be said twice" (Burley, 1990, p. 150). The interpreter and the worker should meet prior to the interview, in order to clear up important aspects of the case and, if the worker is not familiar with working across languages, the nature of communication through an interpreter. Workers should be aware that an interview through an interpreter takes longer and not blame the interpreter for the "waste of time." Without the interpreter, the interview might not take place at all and if it did, it would take *even longer* and would probably be inadequate. Both must remember that they are in an interdependent relationship: The worker depends on the interpreter to commu-nicate, and the interpreter depends on the worker for information. The inter-preter should also remind the worker to speak slowly, to avoid idioms and slang, and to use short sentences to ensure an accurate and complete interpretation. Discussing the nature of the interview is also important because not all situ-ations require the same type of interpretation: It could be a simple question-and-answer session to gather facts or a more complex interview, requiring the inter-pretation of opinions, feelings, or instructions. This pre-interview discussion should also be used by the interpreter to obtain any terminology that will be used.

Client-Interpreter Relationship

Although not always possible, it would be ideal for the interpreter to meet with the client prior to the interview, not only to acquire knowledge of the case but also to build rapport with the client. The interpreter should make the client feel confident that the interview and all case-related materials are confidential unless otherwise indicated by the client. Clients should also be informed about normal interpretation practices, for example, that interpreters alternately as-sume the position of the worker and of the client and thus speak in the first person. Although this might sound trivial, sometimes clients believe that what the interpreter is saying comes from the interpreter and not from the worker and this can be very confusing and frustrating.

There are conflicting opinions as to whether community interpreters should blend into the woodwork as conference interpreters do. I think that this is not possible, given the active role of the interpreter in the worker-interpreter-client relationship. It has been said that interpreters should give a word-for-word rendition and even emulate the tone of the speaker. This was originally intended as a safeguard for misinterpretations, but community interpreters work with two unequal clients: the worker, who uses a high register and rarely gives explanations, and the client, who uses a low register (at times with colloquialisms) that might be totally inappropriate to give word for word. Both assume that interpreters are able to handle any situation and when something awkward ensues, they will be automatically blamed. In this sense, although it is generally accepted that interpreters should not intervene in the exchanges, there are at least three situations that warrant an intervention: (a) if the interpreter did not understand a concept; (b) if the client has not understood a concept; and (c) to alert a client of a concept that may have been assumed but not openly stated. When interpreters are aware of the clients' reactions, they can avoid misunderstandings by intervening when it is necessary.

As we have seen, working face to face, or in a triangular relationship, requires special skills from interpreters, besides the interpretation techniques per se. In this case, the interpretation techniques are based on the same principles as those in the conference setting but are adapted to the needs of the community setting. The most common mode of interpretation used in this setting is consecutive, but a sophisticated note-taking technique is not necessary. Rather, a variation called short consecutive is used, which entails noting basic information (such as names and numbers) and does not require a complicated linkage or vertical-ized system. Simultaneous is used sometimes, but not through a specialized equipment. Rather, a variation of the simultaneous technique is used, called whis-pered interpretation, which was introduced previously. This is used in the courts, for example, during depositions or when a non-English-speaking client is on the witness stand.

The Training of Community Interpreters

Although much has been said about the difficulties of community inter-preting, not much has been done to solve the problem. At present, there are only a few community interpreting programs in the world, and they face basically the same problems: lack of qualified trainers, lack of financial and institutional support (with the exception of Australia, which is quite advanced in this area), and lack of coordination on the training of community interpreting in order to provide a high standard of interpreting across all areas and all language combi-nations. Two of the more important programs are described below.

1. *The Community Interpreter Project*, in England, was started in 1983 under the auspices of the Institute of Linguistics and was funded by the Nuffield Foundation. Its purpose is to develop models to select, train, and use interpret-ers in specific areas (Corsellis, 1987). Training is geared to meet Britain's needs, mostly in Indian languages such as Punjabi, Bengali, Hindi, and Gujarati, followed by Italian, Greek, and Turkish. The targeted areas of application are: *legal services*, such as police, courts, probation, legal advice centers, and immigration; *social and government services*, such as education, welfare, housing, and social services; and *health services*, such as hospitals, clinics, dentists, and medical advice centers.

The program takes into account the lack of qualified community interpreter trainers, so the course is designed to develop interpreters as well as trainers. It is a 3-year program, and students are required to be full-time. Candidates are selected through a written translation test and an interview in both languages, taking into account not only linguistic competence but also knowledge of the cultural background and of the institution they will be working with, as well as interpersonal skills and ability to deal with sensitive issues. The teaching team is formed by the following:

Interpreter trainers: usually conference interpreters with an interest in the community setting
Language trainers: to improve language skills
Teacher trainers: to impart teaching methodologies
Service professionals: such as doctors, lawyers, and social workers, to teach relevant subject content

Training focuses on three main areas: language enhancement, agency knowledge, and interpreting skills, including note-taking and whispered simultaneous. Students are taught to decide which mode of interpretation is appropriate for a given situation and are presented with ethical aspects such as confidentiality, impartiality, and professionalism, including tidiness, punctuality, ensuring adequate working conditions, and deciding when to interrupt proceedings and when to refuse an assignment.

Translation is also a part of the training, given that community interpreters are sometimes required to translate various official forms, information sheets, instructions, and the like. Students receive one of three certificates:

a. *Bilingual Skills Certificate:* for practical, functional language skills in English and another language
b. *Certificate in Community Interpreting:* for specialized options (legal, local services, and health)
c. *Postgraduate Diploma in Community Interpreter Training Techniques:* for trainers of interpreters (this option is offered at the Polytechnic of Central London)

2. Programs were created in Australia in 1978, by the National Accreditation Authority for Translators and Interpreters (NAATI), a regulatory organization created to give interpretation and translation a professional status. It defined five levels of interpretation and translation in Australia, briefly described as follows (Vasilakakos, 1989):

Sub-Professional Levels (for those with some second language competence who can help non-English speaking clients)

- *Level 1:* Language aides and workers in bilingual information services. Offered at highschools and aboriginal institutions.
- *Level 2:* For those who use a second language on the job. Offered at technical colleges and continuing education.

Professional Levels (for those primarily employed as interpreters and/or translators)

- *Level 3:* Community interpreters and/or translators who can deal with any type of interpretation and translation in the medical, legal, educational, welfare, commercial, and industrial areas. Offered at colleges as part of 3-year under-graduate programs leading to a bachelor's degree.

- *Level 4:* Conference interpreters and translators. Accreditation is offered in one direction (usually into their native language) and the candidate selects an area of specialization. Offered at the university level.
- *Level 5:* For those with Level 4 accreditation and extensive experience and leadership in the field.

In Australia, there is a greater need for community interpreters than for conference interpreters, and emphasis is placed on Level 3. Training focuses on enhancing skills in both languages, interpretation skills (mainly short consecutive), translation, cultural background, and supervised fieldwork. In Level 3, students can specialize in either translation and/or interpretation, and students are required to work in both directions (into and out of these native languages).

In the United States, the training of community interpreters is practically nonexistent. The Georgetown University School of Languages and Linguistics offers a course in community interpreting at the undergraduate level. This is a one-semester-long course in which concepts of consecutive interpretation are presented, as well as methods to improve listening skills and public speaking. The course, however, is not intended to prepare professional community interpreters but to present an option for future career development, not only in interpretation but in other careers as well.

Given the scarcity of training programs, the constraints for developing future programs, the lack of regulations on the qualifications of practitioners, and the economic situation, it is unrealistic to expect that community interpreting is going to be performed mainly by professionals, at least in the near future. Because a high-quality interpretation is always desirable, an alternative to having a professional is to upgrade the skills of those bilinguals who are presently working as interpreters and to teach basic skills to interested bilinguals. I want to emphasize that this is not, by any means, the solution to the problem, but it is a way to fulfill a need while other, more permanent, solutions are found and implemented.

Guidelines for Improving the Skills of Nontrained Bilinguals

1. Preselect candidates for the following:
a. Language skills:
  - in both languages
  - in breadth and flexibility of vocabulary
b. Affinity for the work:
  - background knowledge of the agency
  - background knowledge of the culture and of cross-cultural problems
  - relevant work experience, e.g., previous work with foreigners and minorities, which will acquaint them with some of their problems (experience in

interpreting is not always an advantage, because candidates may have acquired bad habits that may be difficult to change)

2. Improve language skills. Encourage reading in both languages to expand vocabulary and familiarize interpreters with common language usage. Writing skills should also be improved.

3. Introduce basic note-taking concepts, such as the importance of analyzing information, as well as writing down numbers, dates, names, and unfamiliar terms to help recall. Exercises such as the one presented below can be used for this purpose.

4. Discuss how to prepare for an interpretation assignment. This includes the development of glossaries of terms used in each area (legal, medical, etc.), and how to find information. Provide information on the agency, frequently used vocabulary, the types of cases, and actual documents used by the agency. Role-playing is useful, especially if workers (doctors, social workers, lawyers) participate with scripts of actual cases so students can have firsthand experiences of interpreting situations. Discussions of the outcome and possible improvements should be encouraged. This can also be a two-way learning situation: By having workers participate, they become aware of the pitfalls and difficulties of the interpreting situation and may become more sensitive to interpreters' needs.

5. Discuss the importance of confidentiality and trust.

6. Make candidates aware of their own limitations; there is no shame in rejecting an assignment if they do not feel competent to carry it out.

Recall Exercises

Introduction

Note-taking is a valuable tool for community interpreters. Most community interpreting situations follow an interview-like format, and regular consecutive note-taking is unnecessary, given that exchanges are short and information is more concise. Nevertheless, the type of note-taking known as short consecutive, in which interpreters take down "kernels" of information, can improve performance, because it will help recall and thus facilitate the exchange.

Notes not only give the interpreter a sense of security, they also ensure that information will be accurate and allow a smoother, less interrupted exchange. For example, if a client is asked to state his name, address, and birthdate, an interpreter taking notes would not have to interrupt the client after each section but let the client answer completely, and then give back the whole information. The fact that the interpreter did not have to interrupt the client also enhances the image of the interpreter as a professional.

Teaching Basic Note-Taking Concepts

There are many advantages in using English to teach skills such as listening, analyzing, and recalling information, as well as basic note-taking skills (e.g., abbreviations and numbers). First, students learn to disengage themselves from any particular language and, second, all candidates can be trained at the same time, regardless of language combination, thus saving time and expense. After candidates are comfortable taking notes and reading them back in English, training can move on to the bilingual stage.

The most important element in note-taking is learning to listen and to analyze information. Several sessions should be devoted to reading short passages that students then repeat as accurately as possible, using their own words. This enhances memory span, increases concentration, and also promotes analytical thinking. Candidates should be encouraged to use their own words, to avoid "phonetic memory" (remembering specific words by their sound). In the beginning this could be accomplished by asking for the main topics or the gist and not a complete retelling of the story. Later, greater accuracy and attention to detail can be required. Passages should not exceed 1 minute and should be read at a normal speed. In a workshop, when one person is giving his or her version, others can compare and at the end give comments or add any missing information.

The length of the passages can be gradually increased and candidates should write down only one or two words that will trigger recall. Passages should not be longer than 2 minutes. This stage further enhances analytical thought, because it forces students to concentrate and decide what to take down in order to enhance recall.

The next phase is to introduce abbreviation techniques. The most useful way to abbreviate words for note-taking purposes is to eliminate as many vowels as possible, while still retaining the "physical appearance" of the word. For example, the word *represent* could be abbreviated as *rprsnt*, all vowels eliminated but still recognizable. Care should be given not to eliminate too many letters. In the above example, candidates could be tempted to write only *rep*, but this could be confused with many words: *republic, repeat, repair, repent, replace,* and so on. It is recommended that candidates find and memorize known abbreviations from various disciplines, such as street markings, weights and measurements, compass directions, days of the week, months, and the like. For example:

avenue	ave
street	st
highway	hwy
place	plce
month	mo
year	yr

Numbers are one of the most important aspects in note-taking and, unfortunately, the greatest problem in any language, for several reasons: (a) Number systems vary from language to language; for example, in Spanish, commas are used for decimals and points for thousands, whereas in English this is reversed. (b) There seems to be a "mental short" between hearing numbers, writing them down, and reading them back—what is heard is not what is written, and sometimes what is written is not what is interpreted. At times numbers are reversed (e.g., 32 and 23), or they sound similar (15 and 50). This phonetic confusion is not limited to numbers and can make for very interesting (and at times embarrassing) situations. I remember being in a conversation where I was told that jazz music had some of its origins in brothels. I was so astonished, that I asked in disbelief: "In Brussels?!!!." Needless to say, I provided quite a bit of amusement.

Several techniques are available to help write numbers. English once again is used as a base, so decimals are noted with points. For numbers beyond 100, a line above the number substitutes for 3 zeros. For example:

One thousand	$\overline{1}$
One million	$\overline{\overline{1}}$
One billion	$\overline{\overline{\overline{1}}}$

Some people prefer to use letters:

One thousand	1m
One million	1M
One billion	1B

Finally, it is important to remember that notes are highly individual, a fact that should be stressed throughout the training. Candidates should therefore be encouraged to experiment and find out what works better for them.

Exercises

The following exercises will be helpful to improve recall and analytical skills of individuals with two languages who will be performing as interpreters. All exercises are in English and could be used as models to develop exercises in other languages.

Simple Recall

The first is a simple recall exercise that will enable you to see some of the difficulties encountered in the interpretation process. The task is very simple. Read the following short text at a normal speed. After finishing, have candidates write it down using as many of the exact words as they can recall. Then ask for a volunteer to read his or her version and analyze what happens.

Anna Thompson of South Boston, employed as a cleaning woman in an office building, reported at the Central Precinct Station that she had been held up the night before on State Street and robbed of 15 dollars. She had four little children, the rent was due, and they had not eaten for two days. The officers, touched by the woman's story, took up a collection for her.

Background Information. This text was taken from the Wechsler (1945) logical memory text, used originally as a standardized memory scale for clinical purposes. The text, modified to Americanize the lexicon, was used for research purposes in a nongraded section of the oral part of the federal court interpreters certification examination, to study recall among interpreters. The text was originally chosen because of the following:

a. It is almost a verbatim recall text.
b. It has been successfully used on research projects studying recall and recognition among interpreters (Gerver, Longley, Long, & Lambert, 1984).
c. It approximates the task done by interpreters when doing consecutive interpretation in the courts (short consecutive).

Gathering from the research done on the interpretation process, several forms of retrieval have been classified. These are, in essence, the following:

a. *Omissions:* including *deletions* of material and *overgeneralizations* (when information has been reduced, e.g., a subject recalls "good teacher" as "teacher").
b. *Embellishments:* including *additions* (*inferences:* made from previous knowledge or from the presented text; *elaborations:* new material is introduced).
c. *Synonymous responses:* including *substitutions, recombinations,* and *paraphrases.*
d. *Veridical or exact recall:* including *permutations,* when the order of information is changed (Arjona-Chang, n.d.).

Analysis. A key to the symbols used in the analysis is provided below. (*Note:* * denotes those phrases or words that have caused the most recall problems among interpreters.)

V	veridical (exact)
O	omission
E	embellishment (addition, change)

Anna Thompson	*employed*
V	V (who works as)
O	O
E (Thomas, etc.)	E (who earns her living as)

*of South Boston	*as a cleaning woman*
V	V
O	O
E (North)	E (as a maid, janitor)

*in an office building
V
O (in a building; in an office)
E (in a large building)

*reported
V (said)
O
E (testified, claimed, informed)

*at the Central Precinct Station
V
O (at the police; at the station)
E

that she had been
V
O
E

held up
V
O
E (attacked)

*the night before
V
O (yesterday)
E

*on State Street
V
O
E

and robbed
V
O
E

*of fifteen dollars
V
O
E (fifty)

She had
V
O
E (the mother of)

*four little children
V (small)
O (four children)
E

*the rent was due
V
O
E

and they had not eaten
V
O
E

for two days
V
O
E

The officers
V
O
E (the police)

touched by
V
O
E (feeling sympathy for; affected by;
        saddened by)

the woman's story
V
O
E

took up
V
O
E

a collection	*for her*
V	V
O	O
E	E

Exercise: A Dialogue

The next exercise is a simple dialogue. Notes should not be used because it is also an introductory memory exercise.

Q: Please state your name.
A: My name is Sumi Ikeda.
Q: Where do you live?
A: I do not remember the address because I do not know English very well.
Q: Ok. Do you live in a house or an apartment?
A: I live in an apartment.
Q: What is the number of the building and of the apartment?
A: The building is 1362 and the apartment number is 34, on the third floor.
Q: On what street is it?
A: Somewhere behind McKinley.
Q: Where?
A: McKinley High School. The apartment is behind the school.
Q: What is your age and date of birth?
A: I will be 31 years old.
Q: When were you born?
A: On December 6, 1961.
Q: Where were you born?
A: In Osaka.
Q: In Japan?
A: Yes, Japan.
Q: What is your occupation?
A: Now?
Q: Yes.
A: I work cleaning gardens, cutting grass, anything I can to live an honest life.
Q: Are you working right now?
A: No. The welfare office helps me because I was in a fight and had to go to the hospital.
Q: Were you seriously injured?
A: Yes, my head was broken with a hammer and they had to put a metal plaque on my skull.
Q: When did this happen?
A: The fight or the surgery?
Q: The surgery.
A: It happened 3 months ago.
Q: Have you worked since the surgery?
A: No.
Q: Are you married?

A: Yes.
Q: Do you have any children?
A: Yes, I have two girls and one boy.

Results can be a analyzed in a manner similar to that for the first memory exercise.

References

Anderson, R.B. (1978). *When two languages meet, who speaks for the interpreter?* Paper presented at the Ninth World Congress of Sociology, Uppsala, Sweden, August 14-19.

Arjona-Chang, E. (n.d.). *Veridical and embellished recall among court interpreters.* Unpublished paper.

Burley, P. (1990). Community interpreting in Australia. In D. Bowen & M. Bowen (Eds.), *Interpreting—yesterday, today, and tomorrow* (vol. 4, American Translators Association Scholarly Monograph Series, pp. 146-153). Binghamton: State University of New York (SUNY) at Binghamton.

Corsellis, A. (February, 1987). Submission for funding to the Nuffield Foundation.

Frishberg, N. (1986). *Interpreting: An introduction.* Silver Spring, MD: RID Publications.

Gerver, D., Longley, P., Long, J., & Lambert, S. (1984). Selecting trainee conference interpreters: A preliminary study. *Journal of Occupational Psychology, 57.*

Herbert, J. (1978). How conference interpretation grew. In D. Gerver & H. Sinaiko (Eds.), *Language interpretation and communication* (pp. 5-9). New York: Plenum Press.

Jones, M. (1985). The community interpreter: A special case. *Australian Social Work, 38*(3), 35-38.

Ozolins, U. (1991). *Interpreting translating and language policy.* Report to the Language and Society Centre, National Languages Institute of Australia. National Languages Institute of Australia, Sydney.

Travillian-Vonesh, A. (1991, February). Recruiting community interpreters from an unexpected source. *The ATA Chronicle*, p. 22.

Vasilakakos, J. (1989). Community interpreting/translating in Australia. *The Jerome Quarterly, 4*(4), 3-6.

Weber, W. (1990). Interpretation in the United States. *Annals, AAPSS, 511*, 145-158.

Wechsler, D. (1945). A standardized memory scale for clinical use. *The Journal of Psychology, 19*, 87-95.

Author Index

Subject Index

About the Contributors

Dr. Elaine K. Bailey, (EdD, University of Southern California) is Assistant Professor of Management and Industrial Relations, College of Business Administration, at the University of Hawaii. She has directed international business programs through the Pacific Asia Management Institute at the University of Hawaii.

Dr. Richard W. Brislin, (PhD, Psychology, Pennsylvania State University) is Senior Fellow and Project Director at the East-West Center in Honolulu, Hawaii. His recent books include *The Art of Getting Things Done: A Practical Guide to the Use of Power* (1991) and *Understanding Culture's Influence on Behavior* (1993). He directs yearly programs for college professors who want to develop intercultural coursework and for cross-cultural trainers who want to expand their skills.

Dr. Kenneth Cushner, (EdD, University of Hawaii) is Associate Professor of Education and Director of the Center for International and Intercultural Education at Kent State University. He is coauthor of the book *Intercultural Interactions: A Practical Guide* (Sage, 1986) and *Human Diversity in Education: An Integrative Approach* (1992).

Ms. Carolina Freimanis is a professional interpreter who has been an instructor at the Center for Translation and Interpretation Studies at the University of Hawaii, Manoa. She is currently living in her home country, Venezuela, and is entering the field of health services delivery.

Dr. Neal R. Goodman, (PhD, Sociology, New York University) is Professor of Sociology and Director of the Intercultural Relations Program at St. Peter's College in Jersey City, New Jersey. He has organized his own consulting firm,

Global Dynamics, Inc, which offers cross-cultural training programs to major international businesses.

Ms. Colleen Mullavey-O'Byrne is Head of the School of Occupational Therapy, Faculty of Health Sciences, the University of Sydney, Australia. She has recently contributed to the case studies component of the instructor's manual that accompanies an Australian text, *The Health of Immigrant Australians: A Social Perspective.*

Dr. Paul Pedersen, (EdD, University of Minnesota) is Professor of Counselor Education at Syracuse University. Among his publications are *A Handbook for Developing Multicultural Awareness* (1986) and *Counseling Across Cultures* (1989). He has also been director of the major grant for the Development of Intercultural Skilled Counselors (DISC). He serves as an adviser to Sage Publications.

Mr. Mark Sawyer is an East-West Center Degree Participant Scholar and a PhD student in second-language acquisition at the University of Hawaii. He has developed and directed language programs at the International University of Japan over a period of 7 years.

Mr. Ted Singelis is a graduate student in the PhD psychology program at the University of Hawaii. He is also an East-West Center Degree Participant Scholar. After leaving his position of president of Pour la France! Inc. in 1985, he lived and worked in both Japan and Korea.

Mr. Larry E. Smith is Dean, Graduate and Undergraduate Curricula, at the East-West Center in Honolulu, Hawaii. He is coeditor of the journal *World Englishes: Journal of English as an International and Intranational Language.* One of his recent books is *Negotiation Training Through Gaming* (1991).

Ms. Tomoko Yoshida is Director of Training, Japanese Programs, ITT Sheraton, Hawaii/Japan Division, in Honolulu, Hawaii. She has been a project fellow at the East-West Center in Honolulu, and she is the coauthor of *An Introduction to Intercultural Communication Training* (Sage, 1994).